Financing Social Policy

Financing Social Policy

Mobilizing Resources for Social Development

Edited by

Katja Hujo

and

Shea McClanahan

UNITED NATIONS
RESEARCH INSTITUTE
FOR SOCIAL DEVELOPMENT

First published 2009 by
PALGRAVE MACMILLAN

Palgrave Macmillan in the UK is an imprint of Macmillan Publishers Limited,
registered in England, company number 785998, of Houndmills,
Basingstoke, Hampshire RG21 6XS.

Palgrave Macmillan in the US is a division of St Martin's Press LLC,
175 Fifth Avenue, New York, NY 10010.

Palgrave Macmillan is the global academic imprint of the above companies
and has companies and representatives throughout the world.

Palgrave®and Macmillan®are registered trademarks in the United States,
the United Kingdom, Europe and other countries.

ISBN 978–0–230–57664–3   hardback

This book is printed on paper suitable for recycling and made from fully
managed and sustained forest sources. Logging, pulping and manufacturing
processes are expected to conform to the environmental regulations of the
country of origin.

A catalogue record for this book is available from the British Library.

A catalog record for this book is available from the Library of Congress.

10   9   8   7   6   5   4   3   2   1
18   17   16   15   14   13   12   11   10   09

Printed and bound in Great Britain by
CPI Antony Rowe, Chippenham and Eastbourne

Contents

v

List of Tables and Figures

Tables

Figures

Foreword

Social policy is a central instrument to achieve an inclusive and democratically anchored development process. Although this is increasingly recognized, the question of the economic and fiscal affordability of social policies tends to dominate policy and scholarly debates.

One of the questions guiding UNRISD research on *Social Policy in a Development Context* has been how best to tap the transformative potential of social policy for economic development, while not forfeiting its intrinsic goals of social protection and equity. Perhaps the key message to emerge was that, in order for social policy to realize its transformative potential, it must shed its residual role and come to occupy a more central position in development efforts. In this research, the issue of financing surfaces repeatedly, in particular with regard to the so-called late industrializers which, confronted with rapid structural change and social mobilization, introduced social policies at a comparatively earlier stage than the pioneers. These studies make clear that the financial dimension of social policy making has to be directly confronted in order to avoid falling into the traps of either not spending (austerity), or engaging in expansionary 'give-but-not-take' policies that are unsustainable in economic terms.

The contributions in this volume approach the financing question from a broader developmental perspective. This approach justifies the inclusion of different sources of revenue, such as taxation, pension funds, rents from natural resources and development aid, as well as remittances. Although the conventional sources of financing like taxation and insurance contributions have the greatest potential to impact positively on state–citizenship relations, not to mention redistribution, income stabilization (at the individual and macro level) and equity, the analyses that follow suggest that revenues generated in foreign reserves from sources like mineral rents, aid and remittances will continue to play an important role for financing developmental states and social welfare in the South, albeit with mixed effects on accountability and macroeconomic stability.

The papers in this volume were presented and discussed at a workshop organized by UNRISD in Geneva in March 2007. UNRISD is grateful to the Ford Foundation for providing financial support for the research on which this volume is based. As is the case with all UNRISD projects, work on the Financing Social Policy project would not have been possible without the core funding provided by the governments of Denmark, Finland, Mexico, Norway, Sweden, Switzerland and the United Kingdom. Let me once again take this opportunity to express our gratitude.

THANDIKA MKANDAWIRE
DIRECTOR, UNRISD

Preface and Acknowledgements

Perhaps at no moment in history has there been a greater need for governments to secure adequate and stable resources for social development: inequalities are on the rise; a severe global financial and economic crisis threatens to wipe out even the small achievements some countries have made over recent years; and the neoliberal policy toolkit, which for over two decades served as a foundation for structural and social reforms in low- and middle-income countries alike, has been largely discredited. Against this backdrop, the United Nations Research Institute for Social Development (UNRISD) initiated a project in 2006 to examine options and constraints for financing social policy in developing countries. UNRISD commissioned the papers for this volume, ten of which were presented at a two-day workshop in Geneva in March 2007, in an effort to explore the developmental impact associated with specific financing techniques and revenue sources, the latter covering taxation, social insurance contributions, social and pension funds, mineral rents, remittances and aid.[1] The project is situated within the UNRISD research programme *Social Policy and Development*, which takes a broad approach to social policy, defining the concept as going beyond basic protection and poverty reduction goals to impact on the productive, reproductive, distributive and protective spheres of society simultaneously.

Once again it has proved to be a highly enriching experience to combine the expertise of different scholarships and to link literatures that usually do not speak to each other, to use the words of Thandika Mkandawire. Looking at different financing sources through the lens of social development, while combining a set of very different revenues, provides us with new insights on how to achieve a more integrated approach to economic and social policy making. Some of these revenues have traditionally been more linked to economic debates, others have generally fallen into the domain of social protection, and still others have fundamentally been associated with political processes and outcomes. Indeed, through this research we remove these resources from the comfort of their predominant disciplines and attempt to open up new lines of thinking about the economic, social and political implications of *each* of the revenues. We do so not in order to emphasize the trade-offs across these dimensions – although we acknowledge that some degree of substitution may be inevitable – but rather to shed light on the importance of balancing the economic, social and political goals and outcomes, both analytically and practically, that are associated with different revenue arrangements.

The editors would like to extend a warm thank you to all of the contributors for engaging in this cross-disciplinary research project and for responding to our numerous requests for revisions. We are also particularly grateful to Thandika Mkandawire for his leadership, intellectual stimulation and support of this project.

Josephine Grin-Yates, Wendy Salvo, Alexander Denis, Véronique Martinez and Sylvie Liu provided excellent organizational and administrative support, and the manuscript would never have gone to press without Jenifer Freedman's guidance and Anita Tombez's gracious copy-editing and scrupulous attention to detail.

Finally, we also thank those who contributed to this project in different ways since its beginning: Huck-ju Kwon for laying the groundwork for the project during his time as research coordinator at UNRISD; Parvati Raghuram, Massoud Karshenas, Roddy McKinnon, Warren McGillivray and Christiane Kuptsch for providing important inputs as discussants and chairs during the first workshop; and Armando Barrientos, Debbie Budlender, Saidakhror Burkhanov, Katrien De Moor, Nora El Qadim, Jayati Ghosh, Martina Metzger, Muhabbat Mahmudova, Naren Prasad, Tom Lavers and Andrés Solimano for reviewing papers, and providing comments and support.

KATJA HUJO AND
SHEA MCCLANAHAN
MAY 2008

Note

1. Contingent on additional funding, a second stage of the project will consist of in-depth and comparative country case studies in different geographical regions on the six major revenue sources around which the project is framed. Thanks to funding from the Ford Foundation, UNRISD had already commissioned eight papers for a project on Social Policy in Mineral-Rich Countries. These papers were presented for discussion at a workshop held in April 2008.

List of Abbreviations and Acronyms

ACU	Asian Currency Unit
ADB	Asian Development Bank
AFESD	Arab Fund for Economic and Social Development
AIOS	*Asociación Internacional de Organismos de Supervisión de Fondos de Pensiones* (International Association of Latin American Pension Fund Supervisors)
ALBA	Bolivarian Alternative for Latin America
APPFs	Approved Private Provident Funds (Sri Lanka)
Asabri	*Asuransi Angkatan Bersenjata Republik Indonesia* (pension scheme for the armed forces)
ASEAN	Association of Southeast Asian Nations
ASSA	ASEAN Social Security Association
AU	African Union
BANDES	Bank for Economic and Social Development of Venezuela
BF	*Bolsa Familia*
BNDES	Bank for National Economic and Social Development of Brazil
CAF	Andean Development Corporation
CAN	Andean Community
CARICOM	Caribbean Community
CPF	Central Government Pension Fund – Global (Norway)
CPIAs	Country Policy and Institutional Assessments
CTF	Child Trust Fund
DC	Defined Contribution
DPR	*Dewan Perwakilan Rakyat* (Indonesian House of Representatives)
ECA	Economic Commission for Africa
ECLAC	Economic Commission for Latin America and the Caribbean
ECOSOC	United Nations Economic and Social Council
ELR	Employer of Last Resort
EPF	Employees Provident Fund (Malaysia)
EPF	Employees Provident Fund (Sri Lanka)
ESAF	Extended Structural Adjustment Facility
ETF	Employees' Trust Fund (Sri Lanka)
EU	European Union
FDI	foreign direct investment
FLAR	*Fondo Latinoamericano de Reservas* (Latin American Reserve Fund)
FTAA	Free Trade Area of the Americas
GAVI	Global Alliance for Vaccines and Immunization
GBS	General Budget Support
G-24	Intergovernmental Group of 24 on International Monetary Affairs and Development

G-77	Group of 77 developing countries
GDP	gross domestic product
GNI	gross national income
GNP	gross national product
GPEF	Government Permanent Employees Provident Fund (Thailand)
GPF	Government Pension Fund (Thailand)
HDI	Human Development Index
HIPC	heavily indebted poor countries
HIV/AIDS	Human immunodeficiency virus/acquired immunodeficiency syndrome
HTAs	hometown associations
IAMC	*Instituciones de Asistencía Médica Colectiva* (Institutions of Collective Medical Assistance)
IDA	International Development Association
IDAF	International Development Aid Fund
IDB	Inter-American Development Bank
IEA	International Energy Agency
IFF	International Financial Facility
IFFIm	International Financial Facility for Immunization
IFIs	International financial institutions
ILO	International Labour Organization
IMF	International Monetary Fund
IMR	infant mortality rate
IOM	International Organization for Migration
ISSA	International Social Security Association
ITO	International Tax Organization
Jamsostek	*Jaminam Sosial Tenaga Kerja* (Private Sector Social Security System, Indonesia)
KVTEL	pension scheme for the municipal employees (Finland)
LAS	League of Arab States
LICs	Low-Income Countries
LMICs	Lower Middle-Income Countries
MDG	Millennium Development Goal
MERCOSUR	*Mercado Común del Sur* (Latin America's Common Market of the South)
MFIs	Monetary Financial Institutions
MSG	Multi Sectoral Growth model (of the Norwegian economy)
MTEF	medium-term expenditure framework
NELM	new economics of labour migration
NGOs	non-governmental organizations
NICs	Newly Industrializing Countries
NIS	National Insurance Scheme (Norway)
NP funds	National Pension funds (Finland)
NPI	National Pension Institution (Finland)

OAP	Old Age Pension
ODA	Official Development Assistance
OECD/DAC	Organisation for Economic Co-operation and Development/ Development Assistance Committee
OLS	ordinary least squares
OPEC	Organization of Petroleum Exporting Countries
PAFs	Poverty Action Funds
PAHO	Pan American Health Organization
PAYG	pay-as-you-go
PF	Provident Fund
PJyJHD	*Programa Jefes y Jefas de Hogar Desocupados* (Programme for Unemployed Heads of Household)
POSTs	Point of Sale Terminals
PPE	pro-public expenditures
PPP	purchasing power parity
PRGF	Poverty Reduction and Growth Facility
PRSPs	Poverty Reduction Strategy Papers
PSPF	Public Sector Provident Fund (Sri Lanka)
PSPS	Public Service Pension Schemes (Sri Lanka)
PT	Perseon Terbatas (state-owned limited liability company, Indonesia)
PVD	Provident (Funds)
RBC	*Renda Básica de Cidadania* (citizen's basic income)
RMF	Retirement Mutual Funds (Thailand)
SAARC	South Asian Association for Regional Cooperation
SADC	Southern African Development Community
SAP	structural adjustment programme
SDP	Social Democratic Party (Finland)
SDRs	special drawing rights
SEC	Securities and Exchange Commission (Thailand)
SEDI	Social and Enterprise Development Innovations
SJSN	*Sistem Jaminan Social Nasional* (National Social Security System, Indonesia)
SME	small and medium-sized enterprise
SOCSO	Social Security Organization
SOEs	state-owned enterprises
SPS	social protection systems
SPS	Seguro Popular de Salud (popular health insurance, Mexico)
SPVs	special purpose vehicles
SSO	Social Security Office (Thailand)
SWAp	Sector-Wide Approach
TEL	pension scheme for employees in the private sector (Finland)
TFP	Total Factor Productivity
TFR	total fertility rate

TRIPS	Agreements on Trade-Related Aspects of Intellectual Property Rights
UK	United Kingdom
UMICs	Upper Middle-Income Countries
UN	United Nations
UNCTAD	United Nations Conference on Trade and Development
UNDESA	United Nations Department of Economic and Social Affairs
UNESCO	United Nations Educational, Scientific and Cultural Organization
UNICEF	United Nations Children's Fund
UNRISD	United Nations Research Institute for Social Development
US	United States
VAT	value added tax
VEL	pension scheme for state employees (Finland)
WHO	World Health Organization
WTO	World Trade Organization

Notes on the Contributors

Mukul G. Asher, Professor of Public Policy at the National University of Singapore, was educated in India and the United States. He specializes in fiscal and pension policy issues, particularly with reference to Asia. He has published extensively and has also been a consultant to multilateral organizations such as the World Bank, IMF, UNESCAP, WHO, OECD and the ADB. His current areas of research include India's pension reforms, including the mainstreaming of micropensions in India. He is also on the Editorial Advisory Board of the *International Social Security Review*.

Hein de Haas is a Senior Research Officer at the International Migration Institute, University of Oxford. His research focuses on the reciprocal linkages between migration and broader development processes, primarily from the perspective of migrant-sending societies. He did extensive fieldwork in the Middle East and North Africa and, particularly, Morocco. He has published widely on issues including migration and development, remittances, migration and environmental change, irregular and transit migration and migration theory. His recent empirical and theoretical research focuses on migration determinants, migration transitions and the effects of migration policy.

Enrique Delamonica, an economist and political scientist, has worked on the impact of macroeconomic policies on children, the financing of social services and budget allocations, socioeconomic disparities and child poverty. He has published and co-edited several articles and books on these issues. He has also taught international development, policy analysis and research methods at Columbia University, the Institute for Social and Economic Development (Argentina) and the New School. Currently he teaches at Saint Peter's College in New Jersey.

Erling Holmøy received an MSc (Cand. Oecon) in 1984 from the Economics Department, University of Oslo. He has worked in the Research Department at Statistics Norway since 1984, except for an engagement in the Norwegian Ministry of Finance 2000–01. His current position is that of Senior Research Fellow and Head of the Unit for Public Economics. His main fields of work include development and applications of applied general equilibrium models to explore long-run growth trends, and to estimate macroeconomic and industry effects of tax reforms, industry and trade policy, environmental policies, population ageing, fiscal policy and public pension reforms.

Katja Hujo is Research Coordinator in the Social Policy and Development Programme at the United Nations Research Institute for Social Development (UNRISD), Geneva. At UNRISD, she manages research projects on *Financing Social Policy* and *Social Policy and Migration in Developing Countries*. She has published on diverse issues such as economic development, pension reform and migration.

Olli Kangas holds a PhD in sociology and is currently Research Professor at the Social Insurance Institution of Finland. Between 1994 and 2003 he was Professor of Social Policy at the University of Turku, and from 2004 to 2007 he worked as Research Professor at the Danish National Institute of Social Research in Copenhagen. His research is focused on comparative studies of the causes and consequences of social policy institutions. Among his current publications is *Social Policy and Economic Development in the Nordic Countries* (co-edited with Jokim Palme) (Palgrave Macmillan, 2005).

Rubén M. Lo Vuolo is Principal Researcher at the Centro Interdisciplinario para el Estudio de Políticas Públicas (Ciepp) in Buenos Aires. He studied at the Universidad Nacional del Litoral (Argentina) and at the University of Pittshburgh (USA). He has been a consultant to different multilateral organizations. He has published and co-edited several articles and books on issues such as social policies, pension reform, development and political economy. His latest books are *Económica para la Argentina: Propuestas* (2003) and *Distribuction y Crecimento* (forthcoming).

Shea McClanahan is a Research Analyst in the Social Policy and Development Programme at UNRISD and is working towards a PhD in Government at the University of Texas, Austin.

Santosh Mehrotra is Head of the Rural Development Division, Planning Commission, Government of India, and is currently engaged in writing India's 11th Five Year Plan (2007–12). He is a human development economist, and his research interests have spanned industry and trade issues, the impact of macroeconomic policy on health and education, the informal sector, and the economics of health and education. After receiving an MA in Economics from the New School for Social Research, New York, and a PhD from Cambridge University (1985), Santosh was Associate Professor of Economics, Jawaharlal Nehru University, New Delhi (1988–91). Since then he has been with the United Nations for 15 years as a policy advisor to the governments of developing countries.

Carmelo Mesa-Lago is the Distinguished Service Professor Emeritus of Economics, University of Pittsburgh as well as having been a visiting professor/researcher/lecturer in 36 countries. Mesa-Lago is currently the author of 74 books and 245 articles/chapters published in eight languages in 33 countries, most of them on the subject of social security, the latest of which is *Reassembling Social Security: A Survey of Pension and Healthcare Reforms in Latin America* (2008). He has worked in every country of Latin America as a consultant with ECLAC, ILO, ISSA, several UN branches, and most international financial organizations. In 2007 he was awarded the inaugural ILO International Research Prize on Decent Work, shared with Nelson Mandela.

Oliver Morrissey is Professor in Development Economics and Director of CREDIT, School of Economics, University of Nottingham. He has published some 60 articles in international journals and co-edited five books, mostly on aid policy and effectiveness, trade policy, conditionality, public finance and the political economy of policy reform. He has conducted many commissioned studies, for example on trade (for the Commonwealth Secretariat, DFID, DGTrade, FAO and the World Bank), aid (for DAC/OECD, DFID, WIDER and the World Bank) and on global public goods (for World Bank and UNIDO).

Manuel Orozco is Director of Remittances and Development at the Inter-American Dialogue, conducting policy analysis of the global flows of remittances. He has managed and advised on technical assistance grant facilities for international development institutions to leverage remittance transfers. He has conducted extensive research on remittances, migration and development worldwide, and teaches at George Washington University. His publications include 'Global remittances and the law – A review of regional trends and regulatory issues', in *International Migration Law: Developing Paradigms and Key Challenges* (2007); and *Remittances: Global Opportunities for International Person-to-Person Money Transfers* (2005).

Isabel Ortiz is a Senior Interregional Advisor at the Department of Economic and Social Affairs, United Nations in New York. She was educated in Spain and the United Kingdom, where she attained a Masters and a PhD from the London School of Economics. Earlier she worked at the Asian Development Bank (1995–2003), the High Council of Spanish Research and Madrid University (1993–95), the European Union (1991–92), and the UN Economic Commission for Latin America in Argentina (1991). Between 2003 and 2005 she undertook a number of freelance assignments for DFID, UNDP, OECD, KfW and the World Bank. Isabel Ortiz has more than 15 years of field experience in 30 countries of Asia, Africa, Eastern Europe and Latin America.

Andrew Rosser is Senior Lecturer in Development Studies at the University of Adelaide. His research interests include the political economy of the resource curse, the politics of state capacity building and the dynamics of economic reform. His publications include: 'Escaping the resource curse', *New Political Economy* (December 2006); and *The Political Economy of the Resource Curse: A Literature Survey*, IDS Working Paper 268 (2006).

Alice Sindzingre is a Research Fellow currently posted at the French agency for research, the National Centre for Scientific Research (CNRS, Paris) and affiliated to the University Paris-X (EconomiX). She is also Research Associate and Visiting Lecturer at the School of Oriental and African Studies (SOAS, Department of Economics, University of London), and associate researcher at the Centre d'Etude d'Afrique Noire (CEAN, CNRS, Bordeaux). She has served as a consultant for international organizations and published in academic journals on a large range of topics in development economics.

1
Introduction and Overview

Katja Hujo and Shea McClanahan

Social policy is a central instrument to promote an inclusive and democratically anchored development process. In recent years the general perception on the costs and benefits of social policy has changed, and policy makers are increasingly aware of the positive potential social policy entails. Despite this recognition, the challenge is to build social programmes on financial arrangements that are themselves sustainable, equitable and conducive to economic development.

One of the key lessons from the previous five-year research project *Social Policy in a Development Context* was that the dominant policy models of the past – populist/redistributive regimes based on soft monetary and fiscal policies, and liberal/conservative regimes based on austerity policies, privatization and the downsizing of public welfare provisioning – have failed to provide a long-term strategy that is developmental, democratic and socially inclusive. There is a growing consensus that economic and social policies have to work in tandem in order to be mutually reinforcing. An integrated approach to development is based on the premise that social policy has multiple roles, which have to be balanced against each other (Mkandawire 2004). An unduly narrow focus on one role, be it redistribution or production, or the outright neglect of others (often gender equality and democratization), can endanger the political or economic viability of the policies, and certainly undermine its success in terms of social development. Conventional debate gives disproportionate weight to the protective function of social policy at the expense of other vital roles. Indeed, the United Nations Research Institute for Social Development (UNRISD) research on late industrializers reveals that the central preoccupation of social policy in successful states has not been poverty reduction; rather, a whole range of social policy measures have been introduced at lower levels of the industrial development process.[1] In this body of research, the importance of finding appropriate financing sources and structures for social policy emerges time and again.

Approaching the topic of financing social policy leads to questions of resource mobilization, resource allocation and the actors and institutions involved in these processes. The current approach is dominated by a microperspective on how best to allocate a given amount of resources. Although efficient allocation of resources for social policy is important, taken in isolation this perspective entails serious

1

shortcomings: it sidelines the impact of welfare arrangements on economic development, and vice versa. In effect, efficiency arguments like these tend to shift the burden of proof regarding the value of social policy to the expenditures side, and at the same time, assume a glass ceiling for state revenues. Accepting that social policy systems are inevitably trapped in conditions of 'permanent austerity' (Pierson 2001) unduly limits the discussion to one of trade-offs based on assumptions of scarce resources. However, what is crucial about social policy *in a development context* is to identify how social policy can actually support and enhance a dynamic accumulation process that allows for the creation of income, which can then be taxed (or pooled in social insurance schemes) and redistributed toward socially desirable ends.

Accounting for the developmental impact of social policy is even more important, considering one of the central dilemmas confronting policy makers: the so-called affordability of public social expenditures.[2] In general, public finance seeks to match revenues and expenditures in the medium and long term. However, in the case of prolonged economic stagnation, social transfers are quickly overstretched. By going beyond demand stabilization and protection, the use of social transfers evolves into a quasi-permanent substitute for the creation of income and formal employment. If this is the case, budgetary pressures and indebtedness tend to increase, and eventually constrain the fiscal and economic space for social policy – even if political commitment is in place. In developing countries with limited capacity for debt-financing, it is often the case that once it reaches this critical stage, the state either fails to deliver on entitlements to citizens or the insured, or it shifts part of the burden towards individuals, families and communities, for example, by increasing the amount of unpaid care work or out-of-pocket payments.[3]

In recent decades there has been an intensification of the debates surrounding the affordability of social policies. Several trends contributing to this process can be identified. The first was the paradigm shift in the 1970s from the Keynesian welfare state model towards the liberal market model. One implication was that social policy was no longer seen as a central instrument for social development and stabilization, but rather was increasingly portrayed as a cost factor and potential cause of fiscal crises, inflation and market distortions.[4] In addition, demographic changes such as ageing and lower fertility rates challenged social insurance schemes that were financed out of contributions from the active working population. Growing inequality, as well as unemployment or increased informal employment, put pressure on revenues and expenditures alike, whereas economic integration and liberalization of goods and capital markets increased competition in general, and, more particularly, tax competition.

Most industrialized countries are in the process of adjusting their tax/welfare regimes to meet these challenges, while also trying to maintain their basic policy regime or social contract.[5] Developing countries, however, face a greater challenge for a variety of reasons. They are confronted with a huge mismatch between means and ends: social investment and transfers are desperately needed, while state revenues and administrative capacities are limited. Institutional legacies present additional difficulties. Existing social protection schemes are often fragmented, stratified and regressive, and social contracts in support of redistribution are weak. Furthermore, adjustment and stabilization policies, plus balance of payments and currency crises, have increased volatility, income and asset concentration, external debt, budget deficits, unemployment and informal sector employment. And last but not least, Washington consensus policies (the triad of privatization, liberalization and deregulation) have frequently resulted in lower administrative capacity; declining revenues due to the substitution of 'difficult-to-collect' taxes for 'easy-to-collect' ones; high fiscal costs related to privatization policies; decreased domestic economic activity to tax; and subsidies or tax exemptions that are designed to attract foreign investors but which squeeze fiscal revenues.[6]

Growing criticism with regard to the theoretical underpinnings of these policy blueprints, together with ample empirical evidence on the development failures they produced, eventually fed into new debates that gradually extended to the global policy-making level.[7] Key events such as the World Summit for Social Development, the declaration of the Millennium Development Goals (MDGs), together with Bretton Woods initiatives such as debt relief for the poorest countries (heavily indebted poor countries/HIPC) and poverty reduction strategies (PRSs), illustrate the rising profile of social issues. The recognition that social policy has highly beneficial effects even in middle- or low-income countries, which were traditionally believed to be 'too poor' to afford welfare policies, opens a window of opportunity for these countries (Pal et al. 2005; World Bank 2005). Unfortunately, the current financial crisis has caused an abrupt reversal of the positive trends in global trade and commodity prices as well as growing remittances and aid flows we had witnessed a few years ago. Theoretically, these external flows have the potential to ease the financing constraints for some countries in the South, as long as macroeconomic stability can be safeguarded and governments are more willing to upgrade their social agenda beyond poverty reduction and emergency measures.

In essence, the current context presents undeniable constraints for developing countries attempting to embark on paths leading to sustainable social development, but it is our view that these constraints are tempered by promising opportunities. The chapters in this volume seek to explore and critically assess some of those opportunities as they are manifest through what we loosely term 'revenue sources'[8] for social policy.

Approaching social policy in terms of revenues

This research project is based on the view that financing social policies is especially challenging for developing countries, given the particular nature of the economic and institutional constraints they confront. However, these challenges will not be overcome if policy debates stagnate around expenditure-based discussions of how best to allocate a given pool of resources. The recent recognition that social policy is also an investment is a positive step forward, but any far-reaching development strategy must also actively seek ways to continually expand the revenue base for developmental purposes. For this reason, UNRISD research on financing social policy departs from previous approaches, which have focused almost exclusively on expenditures, and tackles the revenue side of social policy. Clearly, the social policy commitment of a state is reflected in the structure and volume of social expenditures for health, education, old-age and survivor's insurance, family benefits, labour market policies and social assistance. Furthermore, conventional wisdom holds that redistribution should take place on the expenditure side of the fiscal balance in order to avoid the negative side-effects of complex and redistributive tax systems. However, if social policy is considered to be more than a residual category that merely compensates for market failures and adjustment processes, the financing side has to be treated as an integral part of the problem, and by extension, the solution. An integrated social policy system requires that both revenue and expenditure policies respond to principles of equity and gender equality, progressive redistribution and economic development.

In particular, this book, which reflects the overall structure of a broader research project, examines the challenges and constraints associated with specific revenue sources for social policy, including taxation, social insurance, pension funds, mineral rents, remittances and aid. These topics have been selected on the basis of central contemporary social development concerns, perceived research gaps (taking into account past and current UNRISD research that complements this project as well as research conducted by other United Nations agencies) and themes that are especially conducive to an integrated approach to social policy and economic development. Analyses of different financing instruments complement the studies where appropriate, as for example, when discussing different models and reform options for tax systems or financing methods for social insurance schemes. The overall approach of the project, however, is on the political economy and impact of different revenue sources on social development and social policies.

The book is organized as follows. The first two chapters introduce the current policy environment that both informs and constrains (paradigmatically and financially) social policy making in the developing world. Chapter 1, by Rubén Lo Vuolo, discusses predominant social policy models and reform trends, and their suitability for the developing world. In the second chapter, Isabel Ortiz examines the potential for international resources and redistribution for social development in these countries. Part II builds on the discussion of constraints and challenges for financing social policy in developing countries and delves more deeply into the topics of taxation and aid, drawing primarily on evidence from low-income countries. The chapter by Enrique Delamonica and Santosh Mehrotra deals with the possibilities for creating policy synergies to enhance the financing of pro-poor social services. Then, Chapters 5 and 6, by Alice Sindzingre and Oliver Morrissey, respectively, explore the implications of aid and other forms of external resource dependence (for example, commodity-based taxes) for developing countries' own capacities to finance and implement social policies and to diversify their resource bases. The section on mineral rents follows with two chapters, one by Andrew Rosser and the other by Erling Holmøy, which set out to link the debate on the alleged 'resource curse' with discussions of the political, economic and social conditions necessary for overcoming the challenges posed by natural resource abundance. The chapters on pension funds and social insurance schemes exemplify the wide variety of forms that these systems can take in different contexts. First, Carmelo Mesa-Lago's chapter explores the relationship between labour markets, social insurance (pensions and health) and coverage in Latin America. Next, chapters by Olli Kangas (on Finland) and Mukul Asher (on a selection of Asian countries) highlight the importance of striking the delicate balance between designing pension models that guarantee adequate protection levels for the aged while also contributing positively to economic development and creating appropriate governance structures for these institutions. Finally, the chapters on remittances explore the relationship between these private flows – an increasing and stable source of foreign reserves for many developing countries – and different dimensions of social development, including their implications for social provisioning and social policy more generally. Hein de Haas presents a theoretical and conceptual overview, while Manuel Orozco offers state-of-the-art data and analysis of the Latin American context.

The following paragraphs present a brief introduction of the main issues raised in each chapter. Potential lessons for policy makers and directions for future research are addressed in the concluding chapter.

Global dimensions: Paradigms and resources

Within the development community, the hegemony of neoliberal theoretical and strategic approaches is increasingly challenged and – at least at the level of discourse – more balanced visions of the state–market relationship and of the economic–social nexus are being brought back in. However, a closer look at what could be labelled post-Washington consensus social policy reveals that fundamental shortcomings of the old approaches still persist, as Lo Vuolo illustrates with his analysis of the limits and potential of current approaches to the problems of social exclusion in labour markets in Latin America. He presents a staunch critique of the prevailing conceptual framework around social protection, elsewhere designated 'social risk management' (Holzmann and Jorgensen 2000; World Bank 2001), as illustrated by shortcomings in the areas of pension reform, workfare and microfinance programmes. Social risk management has emerged as a revision of World Bank orthodoxy that attempts to reassert the dominance of the market while acknowledging a legitimate role for the state in attending to the needs of vulnerable groups. The revision lies in a renewed emphasis on state institutions as requisite for reducing market instability, reinforcing competition and improving overall market functioning, ultimately aiding in the reduction of poverty. Lo Vuolo argues that, in essence, this approach retains the orthodox faith that economic growth will produce spillover effects by means of employment generation, while the state provides social protection through a modular system of safety net programmes that are tailored to the specific risk patterns of different groups. These programmes are then expected to function according to a logic of social insurance that diversifies risk and stabilizes individual consumption and savings patterns.

According to Lo Vuolo's analysis, there are clear limits to the application of such mechanisms to a developing context such as that of Latin America. Not only do these policies fail to recognize the disproportionate effect of economic volatility on the poor, but they also overlook the direct link between economic volatility and the economic and social policies supported by the international financial institutions (IFIs). Furthermore, employment alone does not guarantee social security coverage for the very large numbers of informal, semi-formal and temporary workers, or the working poor. In this sense, social risk management's emphasis on individual responsibility in determining one's position in the labour market is misplaced in these contexts; informality is not chosen by workers but rather is imposed by employers and the state. In Lo Vuolo's chapter, these shortcomings are made evident in three policy areas promoted by the World Bank: pension reform, workfare programmes and microfinance programmes. In general, these policies are characterized by incentives based on false premises,[9] low coverage among the poor, a low impact on poverty due to selectivity and targeting, and unjustifiably high administrative costs. He makes a provocative critique in the case of microfinance, arguing that poor people become indebted in exchange for access to impoverished markets, ultimately benefiting financial sectors instead of promoting higher incomes or savings.

Lo Vuolo explores two specific alternatives to the social risk management framework: the Employer of Last Resort (ELR) and the Renda Básica de Cidadania (Basic Citizenship Income). When applied to the Latin American context, these policies suffer from several shortcomings, but, on balance, these alternatives make important strides, on the one hand by encouraging policy makers to rethink the proper role of the state in the economy vis-à-vis employment, and on the other, by vindicating universal and unconditional social policies. Lo Vuolo concludes his chapter by emphasizing the need to advance towards the construction of a universalistic social protection system, one that is based not on 'one' policy, but rather on a 'system of consistently articulated policies' (cited in UNRISD 2007: 5). These policies should place formal employment at the centre of the problem and, more importantly, recognize that unemployment is a pathology of economic, not social, policy. In particular, social policies should be *preventive* and proactive in nature, not reactive, emergency responses, and they should furthermore aim at consolidating long-term support for universalism and unconditionality. Policies that emerge from the prevailing social risk management discourse may seem revisionist at first glance, but, ultimately, they retain fundamentally flawed elements of the orthodoxy.

In her chapter on the international sources and instruments to finance social policy, Ortiz argues that the extreme inequalities in the distribution of the world's wealth call for redistribution at a global scale. To the four conventional pillars of fiscal space for public policies (increased official development assistance, additional international or domestic borrowing, enhanced revenue collection, and improved efficiency and reprioritization of expenditures), Ortiz adds a fifth: 'avoiding South–North transfers through better use of reserves' (chapter 3). Her chapter draws attention to the enormous global wealth disparities, where half of the world's population has access to just 1 per cent of the world's assets, and the returns to globalization are concentrated among a few entities in the North. These inequities impede social development in large part because the costs of social policies are accrued at the national level under conditions of limited resources. Despite rich countries' recurring commitments to provide 0.7 per cent of their gross national product (GNP) in Official Development Assistance (ODA), donors' actual levels consistently fall below this level due to the failure of many countries to adequately prioritize aid over other kinds of expenditures (such as military). Consequently, new international sources of development finance are emerging, some of which already exist (global funds) and others which have been proposed (such as luxury taxes or taxes on activities with negative environmental impacts).

Because ODA in its current form is highly problematic,[10] heated debates over aspects of ODA or new instruments often distract attention away from the more critical issue of international redistribution, and provide donors with convenient excuses to postpone necessary action. Attention should be paid, she argues, to correcting the system's imperfections without discarding the principle of redistribution. Meanwhile, South–South transfers are becoming increasingly important as a means of international redistribution, including ODA by Southern donors (China or Venezuela), regional integration initiatives, or South–South banks. These instruments pose problems of their own (such as lesser resources or a heavy focus on infrastructure rather than social investment), but Ortiz holds that there is cause for optimism with regard to willingness of certain Southern partners to prioritize social objectives.[11]

In her view, perhaps the most striking aspect of the current global economy is the existence of a net transfer of financial resources from poor countries to rich countries. Overall, debt interest payments, investment profit remittances and the portfolio of central bank reserves offset the net financial inflows to developing countries. Rich countries, most notably the United States, are at the receiving end of the vast majority of global savings. Ortiz emphasizes that only by reversing this net transfer of resources can developing countries begin to enjoy the necessary fiscal space for social development. The chapter closes by assessing both the potential and the limitations of each of these specific financial instruments for international redistribution. These instruments include social investment projects, general budget support (GBS), MDG contracts, sector-wide approaches (SWAps), technical assistance, government bonds, municipal/subnational bonds and other securities, such as securitizing workers remittances, and the International Financial Facility (IFF).

Taxation and aid

When identifying possible financing sources for development, taxation and aid are often juxtaposed against each other on account of their different impact on the economic and political system. But, in addition, the extent to which a country finances public expenditures out of taxation revenues versus external aid clearly reflects where that country stands in terms of development and self-reliance.

Reforming tax systems in developing countries is therefore one of the most important tasks for financing social policy in a context of consistent national development strategies and strong state–citizen relationships. Taxation revenue is generally deemed superior to other sources in terms of stability, distributional justice and meeting the goal of universal coverage. Tax systems are also said to enhance ownership and state accountability (Moore 2004; Fjeldstad and Rakner 2003). Whereas the goals of tax reform seem to be widely accepted (for example, increasing the volume of tax funds, enhancing their progressive structure and gender equality, and improving transparency and efficiency), past reforms implemented under the guidance of multilateral donors have been associated with some undesired outcomes like shrinking state revenues or implementation failures.[12]

With regard to aid, as shown in Ortiz's chapter, external funding through international development cooperation remains an important pillar of development finance. International donors agreed to substantially increase ODA for low-income countries in order to accelerate the MDG process. Additional funding for poor countries can ease financial constraints but, as with natural resource rents, increased aid flows pose a variety of political and economic challenges (related to conditionality, accountability and Dutch disease effects), which have to be addressed successfully in order to make aid more effective for development.

Delamonica and Mehrotra's chapter on the 'pro-poor' financing of social services introduces a framework based on a set of interrelated synergies at the macro level, echoing Lo Vuolo's point – indeed a common theme throughout the chapters – that good social policies are those rooted in a system of consistently articulated policies. Economic growth, poverty reduction, reproductive labour and social development are all interdependent and should reinforce each other to produce positive human development outcomes. If it is true that economic growth depends on sound macroeconomic policies, and technological and structural change, it likewise depends on social policy, income poverty reduction and reproductive labour. In the same way, both income poverty reduction and social development cannot be sustained without economic growth working in tandem with socially oriented, gender-sensitive redistributive social policies. In turn, achieving these pro-poor outcomes requires an understanding of the 'complex fiscal causalities' (cited in UNRISD 2007: 6) involved. Just as social policy has multiple roles, the authors remind us that the multiple roles of fiscal policy – including income distribution, output and employment, and social services delivery – should not be overlooked.

In the quest to achieve pro-poor social services, Delamonica and Mehrotra agree that the choice of financing mechanism matters. The authors classify social service financing into the following broad categories: self-provision (where the state is absent and households or individuals must carry the burden); user fees; pre-paid schemes and generalized insurance; earmarked taxes; indirect taxes; and direct taxes. These mechanisms can be assessed according to two criteria: the degree of *progressivity* versus *regressivity*; and the extent to which they are rooted in *solidarity-based* versus *individualistic* principles.

In their chapter, Delamonica and Mehrotra weigh the different financing tools against these two criteria, and the results are instructive. At one extreme, the most regressive and individualistic financing mechanism is, not surprisingly, self-provision, while direct taxation emerges as the most progressive and solidarity-based of the mechanisms. User fees are widely criticized for being detrimental to the poor and, in fact, have been largely reversed since the 1990s. Generalized insurance based on pre-paid contributions poses an alternative to user fees that spreads risks and lowers costs, but high degrees of market segmentation (and regressivity in cases where insurance markets are not income differentiated) make contributory programmes less pro-poor. As concerns taxation mechanisms, indirect taxes such as the heavily promoted value added tax (VAT), are notoriously regressive and, insofar as consumption patterns vary according to gender, are also gender biased. Earmarked taxes, on the other hand, tend to be criticized on the basis of fungibility arguments (whereby general tax funds are diverted away from social services), but, as the authors point out, have the potential to be quite progressive, if one considers the possibility of luxury taxes or taxes on second homes. Moreover, they argue that earmarking has the distinct advantage of shoring up and sustaining political support for redistribution, since the utilization of tax revenues for specific purposes is more transparent. Finally, direct taxes (such as income or property taxes), although the most progressive and solidarity-based, are plagued with implementation challenges since they spark high levels of political resistance and are costly to enforce.

In reference to the political aspects of financing mechanisms, the chapter highlights the fact that *governance* is key to improving the effective utilization of funds for the poor. Not only are Type I (leakage) and Type II (undercoverage) errors pervasive in targeted programmes for social services in developing countries, but the contractual basis for many of these services is an invitation to corruption. The massive evidence of what the authors call 'grand larceny' (cited in UNRISD 2007: 6) by public officials in programmes that are ostensibly for the poor cannot be ignored, but at the same time, social audits and transparency initiatives such as the Right to Information Act in India can paradoxically decrease support for social programmes among the rich, who are reluctant to back government policies plagued with corruption and targeting errors. Overall, for the financing of social services to be more pro-poor, Delamonica and Mehrotra echo the primary justification for this volume, contending that there must first be a shift in focus from the expenditure side of policies towards revenue generation. The tendency to advocate more regressive taxation mechanisms simply because they are easier to implement sidesteps deeper political and technical challenges which, if properly addressed, would pave the way for longer-term, more sustainable, and more equitable financing systems.

In her chapter, Sindzingre explores the conditions and constraints stemming from the finance regime that hinder the contribution of social policies to development in low-income countries. She concentrates on sub-Saharan Africa. While the principal constraints can be traced to processes of state formation and the historical structure of the tax regime in a given country, several additional factors compound the challenges facing low-income countries.

First, the traditional dependence on commodities and trade-based taxation (in some cases representing upwards of one-third of government revenues) implies a high degree of volatility in revenue generation, impeding sound fiscal planning that would be based on predictable inflows. Second, external determinants like trade liberalization and foreign aid also have implications for tax systems. Given

the historical dependence of low-income countries on trade taxes, trade liberalization in many countries severely aggravated existing revenue collection, eroding
fiscal resources without putting in place sustainable alternatives. International
Monetary Fund (IMF) studies show mixed results for the recovery of lost trade
revenues, but the positive trends largely reflect gains in middle-income countries
from the implementation of the VAT. In contrast, low-income countries, by and
large, have not enjoyed revenue gains from the VAT due to problems with the
refund and credit mechanisms, underpayment and high levels of informality.

Sindzingre is also critical of the poverty reduction strategies in many countries.
She argues that the nature of poverty reduction programmes themselves has been
detrimental to low-income states' ability to finance developmental social policies,
as social spending requirements can keep states from investing in productive sectors given the trade-offs that low-income countries permanently face due to budget
constraints. It is important to note here that it is the composition and efficiency
of social spending, rather than the levels *per se*, that is the most significant factor.
Many social programmes are also donor-financed and targeted in nature, which
pose additional challenges for the construction of developmental social policy systems. Finally, dependence on foreign aid makes states vulnerable to aid fluctuations
and can create a disincentive for states to tax their own citizens. Consequently, the
nexus of political accountability shifts from citizens to donors: as policies are perceived to be handed down from external actors, the credibility of governments and
political institutions vis-à-vis citizens is constantly called into question.

According to Sindzingre, developmental states in Asia hold important lessons
for low-income countries in terms of the political economy of taxation. One of
the most important is that it is not the level of taxation ratios that matters, since
many of the developmentalist Asian states exhibited relatively low levels of taxation. Rather, growth-oriented policies, complemented by heavy investment in
education, secured a place for social policies that contributed to economic growth
while simultaneously ensuring political legitimacy. Indeed, low-income countries
get caught in a 'taxation trap' (Chapter 5), wherein low levels of taxation, redistribution and low-level social services are locked into a vicious cycle, and, as a
consequence, political legitimacy is entirely delinked from social policy. While
there is no doubt that the Asian developmental experiences are instructive in a
number of ways, Sindzingre reminds us that their experiences result from a particular set of historical, political and economic processes that may or may not apply
to low-income country contexts.

Morrissey follows with a chapter that examines the role aid plays in increasing
financing for public spending on social service delivery in developing countries.
The primary justification for foreign aid, and one that is often overlooked, is its
role in the provision of public goods in the form of social services. Because there
are international 'spillover ranges' (positive externalities) (ch. 6) associated with
the provision of social services in low-income countries (and, conversely, negative
spillover effects when these services are underprovided), the international community has an interest in 'picking up the slack' where national government efforts fall
short. The principal instrument through which these international public goods

are provided is foreign aid, which may or may not work in tandem with national government social spending.

For this reason, there is a premium on providing evidence that in fact aid does work through national governments to have a positive impact on welfare outcomes. In fact, by Morrissey's calculations, when changes in government social spending (understood to be expenditures in health, education and sanitation) are measured as a function of variations in aid flows, tax revenue as a share of GDP, and GDP per capita over a given period, foreign aid shows, on average, a small but significant effect on government social spending (1.7 per cent increase for every 10 per cent increase in aid).[13] The effect he finds of tax revenue increases on social spending, however, is significantly larger, at 3.2 per cent. Aid has a greater impact on social spending in low-income countries than in middle-income countries, not only because middle-income countries tend to spend more, on average, on social services regardless of aid or tax revenues, but also because aid to middle-income countries is more likely to go towards investments in infrastructure.

In addition to impacting on government social spending, Morrissey's chapter shows that aid also affects measures of aggregate welfare. These effects work through three primary mechanisms. First, aid can influence welfare directly, either by creating income-earning opportunities or through the direct provision of social services. Secondly, aid can improve aggregate welfare indirectly over the long run, by contributing to economic growth. Finally, as mentioned, aid can work through governments, increasing expenditures on social services which, in turn, impact positively on welfare indicators. There is robust evidence that aid indeed does pass through government social spending to reduce poverty and improve the levels of human welfare. Again, the effects on human development indicators are more pronounced in low-income countries; however, government social spending is less likely to impact on aggregate welfare in these same countries. Only in middle-income countries can the positive impact on aggregate welfare be fairly attributed to increases in government social spending. One of the reasons for the disconnect between increasing social spending through aid and aggregate welfare improvements in low-income countries is the low overall quality of public services. Not only are funds often misused or misallocated, but overall social spending tends to remain stubbornly low, despite having grown in recent years. It is likely that any positive effects of aid increases on welfare in poor countries occur primarily through direct impacts on growth, or through aid-financed programmes which tend to bypass governments altogether.

Morrissey's study shows that aid does contribute to poverty reduction, through growth, direct benefits and support to social sector spending, but that the effects are small, mainly due to the lack of effectiveness in social sector spending. However, in his view there is no basis for recommendations that would double the level of aid; rather, more attention should be paid to the effectiveness of government spending, since increasing proportions of aid flows do pass through budgets. There are concerns about the macroeconomic effects of rapid increases in aid, such as effects on prices, competitiveness (through pressures on foreign exchange) and general challenges for disbursement, but he suggests that these are not insurmountable.

Mineral rents

If the lack of sufficient revenues is considered to be a major problem for social policies in developing countries, those countries that are richly endowed with natural resources, especially oil and gas, should presumably be fortunate. For many developing countries, natural resource rents represent a substantial and growing proportion of total government revenues with potentially enormous implications for the design and delivery of social policies. During recent years and before the present crisis, these countries have experienced a mineral 'bonanza' (attributable in particular to skyrocketing oil prices), which potentially could produce a sort of 'big push' for the development process. And yet there is considerable evidence that many resource-abundant countries have not been able to utilize their resources to induce a process of sustained economic growth, let alone social development involving equitable distribution of the fruits of this natural wealth and overall improvements of the welfare of the citizens. Two chapters explore this paradox, one from a comparative perspective, and the other focusing on the particular case of Norway. Both focus on the economic and political challenges that threaten to impede successful social development strategies in mineral-rich countries.

Rosser starts his analysis with a critical evaluation of the evidence pointing to the resource curse, and then examines the conditions under which the resource curse can be overcome. Briefly, the resource curse thesis is based on a correlation between the abundance of natural resources – especially oil – on the one hand, and a set of negative economic, political and social outcomes, on the other. Most commonly, scholars point to the fact that countries rich in natural resources tend to have lower levels of economic growth and are more likely to be authoritarian. A smaller but substantial subliterature examines the association between natural resources and higher levels of poverty or other negative social development outcomes, and one study in particular argues that natural resource wealth is associated with the lower status of women in society. Finally, a sizeable literature explores the relationship between natural resource abundance and the incidence, duration and intensity of civil war.

While much of this literature is persuasive, Rosser shows that it is far from conclusive and that it should therefore be treated with caution. Several serious critiques have been levied against the resource curse thesis, attacking the prevailing evaluation methodologies on the basis of measurement errors, incorrect specification of the models, and the high probability of spurious correlations. For instance, the findings do not appear to be robust across different measures of natural resource abundance. The predominant measures of resource abundance are based on natural resource exports, but causal mechanisms suggest that the problem is caused not by the volume of natural resource exports, but rather by the *rents* from these resources. When measures of rents are used, the relationship is much weaker and is often not significant. Second, it is far from clear whether the type of resource matters, and if so, which resources (for example, point source, lootable, and so on) are 'cursed'. Third, there are several studies that call into question the fundamental claim that there is a relationship between natural resource abundance and negative economic and other indicators. Finally, from a purely methodological perspective, most studies on the resource curse are multiple regressions, statistical studies that draw broad-brush causal conclusions based on what could be mere spurious correlations. As Rosser points out, any number of alternative explanations (missing variables), other than natural resource abundance, could explain the outcomes in question.

Putting to one side the debate about the existence of the resource curse itself, there are numerous examples of resource-abundant countries that do not suffer from resource curse 'symptoms' (examples include Botswana, Indonesia, Chile and Malaysia, among others). Rosser's chapter demonstrates that perhaps the more important question emerges out of the wide degree of variation in the developmental outcomes among these resource-rich countries: under what conditions is the resource curse overcome? Experiences of countries that have achieved both rapid economic growth and moderate levels of social development suggest that intervening variables – such as economic and social policies, or political institutions – can, and do, mediate the relationship between resource abundance and developmental outcomes. It is clear that different types of resource-rich states exhibit different incentive structures for elites, and that these structures, in turn, are also determined by broader historical and structural factors, as well as the location of the countries in the global political economy.

Erling Holmøy's chapter describes how the Norwegian case, in which the resource curse was overcome through a unique combination of economic and social policies, is illustrative for many reasons. Oil money flows into the Central Government Pension Fund (CPF), whose portfolio value amounted to approximately $245 billion[14] in 2006. Since 1998, up to 50 per cent of funds can be invested abroad and, in combination with a strong fiscal surplus, combat 'Dutch disease' and contribute to macroeconomic stability. Oil rents have been used to pay back foreign debt and to finance generous social benefits. The Norwegian example might entail lessons for resource-rich countries concerning how to achieve stability and enhance social protection at the same time. Following this track, Erling Holmøy offers key insights into the experience of his country. He shows how, following the discovery of large petroleum reserves in 1969, long-term planning, and careful investment and expenditure strategies, transformed Norway into one of the world's wealthiest countries on a per capita basis. Specifically, Norway's success can be traced to five features of Norwegian political economy. First, the government savings ratio is high and has even been institutionalized in the form of a legal budget constraint whereby only the expected real return (4 per cent) of the CPF may be used to finance non-petroleum government budget deficits. This fiscal policy rule is a particular feature of the Norwegian system that has been surprisingly well respected since its implementation in 2001. Second, Norway has strong institutions that ensure the protection of property rights, low levels of corruption, and a competent and accountable bureaucracy. In particular, the fact that the CPF is separate from the government budget and is invested according to strict rules has all but eliminated incentives for rent seeking. Third, in this context, petroleum revenues have been instrumental in stimulating rapid economic growth, in large part through spillover effects leading to technological innovations in the petroleum sector. Fourth, some literature suggests that having a parliamentary (rather than presidential) system of government may facilitate Norway's management of natural resource wealth. Finally, Norway's early industrialization (prior to the Second World War) may have eased the pressures to spend rapidly once oil was discovered.

Norway's experience, however, is much more than just a success story. Indeed, questions about the future economic sustainability of the pension fund in the light of ever-increasing government entitlements and rising living standards, illustrates that a country's 'development' is manifested via a never-ending renegotiation of the terms of its social contract. Holmøy's analysis also highlights the sensitivity of resource-abundant political economies to fluctuations in commodity prices, and the intimate relationship between domestic taxation systems and natural resource revenue fluctuations. The outlook for the Norwegian CPF is drastically different when petroleum prices are estimated at $50 per barrel versus projections based on a price of $25 per barrel, and the expected payroll taxes vary inversely with these prices. Whether the nature of the domestic taxation–commodity price nexus is similar for developing countries merits further exploration. Moreover, such complex model-based projections themselves require a great deal of technical expertise, which raises important questions about technical capacity as a necessary condition for weaving together the kinds of institutional complementarities between social and economic policies that characterize the Norwegian experience.

Social insurance and pension funds

Social insurance schemes such as public pensions and health care take a variety of forms in both developing and industrialized countries. A common theme that runs through the discussions is the challenge of reconciling the necessity of financial sustainability in these contributory schemes with the imperatives of ensuring coverage and adequate levels of benefits. Is extension of social insurance programmes a viable option for developing countries? Is it possible to achieve universal access and equitable rules within often-fragmented and stratified schemes covering only a limited fraction of the labour force? Can the beauty of contribution-financed systems, their supposed fiscal neutrality, be maintained in practice in a context of demographic change and shrinking numbers of active contributors? What are the redistributive effects of state subsidies towards these schemes? Social insurance can be organized according to different models, such as public, private or occupationally based insurance schemes, and pre-paid (funded) versus redistributive (pay-as-you-go) schemes. The extent to which the state is involved in social insurance schemes depends on the characteristics of a country's social policy regime, ranging from basically normative and regulative interventions, as in the case of the East Asian developmental state (Kwon 2005), to extensive financial contributions, as in the case of the Western European and some Latin American welfare states. In many countries, employer-based social insurance schemes are offered on a voluntary basis.

In his chapter, Mesa-Lago delivers a thorough analysis of the current state of social insurance (pensions and health) in the context of high degrees of labour market transformation in Latin America. Newly compiled comparative data allow him to draw significant conclusions about the state of social insurance systems throughout the region. Although there are substantial differences in coverage rates between so-called 'pioneer' countries compared with those with less developed welfare systems, increasing informality and labour flexibilization, along with reforms to the health and pension sectors, have contributed to declining rates of coverage in the entire region over recent years. Incorporating 'difficult-to-cover' groups from the informal and rural sectors (such as the self-employed, domestic servants, employees in microenterprises, and non-salaried rural workers, among others) into the pension and health insurance schemes continues to be the key challenge. Indeed, the uninsured informal sector has actually expanded and now averages 47 per cent of the urban labour force for the whole region.

According to Mesa-Lago, Latin American social insurance coverage, besides being low, is highly unequal. These inequalities are largely explained by such factors as income level, gender, geographical location and ethnicity. Not surprisingly, populations showing the lowest rates of coverage tend to be low-income, female, rural and indigenous. Many of the poorest countries lack social assistance pensions altogether, and over the last decade, the IFIs have neglected the poverty-reduction dimension of pensions by placing a heavy emphasis on the mandatory private savings pillar over the public pillar in pension reform. Most of these negative trends can be traced to a combination of several factors external to the pension system itself (including high poverty and unemployment, low government commitment to social policy, scarce fiscal resources, among other things) with the failure of social insurance systems rooted in formal employment schemes to adapt to increasing segmentation, informalization and flexibilization in the labour market. Mesa-Lago's analysis of the Latin American context demonstrates that the challenges of providing adequate coverage and ensuring political sustainability extend beyond the more typical discussions surrounding pensions systems, and in fact, apply to all kinds of social insurances schemes.

As the chapters on pension funds demonstrate, however, where retirement schemes have been designed as pre-funded schemes, a whole new set of issues emerges, as pension funds have been a major financing source for investment in these countries. In this sense they are a good example of how to combine the productive and protective roles of social policy, whereas pay-as-you-go systems constitute an example for combining social protection with social cohesion through forging a generational contract. To assess the developmental impact of social funds it is crucial to look at investment policies: high social returns are desirable from a developmental point of view whereas profitable low-risk investments are necessary from a protective point of view. Privatization policies (usually consisting of a transition from pay-as-you-go financing to funded schemes and decentralized private administration) have performed poorly on both accounts, by imposing high transition costs on governments and substantial social costs in terms of coverage, uncertainty of benefits, greater gender inequality, and so on.[15] Pension funds are confronted with the challenge of reconciling the trade-offs – and maximizing the benefits – implied in the protective and productive functions of these kinds of social security systems. The cases presented in the following chapters highlight the importance of striking a delicate balance between the technical challenges of designing pensions, and the political challenges involved in aligning diverse interests in support of more equitable pension schemes.

Kangas' chapter considers the role that pensions and pension funds played in state formation and the construction of a national economy in Finland. Before the passage of Finland's first pension scheme in 1937, Finland was among the poorest countries in the world. A historically strong and independent state took a nation-building approach to the Finnish welfare state, developing a fully funded, defined-contribution pension scheme, whose primary purpose was the accumulation of capital to spur economic growth. The system underwent significant reform several times, the first of which, in 1956, converted the fully funded system to pay-as-you-go. Because of wide perceptions that the public entity in charge of the funds had confiscated previous funds and distributed them to the rural population, the new plan forfeited the support of trade unions that had been so instrumental in securing the passage of the original scheme. Five years passed before an agreement between conservatives, trade unions and the employers' federation could be reached that would create a totally legislated defined-benefit scheme which was partially funded, and partially pay-as-you-go. Not only did private insurance companies act as insurance carriers, but private funds were then administered by social partners, solidifying political support. Finally, in 1966, two public sector schemes – one for municipal and one for state employees – were created to complement the already existing private schemes.

Notwithstanding the importance of building political support for national pension reforms, the design and investment strategy tied to the funds was a key determinant in Finland's achievement of its desired developmental outcomes. A central part of the investment strategy prior to the 1980s was their 'safe' investment back into the domestic industrial sector. Indeed, up to one-third of all loans went back into industry, while an important amount also went to the construction sector, providing jobs and housing in a context of urbanization. Indeed, during this earlier period, pension funds were explicitly invested in national industries in order to promote national development. The liberalization of credit markets towards the end of the 1980s ushered in an era of high-risk, high-return investments for the pension insurance market. Because foreign investments offered higher dividends, the share of investments in the domestic market has fallen steadily over recent decades, dropping drastically most recently from 60 per cent in 2000 to 30 per cent in 2006. Whereas previous funds were collected and put to use within the national economy, new contributions, although still collected nationally, are invested abroad. The potential benefits of these shifts in investment portfolios on pensioners and pensions (in terms of better interest rates, greater risk sharing, lower contributions, and so on) must be weighed against the implications of investing internationally on the use of resources for national projects.

Although Finland might seem worlds apart from the developing countries of Asia, many of the same issues arise in Mukul Asher's chapter, which gives an overview of social security systems in several Asian countries, including Indonesia, Malaysia, Sri Lanka and Thailand. Any social security system must fulfill certain objectives for both governments and individuals: smoothing consumption over the lifetime of its operation; providing insurance, especially in contexts of longevity and inflation; redistributing income; and relieving poverty. However, given fiscal constraints, these objectives must be traded off against other needs such as economic growth, labour market efficiency, health care, education or infrastructure. According to Asher, the trend rate of economic growth is the most important determinant of the ability of a social security system to meet any of these economic security objectives. Because social security reform is a long-term process, sometimes spanning over a decade, the importance of sequencing and scalability also cannot be overlooked. Within this reform process, organizational effectiveness and policy design are two critical factors for achieving effective reform. There are countless examples of poorly designed systems in Asia, but Thailand stands out with a defined-benefit scheme that is managed through the finance ministry. The minister of finance has complete discretion to change the system's parameters at a whim, which alters the actuarial situation essentially without oversight. The Thai case points to the necessity of establishing a board of trustees which is simultaneously independent and competent. Beyond these, other system design challenges include adequacy of benefits and coverage, affordability (at all levels), sustainability, robustness, and ensuring reasonable levels of income replacement coupled with a safety net for the elderly poor. While there is considerable variety in social security systems across Asian countries, Asher notes that there is general agreement that a multitier framework, one that strengthens the so-called 'zero pillar' of social assistance or flat universal pensions, is most desirable.

In addition, even the core functions associated with any provident or pension fund are often taken for granted and poorly performed in the region. These functions include everything from the reliable collection of contributions and the timely payment of benefits, to securing financial management and productive asset investment, all of which depend upon effective communication, record keeping and financial reporting to ensure fiduciary responsibility, transparency and accountability. Part and parcel of designing and managing pension and provident fund systems is determining the most appropriate ways to invest these resources. Debates boil down to whether or not the objectives should be rooted in broad visions of strategic national interest, or whether the board of trustees responsible for investment should aim at maximizing returns for members, given an established risk tolerance level. Rather than focus on the types of investments (for example, whether or not they are invested in infrastructure), Asher's chapter makes the case that the emphasis should be placed on the quality of the decisions and regulatory environment governing these decisions.

Remittances

If social insurance and pension funds have a clear and direct link with social policy, remittances arguably stand at the opposite end of the spectrum. Nevertheless, in a context where global capital flows are increasingly volatile and aid commitments lagging behind, the steady growth of global remittance flows has led to euphoria in academic and policy circles. Remittances are seen as stable, countercyclical development finance 'from below', providing foreign exchange at the macro level and increasing income, consumption and investment for receiving households at the micro level. Yet problems associated with migration include brain drain, care drain, social disintegration, remittance dependency and 'Dutch disease' effects. Questions therefore arise as to the impact remittances have on the different dimensions of social development, how they shape patterns of social provisioning and what implications for social policy they entail. While the chapters aim to clarify the relationship between remittances and social development, it also becomes clear that there are inherent difficulties that arise when attempting to integrate private flows of money into the financing social policy framework. First and foremost, they produce an increase in migrant households' monetary income, which can then be spent on different purposes, social protection or community projects included. The authors of the two chapters in this volume generally agree that remittances, like any other form of private revenue, cannot be a substitute for social policy; they can merely act as a complement. However, Orozco's analysis reveals that remittances can lead to higher tax receipts, which in turn contribute to the financing of public policies.

De Haas' study addresses the key theoretical questions that emerge when analysing the developmental potential of remittances. Remittances have increased by a factor of 2.5 over the last decade and now far surpass official development assistance, and nearly match foreign direct investment in developing countries. In the face of a surge in international recognition of their potential as bottom-up, North–South financial tools for development, in many policy circles remittances have earned the label 'the new development mantra', even if Kapur (2005) coined the term somewhat dismissively. Although there is a theoretical interest in separating out the impacts of remittances from those of migration more generally, the fact is that remittances are the most tangible tool with which to analyse these effects. Consequently, there tends to be a one-sided focus on the impact of remittances on incomes, such that policies are aimed at facilitating and directing remittances into formal channels. In reality, migrants have multifaceted effects on development in countries of origin, such as changes in delivery of health or education, political debates, culture and the position of women in society, among others. These impacts tend to be neglected when discussions focus too narrowly on remittances.

Current insights into the impacts of remittances on development reveal the need for tempered approaches in order to balance the traditionally opposed views of 'migration optimists' and 'migration pessimists'. Too much optimism about the potential of remittances to remediate structural developmental constraints is premature and misleading since evidence is often mixed or highly context-dependent, and the assessments of the effects can be heavily value-laden. With respect to the protective dimension of remittances, most studies, including Orozco's, confirm the importance of co-insurance and risk-spreading functions among recipients. As for the effects of remittances on poverty, there is general agreement that at the aggregate, remittances reduce poverty (Adams and Page 2003), but the conclusions will vary depending on the level of analysis chosen. The same goes for inequality: comparison across recipient and non-recipient households may reveal inequalities that trace back to the inherent selectivity of migration, but a cross-regional analysis may show remittances to have an equalizing effect.

In turn, debates about remittance expenditure by recipients tend to be misleading since they place too much importance on the distinction between 'conspicuous consumption' versus 'productive investments'. The fact that household incomes are fungible precludes drawing conclusions about how remittances, as compared with other sources of income, are spent. Likewise, determining which sorts of investments are 'productive' is ultimately a subjective exercise, and one that ignores the role of the structural and institutional environment in enabling such investment in the first place. Studies that refer to the 'disruptive' effect of migration on communities and care arrangements are similarly value-laden and miss the more important point that migration almost always implies a trade-off. Similarly, debates about 'brain drain' versus 'brain gain' often fail to disaggregate by type of migration (for example, low-skilled or high-skilled), when in fact, both processes occur simultaneously. Finally, with respect to broader political and economic effects, there is evidence that the power of so-called diaspora communities influences public debate in sending countries, and remittances can impact on economic growth at the national level, though the evidence is mixed.

De Haas concludes by stating that focusing too much attention on the 'positive' impacts of remittances paradoxically distracts from deeper political and economic issues, namely, the failure of the state to provide basic public services and ensure functioning markets. Policies aimed at maximizing the developmental potential of remittances are bound to have negligible effects if they are not accompanied by more general processes of political or economic change.

Manuel Orozco's work offers new data based largely on surveys that he has conducted in various Latin American countries, and contributes substantially to the debate on the relationship between social development and migrants' remittances. He presents a direct and systematic discussion that leaves few questions regarding 'what the data say' about remittances and their potential use for social development in the region. The chapter substantiates the claim that remittances are indeed used for social protection, as recipients use them to invest in nutrition, health and education. But remittances also act as social protection in times of economic downturn or crisis as well as during natural disasters, as evidenced by case studies examining the use of remittances in the aftermath of Hurricane Stan in Guatemala in 2005 and during the banking crisis in the Dominican Republic in 2002. In particular, remittances inflows increased by 15 per cent during the aftermath of Hurricane Stan, and in the Dominican Republic, the fact the remittance flows continued throughout the banking crisis demonstrates that, contrary to conventional thinking, the money transfers occur independently of exchange rate variations.

While the behaviour of individual senders and recipients clearly matters for assessing the impact of remittances, so too do the ways that local economies and receiving countries' governments respond to these flows. Local economic conditions, particularly with respect to the extent to which local businesses cater to recipients of remittances, are paramount for distributing the economic benefits of remittances across wider groups. Moreover, Orozco emphasizes that the social impact of remittance flows depends not only on the capacity of the local economy to absorb the savings from remittances, but also on whether or not governments perceive these funds as a substitute for social spending. In his view, 'expecting governments to see remittances as a measure to ease social spending responsibilities is not only insensible but also irresponsible' (Chapter 13). Perhaps most noteworthy is Orozco's finding that remittances are highly correlated with tax revenue. In particular, for his sample of Latin American countries, a dollar increase in remittances is associated with an average tax revenue increase of $0.16. Typically, remittances triple the income of recipients, thus greatly enhancing their consumption propensity, which in turn leads to greater tax revenue in countries where sales tax is the predominant instrument for tax collection from individuals. The chapter concludes with a set of policy recommendations that would facilitate the leveraging of remittances for broader social uses such as education and health care.

The chapters in this volume seek to shed light on the possibilities for new and greater synergies between economic and social policies, at both the macro and the micro levels. The revenue sources selected for this volume are neither universally available to all developing countries nor is their latent potential by any means easily harnessed. It goes without saying that countries do not control whether they suddenly discover natural resources or benefit from a sudden influx of migrants' remittances. Similarly, the prospect that low-income countries will be able to put in place progressive forms of taxation when such enormous proportions of the population live in extreme poverty, may seem equally improbably or indeed impossible for policy makers. Nevertheless the diversity of experiences presented in this volume illustrates that it would be misleading to think within the sorts of deterministic categories that terms like 'resource curse', 'rentier state' or 'bad governance' would suggest. It would be equally misleading, however, to underestimate the challenges associated with financing social development in a context of rising global inequalities and concentration processes. Very simply, the challenge is to maximize the use of available resources for social ends. The experiences and analyses presented in the coming chapters will hopefully open up new lines of thinking about how to not only increase fiscal space in developing countries, but to do so in ways that are conducive to long-term development goals.

Notes

1. Kwon (2005); Kangas and Palme (2005); Riesco and Draibe (2007); Pierson (2004); Mehrotra (2000).

2. Economic affordability means to spend on social policies without creating macroeconomic imbalances or microeconomic distortions, which in the medium or long term could undermine economic stability and growth. Fiscal affordability or fiscal space depends on the capacity to raise taxes and to incur debt, both of which are constrained options for developing countries. However, International Labour Organization (ILO) studies have shown that basic social protection packages for the poor could be financed with less than 2 per cent of global gross domestic product (GDP) (see Pal et al. 2005).

3. On Latin America, see the chapters in this volume by Mesa-Lago or Lo Vuolo. See also the chapter by Delamonica and Mehrotra in this volume and UNRISD's (2005) flagship report, *Gender Equality: Striving for Justice in an Unequal World*. For discussions of the unpaid care burden, see Razavi and Hassim (2006) and Molyneux (2007) on Latin America.

4. Hujo (2005); ILO (2005); Cichon and Scholz (2006); Mkandawire (2004); Townsend (2004).

5. Pierson (2001); Swank (2002, 2003); Huber and Stephens (2001); Kitschelt et al. (1999); Kangas and Palme (2005).

6. See Sindzingre's chapter in this volume, Ghosh (2007) and Ortiz (2006).

7. Mehrotra and Jolly (1997); Cornia et al. (1987); Mkandawire and Soludo (1999).

8. Although the label 'revenue source' is an obvious fit for some of the topics selected (for example, taxation, aid, and mineral rents), we recognize that the fit is substantially more uncomfortable when applied to, say, private person-to-person flows like remittances. Nevertheless, we employ the term to globally refer to the group of topics we have selected and trust that the understandable knee-jerk reactions to these awkward fits will be softened by the nuanced analyses offered by our contributors on the more 'problematic' revenues. Indeed, in the case of remittances, the choice to include them among the others reflects – precisely – an attempt to critically assess the overexuberance that characterizes much current debate about the potential of remittances as a source of development finance.

9. For example, according to Lo Vuolo, an underlying assumption of these policies is that the problem of alleviating or reducing unemployment falls under the domain of social policy, when, in fact, it is a macroeconomic phenomenon.

10. The author discusses problems of size, concentration, transaction costs, predictability, macroeconomic impacts, tied aid, policy coherence, fungibility and conditionality.

11. Ortiz mentions several promising initiatives, but most notable are the Banco del Sur (Bank of the South) and the ALBA (Bolivarian Alternative for Latin America).

12. See, for example, Tanzi and Zee (2000); Gupta et al. (2004); Addison and Roe (2006); and Sindzingre's chapter in this volume.

13. Based on a sample of over 100 countries from 1980 to 2000.

14. All references to $ are to US dollars.

15. Transition costs arise when pension contributions are channelled into private accounts, whereas governments have to honour past contributions to a public system plus pension benefits for current retirees. In the case of Chile, transition costs have been around 5 per cent of GDP per year over the last three decades. For the Latin American case, see Hujo et al. (2004); on pension privatization for Eastern Europe, see Müller (1999).

References

Adams, Richard H. and John Page (2003) *International Migration, Remittances and Poverty in Developing Countries*, Working Paper No. 3179 (Washington, DC: World Bank Poverty Reduction Group).

Addison, Tony and Alan Roe (2006) *Fiscal Policy for Development* (Basingstoke: UNU-WIDER/Palgrave).

Cichon, Michael and Wolfgang Scholz (2006) *Social Security, Social Impact and Economic Performance: A Farewell to Three Famous Myths*, paper presented at the DFID/GTZ/ILO Research Seminar, Geneva, 4–5 September.

Cornia, Giovanni, Richard Jolly and France Stewart (eds.) (1987) *Adjustment with a Human Face: Protecting the Vulnerable and Promoting Growth* (New York: UNICEF/Oxford University Press).

Fjeldstad, Odd-Helge and Lise Rakner (2003) *Taxation and Tax Reforms in Developing Countries: Illustrations from Sub-Saharan Africa*, CMI Report No. R 2003: 6 (Bergen: Chr. Michelsen Institute).

Ghosh, Jayati (2007) *Macroeconomics and Growth Policies: Background Note*, UNDESA Policy Notes (New York, UNDESA).

Gupta, Sanjeev, Benedict Clements and Gabriela Inchauste (2004) *Helping Countries Develop: The Role of Fiscal Policy* (Washington, DC: IMF).

Holzman, Robert and Steen Jorgensen (2000) *Social Risk Management: A New Conceptual Framework for Social Protection and Beyond*, Social Protection Discussion Paper No. 0006 (Washington, DC: World Bank).

Huber, Evelyn and John D. Stephens (2001) *Development and Crisis of the Welfare State: Parties and Policies in Global Markets* (Chicago, IL: University of Chicago Press).

Hujo, Katja, Carmelo Mesa-Lago and Manfred Nitsch (eds.) (2004) *Públicos o Privados? Los Sistemas de Pensiones en América Latina Después de Dos Décadas de Reformas* (Caracas: Nueva Sociedad).

Hujo, Katja (2005) 'Wirtschaftskrisen und sozioökonomische (Un-)sicherheit in Lateinamerika.' In Barbara Fritz and Katja Hujo (eds.), *Ökonomie unter den Bedingungen Lateinamerikas: Erkundungen zu Geld und Kredit, Sozialpolitik und Umwelt*, Schriftenreihe des Instituts für Iberoamerika-Kunde, Hamburg, Vol. 61 (Frankfurt and Madrid: Vervuert).

ILO (International Labour Organization) (2005) *Social Protection as a Productive Factor*, International Labour Organization Governing Body, Committee on Employment and Social Policy, 294th Session, Geneva.

Kangas, Olli E. and Joakim Palme (2005) *Social Policy and Economic Development in the Nordic Countries* (Basingstoke: UNRISD/Palgrave Macmillan).

Kapur, Devesh (2005) 'Remittances: The new development mantra?' In Samuel Munzele Maimbo and Dilip Ratha (eds.), *Remittances: Development Impact and Future Prospects* (Washington, DC: World Bank).

Kitschelt, Herbert, Peter Lange, Gary Marks and John D. Stephens (eds.) (1999) *Continuity and Change in Contemporary Capitalism* (Cambridge: Cambridge University Press).

Kwon, Huck-ju (ed.) (2005) *Transforming the Developmental Welfare State in East Asia* (Basingstoke: UNRISD/Palgrave Macmillan).

Mehrotra, Santosh (2000) *Integrating Economic and Social Policy: Good Practices from High-Achieving Countries*, Working Paper No. 80 (Florence: UNICEF Innocenti Research Centre).

Mehrotra, Santosh and Richard Jolly (1997) *Development with a Human Face: Experiences in Social Achievement and Economic Growth*, Working Paper (Oxford: Clarendon Press).

Mkandawire, Thandika and Charles C. Soludo (eds.) (1999) *Our Continent Our Future: African Perspectives on Structural Adjustment* (Trenton/Asmara, Eritrea: CODESRIA, IDRC, Africa World Press).

Mkandawire, Thandika (ed.) (2004) *Social Policy in a Development Context* (Basingstoke: UNRISD/Palgrave Macmillan).

Molyneux, Maxine (2007) *Change and Continuity in Social Protection in Latin America: Mothers at the Service of the State?* Programme on Gender and Development, Paper No. 1 (Geneva: UNRISD).

Moore, Mick (2004) 'Revenues, state formation, and the quality of governance in developing countries', *International Political Science Review*, Vol. 25, No. 3, 297–319.

Müller, Katharina (1999) *The Political Economy of Pension Reform in Central-Eastern Europe* (Cheltenham: Edward Elgar).

Ortiz, Isabel (2006) *Social Policy*, Guidance Note (New York: UNDESA/UNDP).

Pal, Karuna, Christina Behrendt, Florian Léger, Michael Cichon and Krzysztof Hagemejer (2005) *Can Low Income Countries Afford Basic Social Protection? First Results of a Modelling Exercise*, Issues in Social Protection, Discussion Paper No. 13 (Geneva: ILO).

Pierson, Christopher (2004) *Late Industrializers and the Development of the Welfare State*, Programme on Social Policy and Development, Paper No. 16 (Geneva: UNRISD).

Pierson, Paul (ed.) (2001) *The New Politics of the Welfare State* (Oxford: Oxford University Press).

Razavi, Shahra and Shireen Hassim (eds.) (2006) *Gender and Social Policy in a Global Context: Uncovering the Gendered Structure of 'the Social'* (Basingstoke: UNRISD/Palgrave Macmillan).

Razavi, Shahra (2007) *The Political and Social Economy of Care in a Development Context*, Programme on Gender and Development, Paper No. 3 (Geneva: UNRISD).

Riesco, Manuel and Sonia Draibe (eds.) (2007) *Latin America: A New Developmental Welfare State in the Making?* (Basingstoke: UNRISD/Palgrave Macmillan).

Swank, Duane (2003) 'Withering welfare? Globalization, political economic institutions, and the foundations of contemporary welfare states.' In Linda Weiss (ed.), *States and Global Markets: Bringing Domestic Institutions Back In*, Cambridge Studies in International Relations (Cambridge: Cambridge University Press).

—— (2002) *Global Capital, Political Institutions, and Policy Change in Developed Welfare States*, Cambridge Studies in Comparative Politics (New York: Cambridge University Press).

Tanzi, Vito and Howell H. Zee (2000) *Tax Policy for Emerging Markets: Developing Countries*, Working Paper No. 35 (Washington, DC: IMF).

Townsend, Peter (2004) 'From universalism to safety nets: The rise and fall of Keynesian influence on social development.' In Thandika Mkandawire (ed.), *Social Policy in a Development Context* (Basingstoke: UNRISD/Palgrave Macmillan).

UNRISD (United Nations Research Institute for Social Development) (2007) *Financing Social Policy* (Geneva, 1–2 March 2007), Conference News, No. 18 (Geneva: UNRISD).

—— (2005) *Gender Equality: Striving for Justice in an Unequal World* (Geneva: UNRISD).

World Bank (2005) *World Development Report 2006: Equity and Development* (Washington, DC: Oxford University Press)

—— (2001) *Social Protection Sector Strategy: From Safety Net to Springboard* (Washington, DC: World Bank).

Part I

Global Dimension: Paradigms and Resources

2
Social Exclusion Policies and Labour Markets in Latin America

Rubén M. Lo Vuolo

Introduction

Social protection systems (SPS) in Latin America, especially in those countries considered to be *pioneers* in the implementation of social insurance, were founded on universalistic aims and followed European models.[1] Despite these aims, SPS developed in a fragmented and unequal manner, with severe limitations on the expansion of coverage (Mesa-Lago 1978, 1989; Lautier 2006). As a result, even when in the 1970s several countries exhibited fairly extensive systems, these were 'hybrids' in comparison to the traditional European welfare state regimes. The experience in Latin America reveals the limitations of comparative studies based on stylized welfare state regime typologies (Esping-Andersen 1990), and the need to conduct a more holistic analysis of each SPS.[2]

During the 1940s and 1950s, the principles of Latin American governments were similar to those that guided most Western European governments. These principles can be briefly summarized as follows.

First, the resources that covered social risks were part of earned wages. The premise was that social protection could be sustained by earned income. It was a matter of the government intervening and mandating the withholdings. In consequence, the implementation of a SPS was not an economic matter, but a political decision about whether or not to create the 'social wage'. The former financing regime in Latin America was based on the idea of the social wage.

Secondly, three variables were identified as impacting on the level and evolution of resources: (i) the evolution of the number of wage earners; (ii) the evolution of wage levels; and (iii) the share of wages reserved for the social wage.

Thirdly, the relative evolution of these variables is likely to be as follows. At the outset, there tends to be a rapid increase in the number of wage earners; thereafter, the increase takes place at a lower rate. Simultaneously, wage increases are regular and self-sustained. As the number of wage earners and the level of wages increase, social wages increase.

From this framework, it was concluded that the SPS sustained itself based on implicit trust in a virtuous circle: social protection increases productivity; productivity increases wages; wages increase social protection. Trust is simultaneously placed and relied upon in economic and political aspects. The economic aspect implies that there is an economic cost associated with social protection, but there is also a benefit: an increase in workers' productivity. The political aspect means that political commitment can be made regarding how the increase in productivity translates into a stable distribution of wages and benefits, and into the increased participation of social wages in total wages. It is essential to determine whether the commitment should be made after the compulsory establishment of social protection mechanisms or prior to it.

The problems of this virtuous circle in Latin America became evident in the 1970s and 1980s. From this period onwards, the region was used as a kind of laboratory in which the recommendations of the Washington consensus were put into practice. The *structural reforms* encouraged by international financial institutions (IFIs) and adopted in almost all countries neglected the tradition of the original SPS. Under the inspiration of a sort of *social liberalism* (Abel and Lewis 2002) a generalized process of welfare state retrenchment (Pierson 1994, 1996) occurred. It was through this process that most of the public institutions were reformed, including those which, like pension systems, were marked 'difficult to reform' in the European case.

During this era of welfare state retrenchment, the universalistic aim of SPS was confronted with the argument that it did not serve the best interests of the poorest members of society. It was believed that to be effective in the struggle against poverty, social policy makers should set aside this universalistic aim and strengthen the relationship between benefits and contributions, preferably through a system of private insurance. The poorest groups would receive direct subsidies by means of social assistance programmes. Public institutions' recognition of the income differences in unequal social sectors turned out to be a dogma that guided administrative management.

In respect of social indicators, the results of the reform experiments were substantially negative. During the 1990s, the Gini index increased in all but two countries in the region (the exceptions being Colombia and Uruguay). At the beginning of this decade open unemployment averaged 9 per cent, showing a marked growing tendency, with peaks of 20 per cent in Argentina and 16 per cent in Uruguay, Colombia and Venezuela. In addition, public employment participation fell and low productivity services increased. Along with the lack of social security coverage, excessive working hours, and so on, two-thirds of the employment generated during this period was informal (including microenterprises), leading to the spread of unstable labour relations. The level of precarious employment conditions increased for both men and women.

SPS exacerbated the problems of labour markets for two specific reasons: (i) the concentration of social security coverage on formal groups with stable contributory capacity; (ii) the pro-cyclical behaviour of social expenditure. The occasionally improved conditions that benefited the most impoverished sectors during short periods of economic boom were worn out by recurring financial crises that had the greatest impact on the largest countries (precisely, those which firmly relied on economic liberalization). Labour flexibility and the privatization of public services (including social services) enhanced the negative impact of the volatile economy on the population.

As in the past, the economic crises transferred to social and political areas. The most recent experience in Latin America of social liberalism does not differ from other experiences of pure market liberalism. Sooner or later it shows an inability to fill in the gaps between the government and the governed, between rhetoric and action. This environment renews contradictions and confrontations that threaten social integration (Abel and Lewis 2002: 51). This in part explains the loss of electoral support experienced by the local representatives of this paradigm. Nevertheless, it is still unclear to what extent the ideological matrix and especially the institutional matrix built in most Latin American countries during the 1980s and 1990s are nowadays being modified.

This doubt is based on three elements. First, if we concentrate mainly on the SPS, most of the governments elected that use an opposite rhetoric to neoliberalism do not seem to make substantial modifications to the institutions created during the retrenchment period. Secondly, international organizations' orthodoxy intends to lead the way to the critical revision of their own recipes, promoting with equal audacity a new *generation* of alternative reforms to correct some of the 'mistakes'. This scenario has to be analysed in the context of the region's new macroeconomic conditions.

The economic and social situation also worsened as a consequence of the crises that affected many countries in 2001–02. Shortly afterwards, Latin America entered a new phase of economic growth,[3] which is taking place within a very favourable international context: a growing global economy, low interest rates and favourable conditions with commodity-producing countries.

Nevertheless, the indicators of wealth distribution and population welfare do not keep pace with economic growth. After years of increasing steadily, unemployment is decreasing but at a low rate and in a heterogeneous manner.[4] Although the level of employment is growing slowly, other variables are increasing, such as informality, precarious labour, and difference in wages between the formal and informal sectors. Other indicators, such as poverty and indigence, reveal minor improvements. It is evident that the increase in productivity and competitiveness in the current bonanza years are not benefiting workers to the same extent as capital owners.

The optimistic view indicates that this unequal redistribution will be solved by maintaining high economic growth rates, thereby guaranteeing a positive impact on the labour market. In addition, the welfare of the most vulnerable groups will be improved if social programmes are reformed under renewed orthodoxy guidelines. The new political environment, involving governments which have more popular roots, is the perfect complement for these policies.

Taking into account this context, and in particular the peculiar functioning of labour markets, this chapter discusses the potential impacts of different approaches to social exclusion in Latin America. First, we will address the recent works of the World Bank, focusing in particular on those that have advanced the revision of orthodox thought. Our starting point will be the new conceptual framework of social protection, *social risk management* (Holzmann and Jorgensen 2000). In order to illustrate the consequences of this conceptual scheme, we give a brief discussion of three specific policies: (i) proposals to reform the reformed pension system established in the region over the course of the past two decades; (ii) workfare programmes; and (iii) microcredit programmes.

Following this, the characteristics and potential of more heterodox proposals that are receiving increased attention are reviewed. We will consider two of the proposals that appear as alternatives to the orthodox revision: the *Employer of Last Resort* (ELR) policy and Brazil's *Renda Básica de Cidadania* (RBC) (citizen's basic income).

This analysis is based upon two criteria. One of them intends to elucidate the extent to which the discussed proposals could serve as a real alternative to policies that have been implemented over the course of the past two decades. The other addresses the connection between the discussed policies and the new macroeconomic conditions, particularly in relation to labour markets.

The revision of the orthodoxy

At present, the orthodoxy of the IFIs and their local representatives admit that it is impossible to reduce poverty without counteracting the pro-cyclical effects that economic instability has on economic growth and the spending capacity of the state. The aim of controlling economic instability, in fact, seeks to reaffirm the market as the institution that coordinates the entire social system; in this way, the orthodoxy claims to endow the analysis with an *institutional dimension*. From this perspective, economic crises and their effects on growth potential and welfare are the result of a lack of institutions that ameliorate market functioning (Rodrik 2003; Marques-Pereira 2006). Thus, the state, in whatever market it intervenes, is forced to continue to play a stimulating role.

Promoting greater financial caution and favouring workers' employment potential appear to be the institutional keys for adjusting markets. This renewal of orthodox thinking completes the *neoclassical restoration* initiated in the 1970s with a refoundation of macroeconomics.

The novelty lies in the definition of a series of rules and institutions that should reinforce competition, giving rise to the idea of a *post-Washingston consensus*. In this manner, the orthodox doctrine attempts to differentiate from the previous consensus and answers the criticism about its naïve confidence in the markets' own capacity to promote development. Under this redefinition, social risk management, the ideology that supports the connection between social and economic policies, plays an important role.

Social risk management

The World Bank is still concerned with trying to prevent social policies from affecting the *healthy macroeconomics* that feed economic growth. The World Bank continues to trust in the spillovers related to the benefits of economic growth, which generates employment. The rationale behind this thinking is that the most vulnerable groups need social assistance policies in order to alleviate their deep sufferings in the transition process to employment. It is believed that the core problem of these groups is their fragility to face the volatility of economic growth.[5]

The World Bank's social risk management concept claims that the problem with poor sectors in Latin America is their inability to protect themselves from social risks. The World Bank claims that poor people are vulnerable because they have more chances of experiencing welfare declines in the case of unexpected economic shocks; this greater vulnerability is the result, for example, of the low availability of resources and the limited possibilities for diversifying risks. To protect the poor, social protection is regarded as public interventions that help individuals to manage social risk; thus, in this respect *safety nets* are defined as a modular system of programmes that adjust to risk patterns of each group.

According to this modular system, through the spreading of social security tied to each risk pattern, the most vulnerable groups could undertake risky activities and reduce the gap between income and the desired level of consumption. The increased capacity to take risks would stimulate *entrepreneurial spirit* and promote the skills that enable people to overcome poverty through their own efforts. Thus, the cause of informal work in the region would be explained by workers' *myopia* to understand the benefits of being insured and by the inefficient social insurance schemes. These factors foster workers to seek employment in the non-regulated market where payroll deductions do not apply.

Ideally, this problem should be solved by private insurance companies, but high premium costs or co-payment makes it impossible for the poorest people to access such services. The solution, therefore, is *mandatory social insurance* schemes, which could be administered by private insurance companies. The mandatory nature of any such system would help to overcome workers' myopia allowing identity breaks between premium and individual risk, and thus incorporating more vulnerable groups. Moreover, in order for social insurance coverage to be universal, mandatory contributions by those who are unable to pay for the premiums would have to be subsidized.[6]

The limitations and potential of social risk management in Latin America

The target of including the entire population in social insurance schemes is reasonable as long as it seeks to include the most vulnerable groups in the same pool as the population that is socially integrated due to formal employment. Nevertheless, the rationale proposed by social risk management in Latin America has clear limits.

First, it is a foregone conclusion that economic instability affects the poor to a greater extent than privileged groups, and that the poor are the group most seriously affected by the economic volatility. However, three issues should not be ignored: (i) the economic and social policies promoted by IFI exacerbate economic volatility (Rodrik 2001) and therefore debilitate the efficacy of social risk management; (ii) in Latin America access to employment does not guarantee social security coverage; (iii) poverty would be solved by preventing random events and by looking for mechanisms to reverse the certainty of great inequality in the region.

A wrong diagnosis exacerbates the problem. The workers' apparent myopia is used as an argument to continue the debate in terms of good *incentives* provided by the social institutions. These arguments have proved to be relatively ineffective in the case of Latin America. Informality in Latin America is the historical result of a regime of accumulation in which the expected profit rate is estimated assuming the persistence of a labour market that presents several pathologies: unemployment, underemployment, unregistered employment, and so on. The responsibility for these pathologies does not lie in workers' myopia, but rather in how easy it is for employers to impose this type of labour relations in the region. Workers do not choose a given job; rather, they accept what society offers them. And this scenario persists in the region both before and after mandatory social insurance.

These realities alert us to the difficulties of accessing social protection coverage experienced not only by unemployed people and unregistered workers but also by *semi-formal* workers: unregistered employees working at formal companies and employees registered for lower hours than the number they actually work, thus earning lower wages and coverage. On the other hand, there is the generalized practice of enacting rules and revoking labour statutes; for example, *temporary* workers in Argentina and Colombia who do not pay contributions and thus are not entitled to social rights. Within the conceptual framework of social risk management there is a huge area of *working poor* earning low and unstable incomes that are excluded from corporate mutualisms of social insurance and targeted assistance policies for unemployed people.

Social mobility channels in the region have been blocked by means of the labour market. This weakens the emergence of generalized interests that could make formal workers accept the reallocation of resources in favour of the precarious workers who cannot contribute. This is done under the assumption that the latter will make future contributions once they have overcome a few years of precarious working conditions. This situation blocks the upward *mobility circuits* of workers and, consequently, the foundations that sustain the principle of mutual aid based on payroll taxes.

Keeping promises: The reform of the reformed pension systems in Latin America

The World Bank's current revision of pension systems is a sound example of the practical application of social risk management postulates. On the basis of this reasoning, the World Bank has been making efforts to demonstrate that, despite the evident problems of the new pension systems, it is still possible to sustain the original promises, providing some administrative adjustments are made (World Bank 2004: 3).

For the World Bank, the problems observed in private pension schemes of individual capitalization established in Latin America in the past few decades are transitory. They are probably caused by low returns from pension funds in recent years, as well as by deficient public regulation. In the revision of policy advice, the

World Bank states that among the poorest sections of the population, the older people are in an advantageous position compared to other groups because they may have accumulated wealth throughout the course of their lives. Sound insurance mechanisms are needed that enable such accumulation and the transformation of accumulated wealth into liquid assets. Precisely, these efficient mechanisms would be pension funds invested in financial markets.

It is surprising to note that the World Bank itself acknowledges that between six and eight of the selected Latin American countries have shown an increase in poverty among people over 65 years of age, notwithstanding the incorporation of privately administered pension systems. In light of this evidence, as a justification World Bank's experts question the quality of the empirical evidence and claim that the data are biased because they only record population *incomes*, leaving *wealth* (and pension funds) aside, and that the retired population tends to underreport their level of income.

According to the World Bank, the problems with reformed pension systems lie in the state's inability to regulate them or to interpret World Bank recommendations appropriately. Specifically, reformed pension systems paid excessive attention to the income-replacement function of pension systems, but little or no attention to the poverty-reduction function. Beyond the fact that privatization and the income-replacement function was a priority encouraged through the widely disseminated 1994 manual (World Bank 1994), the World Bank currently points out that if governments controlled the correct functioning of a poverty-prevention pillar, additional efforts would only have to be made in ensuring the adequate regulation of the performance of private savings and voluntary insurance.

Now it is believed that targeted benefits are perceived as *charity*; therefore families do not take them into account when making an intertemporal optimization of consumption. In addition, governments consider them to be a marginal budget item. Instead, the World Bank prefers a universal and unconditional first pillar, concluding that the cost of this system differs only slightly from the cost afforded by other countries going through the transition towards reformed systems.[7] Nevertheless, the World Bank recommends that they should be of low level in order not to erode *savings incentives* of the second pillar of individual accounts.

Thus, the World Bank suggests that the problems detected in a private system of individual accounts could be solved by increasing the level of competition among private administrators, providing workers with financial education and moving the state from its regulatory role. The World Bank now admits that, instead of a sharp transition from a 'pay-as-you-go' to a funded system, other mechanisms such as notional accounts could also be considered (Disney 1999; Settergren 2001) in order to facilitate the transition towards individual funded accounts that, in the end, will be the most efficient.

The limitations and potential of the World Bank's renewed promises in Latin America

Many of the problems now detected by the World Bank did in fact originate in the reforms promoted by this institution, and were clearly predictable (Lo Vuolo 1996, 2002). After a decade of experience,[8] the level of coverage fell and inequality and fiscal problems increased in those countries that had implemented the World Bank's recommendations. This evidence demonstrates how dangerous it is to use developing countries as laboratories for public policy experiments. *Reforms (and variations) implemented in Latin America have been financially supported and technically assisted by the World Bank and other influential IFIs.*

Therefore, deficiencies originated in the World Bank's recommendations themselves, which still persist at this revision stage. For instance, the World Bank insists on addressing the problem in the context of an incentives theory that cannot be demonstrated, and a catastrophic vision of the relation between government-managed 'pay-as-you-go' retirement systems and *population ageing*. As a result of these mistakes, the World Bank fails to recognize what is shown by the empirical evidence: in Latin America, poor elderly people do not live in better conditions than those in other vulnerable groups. It is unlikely that someone who has been poor throughout the majority of their life has accumulated a substantial amount of wealth. In addition, due to their lower capacity to generate incomes, retired people are left behind in the distribution of family resources. This group, moreover, became more vulnerable with the reforms that reduced coverage and benefits.

The misleading conceptual framework is also evident in the arguments that support the defence of a basic universal benefit. The World Bank claims that the benefit level must be very low in order to avoid discouraging workers' contributions to the individual funded system.

If poverty prevention is the priority, the level of basic universal benefit has to be high enough to fulfil this goal. The justification lies in the need to modify a regressive distribution pattern that has historically characterized pension systems in the region.[9] Furthermore, it is evident that savings are not stimulated by the fear of being poor in the future, but rather when there is security of coverage and certainty of a sufficient benefit. None of these are guaranteed by private pension funds: they have not proved to be more efficient than public systems in the administration of the so-called demographic transition (Barr 2002), and nor have they fostered workers' contributions or ameliorated fiscal problems. Their main effect is to create a financial business and deepen a regressive pattern of income distribution.

What should be justified in Latin America is not an adequate level of basic universal benefits, but the continuity of privately administered pension funds. The existence of these funds is certainly explained by the intention of creating new financial products by absorbing part of workers' salaries rather than for strict social security purposes.

The main problem is how to design a transition in the opposite direction to that proposed by the World Bank: a transition from the unsuccessful privately administered individual accounts systems towards a fiscally controlled pay-as-you-go system. In order to achieve this, the mechanisms of the so-called *notional accounts* are very useful. These mechanisms, designed to shift from a pay-as-you-go system to one centred on individual accounts, could also aid a transition in the opposite direction. By absorbing individual accounts of private systems and turning pension funds into the *buffer fund* required to keep automatic balance in the pay-as-you-go system,[10] this goal can be achieved. A combination of non-contributory universal benefit and contributory notional accounts would allow the objectives of the original pension systems to resume, but in a more efficient manner. The peculiarities of individual cases will hinge on experience and the specific context.

Workfare programmes

In addition to supporting social insurance, the World Bank's revision places *workfare* and microcredit programmes in a central position. The term *workfare* has become an opposing emblematic alternative to the traditional *welfare*. Workfare refers to those policies that, rather than emphasizing *incentives* and *rights* to have a job or receive benefits, place workers under an *obligation* to get a job as the price for receiving a subsidy.

These types of programmes are based on arguments similar to those previously mentioned: to encourage individual responsibility without introducing negative stimuli for seeking a paid job. The idea is neither distributing goods nor giving money for nothing in return, but rather demanding a job done in consideration of the benefit received, justifying the argument that unemployed people are willing to work and therefore are deserving of assistance.

The results expected from workfare programmes in the region can be illustrated through the example of Argentina, a pioneer country in large-scale experiences of this kind (Baker 2000). The period since 2002 has seen the implementation of the most extensive programme in the region: Programa Jefes y Jefas de Hogar Desocupados (PJyJHD) (programme for the unemployed heads of household).[11]

Financially supported by the World Bank, this programme was launched after the hyperdevaluation, which brought an abrupt end to the convertibility regime that had lasted for a decade in Argentina. The PJyJHD was first designed as a transitory measure but then extended. The requirements for qualifying for the programme were: (i) being unemployed and in charge of a household; (ii) having children under 18 (a pregnancy had to be medically verified); (iii) regular school attendance and updated vaccinations of minor children; and (iv) not to be included in any other social programme. In 2005, the number of beneficiaries peaked at 1.8 million (67 per cent of urban unemployed). Then, this amount was reduced due to beneficiaries' transfer to other programmes and to labour market recovery resulting from high economic growth. A fixed amount of money is paid (equivalent to 20 per cent or less of the poverty line for a family of four: parents and two children). Beneficiaries are given a part-time job in projects approved by municipal authorities. If they get a job in a private company the benefit is maintained for a short time as a salary complement.

The results of the PJyJHD have aroused controversy from its very conception: is it an income or an employment programme? Since it questions the link between poverty and unemployment, this is not a minor dilemma. A peculiar feature of Argentina (and Latin America) is precisely the existence of poor workers as a result of labour informality and labour flexibility legislation. The political strategy that is being used by means of PJyJHD is a key aspect. The programme intends to strengthen the idea that incomes can only be guaranteed by employment, thus the programme becomes simultaneously an employment-fostering and income-sustaining plan.

In this sense, the PJyJHD did not represent a modification to the general logic that had been behind social policies over the course of the past decade. The main innovation was the realization that cash benefits are more efficient than in-kind benefits. Another innovation in respect of previous experiences is that this plan promotes self-targeting, whereby beneficiaries acknowledge themselves as eligible participants.

In practice, the programme has a very low impact on the level of poverty.[12] This is explained by a combination of several factors: how beneficiaries are selected; the equal benefit for households of different size; and the exclusion of the working poor.[13] Furthermore, the overall budget of the programme is very low in relation to the *poverty gap*.[14]

Nor are there significant impacts on unemployment,[15] because the programme excludes these groups that have the greatest difficulties in finding a job (young people and elderly adults who do not have underage children). The PJyJHD has control failures[16] that also allows an *unemployment trap* (beneficiaries who perform non-registered work). Simultaneously, the programme stimulates the engagement of non-working people and the substitution of public employment. This effect is also observed in private employment since it is used as a subsidy. Finally, the programme has debatable impacts on male and female division of roles in both the labour market and the family (Rodríguez Enríquez 2005; Pautassi 2004).

Overall, the PJyJHD proved to be an effective political instrument in taking advantage of the 2001–02 crises. Since it became a central element in the surviving strategy of many low-income households, in practice the two evident impacts of this programme are: (i) that it encourages and becomes functional to the generalized environment of precarious labour conditions; and (ii) that it works as a mechanism for attracting political loyalties and capturing votes (Auyero 2004).

The limitations and potential of workfare in Latin America

The problems detected in the PJyJHD are similar to those found in other workfare programmes:[17] they appear to be unresolved hybrids between income sustaining and employment assistance, consequently generating the perverse effects of *poverty traps* and *unemployment traps*. These effects are exacerbated in the precarious labour environment of Latin American countries, because the labour market does not represent a stable solution that guarantees substantial improvements in people's lifestyles. In fact, many beneficiaries of workfare programmes seek complementary incomes in informal labour markets.

In practice, these programmes contribute to the increased fragmentation of the labour market, which is contrary to the World Bank's alleged aim of increasing formality and effectiveness in social security. Workfare programmes consolidate social fragmentation by discriminating between those who deserve assistance and those who do not. The real impact is to isolate the blame for being unemployed and poor, focusing on the personal incapacity to get a formal job in the market. This type of programmes also distorts political practices, enhancing the power of the authorities who have control over benefit assignment, and favours political clientelism.

Under the logic of these programmes, employment is no longer an economic problem; rather, it has become one that belongs to the field of social policy dealing with *emergencies*. In a sense, workfare programmes legitimize a particular class of citizenship. This way of *activating* social policies increases individuals' dependence on the selection criteria of the bureaucracy, thus promoting political indifference, which erodes the basis of citizenship (Habermas 1994).

Microfinance programmes

Microfinance is another proposal of the orthodox revision in Latin America (Goldberg 2006). According to a widespread definition, microfinance involves providing financial services to a low-income population or to economic agents that are excluded from the formal financial sector. While microcredit is the most renowned instrument, in theory, microfinance also includes the provision of financial products such as savings facilities and insurance. The subjects of microfinance would be economic agents who, in addition to having insufficient income, are excluded from the formal financial system, due to a lack of guarantees, the high repayment risk attributed to them or the limitations of the economic activities they perform.

With the purpose of correlating microfinance with productive undertaking, the aim pursued in theory is that self-employed workers start a microenterprise that increases in capacity and size over time, until it consolidates in the market and becomes self-sustained and productive. Thus, poor people do not regard themselves as *beneficiaries* but as *clients* and *debtors* of microfinance institutions. Based on this idea, two approaches stand out (Robinson 2005): *loans to poverty* and *financial systems*.

The first approach aims to reduce poverty by means of loans granted by institutions financed through subsidies from donors, governments or other funds. From this approach, saving is not an instrument that is especially promoted – except when it is a necessary condition for the receipt of a loan. This approach prevailed in Latin America in credit cooperatives that had been established during the 1950s and 1970s and organized by Catholic movements, volunteer organizations and the United States Agency for International Development. They lacked professional management, operated at low and subsidized interest rates and showed themselves to be inefficient in recovering loans and retaining incomes.

Since the mid-1980s, largely as a result of the debt crisis in Latin America, many donors' funds disappeared, and the credit cooperative movement receded. On the basis on this experience, there was much criticism of poverty-focused institutions, which suggested that if they are managed in this way, they become unsustainable. Alternatively, the orthodox revision proposes a different financial system approach, and places an emphasis on the sustainable growth of institutions. The argument is that if an institution records good performance and their loans obtain high repayment rates, one can conclude that clients are improving their well-being and overcoming poverty (Garber and Beard 2003).

This claim corresponds to a particular conception about the causes of poverty in the region: the poor lack *self-confidence* or an *enterprising spirit* that would prevent them from overcoming the situation (Robinson 2005). Access to financial systems would allow the poor to demonstrate that they are capable of borrowing money and of paying it back. By being incorporated into the market's competitive logic, their income would increase, which would allow them to gain self-confidence.

In the early 1990s, institutions that had achieved the so-called *full financial sustainability* through this new modality were already in existence in Latin America and had begun to spread. Simultaneously, *downscaling* processes are produced and commercial banks or traditional financial entities enter the field of microfinance, supported in many cases by the *Microenterprise Global Credit Programme* of the Inter-American Development Bank (Berger et al. 2003).

The orthodox revision in this topic has clearly privileged the financial systems approach: regulated non-governmental organizations have the major share (53.4 per cent), followed by commercial banks that participate with 35.4 per cent of total portfolio in dollars (Marulanda and Otero 2005). Regulated microfinance institutions also absorb the largest number of customers (47.3 per cent), followed by non-regulated ones and banks that equally share the rest of customers' portfolio. These institutions have not developed homogeneously in Latin America. If microfinance coverage relative to the size of the microenterprises sector is considered, small and medium-sized countries in Central America and in the Andes region are the countries that have experienced the greatest penetration of microfinance. On the contrary, the four largest economies in Latin America show the least penetration of microfinance institutions.

The limitations and potential of microfinance in Latin America

The advocates of microfinance in Latin America assess its impact on the basis of repayment rates, risk portfolios, and other indicators that are characteristic of the financing sector. Commonly, these indicators are used to determine the success both of institutions and of beneficiaries. Such a criterion leads to a biased analysis of the effective impact of these programmes (MacIsaac 1996).

Thus, the (apparent) high rate of credit repayment conceals the fact that many customers take loans from diverse institutions to settle previous debts, with no necessary improvement in their social situation. Repayment may also be financed by savings or incomes from activities not related to the credit. The criteria used for defining delays or lack of payment are also questionable.

In contrast, some clients are unable to operate a business or do not have access to a potential market to take advantage of credit. Repayment is often not related to the borrower's payment capacity and debts are often paid by selling the few family assets or with money coming from abroad. This complicates the matter even more as high repayment is considered to be an indicator of increased family well-being. Sometimes the need to obtain incomes in order to comply with repayment implies increased hours of work for spouses and underage children.

In fact, microentrepreneurs have seldom developed into large-scale business owners because of the urgent need to use incomes to satisfy extra basic needs.

Market limits and borrowers' lack of entrepreneurial spirit have also played important roles. The deficiencies of credit programmes mainly oriented to finance working capital have also hindered the ability to provide projects with the fixed assets needed to achieve sustainability and development. This is evident in the strong rotation of clients of microfinance institutions; hence, good technical relations may be established between financial institutions and clients, but these may have a limited impact on the latter's poverty condition.

Success and *self-sustainability* of beneficiaries of financial assistance are not part of the evaluation, leaving many questions with no adequate answer. Among the most important of these are: What is the history of development and performance of microenterprises before and after becoming microcredit borrowers? What activities are most frequently financed and how do they perform? What purposes do beneficiaries have for microcredit? To what extent do microenterprises succeed in developing their businesses and becoming self-sustained or growing to have access to traditional financing services at lower interest rates? To what extent are circles of micro-indebtedness created? Do microcredit borrowers change or are they always the same clients that are not able to get out of the system?

These questions are the basis for the following hypothesis (Pauselli and Villarraga 2006): microfinance is a *financial industry* whose clients are not microentrepreneurs who are trying to develop income strategies by means of self-employment; instead, the real clients are the *investors* providing funds. Microentrepreneurs have become the necessary component for these investors to recover investments with a proper profit through organizations specialized in obtaining financial rent from traditionally *non-bankable* segments of market. The high price of borrowed money masks this situation: such high prices are what justify investors' business instead of reflecting the high risk and administration cost of the activity.

Overall, many doubts arise in respect of the real impact of the present microfinance approach in Latin America, particularly regarding its objective of democratizing and providing massive access to finance services that will reduce the levels of vulnerability and poverty. To place the blame for the condition of poverty on the poor's lack of enterprising spirit is groundless in a region with such unequal life opportunities. This thought begs the question: why should the poor have an enterprising spirit that is absent in qualified wage earners? Or, if they do have this spirit, why will a microcredit be the best way to guarantee the success of a new enterprise? What is really occurring is an effort to place the blame for the social and economic ills of the society on the affected people, thus avoiding society's responsibility to offer formal employment and full insertion in SPS.

Another misconception is the association of *access to income* with *access to credit*. The latter is the result of access to income only if other conditions are met. For instance, a certain level of income has to be guaranteed in order for beneficiaries to devote credit towards productive activity and not towards essential consumption. In addition, microentrepreneurs must have organizational capacities as well as appropriate technologies (Pauselli 2005).[18] Since these elements are not guaranteed, the success of financial institutions does not imply the success of their clients.

Such problems place serious doubts on the statement that 'if a poor person is provided with a loan and adequate training, he or she may become an entrepreneur'. This paradigm is not applicable in the case of Latin America for the majority of vulnerable social groups (Pauselli 2005). Microfinance is more related to the logic of financial globalization than to the struggle against poverty. Instead of promoting higher incomes and savings, the microfinance industry encourages the indebtedness of poor people.

Some alternative proposals

While orthodoxy revision prevails in practice, other policy alternatives are also being promoted in Latin America. To illustrate the contents of these alternatives, I will refer to two proposals that stand on opposite sides in respect of the focus of their strategy. First, the proposal of the state as the ELR,[19] suggests that employment could be offered to anyone requiring it through a government-run programme. Secondly, the proposal of the RBC in Brazil seeks to guarantee a basic income to the population.

The ELR proposal

ELR advocates claim that full employment could be reached in a context of a flexible labour market through the implementation of a programme with the following characteristics:

(i)   The state provides paid employment to anyone willing to work.
(ii) The programme acts as buffer stock, allowing workers to enter or exit the scheme, depending upon the expansion or shrinkage of the labour market. Jobs offered by the programme do not compete with private or public access to formal employment, and beneficiaries would be trained in skills required for formal employment.
(iii) Beneficiaries perform tasks that are considered *useful to society*.
(iv) Wages guarantee a *decent* living standard; the price-wage relationship is stable, and even the provision of health insurance and childcare services can be included.

The central argument that supports these proposals is that unemployment is caused by low demand and that governments could – and should – compensate for insufficient job opportunities allocating public expenditures to ELR. In terms of macroeconomics, this proposal is based on the theory of *functional finance* (Lerner 1947). This theory argues that countries' currencies become a generalized means of payment when the state is 'sovereign' and accepts the currency as tax payment. The state does not need citizens' money to pay for expenditures, because the state creates the money.[20] Taxes would subsequently absorb part of the money supply created by public expenditure. It is concluded that the state should always issue (and spend) more money than it collects, because individuals will always want to retain money.

In other words, under these conditions a fiscal deficit is not an exception but a rule to any economy functioning with a certain degree of *normality*. The fiscal deficit would be equal to the difference between money issued to be spent and a lower amount of money collected from taxes. This is basically money in circulation that economic agents have decided to keep as liquid cash.

Taxes and public bonds are not a useful means to finance public expenditure, but they are rather useful for removing excess money in circulation. Government could and should afford additional expenses by creating money when the aggregate expenditure level is lower than the full employment level, and when there is no excess cash in circulation. When the level of overall expenditure in the economy is excessively high, the state should reduce expenditure and raise taxes. The opposite should occur when overall expenditure is low. Thus, fiscal policy would determine the monetary base, while monetary policy would regulate money excess by placing bonds.

This does not mean that the fiscal deficit has no limits. If it were to become too high, this would imply that public expenditure is higher than is required to maintain an aggregate demand level consistent with full employment. If this were the case, inflation pressure would be generated; otherwise, unemployment would take place.

Based upon this reasoning, ELR advocates assert that any modern economy would be able to provide a job to every unemployed person at a predetermined fixed wage, allowing budgetary deficit to grow as far as is necessary to reach full employment. The programme would perform the function of paying wages to a *reserve army* that, instead of being unemployed, would be permanently available to obtain a better job.

The limitations and the potential of ELR in Latin America

Even if ELR supporters point out that their proposal was designed on the basis of the United States economy (Wray 2000), research has also been conducted in less developed countries. The approach has drawn the attention of many Latin American economists within the macroeconomic environment in which monetary policies privilege inflation targeting over employment (Cibils and Lo Vuolo 2004b), as well as a fiscal surplus that privileges payment of public debt over social expenditure.

Difficulties with this proposal arise when assessing how the functional financing mechanism would work in Latin American countries, especially if we consider that most countries have difficulties sustaining a sovereign currency and have high levels of indebtedness (Reinhart et al. 2003). In this situation, the *cyclical* managing of indebtedness proposed by ELR supporters is very difficult.[21]

In this scenario, economic agents are likely to be reluctant to buy bonds at the offered rates; instead, they would prefer other financial alternatives. Central banks would be very restrained from negotiating interest rates because they would be more concerned with exchange rates. Consequently, handling aggregate demand and taking it to a full employment level with functional finance mechanisms poses considerable obstacles. In addition, it should be noted that aggregate supply is usually inelastic in the short term and could generate greater inflationary pressures than are assumed.

Unemployment in Latin America is not a *cyclical* phenomenon.[22] Unemployment in the region has *structural* roots and multicausal explanations (some of them very peculiar, including rural unemployment, massive rural–urban migration, and so on). In addition, as highlighted, many employed workers are paid very low wages; therefore, ELR could be demanded by employed people and could attract new workers to the labour supply, thereby increasing pressure on unemployment.

With the goal of understanding this point, let us assume that the programme is able to offer *good jobs* (providing social services and a minimum income close to the formal sector's minimum wage). In this case, the programme would attract not only the unemployed but also the underemployed, precarious and informal workers, thus becoming the main employer in the economy. This would affect its own function of *stabilization buffer* and would also turn the programme into a substitute for the current low-quality jobs.

By contrast, if the programme offers very precarious jobs, it would have the same problems that have been cited in the previous discussion of *workfare* programmes. In addition, the ELR could hire workers to perform tasks that are required by the state. The state's capacity to administer programmes of these characteristics and size in Latin America is highly questionable because it requires very complex institutional engineering.

It becomes evident that improving employment conditions in the region needs some re-examination, in particular the macroeconomic policies that regulate effective demand as is the case in countries like Argentina since 2002. This way of generating favourable expectations and of granting credibility to economic policy is much more efficient than the strategy that seeks financial operators' support by means of a monetary policy tied to inflationary goals and unlimited fiscal surplus (Lo Vuolo 2003). However, there are serious limits for the ELR mechanisms in the region both at the macro level and with respect to the kind of jobs offered which could cause distortions that are greater than the existing ones.

RBC in Brazil

In January 2004, Brazil passed a law that institutes – theoretically since 2005 – the RBC programme for all residents and foreigners who have more than five years of residence. The benefit would be uniform, regularly paid and profit-tax free. The fundamentals of the law make reference to the principles of the *Basic Income* proposal.[23]

Although the law recognizes that the right to this benefit is independent of an individual's socioeconomic condition, it states that the programme should be aimed initially at lower-income groups. The intention is that it should be implemented as a *negative income tax* (Friedman 1966). The way to establish the amount of this benefit is not fixed by law, but by the Executive who are supposed to take into consideration the regulations of the Fiscal Responsibility Act. This Act establishes that any expenditure increase has to be accompanied by a justification of the origin of the funds and is not supposed to affect the fiscal goals set out in the budget.

The RBC Act is the result of a long process. Since 1995, Brazil has been experimenting with monetary benefits programmes to poor families in municipal jurisdictions. On the basis of the 1988 Constitution and the *Lei Orgânica de Assistência Social* (Social Assistance Act), numerous programmes have been implemented (including *Bolsa Escola* and *Renda Minima*[24]). These programmes achieved beneficial results in preventing absenteeism from school desertion, but were less effective in terms of poverty reduction.

These and other programmes granting monetary benefits were gradually unified to create the *Bolsa Familia* (BF) programme. BF is focused on the poor; benefits are given on condition that the receivers comply with certain requirements, which do not include getting a job – in contrast to the workfare programmes.

This process triggered a debate about the need to concentrate efforts in a programme that paid direct cash benefits. Senator Eduardo Suplicy from the PT (*Partido dos Trabalhadores*, or Workers' Party) passed several bills that intended to establish a minimum universal income within the *negative income tax* scheme (Suplicy 2002). The result is the recently sanctioned RBC Act that aims strengthen the mechanisms by which the poor gain access to food.

The limitations and potential of RBC in Latin America

At present, the RBC Act appears to be the most important legislative change in income transfer policies in Latin America.[25] This fact is relevant because Brazil is the largest country and the one with the most unequal income distribution. The legal recognition of a universal right to income is a significant conquest. However, many doubts remain about the practical possibilities of applying this universal right.

As an example, the macroeconomic policy in Brazil – a strong primary fiscal surplus devoted to debt payments and monetary policy oriented towards inflationary goals – is not the best environment to put this law into practice. Doubts arise when it is observed that it fails to define how benefits are estimated and also how it is to be financed. In addition, the law explicitly subordinates its practical application to compliance with effective application of the Fiscal Responsibility Act, which establishes very strict limits to the incorporation of additional public expenditure.

Furthermore, Brazil has no tradition of universal social policies. The country's history shows a preference for targeted programmes. This tradition is also expressed in the rules of the RBC Act: it does not set a deadline to obtain the universal coverage and, in reality, is focused on the poorest people. This is not a minor issue, especially if we consider that the Basic Income proposal is difficult to implement even in Europe, where there is a sound universalistic tradition and extended systems of social protection (Van der Veen et al. 2002).

A strongly targeted policy (such as BF) always shows a considerable capacity to extend to other sectors at the beginning, but this capacity is then restricted to certain *categories* of poor people, according either to individual characteristics or to geographical locations. As an increased number of *selection criteria* are introduced, advancement becomes more difficult. The problem is that when the aim is universality, the criteria for selecting policies differ from those of targeted programmes. Organizing a programme in line with universal criteria draws upon a type of solidarity introduced by a given mode of financing and also the capacity of spreading protection mechanisms that is very different from those used to organize targeted programmes.

According to past experiences, building a universal SPS cannot be achieved by employing *targeted technologies* but, rather, by making use of *universalistic technologies*. The problem in Latin America is how to shift the perspective from a technological approach to the struggle against poverty to an approach of (re)constructing the whole system of social protection.

In this sense, some works have already pointed out that, given the mode of implementation of BF, the impact on poverty indicators will be low (Lavinas et al. 2004). In addition, the inconsistency of a law that does not establish funding sources and whose implementation is not associated with a tax reform, particularly with the reform of the income tax, was also mentioned. The proposed alternative is to advance gradually towards universality with other criteria, but first covering the needs of the underage population, since this mode should have a greater impact on poverty indexes and on associating changes to a tax reform.[26]

Regardless of the doubts in relation to the strategy and viability of the programme's implementation under the proposed rules, it is certain that Brazil's RBC Act constitutes a benchmark in the debate about how to build alternative social policies in the region. Its vindication of a universal and unconditional basic income is a turning point in relation to the debate about these issues in Latin America.

A different approach to the social question in Latin America

Current revisions of the orthodoxy of IFIs do not support plausible solutions to the severe social problems that are apparent in the region. Revisions of orthodoxy claim that the essential conception of the Washington consensus is right. They contend that all that is required is some technical correction in order to ameliorate market functioning, which is considered to be the institutional side of the matter. Policy advice points to the need to improve targeting, to establish better regulation of private insurance and to design new programmes in relation to workfare and microcredit. The aim is to individualize the blame for unemployment and to discriminate beneficiaries into those who deserve and those who do not deserve assistance.

The facts do not sustain this approach. The spread of targeted programmes is usually an excuse to justify the dismantling of universal social policies. Economic and social vulnerability increases for those who are and who are not the target of social assistance policies. In addition, the highly pro-cyclical nature of targeted policies and the low levels of public expenditure devoted to them contribute to an instability in internal demand. This way of fighting poverty augments vulnerability and even poverty itself; it is not an unexpected effect, but rather a logical consequence of the mechanics of those policies.

This revision of orthodoxy is what today prevails in Latin America and explains what could be seen as a paradox: the economic growth environment that followed the 2001–02 crises serves to legitimize the institutional order built during the welfare state retrenchment. Although macroeconomic rules changed, the main social policy institutions built under the protection of the Washington consensus have not. Of course, this general assertion has some exceptions to be considered.

Part of the problem is *neostructuralism* gaining ground in the definition of economic policies. Adherents to neostructuralism question some of the economic rules of the Washington consensus but not the role given to the SPS. They share the orthodox distributional trust between the economic growth and the spillover impact on employment, wages and the population's welfare. Their criticism of the policies of the 1990s is focused on the macroeconomic imbalances attached to *market* imperfections; again, the distributional issue is a dependent variable of a sound macroeconomic policy (Marques-Pereira 2006; Bresser-Pereira 2002). As in the original Washington consensus, the view of Latin American neostructuralism places distribution and social protection institutions in a subordinate position in relation to the adequate economic policies.

In fact, this position is opposed to the original structural economic thought in the region[27] which placed an emphasis on the key role of distribution to define the pattern of economic growth. For the original structuralism, little distribution is to be expected as a consequence of the *spilling over* of productivity profits in a growing economy. On the contrary, neostructuralism dissolves the original structuralism into a utilitarian view of institutions: institutions must serve to guarantee the proper functioning of the market.

In contrast, SPSs were not conceived to assist the poor but rather to struggle against social vulnerability by devoting part of a population's income to the social wage. More precisely, this is not about *giving* resources to poor people, but about driving up the social wage and covering risks. The aim of SPSs is to *protect*, to prevent and reduce vulnerability. Secondary income distribution is a means of achieving such protection.

Consequently, the main political problem is not to know whether to distribute or not, but to define the *population* that is to be covered by social protection mechanisms: wage earners? Formal workers? All citizens? This leads to the problem of social mobility. Indeed, in societies where SPSs have expanded broadly, a strong intra- and intergenerational mobility can be observed. This is true for both the European experience and for those Latin American countries that have been pioneers in building SPSs.

It is crucial, therefore, to have clear objectives and to take into account cultural and institutional heritages, avoiding the rise of uncontrolled costs such as irresponsible pension reforms performed by orthodox policy makers. Although it may be too concise, we propose here some guidelines regarding the path that this alternative political project should follow.

First, the existing assistance programmes are to be re-examined in order to simplify and unify them into one programme of direct income transfer to the population. A reasonable way is to begin by the reforming existing family allowance programmes that currently cover only some groups of formal employees and turning these programmes into one that pays a basic income per each underage child. At the same time, it is necessary to reform the pension systems imposed under the financial paradigm of individual capitalization of pension funds and to replace them with schemes founded on a universal and unconditional benefit.

The above policies would have a direct impact on the level of family incomes and would settle an intergenerational distributive agreement necessary for any political project that intends to go beyond the mere objectives of appropriating short-term gains. In addition, these policies would have *externalities* that go beyond the simple aim of distributing incomes. The benefits for childhood would be that it would favour school attendance and put an end to child labour, thereby having positive impacts on present and future labour markets. The basic pillar of pension systems would also have a favourable impact on the regulation of entering and leaving the labour market while offering minimum guarantees that would foster participation in other contributory pillars. In order to achieve this, contributory pillars should abandon the financial capitalization systems in privately administered individual accounts and transform them into pay-as-you-go systems of notional accounts.[28]

Second, income-sustaining policies should be combined with *food sovereignty* policies. The specific character of these policies varies from case to case; in Latin America, strategies are needed to guarantee that popular sectors[29] have access to a healthy food consumption pattern. Actions are required in relation to: distribution channels; the promotion of self-managed cooperatives, society and community-driven undertakings; the education policy intended to change popular sectors' consumption behaviour; and other related matters. Food market regulation policies are also needed in order to avoid supply problems and price increases.

Third, a tax reform reinforcing the implementation of direct and progressive taxes and reducing pro-cyclical behaviour is needed. This is also necessary to ensure the safe financing of public policies to avoid social budget dependence on loans granted by IFIs. This is a necessary condition to recover autonomy in the formulation of public policies. Several countries in the region have demonstrated a capacity to achieve a fiscal surplus under the pressure of paying public financial debt; however, the challenge today is to use this capacity for purposes such as changing the tax and expenditure structure inherited from institutional reforms.

Universal policies of income transfer are also helpful for fiscal reform: (i) they are useful to reform income tax systems, by integrating them as effective fiscal credits;[30] (ii) they are useful for legitimizing tax reforms, since imposing taxes to pay for a financial public debt that benefited some concentrated powerful groups is different from paying universal benefits immediately perceived by the population.

Fourth, the problems of formal employment are to be placed at the core of public policy. Labour relations are the axis that organizes the system of social and economic relations, together with a set of sociocultural values that are indispensable for social cohesion. For this reason, assistance policies are not helpful if they do not create genuine employment.

Employment creation requires multiple integrated economic policies: macroeconomic policies that coordinate monetary and fiscal policies simultaneously, plus recovering the public sector role as employer in essential but increasingly abandoned public service areas such as health, education, community service, social infrastructure, and so on. These activities are all labour intensive and have a very low level of foreign inputs.

Policies that foster the establishment of new enterprises and the support of already established small firms are relevant for the promotion of employment creation. Incentive policies should not be based on the reduction of taxes that finance social insurance, but mainly on financial, administrative and commercial support so that companies have well-grounded expectations in creating their own development capacities once the incentive programme is over.

This is not about proposing *the* good social policy; rather, it discusses how to rebuild the SPS on the basis of other principles. Structural reforms imposed in the region in recent decades showed themselves to be more destructive than constructive. The apologia of individual interest in an extremely unequal society has caused considerable damage, including an environment of corruption in the classical meaning of the word: citizens' inability (and especially that of the government) to recognize and respond to public claims made by the community, always opting to favour individual and corporate interests instead.

The current macroeconomic scenario in the region leaves room for change but needs to be accompanied by an adequate revision of the institutional system built up in previous years. The answer to this is neither a revision of orthodox policies, nor the adoption of alternatives that could be consistent in a laboratory but do not take into account the specific social and economic networks that define the dynamics of each society in the region. The task is to rebuild the SPS on the basis of the identification of general interests which contribute to the consolidation of a more equitable pattern of distribution.

Notes

1. Germany and Italy have probably been the most influential.
2. For critical views of the use of welfare state typologies for comparative purposes, see Théret (1997); Goldberg and Lo Vuolo (2006); Gough and Wood (2004); Ferrera (1996); and Hicks (1991).
3. According to the Economic Commission for Latin America and the Caribbean (ECLAC), growth in Latin America and the Caribbean was 2.2 per cent in 2003, 6.2 per cent in 2004, 4.7 per cent in 2005, and 5.6 per cent in both 2006 and 2007. Projections for 2006 are 4.8 per cent (see www.eclac.cl).
4. According to ECLAC, mean annual rates of unemployment were 11 per cent in 2002, 9.1 per cent in 2005, 8.6 per cent in 2006 and 8 per cent in 2007.
5. These types of paradigms are referred to as static modes for regulating poverty. See Lo Vuolo et al. (1999) and Lautier (1998).
6. For example, the reformed pension system in Mexico.
7. The World Bank supports the analysis on works by Willmore (2001a, 2001b). To safeguard prestige, the World Bank emphasizes that the difference would be relevant in the long term, after transition cost has been paid and increasing life expectancy would make universal benefit even more expensive.

8. To evaluate structural and parametric reforms in Latin America, see Mesa-Lago (2004, 2006).
9. Arza (2002) proposes a method to analyse the Argentine case.
10. In Goldberg and Lo Vuolo (2006), this proposal is justified on the basis of Argentina's experience.
11. Galasso and Ravaillon (2003) offer the World Bank's viewpoint regarding this programme. For a critical analysis, see Barbeito et al. (2003).
12. Without including the programme's beneficiaries, in May 2003 poverty rose to 43.2 per cent of households and 55.3 per cent of the population; including them, poverty was only reduced to 42.6 and to 54.7, respectively.
13. In Argentina, almost 40 per cent of wage earners in the private sector live in poor households, including 25 per cent of full-time workers.
14. This gap is estimated in 2.6 per cent of gross domestic product (GDP); only 1 per cent of GDP is invested in PJyJHD.
15. In May 2003, almost 3 million unemployed workers accounted for 21.4 per cent of the economically active population. If 1.8 million beneficiaries of the PJyJHD were considered employed workers, the rate would go down to 15.6 per cent. By the third trimester of 2006 the open unemployment rate would increase from 10.2 to 12.1 per cent if beneficiaries of PJyJHD that render a service are not considered employed workers.
16. In some regions of Argentina, the number of benefits granted by the PJyJHD plan is greater than the number of unemployed workers statistically recorded.
17. See Rocha (2001) for Brazil and Standing (1999) for the United States.
18. In practice, this paradigm is useful for a lucrative industry that captures financial resources from different parts of the world. At the same time, it absorbs huge resources coming from incentive credits and subsidies granted by the state and by international financial institutions (IFIs), which could be devoted to other programmes with higher impact on vulnerable sectors that remain outside the scope of debate.
19. Wray (1998a, 1998b, 2000); Tcherneva (2003); Cibils and Lo Vuolo (2004a).
20. This would be feasible because money creation and public expenditure always occur before tax collection.
21. If other causes of indebtedness are not considered, the growth rate of GDP should be higher than the real rate of public debt growth originated by the Employer of Last Resort (ELR), for the latter debt not to be explosive (Sawyer 2002).
22. In his original formulation, Lerner (1947) stated that this mechanism served to eliminate cyclical unemployment originated by normal fluctuations in the market economy.
23. Van Parijs (1992, 1995); Van der Veen et al. (2002); Lo Vuolo (1995).
24. Abramovay et al. (1998); Lavinas and Varsano (1997); Caccia Bava (1998).
25. To analyse the process that led to passing this act, see Suplicy (2006).
26. These proposals follow the guidelines supported in Argentina (Barbeito and Lo Vuolo 1996).
27. In this respect, it is worth recalling Furtado's (1964) classic work.
28. For a proposal of reform in Argentina, see Goldberg and Lo Vuolo (2006).
29. See Aguirre (2005).
30. For an exercise applied to Argentina, see Lo Vuolo et al. (1999).

References

Abel, Christopher and Colin Lewis (2002) 'Exclusion and engagement: A diagnosis of social policy in Latin America in the long run'. In Christopher Abel and Colin Lewis (eds.), *Exclusion and Engagement: Social Policy in Latin America* (London: Institute of Latin American Studies, University of London).

Abramovay, Miriam, Carla Andrade and Julio J. Waiselfisz (1998) *Bolsa Escola. Melhoria Educacional e Redução da Pobreza* (Brasilia: Edições UNESCO).

Aguirre, Patricia (2005) *Estrategias de Consumo: Qué Comen los Argentinos que Comen* (Buenos Aires and Madrid: Ciepp/Miño y Dávila Editores).

Arza, Camila (2002) *Distributional Impacts of Social Policy: Pension Regimes in Argentina since c. 1944*, unpublished PhD thesis (London: London School of Economics and Political Sciences).

Auyero, Javier (2004) 'Política, dominación y desigualdad en la Argentina contemporánea. Un ensayo etnográfico', *Nueva Sociedad*, No. 193, September–October, 133–45.

Baker, Judy (2000) *Evaluating the Impact of Development Projects on Poverty – A Handbook for Practioners* (Washington, DC: World Bank).

Barbeito, Alberto and Rubén Lo Vuolo (1996) *Why Begin with a Basic Income for Young People in Latin America?*, paper presented at the 6th International BIEN Congress, Vienna, 12–14 September.

Barbeito, Alberto, Noemí Giosa Zuazúa and Corina Rodríguez Enríquez (2003) 'La cuestión social en Argentina y el Plan Jefes y Jefas de Hogar desocupados.' In *Proyecto Enfrentando los retos al trabajo decente en la crisis argentina*, mimeo (Buenos Aires: OIT – Gobierno Argentino, Ministerio de Trabajo y Seguridad Social).

Barr, Nicholas (2002) 'Reforming pensions: Myths, truths and policy choices', *International Social Security Review*, Vol. 55, No. 2, 3–36.

Berger, Marguerite, Alison Beck Yonas and María Lucía Lloreda (2003) *The Second Story: Wholesale Microfinance in Latin America*, Best Practices Series (Washington, DC: Inter-American Development Bank, Sustainable Development Department).

Bresser-Pereira, Luiz C. (2002) 'Incompatibilidade distributiva e desenvolvimento autosustentado'. In Ricardo Bielschowsky and Carlos Mussi (eds.), *Políticas para a Retomada do Crescimento: Reflexões de Economistas Brasileiros* (Brasilia/Rio de Janeiro: IPEA–Escritório da Cepal no Brasil).

Caccia Bava, Silvio (1998) *Programas de Renda Mínima no Brasil* (São Paulo: Polis).

Cibils, Alan and Rubén Lo Vuolo (2004a) *El Estado como Empleador de Ultima Instancia*. Documentos de Trabajo Ciepp 40. www.ciepp.org.ar/trabajo.htm, accessed on 9 April 2007.

—— (2004b) *Régimen de Metas de Inflación: ¿El Nuevo Consenso Ortodoxo en Política Monetaria?* Documentos de Trabajo Ciepp 41. www.ciepp.org.ar/trabajo.htm, accessed on 9 April 2007.

Disney, Richard F. (1999) *Notional Accounts as a Pension Reform Strategy: An Evaluation*, Pension Reform Primer Series, Social Protection Discussion Paper No. 9928 (Washington, DC: World Bank).

Esping-Andersen, Gøsta (1990) *The Three Worlds of Welfare Capitalism* (Princeton, NJ: Princeton University Press).

Ferrera, Maurizio (1996) 'The "southern model" of welfare in social Europe', *Journal of European Social Policy*, Vol. 6, No 1, 17–37.

Friedman, Milton (1966) 'The case for the negative income tax: A view from the right.' In John H. Bunzel (ed.), *Issues of American Public Policy* (Englewood Cliffs, NJ: Prentice Hall).

Furtado, Celso (1964) *Desarrollo y Subdesarrollo* (Buenos Aires: Editorial Universitaria).

Galasso, Emanuela and Martin Ravaillon (2003) *Social Protection in Crisis: Argentina's Plan Jefes y Jefas* (Washington, DC: World Bank, Development Research Group).

Garber, Carter and Brian Beard (2003) *New Approaches to Microfinance Client Assessment in Latin America* (Miami, FL: The Dante B. Fascell North-South Center).

Goldberg, Laura (2006) *Lo que Dice y lo que Calla la Literatura sobre Microfinanzas*, Documentos de Trabajo Ciepp 54. www.ciepp.org.ar/trabajo.htm, accessed on 9 April 2007.

Goldberg, Laura and Rubén Lo Vuolo (2006) *Falsas Promesas Sistema de Previsión Social y Régimen de Acumulación* (Buenos Aires and Madrid: Ciepp/Miño y Dávila Editores).

Gough, Ian and Geof Wood (eds.) (2004) *Insecurity and Welfare Regimes in Asia, Africa and Latin America* (Cambridge: Cambridge University Press).

Habermas, Jurgen (1994) 'Citizenship and national identity'. In Bart van Steenbergen (ed.), *The Condition of Citizenship* (London: Sage).

Hicks, Alexander (1991) 'A review of G. Esping-Andersen, The three worlds of welfare capital-
    ism, Princeton: Princeton University Press, 1990', *Contemporary Sociology: An International
    Journal of Review*, Vol. 20, No. 3, 399–401.
Holzman, Robert and Steen Jorgensen (2000) *Social Risk Management: A New Conceptual Frame-
    work for Social Protection and Beyond*, Social Protection Discussion Paper 0006 (Washington,
    DC: World Bank).
Lautier, Bernard (2006) 'Una protección social mutualista y universal. Condición para la
    eficacia de la lucha contra la pobreza.' In Rubén M. Lo Vuolo (ed.), *La Credibilidad Social de
    la Política Económica en América Latina* (Buenos Aires and Madrid: Ciepp/Miño y Dávila).
—— (1998) 'Représentations et régulations statiques de la pauvreté en Amérique Latine.' In
    Richard Poulin and Pierre Salama (eds.), *L'Insoutenable Misère du Monde, Économie et Sociologie
    de la Pauvreté* (Quebec: Éditions Vents d'Ouest).
Lavinas, Lena and Ricardo Varsano (1997) *Programas de Garantia de Renda Mínima e Ação
    Coordenada de Combate à Pobreza* (Rio de Janerio: IPEA).
Lavinas, Lena, Marcelo Nicoll, Cristiano Duarte and Roberto Loreiro Filho (2004) *Exception-
    ality and Paradox in Brazil: From Minimum Income Programs to Basic Income*, paper presented
    at the Tenth Congress of the Basic Income European Network (BIEN), Barcelona, 18–21
    September.
Lerner, Abba P. (1947) 'Money as a creature of the state', *American Economic Review*, Vol. 37,
    No. 2, May, 312–17.
Lo Vuolo, Rubén (2003) *Estrategia Económica para la Argentina* (Buenos Aires: Siglo XXI/Ciepp/
    Osde).
—— (2002) 'Ideology and the new social security in the Argentine.' In Christopher Abel and
    Colin Lewis (eds.), *Exclusion and Engagement: Social Policy in Latin America* (London: Institute
    of Latin American Studies, University of London).
—— (1996) 'Reformas previsionales en América Latina: Una visión crítica en base al caso
    argentine', *Comercio Exterior*, Vol. 46, No. 9, 692–702.
—— (ed.) (1995) *Contra la Exclusión: La Propuesta del Ingreso Ciudadano* (Buenos Aires and
    Madrid: Ciepp/Miño y Dávila).
Lo Vuolo, Rubén, Alberto Barbeito, Laura Pautassi and Corina Rodríguez (1999) *La Pobreza...
    de la Política contra la Pobreza* (Buenos Aires and Madrid: Ciepp/Miño y Dávila).
MacIsaac, Norman (1996) *Micro-Enterprise Support: A Critical Review*, background paper for
    the CCIC Learning Circle on Microenterprise Development (Ottawa: Canadian Council for
    International Cooperation/CCIC).
Marques-Pereira, Jaime (2006) 'Teoría económica y credibilidad de la política anti-cíclica: La
    distribución del ingreso y los límites al crecimiento económico.' In Rubén Lo Vuolo (ed.), *La
    Credibilidad Social de la Política Económica* (Buenos Aires and Madrid: Ciepp/Miño y Dávila).
Marulanda, Beatriz and María Otero (2005) *Perfil de las Microfinanzas en América Latina en 10
    Años: Visión y Características* (Boston, MA: Acción Internacional).
Mesa-Lago, Carmelo (2006) 'Private and public pension systems compared: An evaluation of
    the Latin American experience', *Review of Political Economy*, Vol. 18, No. 3, 317–34.
—— (2004) 'Evaluación de un cuarto sigo de reformas estructurales de pensiones en América
    Latina', *Revista de la CEPAL*, No. 84, 59–82.
—— (1989) *Ascent to Bankruptcy: Financing Social Security in Latin America* (Pittsburgh, PA:
    University of Pittsburgh Press).
—— (1978) *Social Security in Latin America: Pressure Groups, Stratification and Inequality*
    (Pittsburgh, PA: University of Pittsburgh Press).
Pauselli, Emilio (2005) *Microcrédito: Una Industria sin Clientes o Sobre Paradigmas y Negocios*
    (Buenos Aires: Documento Organización Poleas).
Pauselli, Emilio and Jaime Villarraga (2006) *Microfinanzas Vinculadas al Desarrollo de Población
    Pobre y Excluida: Otra Visión. Reflexiones para que las Microfinanzas Contribuyan Efectivamente
    al Desarrollo de Nuestra América* (Buenos Aires: Documento Organización Poleas).

Pautassi, Laura (2004) 'Beneficios y beneficiarias: Análisis del programa Jefes y Jefas de Hogar Desocupados de Argentina.' In María Elena Valenzuela (ed.), *Políticas de Empleo para Superar la Pobreza* (Santiago de Chile: Oficina Regional de la Organización Internacional de Trabajo).

Pierson, Paul (1996) 'The new politics of the welfare state', *World Politics*, Vol. 48, No. 2, 143–79.

—— (1994) *Dismantling the Welfare State? Reagan, Thatcher, and the Politics of Retrenchment* (Cambridge and New York: Cambridge University Press).

Reinhart, Carmen, Kenneth Rogoff and Miguel Savastano (2003) 'Debt intolerance', *Brookings Papers on Economic Activity*, Vol. 1, 1–74.

Robinson, Marguerite S. (2005) 'La oferta y la demanda en el microfinanciamiento.' In Alberto F. Sabaté, Ruth Muñoz and Sabina Ozomek (eds.), *Finanzas y Economía Social: Modalidades en el Manejo de los Recursos Solidarios* (Buenos Aires: Universidad Nacional de General Sarmiento/Altamira/Fundación Osde).

Rocha, Sonia (2001) *Workfare Programmes in Brazil: An Evaluation of Their Performance* (Geneva: ILO).

Rodrik, Dani (2003) 'Introduction: What do we learn from countries narratives?' In Dani Rodrik (ed.) *In Search of Prosperity* (Princeton, NJ: Princeton University Press).

—— (2001) '¿Por qué hay tanta inseguridad económica en América Latina?', *Revista de la CEPAL*, No. 73, 7–31.

Rodríguez Enríquez, Corina (2005) *Gender Aspects of Social Policy in Argentina: The Case of Money Transfer Policy*, paper presented at the 6th International Conference Engendering Macroeconomics and International Economics, GEM-IWG – University of UTAH, 12–13 July.

Sawyer, Malcom (2002) *Employer of Last Resort: Could It Deliver Full Employment and Price Stability?*, mimeo (Leeds: University of Leeds).

Settergren, Ole (2001) *The Automatic Balance Mechanism of the Swedish Pension System: A Non-Technical Introduction* (Stockholm: Swedish National Social Insurance Board).

Standing, Guy (1999) *Global Labour Flexibility: Seeking Distributive Justice.* (London: Macmillan Press).

Suplicy, Eduardo M. (2006) *Renda Básica de Cidadania: A Resposta dada pelo Vento* (Porto Alegre: Coleção L&PM Pocket).

—— (2002) *Renda de Cidadania. A Saída é pela Porta* (São Paulo: Perseu Abramo Editora e Editora Cortez).

Tcherneva, Pavlina R. (2003) *Job or Income Guarantee?*, Working Paper No. 29 (Kansas City, MO: Center for Full Employment and Price Stability, University of Missouri).

Théret, Bruno (1997) 'Méthodologie des comparaisons internationales, approches de l'effet sociétal et de la régulation: Fondements pour une lecture structuraliste des systèmes nationaux de protection sociale', *L'Année de la Régulation*, Vol. 1, 163–228 (Paris: Éditions La Découverte).

Van der Veen, Robert, Loek Groot and Rubén Lo Vuolo (eds.) (2002) *La Renta Básica en la Agenda: Objetivos y Posibilidades del Ingreso Ciudadano* (Buenos Aires and Madrid: Ciepp/Miño y Dávila Editores).

Van Parijs, Philippe (1995) *Real Freedom for All: What (If Anything) Can Justify Capitalism?* (Oxford: Clarendon Press).

—— (1992) 'Competing justifications of basic income.' In Philippe Van Parijs (ed.), *Arguing for Basic Income: Ethical Foundations for a Radical Reform* (New York: Verso).

Willmore, Larry (2001a) *Universal Pensions in Low-Income Countries*, paper presented at the Meeting of Asociación Internacional de Organismos de Supervisión de Fondos de Pensiones, San José, Costa Rica, 19–23 November.

—— (2001b) 'Three pillars of pensions: Is there really a need for mandatory contributions?' In *OECD Private Pensions Conference*, Private Pension Series, No. 3, 385–97.

World Bank (2004) *Keeping the Promise of Social Security in Latin America* (Washington, DC: Office of the Chief Economist Latin America and Caribbean Region, World Bank).

—— (1994) *Averting the Old Age Crisis: Policies to Protect the Old and Promote Growth* (Washington, DC: World Bank).

Wray, L. Randall (2000) *The Employer of Last Resort Approach to Full Employment*, Working Paper No. 9 (Kansas City, MO: Center for Full Employment and Price Stability, University of Missouri).

—— (1998a) *Understanding Modern Money: The Key to Full Employment and Price Stability* (Cheltenham: Edward Elgar).

—— (1998b) *Modern Money*, Working Paper No. 252 (Annandale-on-Hudson, NY: Levy Economic Institute of Bard College).

3
Financing for Development: International Redistribution

Isabel Ortiz

Conventionally, it is argued that there are four pillars of fiscal space for public policies: increased official development assistance (ODA), additional international or domestic borrowing, enhanced revenue collection, and improved efficiency and reprioritization of expenditures. To these, we add another way to win fiscal space, avoiding South–North transfers through the better use of reserves. Three of the five areas have an international nature.

This chapter presents the international sources and instruments to finance social policy. It is argued that the extreme inequalities in the distribution of the world's wealth require redistribution at a global scale. ODA is the official channel for North–South redistribution; however, ODA in its current form presents problems of size, concentration, transaction costs, predictability, macroeconomic impacts, tied aid, policy coherence, fungibility and conditionality. Some alternative options for ODA are explained. Given that North–South transfers are minimal and often loaded with conditions, developing countries are increasingly cooperating among themselves, either as bilateral South–South ODA, regional integration, or as South–South banks. However, investments to date have focused on infrastructure, and not on social policies, with the only exception being regional associations in Latin America, particularly the Bolivarian Alternative for Latin America (ALBA) and the proposed alternative Bank of the South and Bank of ALBA. The chapter follows with an analysis of the world's net financial flows that puts ODA into perspective: actually, it is the South that finances the North. Developing countries must start by reducing transfers to the North and use resources for their own development and welfare, instead of the welfare of rich Northern countries. The chapter closes with specific financial instruments, from Sector Wide Approach (SWAp) and Millennium Development Goal (MDG) contracts to bonds and securities, including the International Financial Facility, as potential channels to finance social policy in developing countries.

International sources of development finance

North–South transfers
World distribution asymmetries: The need for international redistribution

The extreme inequality in the global distribution of income and assets seriously undermines governments' capacity to finance social policy. In 2000, the richest

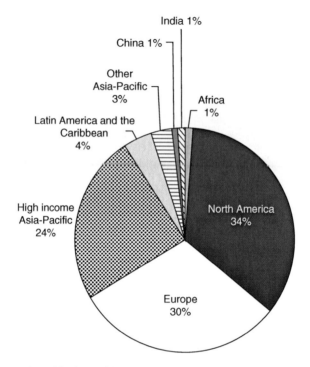

Figure 3.1   Regional wealth shares (%)
Source: Based on UNU-WIDER (2006).

1 per cent of adults owned 40 per cent of total global wealth, and the richest 10 per cent of adults accounted for 85 per cent of total world income and assets; in contrast, the bottom half of the world adult population owned barely 1 per cent of global wealth.[1] While the economic benefits of globalization go to a few countries, companies and individuals, the cost of social policies must be dealt with at the national and local levels, with fewer resources, within a diminishing policy space.

The justification for international redistribution could not be stronger. For globalization to be accepted, it will have to be a globalization that benefits the majority, a globalization for all, rather than a few. The magnitude of the concentration of income in Northern countries is so gross, that authors such as Samir Amin have claimed that this is apartheid on a global scale. North America, the European Union, and the high-income countries of Asia and the Pacific[2] hold 84 per cent of the world's wealth, or 79 per cent of the world's gross domestic product (GDP) (UNU-WIDER 2006); redistributing a significant part of it to Southern regions is a legitimate goal.

Official Development Assistance (ODA)

The official channel for international redistribution is ODA. ODA has existed since colonial times, but in its current form, it can be traced to the postwar period, when the Bretton Woods institutions were created.[3] A large number of European colonies became independent and were in dire need of assistance. The good experience of the Marshall Plan in Europe[4] led to the idea of a 'Marshall Plan for the South', which finally won official support from Northern governments in the late 1950s. It was adopted by the General Assembly of the United Nations (UN) in 1960: 1 per cent of the gross national product (GNP) of rich countries should be devoted to aiding the South. Interestingly, today Jeffrey Sachs argues that poverty could be eradicated with 1 per cent of the combined GDP of Organisation for Economic Co-operation and Development (OECD) countries.

However, aid never reached its target of 1 per cent of GNP; furthermore, there were notorious accountability problems in the determination of what was included under aid expenditures. In 1969, a Commission led by the then Canadian Prime Minister Pierre Trudeau called for 0.7 per cent of rich countries' GNP to be given in aid, excluding commercial loans and military expenditure. This was adopted by all developed countries at the UN General Assembly in 1970. Since then, Northern governments have made repeated commitments to contribute 0.7 per cent of GNP to ODA, but the international effort is well below this target, at just 0.3 per cent.[5] Of the total ODA, about 15 per cent is dedicated to education and health; this is because of donors' efforts to support Africa in order to achieve the MDGs. The percentage has remained constant over recent years.

Exceptionally, in 2005 aid rose to 0.33 per cent of GNP as the result of extra personal donations sent for relief efforts for the Asian Tsunami and Iraq war, but in 2006 ODA fell back to 0.30 per cent. Rich countries are becoming richer – and meaner. In real terms, their contributions have decreased (relative to their income) as compared to one decade earlier; in the early 1990s, contributions were 0.32 per cent of OECD's gross national income (GNI) on average. The United States' (US) contribution in 2006 was 0.17 per cent, Japan's 0.25 per cent and the European Union's 0.54 per cent. Only Denmark, Luxemburg, the Netherlands, Norway and Sweden have met the 0.7 per cent commitment. Several governments have claimed that the 0.7 per cent commitment is outside their budget envelope. However, comparing expenditures on military defence and aid, for instance, shows that it is really a question of priorities.[6]

Donors argue that this reduction in ODA comes from a fatigue of the limited effectiveness of development aid. Over recent decades, development assistance did not contribute sufficiently to the reduction of poverty or the creation of sustainable conditions for economic development. In part, this is a self-fulfilling prophecy: rich countries never invested in a Marshall Plan for the South but instead gave tiny resources, so that the world's 180 developing countries have never been developed fully.

Private flows and remittances

Some argue that private sector flows and workers' remittances have made ODA irrelevant. Net private debt and equity flows to developing countries have risen from a little less than $170 billion[7] in 2002 to close to $647 billion in 2006. While private sector flows to developing countries are certainly much larger than the

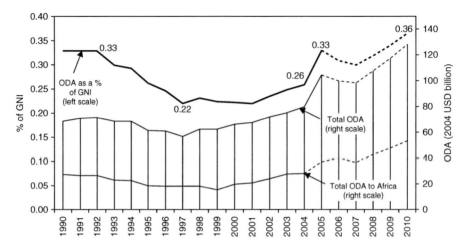

Figure 3.2   Official development assistance, 1990–2010
Source: Based on OECD DAC (2007b).

level of ODA, it should be noted that 70 per cent of them benefit only a few middle-income countries such as Argentina, Brazil, China, India, Malaysia, Mexico, Singapore, the Republic of Korea, Taiwan Province of China and Thailand; private flows are insignificant in the least developed countries of Africa and elsewhere (Chandrasekhar 2007; Ortiz 2005). In addition, the contributions of international private investments to social policy are poor.

Workers' remittances are another important source of transfer to developing countries, reaching $193 billion in 2006 (compared to $106 billion ODA in the same year) (World Bank 2007a; NEF 2006). However, remittances are informal flows of finance. They are fundamental to sustaining migrant families' private consumption, and a good source of foreign exchange for governments, but they are not a good financing mechanism to support public policies for long-term sustainable economic development in a country. The main recipients are India, Mexico and the Philippines; remittances are spread unevenly among developing countries, and they rarely benefit the poorest population groups.

New sources of development finance

The failure of donors to meet the commitment to provide 0.7 per cent of GNP as aid has led to proposals to develop new international sources of development finance. These have focused principally on the taxation of luxury activities or activities with negative social or environmental externalities. The proposals include: (i) taxing the arms trade; (ii) global environmental taxes (carbon-use tax); (iii) a tax on speculative short-term currency flows (the so-called 'Tobin tax'); (iv) taxes on airplane tickets; or (v) increasing voluntary donations using new methods (percentage of credit card sales, lotteries and so on) (Atkinson 2004). In 2006, a Leading Group on Solidary Levies to Fund Development was officially established in Paris, and its first action has been to implement the Air Ticket Solidarity Levy, to which at the time of writing 28 countries have committed. Proceeds will be used to scale up access and treatments for HIV/AIDS, tuberculosis and malaria, using an international new drug purchase facility, UNITAID (United Nations 2007). If operative, these could become additional sources of funding for social policies.

Since the 1990s a number of public–private partnerships and foundations, mostly in the area of health, have appeared. Such is the case of the Global Health Programme of the Gates Foundation (started in 1994), the Global TB Vaccine Foundation (1997) or the Drugs for Neglected Diseases Initiative (2003), among others. They tend to be issue-focused (for example, on malaria, tuberculosis or HIV/AIDS) and financed by private donations which often surpass the level of funds for similar UN programmes and bilateral ODA (Conceiçao 2006).

These new sources of development finance are good initiatives but they should be as complements to – rather than replacements for – ODA. Ultimately, what is needed is an enforceable and progressive multilateral system to transfer resources from richer to poorer governments, thereby sharing responsibility for development.

Proposals for an International Tax Organization (ITO)

Proposals for an ITO have been suggested by the United Nations Panel on Financing for Development in order: (i) to avoid tax competition and its pressures to make tax systems less progressive and equitable; (ii) to coordinate efforts to fight tax evasion and tax havens; and (iii) to study a global formula to levy taxes on multi-national enterprises (United Nations 2001).[8] The idea of an ITO was not received with enthusiasm by the United States and other Northern governments in the later Monterrey Conference on Financing for Development (2002), despite the fact that it would involve a high degree of distributional justice and – in technical terms – would not be difficult to implement, as multinational corporations are already taxed. With the votes of 115 countries, in 2004 the UN General Assembly adopted a resolution calling for an examination of international taxes as an instrument of development financing, but again no agreement was reached on an ITO. However, the creation of an ITO is ultimately a correct step towards improving global governance and redressing the erosion of the nation-state's tax base and policy space (Wahl 2006).

South–South transfers

South–South cooperation is becoming increasingly important. Since the nineteenth century, non-hegemonic countries and regions have forged alliances as a strategy to reduce dependency and dominance from Northern powers. At the beginning of the twenty-first century, Southern countries are still associating to promote South–South cooperation in two main forms: international groups (for example, the G-77 or the G-24)[9] and regional integration (for example, the Mercado Común del Sur/MERCOSUR, the Southern African Development Community/SADC, the Association of Southeast Asian Nations/ASEAN, and so on).

South–South bilateral ODA and investments

South–South aid and investment tend to occur on a bilateral basis. The main non-OECD donors are Brazil, China, India, Kuwait, Mexico, the Russian Federation, Saudi Arabia, South Africa, the Republic of Korea, Taiwan Province of China and Turkey. Precisely because they are beyond the sight of the monitoring lens of OECD Development Assistance Committee (DAC), data on South–South transfers are unreliable. The World Bank (2007c: 243), based on DAC data, estimates that in 2005, 4.4 per cent of total ODA was provided by non-OECD countries, but this is an underestimation. Interestingly, the bulk of this aid goes not to social sectors but to large infrastructure projects, given that infrastructure is what many developing governments think as priority. Nevertheless, South–South transfers are a potential source of financing for social policies.

In this instance the case of China must be mentioned, given the magnitude (and controversy) of its investments in developing countries, particularly in sub-Saharan Africa and East Asia. Beijing does not officially report on its ODA but estimates to have spent $5.7 billion on assistance for Africa in the period to 2006 – though it is unclear what this figure includes.[10] In 2003, China set an important example by honouring the commitments made by the world community at the Monterrey Conference on Financing for Development by reducing or cancelling $1.2 billion of debt in favour of 31 African countries, arguing that world peace and development cannot possibly be sustained if the North–South divide grows wider and the developing nations grow poorer. In 2006, President Hu Jintao announced that China would double its assistance to Africa by 2009, and provide $5 billion additional in loans.

The Export-Import Bank of China plays a strategic role. Since its foundation in 1994 to 2006, Exim Bank China developed 259 loans in Africa alone (concentrated in Angola, Nigeria, Mozambique, Sudan and Zimbabwe), most of them for large infrastructure projects:[11] energy and mineral extraction (40 per cent), multi-sector (24 per cent), transport (20 per cent), telecoms (12 per cent) and water (4 per cent) (Broadman 2007). According to the Exim Bank China Annual Report 2005, only 78 loans of the total bank loan portfolio were concessional, below-market rate loans. When the terms are concessional, interest rates can go as low as 0.25 per cent per annum, subsidized by the Chinese government; however most of the procurement has to be imported from China, that is, tied aid. Apart from the condition to procure inputs from China, there are no other strings attached to these loans, that is, no policy conditions, no environmental or social standards required.[12]

International and national organizations, including civil society groups, have made critical remarks that China is supporting highly repressive regimes (for example, Myanmar, Sudan, Uzbekistan or Zimbabwe) to satisfy China's need for natural resources, particularly oil; creating new debt in low-income countries to promote Chinese exports; undermining the fight against corruption and the promotion of environmental and social standards (Bosshard 2007). Exim Bank China recently approved an Environmental Policy (its quality remains to be evaluated); it has no social safeguards yet but there are signs that this may be reversed.[13]

Intraregional transfers

Intraregional transfers are another source of financing for social policies. This requires, of course, the existence of at least one higher-income country in a regional association, as well as the willingness to pay for regional solidarity. Such is the case of the European Union, MERCOSUR, ALBA and the League of Arab States (LAS).

Regional integration is a major form of South–South cooperation, and a constructive alternative to the current pattern of inequitable globalization. Regional formations offer a means of 'locking-in' finance for the development of its member countries. Regionalist trading strategies are an effective means of protecting, promoting and reshaping a regional division of labour, trade and production. While the European Union is the best existing example of how regional solidarity may be articulated, there are increasing experiences in developing countries. Virtually every country in the world falls into some regional bloc: the Association of South East Asian Nations (ASEAN), the African Union (AU), the Andean Community (CAN), the Caribbean Community (CARICOM), the League of Arab States (LAS), the South Asian Association for Regional Cooperation (SAARC), the Southern Africa Development Community (SADC), to mention some. The most mature Southern regional integration case is MERCOSUR, and the most radical, the recently created ALBA, is also in Latin America.[14]

MERCOSUR has evolved slowly but steadily, from a mere trade agreement in 1991 to the establishment of a Common Parliament in May 2007. The importance of MERCOSUR comes in its being the best example of regional integration after the European Union, which is meritorious, given the high growth volatility in the region and the fact that several economies collapsed during the period. Countries also managed to resist external Northern pressures that would have eroded MERCOSUR's potential, such as the US-led Free Trade Area of the Americas (FTAA) – 'Our North is the South' says MERCOSUR's motto. MERCOSUR has progressively expanded its role, from common external tariff agreements to a more comprehensive economic and political integration of its member states. In social policy, it has an important labour and social declaration, harmonized regulations on pharmaceuticals, education degrees, social security entitlements, and joint health and safety inspections. In January 2007, its Council approved the establishment of MERCOSUR Social Institute, to be based in Paraguay, with the mandate to elaborate regional social policies and promote the exchange of good practices in the social field and cooperation mechanisms. However, intraregional transfers for social policy remain low, as compared to the European Union, where the Social Cohesion Funds absorb 36 per cent of the EU budget (Deacon et al. 2007).

This is different in ALBA, which was created in 2006 to address the 'social debt' of Latin America, that is, to address the needs of those who have lost out in the process of globalization, and as an alternative to the neoliberal FTAA. ALBA countries argue that a new set of public policies is needed to redress social asymmetries and raise living standards, based on social spending, public investment, and macroeconomic policies geared towards employment and the expansion of national markets. Because ALBA countries are standing against the orthodoxy of Northern powers and the international financial institutions (IFIs), they feel that the only chance of success comes by associating and uniting efforts, creating a new political bloc that provides support to its members. ALBA is using policies of regional solidarity to pursue social transformations at both national and regional levels; oil-rich Venezuela has been funding a number of social policies among neighbouring countries, such as under the Petrocaribe or Petrosur initiatives. The largest is *Project Grand National*, signed in April 2007,[15] which includes multiple proposals from literacy programmes and regional universities to the promotion of industrial technology policies; from radio/TV media with indigenous content to regional fair trade agreements and the issuance of an ALBA bond.

Critics argue that ALBA's redistributive policies depend upon the price of oil; if oil prices were to plummet, regional integration may fall apart. While diversification of regional contributions and lesser dependency on a single resource is advised, it must be pointed out that oil prices are likely to remain high. Venezuela is doing with ALBA what was hardly done earlier by the Organization of Petroleum Exporting Countries (OPEC): using funds to develop the region. In the past, OPEC countries lost a golden opportunity for development, as a large majority of petrodollars coming from the oil bonanza ended up in Northern banks.

South–South banks

The most elaborate South–South multilateral banks are to be found in the Arab and Islamic world. Most of these institutions began to operate in the 1970s as vehicles to transfer resources from the oil-rich countries to poorer countries in the region and Africa. The Islamic Development Bank's objective is to foster the economic development and social progress of Muslim communities in accordance with the principles of *shari'ah*. In 2006, it announced a major funding operation in support of MDG-related expenditures among its member states. The second-largest is the Arab Fund for Economic and Social Development (AFESD), which provides soft lending for Arab League countries, but mostly for infrastructure projects (UNDESA 2007b).

The Andean Development Corporation (CAF in its Spanish acronym) is also a successful case of a Southern multilateral bank. In recent years its portfolio ($3 billion), mostly in infrastructure, largely surpasses investments by the World Bank and the Inter-American Development Bank (IDB) in the Andean region. Its board includes 17 Latin American members, plus Spain, and 12 commercial banks; most of the Andean borrowing members value CAF's proximity, its lack of conditionalities and its rapid processes (as low as three months for loan approval). However, the lack of transparency regarding the most basic of CAF functions and the pricing of its loans are cause for some criticism of the institution (McElhinny 2007).

South–South banks appear friendly to governments, given their lack of policy conditionalities and lesser requirements. However, unless these are created with a different set of principles, they will replicate the same problems that exist in the Northern ODA banks presented later in this chapter (including tied aid, the concentration of ODA, inequitable outcomes, residual social investments, and so on).

In 2007 and early 2008, countries from MERCOSUR and ALBA came together to create alternative banks – the Banco del Sur (Bank of the South) and the Banco del ALBA (Bank of ALBA).[16] Several member countries, who were very critical of the roles of the International Monetary Fund (IMF) and the World Bank, intend for Banco del Sur/ALBA to become an instrument of South–South solidarity and fair development. This alternative to the IFIs is expected to be combined with either a 'Fund of the South' or a revamped Latin American Reserve Fund (known by its Spanish acronym FLAR), to create a regional monetary fund that would ensure 'collective insurance' for its members, pooling funds against financial risks. The founding charts of both Banco del Sur and Banco del ALBA adopt the system of one-country–one-vote, which is an important advance as compared to the rest of multilateral banks which assign votes according to contributions (so richer countries remain in control). The Bank of the South intends to raise $7 billion in paid-in capital.

The Bank of the South and Bank of ALBA are likely to expand the model of BANDES (Bank for Economic and Social Development of Venezuela, created in 2001) on a regional scale. BANDES, under the Ministry of People's Power for Finance of Venezuela, supports advice and investments in less developed areas, fostering local economic and social development, and offering concessional rates to public/social enterprises such as state-owned enterprises (SOEs), cooperatives or community ownership) according to the priorities of Venezuela's National Development Strategy. In 2005–06 most of the BANDES portfolio ($1.2 billion for the biennium) was lent on to rural, industrial, small and medium-sized enterprise (SMEs) and mutual banks, supporting everything from milk producers to health services. There are, however, some pressures to use the model of the Brazilian BNDES (Bank for National Economic and Social Development of Brazil, created in 1952), which has a much more traditional portfolio, principally supporting large infrastructure projects and Brazilian exports.

Many questions remain for the new Banco del Sur and Banco del ALBA, such as the lending framework, the type of loan guarantees expected, the criteria for selecting investments to ensure equitable development, and its social and environmental safeguard policies. The fact that these banks were founded with the intention of becoming alternative banks will hopefully bring transparency and accountability to their processes, and question the drive of most Southern institutions to spend resources on large infrastructure projects with either no, or limited, social standards. Their objectives, specified in the founding charters, are to 'finance the economic and social development of their member countries, to strengthen regional integration, to reduce asymmetries and to promote an equitable distribution of investments'. With their egalitarian principles, Banco del Sur and Banco del ALBA could well be the first Southern institutions that do not consider social development as a residual investment.

Avoiding South–North transfers

Development institutions normally argue that there are four pillars of fiscal space for public policies: increased ODA, additional borrowing, enhanced revenue collection, and the improved efficiency and reprioritization of expenditures. Two of

Table 3.1   Net financial transfers to developing countries, 1995–2006 (selected years/billions of dollars)

	1995	1998	2000	2002	2004	2006
Africa	5.9	15.6	−27.7	−6.7	−35.0	−95.3
Sub-Saharan*	7.5	12.1	2.8	5.3	4.5	−10.1
Eastern Asia	21.8	−128.4	−119.1	−146	−162.1	−244.7
Western Asia	20.1	34.8	−29.7	−18.4	−69.8	−194.7
Latin America	−1.7	44.3	−1.6	−31.6	−80.0	−123.1
Transition economies	−2.7	3.6	−49.4	−26.1	−54.6	−125.1
Memorandum						
– HIPCs	6.7	8.5	7.8	10.3	10.2	9.8
– Least developed countries	11.8	12.5	5.7	7.1	5.4	−4.3

Note: * Sub-Saharan Africa excluding Nigeria and South Africa.
Source: UNDESA 2007b, based on IMF World Economic Outlook database (2006) and IMF Balance of Payment Statistics. 2006 figures are estimates.

the four pillars refer to the transfer of resources from richer to poorer countries. However, when analysing the net financial flows, the reality is that poor countries transfer resources to rich countries.

Net financial flows show a different picture

Looking at the bigger picture, debt interest payments, profit remittances, and public/private investments in capital markets in developed economies, offset net financial inflows to developing countries. According to the United Nations Department of Economic and Social Affairs' (UNDESA's) latest *World Economic Situation and Prospects 2007*, the net financial flows in developing economies have gone from a positive net inflow of $40 billion in 1995 to a negative net outflow of $657 billion in 2006 (Table 3.1). The net transfers to sub-Saharan Africa have also become negative in 2006, having been the only region with positive net transfers in previous years. If we add the accumulation of foreign-exchange reserves in developing countries, the figure goes up to $3 trillion. Most of this goes to the US economy, which monopolizes two-thirds of world savings, followed by countries like Spain, the United Kingdom and Australia. In other words, poor countries are transferring resources to rich countries.

Global savings are flowing in the wrong direction, overwhelmingly to the richest country in the world, while poor countries are crowded out of global resource transfers. The United States borrows $2 billion a day from poorer countries (Stiglitz 2006a). Thus, the global distribution of net savings is very inequitable, and poor countries, the most in need of more capital, export their net savings to rich countries. This challenges all conventional economic logic, as in theory capital is abundant in the North, having lower rates of return, and therefore it should have an interest in investing in the South, where capital is scarce and rates of return higher. Beyond this, the situation questions the whole logic of the current international financial system: poor countries should not be financing rich countries.

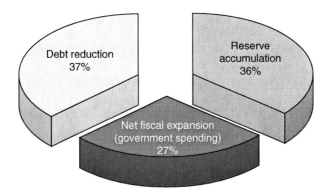

Figure 3.3 How official development assistance is used in sub-Saharan Africa
Source: Based on IMF (2007).

As McKinley and Izurieta (2007: 1) point out:

> Based, in effect, on borrowing money from other countries, US households have monopolized goods and services that could have a greater impact on global human welfare if they were consumed in poorer countries . . . the US economy is enjoying a gargantuan inflow of financial resources that could be invested at a higher social rate of return by low-income and middle-income countries in their own development.

Even the IMF Evaluation Office warns that since 1999, nearly three-quarters of the aid to the poor countries of sub-Saharan Africa is not being spent; rather, at the IMF's request, aid is used to pay off debt and accumulate reserves, instead of being used for much needed economic and social investments to eradicate the overwhelming poverty and human deprivation of the region (IMF 2007).

Options to curtail South–North transfers

Winning fiscal space for social development should start by stopping this net transfer of resources from South to North. This may be done by:

(i) reducing outflows below the level of inflows (for example, through significantly expanded debt relief, or increased taxation of investment profit remittances);

(ii) increasing substantially non-liable inflows above the level of outflows (for example, through ODA grants); or

(iii) diversifying central bank reserves away from liabilities in the United States like treasury bills (for example, through building reserves in regional local currency bonds, or bonds of development banks that invest at national level contributing to achieve the MDGs, or issuing new special drawing rights/SDRs under a new global reserve system).

All of these options have drawbacks, and the best solutions would require international coordination. Indeed there is a need for a new global financial architecture. Recent trends in financial liberalization, opening up capital accounts when incentives are distorted and the level of domestic regulation/supervision is inadequate, have increased financial flows to the North, as well as the frequency and severity of currency and financial crises. Ocampo and Griffith-Jones (2007) point out that over the course of the past 25 years, the income of developing countries has been 25 per cent lower due to currency and banking crises. A new financial architecture should also address an increase in the availability and provision of ODA, as is presented later in this chapter, not only in terms of quantity but also in terms of the areas and approaches, that is, by promoting expansionary, growth-oriented and equitable macroeconomic and sector policies geared towards employment and the expansion of national markets. However, even an MDG-inspired doubling of ODA to poor countries will not offset the current scale of South–North transfers (McKinley 2006; Stiglitz 2006a).

With respect to debt reduction/forgiveness, there are many arguments to support further action. The heavily indebted poor countries' (HIPC) initiative (1996) has been generally positive, but too slow to deliver results. In 2006, only 22 countries had reached the completion point at which debt relief is delivered (World Bank 2007b). Many object to the fact that HIPC targets only highly indebted low-income countries; there are strong arguments to condone debt in a larger group of countries, shifting the responsibility away from debtor governments to rich creditors who should also share liability for the irresponsible lending they incurred in earlier decades. Many question the legitimacy of this debt as it was often created by former (often non-democratic) governments who spent loans in military/defence and grandiose infrastructure projects with little or no social returns. However, current democratic governments need to service debt, consuming fiscal space to achieve social and economic development (George 1988). Additionally, critics argue that the neoliberal conditionalities attached to HIPC impede national development, by deepening financial liberalization, the privatization of strategic economic sectors, increases in regressive value added tax (VAT) tax and so on. Faster and wider efforts for debt relief are necessary (Pettifor 2003a, 2003b; Tan 2007).

Regarding the highly inequitable global reserve system, as pointed out earlier, developing countries finance the US current account deficit by accumulating US dollar-denominated international reserves as a 'self-insurance' mechanism to protect themselves against a potential future financial crisis, and as a way to keep currencies away from appreciation. For the United States this is beneficial as its deficit is sustained, and the country expands its consumption and imports based on debt. The United States promotes economic growth based on domestic consumption, and developing countries (particularly Asian) based on exports. The situation provides asymmetric benefits for all (Eichengreen 2004). But how long can these imbalances be maintained? And to what extent are they an obstacle to achieving the MDGs and other development goals?

The better use of reserves for development is suggested as another source of fiscal space for public policies. For developing countries, there are major arguments for the use of resources to expand domestic consumption instead of financing consumption in the United States and other rich countries. Expanding domestic markets could be an effective means of reducing poverty and achieving national development. There have been moves towards using Central Bank reserves to promote national development in developing countries, mostly by launching regional bonds, such as the regional Asian Bond Funds[17] or the proposed ALBA bond. In early 2005, China announced that it was no longer committed to holding reserves in dollars and used them to recapitalize its public banking system. Singapore, the Republic of Korea and the Arab Emirates have created investment funds to support national and regional companies. In Latin America, the proposed Banco del Sur and Banco del ALBA intend to use reserves to finance development in the region.

Additionally, there are better means to protect against future financial crises than through 'self-insurance', accumulating foreign reserves at the national level. Precisely, the IMF was created as a 'collective insurance' system, pooling funds against financial risks. 'Collective insurance' is a reinforced objective of the proposed Asian Monetary Fund[18] and the Fund of the South/FLAR,[19] supported by developing countries dissatisfied with IMF's current lending decisions and conditionalities.

New mechanisms, such as a global fund for pooling liquidity, could also be an alternative to reverse South–North transfers. There are proposals for a new global reserve system to issue a pool of reserves each year (such as Special Drawing Rights) that could be distributed disproportionately to poor countries in order to help overcome the deflationary bias of the current international reserve system and used to promote human development.[20] Ultimately, rich countries will have to restructure their expenditures in order to adequately correct global imbalances.

ODA: Trends, issues and options

According to OECD DAC, of the total ODA, 64 per cent is bilateral (with an upward trend) and only 36 per cent given to multilateral institutions, United Nations and IFIs (and the trend is to remain cutting contributions to them). The problem resides in powerful countries not agreeing on a common agenda.

The re-emergence of bilateralism in the early twenty-first century is a worrisome trend. Global problems such as migration, transmittable diseases or the 'race to the bottom', to mention a few, require global solutions. Moving towards smaller bilateral deals may benefit donor countries (in terms of political or economic influence), but it will not bring the much-needed long-lasting results.

Furthermore, in this situation of increased bilateralism, as they lack a common agenda, donors finance their own preferences, without an assessment of what is missing at the global level. Using a metaphor, this is as if a government were financed by charitable contributions (instead of a proper taxation system), and philanthropists would pick the areas to which they wanted their donations to be directed, leaving significant regions and public policy sectors uncovered, with no funds. For instance, in recent years there has been an increase in short-term emergency relief, while longer-term investments in agriculture that can help millions out of poverty are decreasing. The need for multilateral coordinated action to address global development is overwhelming.

The drawbacks of ODA and possible solutions

Concentration of ODA – The problem of the 'orphans and darlings'

Given limited development resources and increasing bilateralism, donors pick their favourite allied developing countries (the 'darlings'), leaving other countries 'orphan'. This concentration of ODA makes international redistribution unfair. Main aid recipient countries at the beginning of the twenty-first century are Iraq, Nigeria, China, Afghanistan, Indonesia, India, the Democratic Republic of the Congo and Egypt. These countries are linked tightly to the economic and political interests of the world's main powers. Critics point to a revival of neocolonialist attitudes in this first decade of the twenty-first century.

For the remaining developing countries that are not among the 'darlings' or the 'orphans', donors tend to move in and out together, causing herding behaviour. The Poverty Reduction Strategy Papers (PRSPs), Country Policy and Institutional Assessments (CPIAs),[21] elaborated by the IFIs for low-income developing countries, function like a rating signal for donors – somewhat similar to the reactions of private creditors to international credit rating agencies. Sometimes there are good reasons for donor withdrawal, such as a shift in domestic policy making or capture by some interest group who benefits disproportionately from public policies instead of ensuring development for the majority of the population (see 'fungibility' below). However, on many other occasions, IFIs base their ratings on compliance to their orthodox policy prescriptions (see 'conditionality'), not allowing governments to have a policy space and ultimately punishing governments trying alternative employment-generating development policies.

Agreeing on a new, universal and equity-promoting ODA allocation criteria that would not restrict developing countries' policy space is the way forward to solve the problem of the 'orphans and darlings', and concentration of ODA.

Lack of donors' policy coherence

Critical voices from both North and South have denounced donors' double standards when defending a poverty reduction agenda through ODA while often pursuing international policies that undermine poverty reduction efforts. For instance, a donor such as the United States actively supports developing countries' fight against HIV/AIDS through ODA programmes, its government pushes for free trade agreements with a clear conflict of interest between multinational companies and the generally poor populations of developing countries, to the benefit of the first, in life-saving anti-retroviral drugs. Most Agreements on Trade-Related Aspects of Intellectual Property Rights (TRIPS) tend to perpetuate asymmetries to the disadvantage of developing countries in important social areas such as health, given that patents protect the rights of corporations in research and development (R&D), at the expense of consumers in developing countries who cannot afford life-saving drugs from international pharmaceutical firms, but could afford cheap generic drugs (Stiglitz 2006a).[22] Patents cause health costs to escalate, generating a real problem for financing social policy; beyond this, thousands of people die daily in Africa because of a lack of access to cheap generic drugs – virtually, the signing of certain trade agreements means their death warrant.

But the major policy contradiction comes in holding to an orthodox neoliberal agenda, while simultaneously promoting the MDGs. By the mid-1990s, it had become clear that the standard neoliberal agenda, the so-called 'Washington consensus',[23] had failed to deliver. Many questioned whether containing inflation, paying debt and building reserves (mostly in US bonds) should be major development priorities. As the Tanzanian President Julius Nyerere demanded publicly, 'Must we starve our children to pay our debts?' Critics argued that structural programmes' primary purposes in the 1980s–1990s were to protect banks in developed countries and to sustain the US dollar, at huge social costs. Poverty and civil conflicts increased throughout the world, and social indicators worsened. Epidemics such as HIV/AIDS spread. Rich countries spent more heavily on peacekeeping and emergency missions, while much-needed development aid remained low.

In 1995, the international community set a new agenda at the World Summit in Copenhagen, later consolidated in targets, the MDGs, endorsed by all countries at the 55th Session of the United Nations General Assembly (2000). These targets are proxies/symptoms of development, halving hunger and extreme poverty by 2015, improving on a basic set of development indicators, such as achieving universal primary education, reducing infant mortality rates, and improving maternal health. To address these symptoms of development, a new agenda was put forward to promote development for all, fast-tracking employment-generating growth and equity, building state capacity to actively promote national development and integrating social and economic issues in all policy domains.[24]

However, many donors – notably the IFIs – kept their faith in the orthodox policies of earlier decades, and simply added more funds to social sector capital investments in order to accomplish the MDGs. Developing countries complain that development policies need to be realigned with the objectives of rapid growth and social development rather than being focused on achieving macroeconomic stability at all costs with some added social investments. Despite rhetoric, most developing countries have been 'over-stabilized', required to adopt excessively restrictive macroeconomic and financial policies that slowed down broad-based growth (Ghosh 2007; McKinley 2006). With so many pressing needs, why should the priority of developing countries be on fiscal discipline and the control of inflation? Many economists are tolerant to some inflation and fiscal deficit and have pointed out that holding rigidly to these principles blocks efforts to reduce poverty.[25] Clearly no one is encouraging governments to spend irresponsibly; however, the key is to make informed economic decisions and to be aware of their social impacts. Additionally, in the economic areas, the multilateral banks and bilaterals have either abandoned or sharply reduced industrial financing, thus limiting the likelihood that developing countries will develop new manufacturing capacities and capabilities that are so necessary for sustainable development and employment (Jomo 2005; Akyüz 2007). In the social areas, investments have often remained too targeted, focused on the delivery of limited services and safety nets, instead of being used to promote faster universal social polices that benefit all, not understanding that redressing inequalities requires maximizing equitable distributional impacts at all policy levels (Mkandawire 2006; Ortiz 2007).

The IMF remains the most influential institution, holding to orthodox principles at any cost. But it is not the only one. When – following pressure from progressive governments and civil society groups – the World Bank and the regional development banks officially embraced poverty reduction as their overarching goal and the MDGs in their agendas, the banks' Finance, Infrastructure and Private Sector Departments were replicating the old orthodox neoliberal policy conditionalities in their loans, often causing poverty rather than reducing it. Often PRSPs had a correct diagnosis of poverty, but many of their economic prescriptions (mostly contributions from the Finance, Infrastructure and other relevant bank departments) were the old standard policy advice, instead of economic strategies to fast-track broad-based, employment-generating growth and poverty reduction. Even the staff of the Social Sector Departments often kept promoting private services combined with safety nets for the poor, instead of studying options to achieve universal policies for all. The same contradictions exist among most bilateral donors. Efforts towards policy coherency are critical both among bilateral and multilateral donors.

Conditionality

A huge controversy exists around the conditionality of ODA.[26] Some donors, notably the IFIs, demand policy reforms in exchange for the funds provided as budget support. The main criticism is the neoliberal nature of these policy reforms, with which governments have to comply; other types of employment-generating, broad-based and pro-poor policy reforms could be put on the agenda. But many critics also argue that conditionalities should disappear altogether, as they are an intrusion in a country's self-determination, policy making and social coalitions/pacts.

Conditionality is such a loaded term that it should simply be abandoned. Whatever the term, there are issues of attribution and accountability. Donors naturally want to see their funds well utilized, achieving results and positive outcomes, but how then to penalize failure? The ODA system could work like intergovernmental finance works in most countries: rich regions transfer to poor regions through an equalization formula based on the number of people below an income threshold, the capacity to raise resources, and so on; and, if regional authorities are negligent or mismanage funds, they are penalized/replaced. However, this cannot happen internationally, as the heads of government cannot be replaced even if they mismanage funds or are negligent. Therefore, some type of results-based accountability needs to be in place. Some General Budget Support (GBS) donors, such as the European Union, believe in linking disbursements to results and outcomes, instead of policy conditionalities – that is, providing budget support to a government as long as it keeps on track achieving development results (for example, in achieving the MDGs – see later 'MDG contracts'). This outcome-based budget support appears to be a much better alternative, allowing countries to have policy space and to take ownership of their own policies.

However, a number of concerns with aid effectiveness are closely linked to the implementation of outcome-based conditionality:

- To date donors have been very cautious about outcome-based budget support, ranging between 2 and 3 per cent of the overall budget support, so developing countries do not find any incentive to take this approach seriously. Furthermore, disbursement assessments are done on a yearly basis, which implies a significant amount of work for very limited resources (EURODAD 2008).
- Outcome indicators need to be feasible and carefully identified; otherwise governments will be unable to accomplish results (for example, education and health outcomes tend to be achieved in the long run).
- Harmonizing outcome-based conditionality among donors is necessary. Currently, the IFIs say they are also moving to 'Results-Based Conditionality'; however, in practice IFIs' strategy to date is moving away from micromanagerial policy prescriptions towards a 'hands-off' attitude in which countries will have to attain benchmarks that support the same policy prescriptions as before (as, for example, along the lines of IDA Resource Allocation Index, or IRAI, criteria). The difference with the European Union is that, at least in principle, it supports social results as a priority.
- Ultimately, the key is that budget support in any of its forms (general budget support/GBS, SWAps) is used as an instrument of development, redistribution and social justice, that is, that reaches people and is not utilized to sustain institutions (for example, a ministry) or processes (for example, the completion of a PRSP or a medium-term expenditure framework/MTEF), or is simply used as a fast disbursing mechanism of ODA by donors (Booth and Curran 2005).

High transaction costs of ODA

The multiplicity of donors creates problems for governments in developing countries. Each donor comes with different procedures and mechanisms to identify, plan, implement, monitor and evaluate its activities, and different reporting requirements. This represents a lot of paperwork that consumes time and resources from government officials. Each donor has its own policy priorities, often contradictory, such that governments in developing countries find themselves in the middle of inconsistent policy reforms. Sometimes, donors negotiate their projects directly with ministries, bypassing central planning authorities and thus creating tension within national administrations. Frequently, donors use a joint-piecemeal approach, splitting areas of intervention among them (for instance, a donor contributes to the health sector and another to the education sector, or donors distributing different geographical regions among them) regardless of the magnitude and reliability of their assistance, leaving governments with unbalanced support in the different areas.

To remedy these numerous pitfalls resulting from donor multiplicity, an important initiative on Aid Effectiveness, Harmonization and Alignment was launched in 2003, coordinated by OECD DAC (see OECD DAC 2007a). In addition, new aid instruments were created to pull funds together under the same roof: SWAps and GBS that would allow countries a policy space for both new investment and recurrent costs, explained later in this chapter. This is, however, only an attempt to patch up an inconsistent ODA system; ultimately, the solution is to be found in increased multilateralism and concerted international action.

The predictability and longevity of ODA

Donor agencies have their own disbursement processes, different from the developing countries' budget cycles; and worse, sometimes their funds are unreliable, the disbursements are delayed, and the programmes are discontinued. Aid flows tend to rise and fall with economic cycles in donor countries and policy assessments of the recipient countries, as well as with shifts in donor policies. This volatility is exacerbated by the gap between commitments and disbursements. The volatility of aid flows often exceeds that of other macroeconomic variables, such as GDP or fiscal revenue. When aid falls, it leads to costly fiscal adjustments in the form of increased taxation and spending cuts that reinforce the cyclical impact of declining aid flows. Giving the increasing magnitude of world income disparities, donors should make medium- and long-term ODA commitments and fulfil their obligations to contribute 0.7 per cent of their GNP as they have repeatedly endorsed at the United Nations since 1970.

Tied aid

Most ODA remains tied. Tied aid means that development funds are given with the condition that all goods and services have to be procured exclusively from the donor country, no matter what the price. For instance, a lot of humanitarian aid to mitigate food emergencies acquires foodstuffs from companies in developed countries, instead of buying it more cheaply from neighbouring developing countries. The World Bank calculates that tied aid causes the loss of about 25 per cent of aid, given that cheaper and better-quality goods and services could be bought in the international market. Beyond this, procuring goods and services locally develops the domestic economy. Tied aid brings up the question of who benefits from development aid, as tied aid is a de facto subsidy to companies in the donor country. This is particularly unacceptable in the case of development loans which the poor country must repay; taxpayers in poor countries should not be supporting companies from rich developed countries. In 2005, only a few donor countries have fully untied their aid contributions – Finland, France, Germany, Ireland, Japan, the Netherlands, Norway, Portugal, Sweden, Switzerland and the United Kingdom. DAC continues to monitor progress and, together with development organizations, to raise awareness.

Fungibility

Fungibility refers to a substitution effect. Sometimes, when ODA is allocated to a particular sector, for instance social sectors, instead of being utilized to top up government spending, a government may consider domestic resources to be freed and put them to some other use – for example, for military/defence spending. Fungibility may be corrected by better governance and public accountability.

Debates on the 'Dutch disease' and other macroeconomic impacts

The many positive macroeconomic effects of ODA are obvious, especially for poor developing countries. ODA can reduce three gaps that keep domestic investment and growth below potential: the savings gap, the foreign exchange gap and the fiscal gap. Some regard thinking in terms of these gaps as inappropriate for developing countries, given international capital mobility and the argument that ODA is not effective.[27] However, a large number of developing countries do not have easy access to international capital markets and continue to experience shortages of foreign exchange. ODA is an important mechanism to fill the abovementioned gaps for developing countries. It effectively amounts to an addition to domestic savings and allows governments to spend more than the revenues raised through taxation and other means, allowing for more public investment, including critical social spending.

The recent debate on scaling up ODA has led the IMF to appraise ODA in terms of its impacts on inflation and exchange rate appreciation – if the latter is sustained over a length of time, it could lead to an overvaluation phenomenon known as the 'Dutch disease'. McKinley (2005) and Foster and Killick (2006), following the IMF analysis in terms of government's capacity to 'spend' and 'absorb' ODA, conclude that both inflation and exchange rate appreciation can be mitigated if ODA is properly spent and absorbed.[28]

From the perspective of a post-Washington consensus, the real issue is not about having a perfect macroeconomic balance (Stiglitz 2006b). Precisely, the problem in many developing countries today is that the fear of the adverse effects of currency appreciation or inflation is so great, and the need to keep high levels of foreign exchange reserves to guard against potential financial crises so acutely felt, that ODA inflows are not put to good use, that is, to promote expansionary, growth-oriented and equitable macroeconomic and sector policies geared towards employment and the expansion of national markets (McKinley 2005). However, if recipient governments can use ODA to increase public investment in important areas in order to ease supply constraints and improve aggregate productivity, ODA will not be inflationary and can have expansionary effects. These effects could spill over into positive balance of payments effects through a higher level of exports or a reduction in the level of imports. Reddy and Minoiu (2006) find a strong correlation between development-oriented ODA and growth. So it is important to ensure that ODA translates into higher public investment, preferably in areas where there are shortages, or which form bottlenecks for production, or in areas where existing levels of provision are socially suboptimal (Ghosh 2007).

ODA: Some alternatives

The long list of problems presented above offers two main solutions: to dismantle ODA, or to reform it. Interestingly, the first option is defended by opposite extremes: (i) conservative voices in the North which dislike multilateralism; and (ii) assertive nationalist voices in the South which distrust Northern institutions, defend the need for increased policy space in the South, some claiming that international redistribution is not essential.

Proposals to reform multilateral ODA are based on the need to redistribute the world's wealth, given that ODA distributional impacts are progressive and equality enhancing. The degree of reform varies, from most radical to more moderate:

(i)   The most radical proposals relate to institutionalizing a new system of global governance – ultimately, a world government – that would effectively deal with global issues, including enforcing a global taxation system, a new global reserve and financial system, and so on.

(ii) A second set of proposals relate to the reform of all Bretton Woods institutions, and empowering governments in developing countries and the United Nations (where developing countries have a voice) by making the UN Economic and Social Council (ECOSOC) the main forum to transparently discuss/agree on development aid matters.[29]

(iii) The creation of a new International Development Aid Fund (IDAF) for the poorest countries, to be funded by compulsory contributions made by each of the world's wealthiest governments, with the amounts contributed by each determined by their relative wealth and distributed according to governments' commitment to development (Riddell 2007).

(iv) The least radical proposal, the patching-up (but meaningful, given circumstances) OECD DAC attempt to harmonize and align donors, explained earlier.

Bypassing governments: A Global Welfare Agency/Social Trust?

The four options explained above are based on multilateral systems coordinating aid from governments in the North to governments in the South. Some commentators have suggested alternatives that would bypass governments. Milanovic (2006) suggests that current mechanisms of global redistribution – intergovernmental transfers between rich and poor countries – could be enhanced by a global system in which taxes raised from rich individuals in rich countries are used as transfer to poor individuals in poor countries:

A global redistribution through taxes that would be levied by an international body is an idea that may seem farfetched today, but which the logic of development we have recently witnessed – away from the nation state – suggests may eventually come to pass. Such a body should not be another inter-governmental organization like the United Nations or the World Bank. Indeed the new agency should take its cues from globalization. If it is empowered to raise its own funds, it should also eschew dealing with governments that have often wasted foreign aid. Instead, in the spirit of global citizenship, it should deal directly with national NGOs [non-governmental organizations] and individual citizens in poor countries and distribute collected funds in the form of cash grants. (Milanovic 2006: 24)

The Russian case is often cited as an example in which a large amount of ODA that was disbursed to the central governments was lost, and in which citizens could have received more benefit from direct cash transfers (for example, pensions) to buffer the social costs of transition. The proposal takes away some of Northern countries' control of ODA and at the same time it also takes away some of Southern countries' sovereignty since Milanovic's proposed Global Welfare Agency could help poor citizens in those countries directly – without requiring authorization from their governments.

Given its relevance for social policies, the International Labour Organization (ILO) proposal for a Global Social Trust must be mentioned at this point. In 2002, the ILO proposed a trust to extend coverage of social security benefits to populations that are not covered. The underlying principle is the global social responsibility of individuals in the North, and the acceptance of global citizenship and solidarity to support poorer citizens in the South. People in developed countries may contribute on a voluntary basis a rather modest monthly amount (for example, €5 or $7 per month) to the Global Social Trust, which will then invest these resources to expand national social insurance schemes in developing countries (ILO 2002). A pilot scheme has been launched in Ghana.

Instruments to finance social policy

This section will present a variety of currently operational funding instruments for social policies in developing countries. Typically, these instruments are either grants or debt.

Grants versus debt

(i) *Grants*: Grant financing is a preferred first option given its lesser cost to governments; in addition, it is fully justified given the unequal distribution of income resulting from globalization processes.

(ii) *Debt*: Loans and securities are a least preferred option given that they build debt in a country. Loans provided by multilateral banks (such as the World Bank, regional development banks such as the Asian Development Bank/ADB or IDB and South–South banks), funds (such as OPEC or AFESD) and Northern/Southern donors, must be repaid according to either commercial or concessional interest rates. Concessional loans are a preferred option in this category, as their conditions are beneficial to developing countries (around 1 per cent interest rate per annum, with a maturity period of about 20 years depending on the institutions). The World Bank, ADB and IDB only give commercial loans to developing countries with higher GDP per capita, like Mexico or India. Bonds are generally preferable to regularly priced commercial loans at market rates.

Table 3.2   International instruments to finance social policy

Instrument	Predetermined expenditures	Sector specific	Redistributive
Investment projects	Y	Y	If grant or concessional loan
GBS including MDG contracts	N	N	If grant or concessional loan
SWAps	N	Y	If grant or concessional loan
TA	Y	Optional	If grant
Subnational bonds	N	Y	N
Other securities	N	N	N
IFF	Optional	Y	Y

Notes: GBS: General Budget Support; IFF: International Financing Facility; SWAps: Sector Wide Approaches; TA: Technical Assistance; Y/N: Yes/No.

The different instruments are presented below, and summarized in Table 3.2.

Social investment projects

Projects are the traditional ODA instrument to finance social policies. They consist of specific investments set in components with predetermined expenditures (for example, a typical education project may consist of the construction of a number of schools, the procurement of X amount of textbooks and classroom materials, the delivery of refresher training to Y number of teachers and so on). Currently, the tendency is to avoid donor-managed projects – since it is believed that they undermine a government's capacity – and instead to support government-owned social policies/strategies with budget support.

General Budget Support (GBS)

GBS consists of direct, unallocated transfers from international donors/organizations to a developing country's general budget (for example, a multi-donor GBS, provided donors agree with the quality of a country's National Development Strategy[30] and a MTEF).

The importance of GBS and SWAps comes in the harmonization of objectives between donors, international organizations and a developing country government – all focused on the country's National Development Strategy. By harmonizing policy objectives and providing direct support to the government, donors ensure that national priorities are addressed in a transparent manner and their funds are well utilized; otherwise they could withdraw their support. On the other hand, governments from developing countries find strong support to fight the internal obstacles to transparent policy making, minimize the transaction costs of development aid and strengthen their capacity to develop a modern administration.

MDG contracts

MDG contracts are a type of GBS promoted by the European Union. The European Union, the world's largest donor,[31] is reducing its project and sector-based ODA and increasing GBS to developing countries. This will reflect, at least in theory, a decrease in the EU's contributions to social policies. However, in 2006 the EU proposed a new development policy based on outcome-based budget support and the MDG contracts. An MDG contract ties a country not to the orthodox policy conditionality (such as privatization, liberalization and so on), but rather to the accomplishment of results in education, such as progress on literacy rates; in health, such as the reduction of infant and maternal mortality; and generally, in terms of a government's successful achievement of the MDGs. In order to be effective, MDG contracts will have to address the issues presented earlier on outcome-based conditionality.

Sector-wide approaches (SWAps)

SWAps are based on multi-donor support to a government sector strategy and budget. Once there is an agreement/partnership between a government and major donors/institutions, donors pool funds and release them to the government's budget, relying on government procedures to disburse and account for all funds. In early 2004 there were about 100 SWAps in the developing world, 85 per cent of them in Africa, mostly in health and education, but increasingly in other areas such as water supply. SWAps are critical instruments for social policies in developing countries. Figure 3.4 shows how SWAps should work.

In practice, however, because donor procedures are not harmonized, SWAps often resemble Figure 3.5. Some donors may pool funds to support a government's budget, but others may remain with a narrow project approach. There is an important loss of benefits with the current implementation of SWAps, as they keep incurring high transaction costs to governments. Nevertheless, it is a step forward, as at least all stakeholders agree on a sector policy and contribute to it.

Technical assistance (TA)

Technical assistance is increasingly important with GBS and SWAps; it is important that their terms of reference are drafted by the government, to allow for policy space, and that technical assistance is untied.

Government bonds

Since early modern history, governments in Europe have issued bonds to cover financing gaps in the national budget, that, is, borrowing, although this is generally a lower-cost alternative than commercial bank loans. A government bond is a debt security. Investors lend money for a fixed period of time and at a predetermined interest rate; governments incorporate funds into the national budget, pay interest during the term of the bond and repay the principal after the maturity period. An interesting development in recent years in developing countries has been the growth of local currency bond markets, which are concentrated in a few countries such as Brazil, China, India, Malaysia, Mexico, the Republic of Korea, Turkey and South Africa; their development has been driven by governments' desires to limit levels of foreign currency debt (UNDESA 2007b).

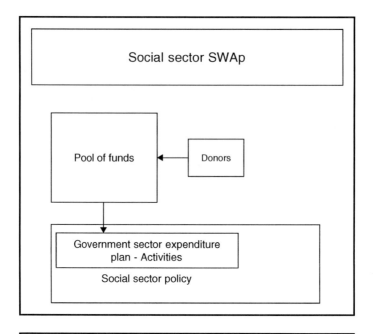

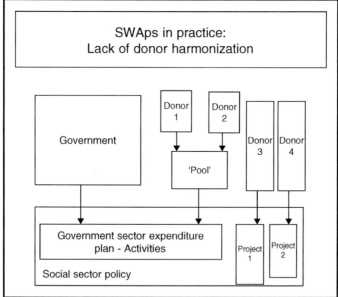

Figures 3.4 and 3.5   SWAPs in theory and practice

Municipal bonds (subnational bonds)

Municipal bonds are issued for specific purposes, many of which make considerable contributions to social development. In the nineteenth century, developed countries began to use bonds for local public investments. The issuers could include cities, school districts, fire departments, water supply agencies or publicly owned airports and seaports. These entities issued specific bonds which were dedicated to specific schemes such as urban development or the expansion of school systems.

Although municipal bonds do not have a long-standing precedent in developing countries, their use has been generalized in recent years in major countries in Latin America, Eastern Europe, the former Soviet Union and Asia. Cities, municipalities, districts and regions in these areas have issued bonds both in local and international currencies to have more fiscal space. Municipal bonds normally cater to the domestic market, but they may be part of the portfolio of investment funds provided they are rated investment grade ('BBB') by a rating agency as most international investors cannot invest in subinvestment grade rated financial instruments.[32] This could become an important source of finance for social development, given the increasing demand for ethical investment funds among investors.

Municipal bonds also have some limitations. They mobilize private capital to support social policies, but they are not redistributive instruments; they build local and national debt (if central government guarantees), therefore creating fiscal stress that could potentially lead to either increased borrowing to support a revenue deficit, or to default/crisis, as occurred in Argentina in 2001. In addition, subnational bonds are difficult to develop in poor municipalities/regions in low-income countries.

Other securities

Raising funds in the international capital market through securities, beyond the traditional government obligation bonds, is another recently explored source of development finance. Project or revenue bonds and securities are not backed by government general taxation as in the case of traditional obligation bonds, but rather by future incoming revenues, for instance from a power plant or a toll road. These are corporate bonds, that is, they are not issued by a municipality or government. It is important for the success of a project bond to have the backing and guarantee of reputable financial institutions. They are increasingly used to raise development funds (Conceiçao et al. 2006). However, these new sources of development finance are generally not funding social sectors, given that they yield few private returns attractive to investors.

Securitizing remittances

Securitization has emerged as an important means of capital formation in developed economies, particularly in the United States, and is expanding in developing countries. Workers' remittances tend to be a steady flow of foreign exchange in developing countries. Like any other predictable revenue flow, remittances can be securitized. Private banks in Latin America, Turkey and Kazakhstan have launched bonds based on remittances' future revenue flows, tapping global capital markets to get financing for development of the domestic private sector in developing countries (Willms 2004). Like any security instrument, it must be noted that remittance securities build national debt. The most controversial aspect of these securitization schemes consists of the use of offshore Special Purpose Vehicles (SPVs) to manage the fund flows. To date SPVs have been set in offshore tax havens, which should

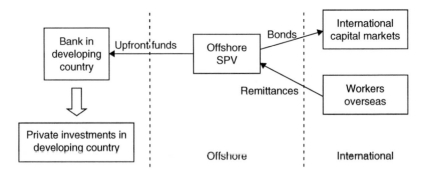

Figure 3.6   Securitizing workers' remittances

be avoided from a developmental point of view. Leaving this contentious issue aside, the proceeds from securitizing remittances can provide national banks with upfront funds to onlend to productive national investments such as financing small and medium-sized companies – though rarely are these investments in the social sectors.

The International Financial Facility (IFF)

As mentioned earlier, bonds and securities incur debt and are non-redistributive. Exceptionally, the IFF is a redistributive securitization scheme. IFF issues AAA-rated bonds based upon donor commitments to aid. The scheme is thus guaranteed by donor countries, and donor payments also fund bond interest and IFF administration. The IFF uses bond proceeds to fund grants to official aid agencies and these are then disbursed to beneficiaries (Rogerson 2004). In addition, the IFF forces donors to disburse aid commitments.

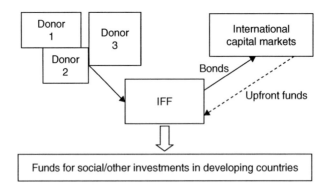

Figure 3.7   The International Financial Facility

To date IFF has only mobilized resources for health immunization through the International Financial Facility for Immunization (IFFIm).[33] IFFIm was launched by seven countries in London in November 2006. IFFIm funds GAVI (Global Alliance for Vaccines and Immunization). Given the strength of its backing from largely AAA-rated sovereigns and its conservative financial policies, IFFIm has been rated AAA. The World Bank is acting as Treasury Manager for IFFIm. The problem with IFFIm, like the Global Funds, is the very narrow focus; achieving social development requires much more than these specific health interventions. The further expansion of IFF beyond IFFIm, and the basis on which some development programmes are to be chosen, remains to be agreed, but funds raised by IFF could be used for a wider portfolio of social investments.

Conclusion

There are four pillars of fiscal space for social policy: increased ODA, additional borrowing, enhanced revenue collection and improved efficiency/reprioritization of expenditures. To this, we add avoiding South–North transfers through better use of reserves. This chapter presents the mechanisms, advantages and disadvantages of a variety of international instruments to finance social policy, providing a menu of options for governments.

What is important, however, is not to lose perspective. Sometimes debates over an aspect of ODA or a new instrument create much ado, distracting attention away from critical issues. Some of these debates may actually be a convenient way to postpone necessary action. The current ODA system is imperfect, but its drawbacks in terms of size, concentration, transaction costs, predictability, macroeconomic impacts, tied aid, policy coherence, fungibility and conditionality, can be corrected, and better options put in place.

The reality is that the gross inequities in the distribution of wealth are an obstacle for social development. While the economic benefits of globalization go to a few companies and individuals in Northern countries, who own 84 per cent of the world's wealth, or 79 per cent of the world's GDP, social policies and their costs must be dealt with at the national level, with very limited resources and a diminished policy space – apartheid on a global scale.

This situation is worsened by the unbelievable fact that poor countries transfer resources to rich countries. Looking at the big picture, net international financial flows show that debt interest payments, investment profit remittances and the portfolio of central bank reserves offset net financial inflows to developing countries. Winning fiscal space for social development should start by stopping this net transfer of resources from South to North.

Given the limited North–South transfers due to failure of donors to meet their ODA commitments, developing countries are trying alternative South–South integration experiences and South–South banks, presented in this chapter. However, South–South resources are fewer; developing countries only hold 16 per cent of the world's wealth, or 21 per cent of the world's GDP. Additional South–South cooperation tends to focus on infrastructure investments. Awareness needs to be raised among Southern governments about the importance of social policy for national development. The ALBA and the Bank of the South/ALBA are formulating a different set of priorities given their drive for social equity, but this is still in the making.

The justification for international North–South redistribution cannot be stronger. For globalization to be accepted, it will have to be a globalization that benefits the majority, a globalization for all. This requires multilateral coordinated action, increased and improved ODA, with more grants and fewer loans, with more budget support and less micromanagement, with more effective results to bring half of the world's population out of poverty, sharing responsibility for social development.

Notes

1. See UNU-WIDER (2006); UNDESA (2005); Jomo and Baudot (2007).
2. Japan, the Republic of Korea, Taiwan Province of China, Australia and New Zealand.
3. The United Nations and the international financial institutions (IFIs) – the International Monetary Fund (IMF), the World Bank and the African, Asian and Inter-American Development Banks. These different stakeholders in multilateral aid have different policy approaches and aid conditions. The United Nations (UN) agencies provide grants. The IFIs work mostly through loans (either on a commercial or a concessional basis), normally under conditionalities that respond to their Northern-dominated Executive Boards (voting power is assigned according to the amount of funds provided).
4. In 1948, the United States (US) Congress approved the use of 2–3 per cent of US gross domestic product (GDP) per annum to finance grants for the reconstruction of Europe until 1953. This became known as the Marshall Plan. It disbursed $13 billion to 16 European beneficiary countries (or $87 billion in 1997 dollars, an interesting comparison to the current average of 0.2 per cent gross national income (GNI) that rich countries spend in aid for more than 180 developing countries). The Marshall Plan was channelled through newly created institutions in 1948, the Organization for European Economic Cooperation (later the Organisation for Economic Co-operation and Development/OECD) and the European Payments Union (Ocampo 2006).
5. Source: OECD Development Assistance Committee (OECD DAC) data (2000–05) (see www.oecd.org/dac/stats).
6. Jolly (2004) estimates that US military expenditures were 6 per cent of gross national product (GNP) in 2003, compared to 0.1 per cent expenditure on (tied) official development assistance (ODA) the same year.
7. All $ amounts refer to US dollars.
8. The International Tax Organization (ITO) was originally proposed in 1999 by former IMF director of fiscal affairs, Vito Tanzi.
9. The Non-Aligned Movement, consisting of more than 100 countries not politically allied to any Northern power, established the Group for South-South Consultation and Coordination in 1989; the Group of 77 allied developing countries declared a Framework for South-South Cooperation in Marrakesh in 2003.
10. OECD DAC ODA statistics do not include OECD countries Export-Import Banks non-concessional loans; a major international effort is needed to start monitoring non-OECD ODA. Simply for reference, total ODA in year 2005 was estimated at $111 billion.
11. The most well-known examples include oil facilities (Nigeria), copper mines (the Democratic Republic of the Congo and Zambia), railways (Benguela and Port Sudan), dams (Merowe in Sudan; Bui in Ghana; and Mphanda Nkuwa in Zambia) and thermal power plants (Nigeria and Sudan). Social sector investments have not been a Chinese priority; however, on a lesser scale, China has offered free technical assistance and goods such as anti-malaria drugs.
12. Policy conditionality must be distinguished from social/environmental standards. Policy conditionality refers to reforms that a government must implement in order to get

funds disbursed by a donor; criticisms of the neoliberal agenda (for example, privatization or liberalization) associated with policy conditionalities are presented later in the chapter. Social/environmental standards are not related to this; they consist of progressive minimum safeguards such as respecting the core labour standards in development projects, such as not employing children or slaves/bonded workers. See section on 'Conditionality'.

13. Given donor concerns over the fungibility of ODA, additional debt and the low environmental and social standards of Chinese infrastructure loans, the World Bank (including its private sector arm, IFC) signed a Memorandum of Understanding with Exim Bank China in May 2007 to ensure coordination in issues such as financial management, procurement, environmental and social safeguards.

14. MERCOSUR or Southern Common Market (1991) among Argentina, Brazil, Paraguay, Uruguay and Venezuela (Bolivia, Chile, Colombia, Ecuador and Peru currently have associate member status); ALBA is the Bolivarian Alternative for Latin America (2006), including Bolivia, Cuba, Honduras, Nicaragua and Venezuela.

15. *Proyecto Grannacional*, signed by the Presidents of Bolivia, Cuba, Nicaragua and Venezuela at the 5th ALBA Summit on 30 April 2007. It comprises numerous regional agreements on the areas of culture, education, energy, fair trade, finance, food security, health, industry, mining, telecommunications, tourism and transport. See www. alternativabolivariana.org.

16. The Bank of the South was founded on 9 December 2007 by the governments of Argentina, Bolivia, Brazil, Ecuador, Paraguay, Uruguay and Venezuela. The Bank of the Bolivarian Alternative for the Americas (Bank of ALBA) was founded on 26 January 2008 by the governments of Bolivia, Cuba, Nicaragua and Venezuela. Both banks will have their headquarters in Caracas (Venezuela).

17. Asian Bond Funds are being developed by East Asia's central banks after the 1997–98 Asian crisis, with the support of the Bank for International Settlements and Asian Development Bank (ADB).

18. The Chiang Mai Initiative, which includes all ASEAN countries (Brunei, Cambodia, Indonesia, Laos, Malaysia, Myanmar, the Philippines, Singapore, Thailand and Viet Nam) plus China, Japan and the Republic of Korea, was launched in the aftermath of the Asian crisis, and holds about $80 billion. However only 10 per cent is usable without IMF approval. In May 2006 Asian ministers decided to study the idea of an Asian Currency Unit (ACU, similar to the former European ECU), based on a basket of currencies.

19. Latin American Reserves Fund (created 1978), a regional 'monetary fund' for Bolivia, Colombia, Costa Rica, Ecuador, Peru and Venezuela.

20. Keynes already proposed an International Clearing Union, the 'bancor', in 1942, with a form of fiat money to act as reserves. See Soros (2002); McKinley (2006); Stiglitz (2006a, 2006b).

21. The CPIAs are the base of the World Bank's International Development Association (IDA) Resource Allocation Index (IRAI) for IDA eligible countries (concessional loans). Countries are ranked against a set of 16 criteria grouped in four clusters: economic management; structural policies; policies for social inclusion and equity; and public sector management and institutions. Designing a universal rating system for allocation resources is very correct, but criticisms come regarding the criteria. For instance, macroeconomic criteria measure if 'aggregate demand policies are inconsistent with macroeconomic stability; monetary and exchange rate policies do not ensure price stability; and there is significant private sector investment crowding out' (World Bank 2005: 6), or trade criteria if 'average tariff [is] less than seven percent; maximum tariff rate 15 percent ... [or if] internal taxation discriminates heavily against imports' (World Bank 2005: 11–12). Many argue that these criteria are based on contractionary policies that, combined with trade liberalization, are obstacles to pro-poor growth and employment in developing countries.

22. As an example of different pricing of drugs, in 2000 a standard yearly anti-retroviral treatment provided by international pharmaceutical firms was $10,500. CIPLA, an Indian leading generic drug producer, offered the same treatment for $350, that is, 30 times cheaper. In 2001, 39 international drug corporations took the South African government to court in a lawsuit over its Medicines Act, designed to provide South Africans with affordable drugs and to lessen health costs; more recently, other developing countries have come under pressure to implement TRIPS protection rules (Hoen 2005).

23. The Washington consensus was a development agenda based on promoting growth through deregulation, free markets, supply-side economics, tight monetary and fiscal policies, independent central banks, privatization of state-owned enterprises, trade and financial opening, minimal regulations, huge infrastructure projects absorbing the very limited national development resources, forcing governments to have residual and targeted social policies.

24. For a recent formulation of the new agenda, developed with Nobel Laureate J. Stiglitz, Jomo K.S., J.A. Ocampo and other international development specialists in coordination with UN agencies, including UNRISD. See UNDESA (2007a).

25. For a review of the inflation literature, see Action Aid (2007). While IMF standard inflation threshold is about 5 per cent to 8 per cent per annum, empirical studies by economists like Gylfason and Herbertsson put it up to 20 per cent, Bruno and Easterly to 40 per cent. Action Aid makes a strong case showing how fiscal discipline keeps recurrent social expenditures low, such as recruitment and salaries of health and education staff, therefore being an obstacle to achieve the Millennium Development Goals (MDGs) (Action Aid 2007; Rowden and Thapliyal 2007).

26. A distinction must be made between policy conditions (such as policy reforms in exchange of funds) and environmental and social standards or safeguards (such as mitigation of negative involuntary outcomes such as resettlement of displaced populations because of construction work, compensation/redeployment of labour layoffs, and so on).

27. See, for instance, Easterly (2003, 2006).

28. The critical points consist on focusing increased government spending on public investment, and increased imports focused on capital instead of consumption goods (McKinley 2005; Foster and Killick 2006).

29. Currently discussed at many international fora. For a written formulation, see Burall and Maxwell (2006).

30. This chapter refers to National Development Strategies as the main planning documents that a country has. The Poverty Reduction Strategy Papers (PRSPs) can be a type of National Development Strategy, but not all countries develop PRSPs, only those low-income countries with access to World Bank's concessional IDA funds. Middle-income countries do not develop PRSPs, therefore it is more inclusive (and less Bank biased) to refer to the generic term National Development Strategies.

31. The European Union is the world's leading aid donor, €36 billion in 2004, over 50 per cent of global ODA. In June 2005 the EU Council endorsed EU Commission proposals to increase ODA to an average of 0.56 per cent of member countries' GNI by 2010, with a vision to reach 0.7 per cent in 2015 and commitment to increase aid effectiveness; this increase in ODA translates into €20 additional billion per year.

32. Private independent rating services such as Standard & Poor's or Moody's evaluate the quality of bonds based on the issuer's ability to pay a bond's principal and interest in a timely fashion. Bond ratings are expressed as letters ranging from 'AAA' (highest quality investment) to 'C' ('junk').

33. This occurred in mid-2007, supported by the governments of Brazil, France, Italy, Norway, South Africa, Spain, Sweden and the United Kingdom.

References

Action Aid (2007) *Confronting the Contradictions: IMF, Wage Bill Caps, and the Case for Teachers* (Johannesburg: Action Aid).

Akyüz, Yilmaz (2007) *Global Rules and Markets: Constraints over Policy Autonomy in Developing Countries* (New Delhi: International Development Economics Associates (IDEAs).

Atkinson, Anthony (ed.) (2004) *New Sources of Development Finance* (Oxford: Oxford University Press).

Bosshard, Peter (2007) *China's Role in Financing African Infrastructure* (Berkeley, CA: International River Network and Oxfam).

Booth, David and Zaza Curran (2005) *Aid Instruments and Exclusion*, Report for the UK Department for International Development (London: Overseas Development Institute).

Broadman, Harry (2007) *Africa's Silk Road: China and India's New Economic Frontier* (Washington, DC: World Bank).

Burall, Simon and Simon Maxwell (2006) *Reforming the International Aid Architecture: Options and Ways Forward*, ODI Working Paper No. 278 (London: Overseas Development Institute).

Chandrasekhar, Chandru (2007) *Global Finance Today: Déjà Vu?* (New Delhi: IDEAs).

Conceiçao, Pedro (2006) 'Accommodating new actors and new purposes in international cooperation: The growing diversification of financing mechanisms.' In Inge Kaul and Pedro Conceiçao (eds.), *The New Public Finance: Responding to Global Challenges* (New York: Oxford University Press).

Conceiçao, Pedro, Hari Rajan and Rajiv Sha (2006) 'Making the right money available at the right time for international cooperation: New financing technologies.' In Inge Kaul and Pedro Conceiçao (eds.), op.cit.

Deacon, Bob, Isabel Ortiz and Sergei Zelenev (2007) *Regional Social Policy*, United Nations Department for Economic and Social Affairs (UNDESA) Working Paper No. 37 (New York: United Nations).

Easterly, William (2006) *White Man's Burden: Why the West's Efforts to Aid the Rest Have Done So Much Ill and So Little Good* (Oxford: Oxford University Press).

—— (2003) 'Can foreign aid buy growth?', *Journal of Economic Perspectives*, Vol. 17, No. 3, 23–48.

Eichengreen, Barry (2004) *Global Imbalances and the Lessons of Bretton Woods*, NBER Working Paper No. 10497 (Cambridge, MA: National Bureau for Economic Research).

EURODAD (2008) *Outcome-Based Conditionality: Too Good to be True?* (Brussels: Europe Debt and Development).

Exim Bank (2005) *Export–Import Bank of China Annual Report* (Beijing: Exim Bank China).

Foster, Mick and Tony Killick (2006) *What Would Doubling Aid Do for Macroeconomic Management in Africa: A Synthesis Paper*, ODI Working Paper No. 264 (London: Overseas Development Institute).

George, Susan (1988) *A Fate Worse than Debt: The World Financial Crisis and the Poor* (London: Penguin Books).

Ghosh, Jayati (2007) *Macroeconomics and Growth Policies: Background Note*, UNDESA Policy Notes for National Development Strategies (New York: United Nations).

Hoen, Ellen (2005) *A Guide to the Post-2005 World: TRIPS, R&D and Access to Medicines* (Geneva: Medécins Sans Frontières).

ILO (International Labour Organization) (2002) *Recommendations to the Director General and the Governing Body of the International Labour Organization on the Feasibility of a Global Social Trust* (Geneva: International Labour Organization).

IMF (International Monetary Fund) (2007) *The IMF and Aid to Sub-Saharan Africa* (Washington, DC: IMF). www.imf.org/external/np/ieo/2007/ssa/eng/pdf/report.pdf, accessed in February 2008.

Jolly, Richard (2004) *Disarmament and Development*, DDA Occasional Paper No. 9 (New York: United Nations Department for Disarmament Affairs).

Jomo, K.S. (2005) *Sovereign Debt for Sustained Development*, IDEAs Analysis (New Delhi: IDEAs).

Jomo, K.S. and Jacques Baudot (eds.) (2007) *Flat World, Big Gaps: Economic Liberalization, Globalization and Inequality* (London: Zed Books).

McElhinny, Vince (2007) *Banco del Sur: A Reflection of Declining IFI Relevance in Latin America*, BICUSA Update (Washington, DC: Bank Information Center).

McKinley, Terry (2006) *The Monopoly of Global Capital Flows: Who Needs Structural Adjustment Now?*, UNDP/IPC Working Paper No. 12 (Brasilia: International Poverty Centre).

—— (2005) *Why Is the Dutch Disease Always a Disease? The Macroeconomic Consequences of Scaling Up ODA*, UNDP/IPC Working Paper No. 10 (Brasilia: International Poverty Centre).

McKinley, Terry and Anibal Izurieta (2007) *The Gross Inequities of Global Imbalances*, UNDP/IPC One Pager No. 12 (Brasilia: International Poverty Centre).

Milanovic, Branko (2006) *Rules of Redistribution and Foreign Aid: A Proposal for Change in Rules Governing Eligibility for Foreign Aid*, paper presented at the conference Equality and the New Global Order, JFK School of Government at Harvard, 11–13 May.

Mkandawire, Thandika (ed.) (2006) *Social Policy in a Development Context* (Basingtoke: UNRISD/Palgrave Macmillan).

NEF (New Economics Foundation) (2006) *Migration and the Remittance Euphoria: Development or Dependency?* (London: NEF).

Ocampo, José Antonio (ed.) (2006) *Regional Financial Cooperation* (Washington, DC and Santiago de Chile: Brookings Institution Press and UN ECLAC).

Ocampo, José Antonio and Stephany Griffith-Jones (2007) *A Counter-Cyclical Framework for a Development-Friendly International Financial Architecture*, UNDESA Working Paper No. 39 (New York: United Nations).

OECD DAC (Organisation for Economic Co-operation and Development/Development Assistance Committee (2007a) *Aid Effectiveness.* www.oecd.org/dac/effectiveness, accessed in July 2007.

—— (2007b) *Aid Statistics.* www.oecd.org/dac/stats, accessed in July 2007.

Ortiz, Isabel (2005) *Development Aid*, Initiative for Policy Dialogue Backgrounders (New York: Columbia University).

Ortiz, Isabel (2007) *Social Policy*, UNDESA Policy Notes for National Development Strategies (New York: United Nations).

Pettifor, Anne (2003a) 'Resolving international debt crisis fairly', *Ethics & International Affairs*, Vol. 17, No. 2, 2–9.

—— (ed.) (2003b) *Real World Economic Outlook* (London: Palgrave).

Reddy, Sanjay and Camelia Minoiu (2006) *Development Aid and Economic Growth: A Positive Long-Run Relation*, UNDESA Working Paper No. 29 (New York: United Nations).

Riddell, Roger (2007) 'Effective aid requires new structures', *Poverty in Focus*, No. 12 (Brasilia: UNDP/IPC).

Rogerson, Andrew (2004) 'The International Financing Facility: Issues and options', *Opinions*, No. 15 (London: Overseas Development Institute).

Rowden, Rick and Nisha Thapliyal (2007) 'IMF still blocking progress on HIV/AIDS, health, and education', *Policies and Priorities*, Vol. 2, No. 1 (Washington, DC: Action Aid).

Soros, George (2002) *Special Drawing Rights for the Provision of Public Goods on a Global Scale*, presentation at the roundtable on New Proposals on Financing for Development, Institute for International Economics, Washington, DC, 20 February.

Stiglitz, Joseph (2006a) *Making Globalization Work* (New York: W.W. Norton).

—— (2006b) 'Global public goods and global finance: Does global governance ensure that the global public interest is served?' In Jean-Philippe Touffut (ed.), *Advancing Public Goods* (London: Edward Elgar Publishing).

Tan, Celine (2007) *Debt and Conditionality: Multilateral Debt Relief Initiative and Opportunities for Expanding Policy Space*, TWN Global Economy Series No. 9 (Penang: Third World Network).

UNDESA (United Nations Department of Economic and Social Affairs) (2007a) *Policy Notes for National Development Strategies* (New York: United Nations). esa.un.org/techcoop/policyNotes.asp, accessed in February 2008.

—— (2007b) *World Economic Situation and Prospects, 2007* (New York: United Nations).

—— (2005) *The Inequality Predicament: Report on the World Social Situation 2005* (New York: United Nations).

United Nations (2007) *Follow-up To and Implementation of the Outcome of the International Conference on Financing for Development*, Sixty-second session of the General Assembly. Document No. A/62/217, 10 August (New York: United Nations).

—— (2001) *Report of the High-Level Panel on Financing for Development: Recommendations* (New York: United Nations). www.un.org/reports/financing/recommendations.htm, accessed in March 2008.

UNU-WIDER (United Nations University-World Institute for Development Economics Research) (2006) *The World Distribution of Household Wealth* (Helsinki: UNU-WIDER).

Wahl, Peter (2006) 'International taxation: The time is ripe.' In *Social Watch Report 2006. Impossible Architecture: Why the Financial Structure Is Not Working for the Poor and How to Redesign It for Equity and Development* (Montevideo: Third World Institute).

Willms, William (2004) *ADB's Role in Encouraging and Facilitating the Securitization of Worker Remittances*, presentation at the Asian Development Bank, Manila, 16 December.

World Bank (2007a) *Global Development Finance* (Washington, DC: World Bank).

—— (2007b) *HIPC and MDRI Initiatives*, presentation at the Spring Meetings (Washington, DC: World Bank).

—— (2007c) *Global Monitoring Report: Millennium Development Goals* (Washington, DC: World Bank).

—— (2005) *Country Policy and Institutional Assessments: 2005 Assessment Questionnaire* (Washington, DC: World Bank).

Part II
Taxation and Aid

4
How Can the Financing of Social Services Be Made Pro-Poor?

Enrique Delamonica and Santosh Mehrotra

Introduction

The mainstream view of development posits that if economic growth is maximized, the levels of poverty will be reduced, and this will result in increases in welfare (in a more or less automatic fashion). Thus, much policy making occurs under a leader/follower hierarchy model, where macroeconomic policy is determined first, while social policy is derivative and left to address the social consequences of economic policies (Atkinson 1999). This separation of the 'economic' from the 'social' discourse is inherent to the Washington consensus and the neoclassical theory which underpins it. Moreover, under this view, only certain policies ensure economic growth. In contrast, social policy can and should be understood as 'collective interventions in the economy to influence the access to and the incidence of adequate and secure livelihoods and income' (Mkandawire 2004: 1).

The core of the chapter in the second section deals with issues of financing these collective interventions. We present recent good and bad experiences from various countries and contexts and assess how progressive and solidarity based these reforms have been. First, however, we provide the context in which tax revenues are needed. Once the case for additional tax revenue is made, we address different ways in which tax revenue can be raised (second section). In the third section we deal with the role of taxes in the poverty reduction, human development, economic growth synergy.[1] This section concludes by highlighting the fact that social and economic policies cannot be divorced. Taxation should be assessed from the point of view of whether or not it contributes to a pro-poor policy context.

Taxation

In order to provide the context for the discussion of taxation, it has to be remembered that the existence of large budget deficits has forced governments to undertake macroeconomic stabilization and adjustment aimed at achieving cuts in budget deficits and public expenditure. Since the early 1980s, these adjustment policies have unfortunately been characterized by an almost exclusive emphasis on public expenditure cuts in the quest for budget deficit reduction. In an external review of Extended Structural Adjustment Facility (ESAF) programmes, a group of independent experts noted in the late 1990s[2] that public spending limits have often been set too tightly, with detrimental effects on human development. This was again the case in the policy conditions laid down in the International Monetary Fund's (IMF's) response to the Asian economic crisis. Evidence shows that, for all cases, real per capita basic social services expenditure only declined when the public expenditure share in total output declined.[3] Obviously, it is not possible to pre-judge what shares should go to different government services such as administration, justice, defence or economic services.[4] Nevertheless, the ability to undertake public expenditure on social services is thus affected by revenues, that is, primarily taxation.

On the tax side, the general approach in structural adjustment was that an increase in tax rates was recommended only if it was unavoidable. On the assumption that lower rates would ensure better compliance with tax laws, lower rates were expected to raise revenues (Williamson 1989). When combined with the broadening of the tax base, the tax to gross domestic product (GDP) ratio was supposed to rise. However, in the vast majority of countries in sub-Saharan Africa and Latin America the tax to GDP ratio stagnated or declined (Mehrotra 1996; Agbeyegbe et al. 2004).[5] This is not surprising, given that trade taxes account for the largest share of tax revenues in developing countries; and with tariffs declining under the World Trade Organization (WTO) regime, the share of trade taxes was bound to fall. Unfortunately, other taxes have not grown to compensate for the fall in the contribution of trade taxes. Even India in the 1990s following its period of economic reform experienced a decline by two percentage points in the central government's tax to GDP ratio, as the result of declines in the contribution of trade taxes (Rao 2005).

Substantively, what has changed generally is that, on average, for the low-income countries, Poverty Reduction and Growth Facility/PRGF-supported programmes target a smaller and more gradual fiscal consolidation than programmes under the erstwhile ESAF, and give more weight to increases in revenue than contractions of expenditure (IEO 2004). However, even in this instance the Internal Evaluation Office of the IMF finds that the outcomes are not very different between ESAF loans and its renamed successor, the PRGF.

During the 1980s many middle-income countries, particularly those in Latin America, undertook tax reforms. The initial efforts, which were consistent with the requirements of the Washington consensus, emphasized lower tax rates, indexing for inflation and a broadening of the tax base. These reforms were typically unsuccessful in substantially increasing revenues (Das-Gupta and Mookerjee 1998).[6] As a result later in the 1980s and 1990s significant changes in tax administration were introduced in a handful of Latin American countries, and also in Indonesia and the Philippines.

There is an urgent need to reverse this phenomenon of fiscal inertia through a greater focus on revenue generation as a means of increasing social spending. Low revenue collection is the combined outcome of institutional weaknesses, dependence on trade taxes for many developing countries, and low incomes.

We recognize that none of these factors can be altered in the short run. Domestic revenues can only be increased over a longer time horizon. In fact, one has to acknowledge that over the short to medium run budgets cannot be balanced via increased taxes.[7]

However, there needs to be more explicit international recognition of the fact that adjustment has focused much more on expenditure reduction than revenue generation. A fiscal system can only be progressive and pro-poor[8] if, first, the revenue system is progressive in its overall structure and, second, the revenue base is growing to enable pro-poor expenditures to be undertaken. For this reason, much more could be done to strengthen tax collection in order to prevent tax evasion and tax avoidance. Moreover, much more could be done to enhance tax collection, by enlarging the tax net to catch those who are currently escaping. The international financial institutions (IFIs) need to pay much greater heed to the technical support requirements of most developing countries, but especially those in sub-Saharan Africa and Latin America, in the area of tax administration and collection.

For developing countries, the total tax revenues are derived almost equally from three sources: domestic taxes on goods and services (general sales tax, excises); foreign trade taxes (mostly import duties); and direct taxes (mostly from corporations, rather than individuals).[9] Wealth/property taxes and social security contributions make a marginal contribution. However, for industrialized countries, income taxes (mostly from individuals) make the largest contribution, with domestic taxes on goods and services and social security contributions accounting for slightly over a quarter each of total tax revenue, while trade taxes are quite insignificant (Burgess 1997). It is clear, then, that additional tax revenues are needed to meet the resource requirements for basic services. The questions which are relevant to our purposes are: how do these taxes fare in terms of promoting solidarity?[10] How do they fit in terms of helping or hindering the unleashing of development synergies? In other words, are they pro-poor?

Assessing whether and how taxes are pro-poor

In this section, we analyse various types of revenue generating mechanisms and we assess them in terms of their impact. In particular we look at how progressivity and solidarity in the revenue-generating mechanism affect income poverty and income distribution (which in turn are necessary to help set in motion development synergies). In general, the following sources of financing for social services exist:

- self-provision (involving a time-burden tax);
- user fees;
- pre-paid schemes;
- generalized insurance;
- indirect taxes;
- earmarked taxes; and
- direct taxes.

When describing the sources of government revenues, it is customary to assess their level of progressivity. Progressivity measures the percentage of personal income which is used to pay the tax. If the poor contribute 10 per cent of their income as tax, and the rich also contribute 10 per cent of their income, obviously, the rich are paying more in absolute terms because their income is larger. However, both groups are paying 10 per cent. In this case, the tax is neutral. For the tax to be progressive, the rich must pay a higher *proportion* of their income (not just pay more taxes). It could be the case that the rich pay a smaller *proportion* of their income than the poor, which is a regressive tax, and still pay a higher amount. The focus when we assess the progressivity or regressivity of the tax is on the *percentage or proportion* of their income which is being paid in tax.

Another issue relevant to the financing of social policy is that of the relationship between the state, the individual and society. One approach, which could be labelled 'individualistic', is to make every person pay for the services they use at the moment the service is rendered. When an individual is ill, he or she goes to the doctor and pays for treatment. If the individual is feeling well, he or she stays home and saves the money. That is one way of looking at the issue.

The opposite way of considering the financing of social policy in terms of the relationship between individuals, the state and society is the solidarity approach. The individual is healthy today, but nevertheless contributes to some kind of generalized insurance mechanism which uses the money, so whoever is ill today receives health care. The solidarity approach means financing social services through taxes.

Each of the types of revenue mentioned above (user fees, pre-paid schemes, and so on) can be classified along these two axes of progressivity/regressivity and solidarity/individualism. In general, the most regressive types are self-provision (involving a time-burden tax[11]) and user fees, and the least regressive are direct taxes. Assuming that there is a reasonably well-functioning direct tax system, the rich tend to pay proportionally more, so direct taxation is the most progressive (that is, pro-poor) while user fees are the most regressive. In terms of solidarity, self-provision and user fees are the least reflective of the principle of collective solidarity and the direct taxes are at the other end of the spectrum.

Thus, the types of revenue mentioned above can be classified along these two principles of financing social policy (progressivity and solidarity), wherein the bottom and the peak of the respective pyramids are the goals towards which systems of financing social policy should aim, as shown in the inverted pyramid figure.

Time-burden tax (self-provision)

User fees (most regressive, least solidaristic)

Pre-paid schemes

Generalized insurance

Indirect taxes

Earmarked taxes

Direct taxes (most progressive, most solidaristic)

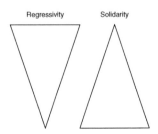

Self-provision

When the state fails in its responsibilities to provide for the well-being of the population, the slack is taken up by the individuals and households themselves. This is the way it was done until roughly the end of the nineteenth century when in Western Europe the first steps were taken towards the establishment of a welfare state.[12] Under these circumstances, wealthy families could try to avail themselves of the services of private doctors or tutors, as well as buying the minimally necessary infrastructure (for example, individual dwellings). The vast majority of the population, however, remained in a state of despair. Similar conditions currently exist in most developing countries.

Two important elements need to be mentioned in respect of self-provision. First, it is inequitable not only from a class or wealth perspective, but also in terms of gender. In most societies, the burdens (of fetching water, taking care of the ill, and so on) fall disproportionately on women. Thus, the inability of the state to implement social polices results in a time-burden tax on women.

Second, besides equity (across class and gender[13]), there are efficiency issues. Self-provision – whether directly through 'invisible'/reproductive female labour or indirectly the purchase of services or goods – is inefficient. The unit costs are much larger than they would be if it were possible to spread the total cost among more users (for example, the difference between a private tutor and a teacher for 15 children). Often, these costs would be so high as to make the provision of the service impossible (for example, sewerage), so they would not be available for anyone.

User fees and pre-paid schemes

In the presence of user fees there is no solidarity. Nor is there any progressivity in the financing of social policy.[14] User fees are not pro-poor, at least from a financing perspective. This was recognized explicitly by representatives of the World Bank, the United Nations Children's Fund (UNICEF) and the United Nations Economic Commission for Africa (ECA) at a meeting in Addis Ababa in 1997, which established that no user fees should be charged for (at least) basic education and primary health care (ECA et al. 1998).

Evidence from several African countries[15] over the past decade demonstrates that the elimination of fees has led to a dramatic increase in the number of enrolments at the primary education level. Thus, the elimination of user fees is a pro-poor intervention. Moreover, this may help to unleash some synergies. For example, in Tanzania not only did school attendance increase, but the level of undernutrition also declined between 2000 and 2004.

The case for cost recovery in health was voiced strongly in a World Bank policy paper in 1987, which called for user charges, insurance, decentralization and a greater role for the private sector (Akin et al. 1987). It assumed that user charges offered the possibility of reducing excess and the unnecessary demand for free services, and that a graduated fee system would encourage citizens to make first use of lower-level health services. The 1993 *World Development Report* (World Bank 1993) presented a more refined position. Market failure arguments were used to advocate public financing of public health services and some essential clinical services (Stiglitz 2000). In countries where the cost of the basic package of essential clinical services was financially infeasible for government, selective user charges and targeting mechanisms were suggested. The argument in favour of user charges was that charging fees can improve equity if fees are used to improve quality.[16]

Nevertheless, cost recovery in some form or other characterizes the present-day health systems found in most African countries. The Republic of Korea, Thailand, Malaysia, Singapore and Indonesia also have some user charge policy in place for health; these coexist as cost-sharing provisions with national or partial social insurance. In Latin America as well, cost sharing is also an important component of health insurance systems. However, as Creese and Kutzin (1997) rightly point out, establishing or raising fees is not the same thing as getting a user charge system to operate as a means of improving efficiency, nor is it a basis for ensuring equity in the provision of services. Out-of-pocket costs (or private expenditures) account for the majority of the health spending in most developing countries. In India, the majority of contacts between the sick and a health provider are with private providers – a majority of them poorly qualified – at considerable cost, both in financial and health terms, for the population (Rohde and Viswanathan 1995).

In most industrialized countries, user charges are not part of the reform agenda; in fact, performance improvement in the health sector has been seen to depend more upon changing the behaviour of providers than of consumers. However, this is in the context of universal access to health care (except in the United States). Not only is there a well-implemented scheme for solidarity and redistribution, but there is also the technological infrastructure to easily implement a sliding scale system to maintain the pro-poor aspects of the system, even if some type of minimal user fees exist.[17]

Several conditions must coexist if increased user charges at government health facilities are to lead to an *increase* in access to the poor. Local revenue retention is one of these. There is evidence that this has led to improved quality in service, and hence the greater utilization of services. Secondly, appropriate management skills and financial institutions need to be in place in order for local fee retention to lead to an improved quality of service. This involves having staff trained in basic financial management, the existence of banks to deposit the funds, the use of simple audit procedures, and community committees for oversight over the use of funds (WHO 1999). Finally, if the increased revenues (from user fees) and improved quality actually *reduce* the cost to the poor of accessing effective care, there could be a basis for levying such fees (Creese and Kutzin 1997). This last condition may be met if the 'exit' option for the poor involves higher levels of payment to a private provider (for example, as is common in much of South Asia, where private providers are abundant), or if the community in question is relatively isolated (for example, as in many parts of low-density parts of Africa or even certain parts of South Asia).

There is a qualitative difference between education and health in terms of the nature of the demand for them that makes user fees even less appropriate for the health sector. For education, parents can anticipate and plan for the costs of schooling. However, health care costs are unpredictable – in terms of both their incidence and their magnitude (Colclough 1997). Catastrophic health costs can wipe out a family's savings, and a vulnerable family is likely to fall below the poverty line under such circumstances. For instance, in India medical costs are said to be the second most important cause (after a dowry for a girl's marriage) in pushing vulnerable families below the poverty line. Hence, while user fees at higher levels might be justified as a short-term, temporary measure if a government faces a particularly resource-constrained environment (as in all low-income and most middle-income countries), the case is rather different in respect of basic health services. On account of the unpredictability of health costs, insurance mechanisms or public finance are the appropriate means for financing health services for the majority of the population, and especially for the poor.

The arguments in favour of user fees included the following: they may raise revenue, improve efficiency and quality, and improve access and equity. The evidence, however, suggests that increased use of user fees since the World Bank advocated them has not contributed any of these potential benefits.[18] While the Bank expected that revenues in the order of 10–20 per cent of recurrent expenditure would be raised, net revenues have been much lower than gross revenues on account of collection costs. Secondly, user fees do not promote efficiency, since there is little evidence of moral hazard in the form of an excess of free facilities. Users, particularly poor ones, already have to take account of the cost of time and transportation when visiting a health facility, which minimizes excess use. In fact, after the imposition of user fees, the level of utilization actually falls, with adverse equity effects. Nor does the evidence suggest that differential pricing of lower and tertiary facilities has resulted in more effective utilization of primary, as opposed to tertiary, facilities, as was expected.

Generalized insurance

A widely used alternative to user fees is a system of pre-paid contributions, especially for health.[19] This provides the advantage of not having to wait to pay until the service is required. Also, by regularly contributing small amounts, the impact of the contribution on households' budgets is diluted.

In addition, by spreading the risk among a larger number of individuals, an insurance system lowers the unit cost. Certainly a pre-paid scheme would be much more progressive than user fees. It would also involve the principle of solidarity. However, they cannot be said to be truly pro-poor.

At least two reasons support this claim. First, unless the insurance is mandatory and universal, it would cater only to the richer sections of the population, who would pay a premium for their services. This not only increases the unit costs (due to the small number of individuals to spread the risk), but also introduces the possibility of segmenting the market. Thus 'premium' high-end services would exist for the richer members of society while the poorest would receive lower-quality services (or none at all). Second, if everybody pays the same premium, in essence, the contribution is regressive. As one or the other must be the case, an insurance mechanism cannot be based simultaneously on solidarity and progressivity.

Indirect taxes

While sales and excise taxes have accounted for most of the indirect domestic taxes in developing countries, the introduction of value added tax (VAT) as a means of raising revenue is a more recent trend.[20] Burgess (1997) argues that since VAT covers a large share of the value added in an economy, the revenue from VAT is buoyant; that is, it tends to rise in line with (or faster than) economic growth. VAT systems have been introduced in over 30 developing countries, and more are in the pipeline. China introduced one in 1994, and India did so in 2005. To maximize the revenues from a VAT, countries need to ensure that the tax base is as broad as possible and that the rate structure is simple.

It is notable that there is little variation in the role of indirect domestic taxes across different low-income countries, but that these taxes are substantially more important for middle- and high-income countries (Das-Gupta and Mookerjee 1998). They have been implemented in countries with low administrative capacity.

The buoyancy of VAT can be contrasted with foreign trade taxes, which are known to be sensitive to fluctuations in world prices. Given that for a large number of low-income and even middle-income countries the export structure is character-ized by a high commodity concentration of exports, an excessive reliance on trade taxes can destabilize the revenues and spending in such countries. In Latin Amer-ica, for instance, the contribution of VAT has been increasing over time, and by the mid-1990s accounted for between 1 and 5 per cent of GDP for Uruguay, Peru, Mexico, Guatemala and Colombia, and for 9 per cent of GDP in Chile. In nearly all of the developing countries in which it has been introduced, its contribution to tax revenues has been increasing (Burgess 1997).

Excise taxes are another important source of revenues in developing countries. They are levied particularly on a few products – alcohol, tobacco, petroleum, vehicles and spare parts. They exhibit several positive features from a revenue per-spective: few producers, large sales volume, relatively inelastic demand, and are easily observable. Excises may be levied on the basis of quantities leaving the fac-tory or at the import stage, thus simplifying measurement and collection, enabling extensive coverage and limiting evasion and better physical monitoring. Currently, excise taxes amount to less than 2 per cent of GDP in low-income countries, com-pared to about 3 per cent in high-income countries. They have a buoyant base and can be administered at a low cost.

However, VAT and excise taxes, like all indirect taxes, tend to be regressive.[21] They are not a pro-poor tax reform. They do not assist with redistribution from the rich to the poor. While efforts have been made to protect the consumption of the poor through the introduction of a number of exemptions, these are difficult to implement and are easily abused. Others argue that the consumption needs of men and women are different and that a VAT system (or other indirect taxes) should take this into account. Nevertheless, the logistics of such differentiation are almost insurmountable.

Earmarked taxes

Normally when a new tax is imposed, there is a considerable amount of public resistance. However, when a source of revenue is identified for specific programmes that are known or seen to have a high social benefit, the normal resistance of taxpayers to new levels of taxation can be overcome. This is one major factor in favour of hypothecated (or earmarked) taxes. Another factor, discussed below, is that these taxes could be progressive and pro-poor. Such earmarked taxes have been used in many countries at different times in their histories. They have taken a variety of forms:

- taxes on property;
- taxes on business;
- taxes on certain commodities, especially intoxicants or cigarettes;
- taxes on imports; and
- taxes on interest or dividends.

One argument that is used against earmarked taxes has been that they might not add to resources for the particular purpose they are meant, as the government may simply divert resources hitherto devoted to say, education, to other purposes. Government resources are fungible, and the possibility of diversion has also been the argument made against project aid from external sources. Earmarked taxes may simply make it easier for the government to divert its own resources, for instance, for military purposes. Clearly, if earmarking is to be used for elementary education, specific safeguards have to be built into the spending mechanism.

Despite the risks associated with it, in a number of industrialized countries the earmarking of revenues has been implemented to fund parts of the education system: for example, in the United States earmarked taxes have been used for education at the state level (Lockheed et al. 1991). There are also examples of earmarking from every region of the developing world. The Republic of Korea, which was a high achiever in terms of mass schooling very early in its development process, has used earmarking to good effect. In 1982 the government found that the general budget was unable to meet the costs of the education system. The government introduced a five-year education tax on spirits (liquor), tobacco, interest and dividend income, and the banking and insurance industry. Five years later the tax accounted for 15 per cent of the education ministry's budget. Other Asian countries, such as China, Nepal and the Philippines, have implemented earmarking for education. India introduced a surcharge on income taxes of 2 per cent in 2004 to be earmarked for elementary education – the surcharge came after the Indian government committed itself (through a constitutional amendment) to making elementary education a fundamental right of every citizen (Mehrotra 2005).

Earmarked taxes for education have also been used in Latin American and African countries. Brazil imposed a 2.5 per cent salary tax on the wages of employees in the private sector, and the funds are used exclusively for primary education. The federal government collects the tax, two-thirds of which go to the states. Alfonso and de Mello (2000) argue that the earmarking of revenues in the areas of both education and health have yielded good results in Brazil. This experience from a wide variety of countries seems to suggest that, when designed appropriately, earmarked funds from dedicated revenues for specific purposes for a sector can play a useful supplementary role in general budgetary allocations to the sector.

Nevertheless, the international experience does point to certain pitfalls that should be avoided if earmarking is adopted. Potter and Diamond (1999) point out that in most Organisation for Economic Co-operation and Development (OECD) countries, comprehensiveness and transparency are achieved by designing a budget system with three key characteristics: annuality,[22] unity[23] and universality. The last principle – universality – states that all resources should be directed to a common pool or fund. In other words, the earmarking of resources for specific purposes is to be generally discouraged. All three characteristics are needed to ensure that all proposals for government expenditure will be forced to compete for resources, and also that priorities will be established across the whole range of government operations. It will be immediately obvious from these principles that they are derived mainly from the macroeconomists' concern for budgetary control, and the fear that extrabudgetary funds (into which earmarked resources are placed) might diminish the Finance Ministry's ability to determine resource allocation. Given the experience of runaway budget deficits since the early to mid-1980s in many developing countries, this concern is by no means illegitimate.

However, if adherence to these principles ignores the institutional development needs of certain sectors, which have tended to get traditionally ignored in many developing countries, then the case for earmarking is a legitimate one. The case also gains strength from the proposal that it is not existing financial resources that would be earmarked, but rather that new resources would be mobilized and then dedicated to pro-poor social policy.

Too many extrabudgetary funds should indeed be discouraged.[24] In other words, one cannot make the case that policy makers should resort to earmarking in order to ensure the delivery of *all* basic social services. Much of the IMF critique of extrabudgetary funds derives from the indiscriminate use of funds that was rampant in many African as well as post-communist countries. Nevertheless, a selective use of funds should be encouraged. Thus, it will be appropriate to use, for instance, part of the proceeds from the disinvestment of state-owned enterprises for creating a fund for some social service, say, for example, meeting maternal or child nutritional needs. Similarly, social security funds are a feature of many countries. Second, we have given several examples above of the earmarking of funds for education and health services. Third, the earmarking of funds for infrastructure, especially road maintenance, is good if it prevents the diversion of resources needed for road maintenance (often seen as not politically attractive) to other purposes; poor road maintenance can lead to higher capital expenditures in the long term. The World Bank has encouraged, as part of its Roads Management Initiative, a 'second-generation road fund', emphasizing their transparency and accountability and their financing by user charges. Gwilliams and Shalizi (1997) note that these funds allow the allocation of resources to activities and programmes with relatively high returns, but which ordinarily have little, if any, political support.

Another advantage of instruments such as earmarked taxes on interests, assets, and so on, as seen in the above discussion, is that they can be implemented in a way which makes them inherently progressive.[25] This is important in terms of the distributive function. In other words, taxing the wealthy provides the funds with which to fund universal basic social services, the pro-poor aspect of fiscal policy.

Direct taxes

Atkinson (1989) has argued that in industrialized countries, personal income and social security taxes are normally seen as key instruments for the redistribution of income. However, in developing countries these account for only a small proportion of revenues; hence their use as instruments for redistribution of income is likely to be restricted (Burgess 1997). The IMF subscribes to this point of view: 'In view of the high share of agriculture and informal economic activity in many countries, corporate and personal income taxes are unlikely to be a major source of domestic revenues in the short- to medium-term' (2004: 5). However, a growing literature suggests that while social security taxes will remain marginal to the redistribution objective in developing countries, the same may not necessarily be true for income taxes. Thus, we do not subscribe to the pessimism about redistributive income taxes to finance pro-poor social policy and unleash the synergies described in the second section. Burgess and Stern (1993) find that in some countries tax reform has led to significant improvements in the contribution of direct taxes to overall revenue. Moreover, the point is not only to improve income distribution, a valuable goal in itself, but also because greater income equality is an important instrument to reduce poverty, expand social development and promote macroeconomic growth.

Optimal tax theory[26] is traditionally concerned with the tax structure, and its efficiency and incidence. The traditional approach uses a general equilibrium framework, and is primarily concerned with 'getting prices right'. While this approach is important, there is almost total neglect here of administrative feasibility. An alternative, though complementary, approach is to focus on taxpayer incentives and the design of tax administration, where the principal concern is to 'get incentives and institutional arrangements right' (Das-Gupta and Mookerjee 1998). Issues of administrative feasibility acquire particular significance in developing countries, where corruption in the tax departments of governments is known to be widespread. It is useful, therefore, to examine the literature on tax compliance and issues of enforcement of existing tax law.

For instance, the performance of Indian income tax collections is particularly poor. Economic development is normally associated with an increase in the relative contribution of personal income taxes to government revenue. This is caused by factors such as the widening of the taxpayer population, increases in personal income, and improvements in enforcement technology and administration. However, the experience in India (and in many other countries, but especially in Latin America) has bucked this normal trend. In India during the period from 1970 to 1990 the share of income taxes in total central tax revenue actually fell from 14.7 per cent to 9.7 per cent, as did the proportion of personal income tax in non-agricultural GDP.[27] The evidence suggests that the proximate cause for the poor and deteriorating performance of Indian income tax revenues during that period was tax evasion (Das-Gupta and Mookerjee 2000). It was poor revenue performance and a fiscal crisis that had forced Latin American countries to undertake large-scale tax administration reforms in the late 1980s and 1990s. Countries such as Colombia, Costa Rica, Ecuador, Peru[28] and Jamaica achieved significant gains from comprehensive reforms that included administrative reforms.

Meanwhile, one of the main implications of low (and in certain countries, like India, falling) income tax collection is that the government is compelled to rely on indirect domestic taxes and trade taxes for its revenue. As mentioned before, these taxes are regressive and hinder the synergies described in the second section. Moreover, in large federal countries they create problems of coordination of indirect taxes between central and subnational governments. The resulting cascading effects distort relative prices, in addition to encouraging excessive vertical integration. Imports are discouraged by the high levels of tariffs (that must compensate for poor income tax collections) and correspondingly, expenditure on essential infrastructure and basic social services is restricted.

While it is clear we are advocating a much larger share of direct taxation of wealthy groups through more progressive income taxes, it has to be acknowledged that developing countries could substantially increase government revenue through better compliance with, and higher collection of, currently existing taxes. For instance, as part of a comprehensive reform of its tax administration during the period 1988–92, the Mexican system awarded a bonus to theist tax collectors. This represented about 60 per cent of additional collections. As a result of the bonuses, the number and yield of audits increased almost overnight. The share of audits generating additional revenue increased from 38 per cent in 1988 to 90 per cent in 1990. Limiting the discretionary authority of tax officials would also help to improve compliance and reduce the level of evasion. Computerization of tax administration can help control corruption as it makes it harder to tamper with records.[29]

Improved tax administration has also resulted in an increase in the share of personal income taxes in total tax revenues even in India during the 1990s, in contrast to the 1970–90 period mentioned above. A number of innovations have accounted for this shift. The xpansion of the scope of tax deduction at source has been very effective in reaching the hard-to-tax group (Rao 2005). Moreover, every individual living in large cities covered under any one of six conditions which are associated with high income/consumption[30] is necessarily required to file a tax return.

Thus, as we mentioned above, if they intend to help the poor the IFIs must seriously focus technical support for tax administration and collection requirements in most developing countries, rather than meddling with their expenditure levels. This is especially the case in sub-Saharan Africa and Latin America.

Trade taxes

There are many a priori reasons for believing that there may be revenue losses due to trade reforms, and these need to be addressed if new resources are to be found for social purposes. There are three grounds for this fear. First, capital movements increase opportunities for evasion because of the limited capacity that any tax authority has to check the overseas income of its residents. Evasion is also encouraged since some governments and other institutions systematically act to conceal relevant information. Where dividends, interest, royalties and management fees are not taxed in the country in which they are paid out, they may easily escape notice in countries where the recipients of such income live. There have been large non-resident aliens' bank deposits in countries like the United States that charge no taxes on the interest from such deposits.[31]

Second, avoidance (as opposed to evasion) may increase, given the differences internationally in tax rules and rates, because of the element of effective choice of tax regime that the international tax treatment of enterprise income commonly offers (Clunies-Ross 1999). This is likely for the taxation of the profits of corporations and other enterprises that have international operations. Transfer prices for goods, services and resources, or moving between branches of a company, provide opportunities for shifting income for tax reasons to minimize the revenue due.[32]

Third, the competition for international inward investment may lead governments to reduce the income tax rates, and increase the income tax concessions, that fall on international investors (Clunies-Ross 1999). Income tax rates have fallen sharply since the late 1970s. Tanzi (1996) notes evidence that there have been sudden outflows of capital in response to certain changes in tax policy. This suggests that governments find themselves constrained by international competition in the rates that they can apply. There has been a decreasing readiness of countries to raise rates or to tax dividend and interest income on the ground for fear that doing so would encourage capital flight. Yet it has been well known for a considerable time that granting direct tax concessions has little or no effect even in diverting investment internationally, let alone in increasing its global levels. Hence, concessions are an unnecessary loss of revenue. 'Beggar-thy-neighbour' policies will lead to losses of revenue for all developing countries in a mirror image of the 'race to the bottom' in respect of labour and environmental standards, which also negatively affect the possibility of achieving inclusive, sustainable social development.

The literature is relatively silent on the relationship between trade tax reform and gender.[33] Nevertheless, it should be clear, for example, based on the structural adjustment programme (SAP) and gender literature, that when men and women engage in different economic activities,[34] policy initiatives affect them differently. Thus, the relative rates of return of these activities (and trade tax reforms is primarily geared towards altering different rates of return) must be analysed from a gender perspective.

Moreover, trade tax reforms that result in the shifting of output into activities with lower levels of employment or with less value added per worker (and thus lower wages) are not pro-poor. Sadly, these are typically the kinds of reforms that have been implemented in most developing countries since the late 1980s and early 1990s.

Tax revenues, social development, poverty reduction and economic growth

Preliminaries

In the positive experience of recently industrialized countries or of high-achieving developing countries, it is difficult to establish causal relationships between human development and economic growth. For example, despite widespread literacy within a population, many countries have not achieved rapid growth, although education is a major determinant of such economic growth.[35] There are also examples of countries with relatively rapid economic growth but persistent income poverty. Indeed, the relationship between economic growth, income poverty, and health/education development is a complex one. A framework to describe these linkages is presented below.[36]

The lingering question remains: if there are no sufficient or necessary conditions linking these elements, are they unrelated? The answer is, no, they are indeed related, but in a complex way. Although no particular element is necessary or sufficient for the advancement of the other, they help each other.[37]

Describing complexity, the development synergy and the role of taxes therein

A synergy or feedback loop can be succinctly expressed as the enhanced impact a change in an independent variable has on the growth rate of a dependent variable, given the presence of a third variable (Haken 1977).[38] This leads to several important, and often overlooked, interrelated effects in terms of policy. The impact of a policy (for example, redistribution to directly reduce poverty) on another variable (say economic growth) crucially depends on the level and rate of change of a third variable (for example, health and educational status). In other words, economic growth will be faster and longer-lasting if (income) poverty is reduced simultaneously through direct policies, and the health and educational status of the population is higher and increasing.[39] What we have in mind can be expressed in a set of three relationships (income growth, income poverty reduction, and social development), the determinants of each of which are discussed below.

$$GNP \text{ per capita growth} = f_1 \text{ (macroeconomic policies, social policy, income poverty reduction, technical/structural change, reproductive labour)} \quad (4.1)$$

Gross national product (GNP) per capita growth is not chosen by governments, but rather is the result of the combination of public policies and private decisions. GNP per capita growth is influenced by social policy, that is, by the provision of social services, and reproductive labour. This does not imply that they are the same or that one is a perfect substitute of the other one. On the contrary, when the government does not provide the services through social policy and women have to provide care, there is a time-burden tax on women (as discussed in the previous section). Thus, both aspects of social policy are important: the provision of basic social services and their financing.

The pace of poverty reduction, the nature of macroeconomic policies, and, most importantly in the medium to long run, technological change (that is, the introduction of value-adding activities and productivity increases through technical/structural change) also affect economic growth. Low unemployment and high wages reduce poverty, leading to higher levels of consumption, internal demand and economic growth.[40] Stable prices and low interest rates also contribute to a favourable context in which firms would want to invest and create well-paid jobs

However, this does not mean that macroeconomic stability per se results in economic growth, as evidenced by the standard error of the regressions that try, but fail, to establish this point.[41] Nor does this imply that a privately led boom will not result in imbalances. Here we want to stress that innovations are introduced through investment – which is financed by profits or by inflows from abroad. The latter may be more volatile than the former and both are influenced by macroeconomic policy.[42]

Technological change, the engine of growth,[43] follows an evolutionary path, rather than one involving firms with absolute knowledge concerning static production functions, as posited by the traditional model underpinning the Washington consensus. Inventing and adapting new technologies is a process of discovery characterized by uncertainty, rather than by probabilistic risk (Nelson and Winter 1982). In this case, markets are not efficient and have no tendency to reach equilibrium, as they tend to change.[44] This different theoretical perspective leads to alternative policy recommendations.

For instance, if markets are in constant flux as firms try to alter those constraints through innovation, then the very notion that taxes or import restrictions introduce distortions lacks foundation. Taxes do, however, play another (apart from generating revenue) important role that is usually unnoticed. Taxes affect the distribution of income (especially the progressive ones discussed in the second section), with concomitant effects on income poverty, as we see next.

$$\textit{Income poverty incidence reduction} = f_2 \textit{ (GNP per capita growth, social policy, asset re-distribution policies, reproductive labour)} \qquad (4.2)$$

As with economic growth, the primary income distribution is not in the hands of governments to decide, but instead emerges from market results and relative bargaining power between the owners of factors of production. The distribution of income, in turn, affects the incidence of income poverty. Nevertheless, both through regulation and overall management of macroeconomic conditions (captured in the GNP per capita growth variable) and polices (that is, taxation), the government can affect income distribution.[45]

Moreover, the distribution of assets can also be altered (for example, through land reform, titling, distribution of shares), which, in turn, will affect the primary income distribution and other determinants of poverty, such as the status of women. In rural South Asia, for instance, few women own land and even fewer control it (Agarwal 1994). Evidence from sub-Saharan Africa has also argued that one of the factors constraining growth and poverty reduction is the gender inequality regarding access to, and control of, a diverse range of assets (World Bank 1999).

Gender discrimination not only affects the ownership of physical assets, it also influences the allocation and pay rates of labour. This explains the need to include reproductive labour in the equation. The negative impact in terms of poverty reduction opportunities can be seen, for instance, in wage differentials by gender for the same job, allocation of time in care (which reduces the available time for earnings-related activities), and the contribution to production for self-consumption by women rather than for the market.[46] This contribution is similar to a tax burden, as we have shown in the previous section.

Finally, another fundamental way in which the government can influence distribution is through public expenditure on the provision of services and transfers through social assistance and social insurance (the tertiary income distribution), that is, through elements of social policy, the final determinant of the level of the income poverty ratio and its rate of change.[47] Thus, we turn to the determinants of social development.

$$\textit{Social development} = f_3 \textit{ (GNP per capita growth, income poverty reduction,}$$
$$\textit{social policy, reproductive labour)} \qquad (4.3)$$

Education, health and sanitation – the elements which enable people to live a dignified life – have myriad interaction effects among them. Obviously, additional resources (at the household level and nationally) through poverty reduction and economic growth helps. However, as many country experiences show, 'unaimed opulence' is not sufficient. Public action in terms of social policy is fundamental in this regard.[48]

Our contention is that human development outcomes are the result of synergies between income poverty reduction, social development and economic growth. A fundamental point of the notion of synergy among the three types of interventions is that in strategies where one is absent, the effect of interventions in the other three spheres is less than what it would be otherwise. Policies which focus largely on *economic growth* (without much regard for income poverty reduction or social policy) are doomed to generate unequal income distribution (and thus higher income poverty) as well as lower levels of social development, which will dampen economic prospects in the long run (Mkandawire 2004).

Policies that focus only on *social development*, but ignore income poverty reduction or economic growth are unsustainable. A 'growth-mediated' strategy, following Sen's terminology (see Sen 1985), could be translated into the expansion of social services through supportive social policy (for example, direct provision or transfers) which could lead eventually to a reduction in income poverty. A growth-mediated strategy may also help people to access social services as higher levels of national income are attained may enable command over (social) goods and services. However, a growth-mediated strategy is a risky proposition, as many elements may not materialize in this long causal chain. Moreover, it could represent unconscionable delay for those at the bottom of the social pyramid. This is particularly important for women and girls who often have to tackle the 'gap' created by insufficient government policy.

Thus, economic and social policies cannot be separated, whether in terms of analysis or policy making. Moreover, fiscal policy, in particular taxation, is at the centre of the synergies which ensure the complementarities between social development, economic growth and poverty reduction.

The role of taxation

Social policies, which are present in all three of the equations described in the previous subsection, basically consist of government expenditures, which are, in turn, determined by government revenue. The way this revenue (including the time-burden tax mentioned earlier) is collected has implications both in terms of the level of expenditure that can be financed and also for income distribution, an important element in expanding equality and reducing the level of income poverty.

Fiscal policy in general has many tasks and thus different objectives, all of which are directly affected by the level and type of taxation. One objective is income redistribution (for example, through taxes and subsidies) and another is striving for full employment (that is, through the size and structure of taxation and expenditure). A third objective is the delivery and affordability/access of services (both social and other ones).

All three of these are important components of social development (and social policy) and contribute to the reduction in inequality, decreases in income poverty

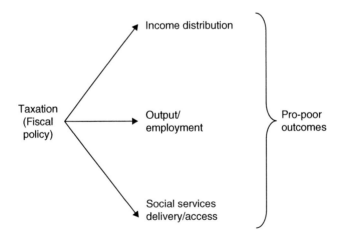

Figure 4.1   Complex causalities

and the acceleration of economic growth. Full employment and stable family incomes are crucial for the well-being of all members of society. Income distribution is also related to income poverty. However, as there are some non-income dimensions of poverty, the allocation of expenditures among various social sectors is also important. The impact on well-being of the level, composition and efficiency of government expenditures, as well as their financing (whether through taxation or self-provision/user fees), are interrelated. For instance, a policy of building schools to increase access to primary education can be undermined by the introduction of user fees.[49]

Conclusions and policy recommendations

As fiscal policy (through both spending and taxation) affects employment, the distribution of income and the provision of social services, it is impossible to discuss pro-poor social policies without paying careful attention to their financing. Moreover, the existence of synergies (both within the sectors constituting social policy as well as among poverty reduction policies, economic growth and social development) requires that a framework making these connection and feedback loops be made explicit. Our argument is that analysing these synergies points to particular policy recommendations, which are at variance from the traditional/orthodox approach of the IFIs and most governments in developing countries, the majority of whom pursue a neoliberal agenda.

In particular, we posit that social and economic policies cannot be divorced. Thus, when analysing social policy, for instance, we need to include the mode in which it is financed. Otherwise, there is the possibility that the pro-poor benefits of social service provision may be undermined by 'anti-poor' revenue-raising strategies. Taxation should be assessed from the point of view of whether or not it contributes to a pro-poor policy context. In other words, the tax structure should be progressive and should promote the principle of solidarity.

Since the inception of structural adjustment programmes in the early 1980s, the wave of reforms in the 1990s, and also among most recent Poverty Reduction Strategy Papers (PRSPs) and similar plans, there has been a push towards the elimination of trade taxes and the promotion of VATs (and other indirect, regressive taxes). The shortfalls generated by reductions in trade taxes have not been compensated for by increases in other forms of taxation. Thus, from the point of view of solidarity and progressivity, recent trends are not very encouraging.

Nevertheless, not all of the reforms have had negative effects. In particular, within the last ten years or so, there has been a growing recognition among policy makers in developing countries as well as among donors and international advisors about the detrimental effects of user fees. Several success stories in education attest to this. In the health and water and sanitation sectors, however, the situation is not as encouraging (Prasad 2006). In any case, recent attempts at converting the user fees into pre-paid insurance schemes are steps in the right direction. This is the case, in particular, when such insurance schemes are nationwide and provide subsidies to help the poor, or the premium is established using a sliding scale whereby the contribution is proportional to income.

In terms of future steps, countries should be encouraged to implement direct, progressive taxes. As it is well known that these taxes are harder to collect, the United Nations and the IFIs should take a leading role in capacity building. Donors should help to foot the bill for training and the required infrastructure to ensure compliance with these taxes. External partners and the international community should also strengthen their efforts to provide financing, including through the introduction of innovative sources of funding.

These steps (progressive taxation, fiscal policies to maintain full employment, solidarity-based revenue raising, the elimination of user fees for basic social services, and an improved capacity to enforce tax compliance) would contribute to the adequate financing of pro-poor social policies. Moreover, by unleashing the synergies among social development, poverty reduction and economic growth, they would also help to construct inclusive societies.

Notes

1. Our model of synergy explicitly integrates economic and social policies. It is associated in the economics literature with different heterodox approaches: Post-Keynesian, Evolutionary, Structuralism and Transformational Growth. See, among others, Hirschman (1958); Taylor (1991, 2006); Nell (1998a); Chang and Grabel (2004).
2. One of the members of the group was Kwesi Botchwey, a former Ghanaian Finance Minister.
3. See Mehrotra and Delamonica (2007).
4. Even the leading proponents of orthodox general equilibrium and market failure approaches recognize this. See, for example, Diamond (2002), Laffont (2002) and Stiglitz; (2000). In addition, Paternostro et al. (2007) address the lack of theoretical foundation in most of the literature on public expenditures. See also Lindert (2004).
5. The latter, however, support the notion that trade liberalization accompanied by appropriate macroeconomic policies can be undertaken in a way that preserves overall revenue yield.
6. Also, see Carciofi and Cetrángolo (1994), where evidence is cited that at the end of the 1980s Latin American countries still had tax to gross domestic product (GDP) ratios which were well below what might have been anticipated from their level of per capita income.
7. For the least developed countries, it should be possible for donors to alter their disbursement profiles over time so as to accommodate shocks and to create bigger and better compensatory financing mechanisms.
8. By 'pro-poor' we mean policies which attempt to increase the standard of living of the poor. These should not be confused with targeted programmes which all too often are of such limited or weak scope that are not necessarily 'pro-poor' in this sense (Tendler 2004).
9. The International Monetary Fund (IMF) notes that for Low-Income Countries (LICs), its 14 per cent tax revenue to GDP is accounted for by foreign trade taxes (4.2 per cent), excises (1.8 per cent), general sales tax (3.1 per cent), and social security (1.8 per cent). For Lower Middle-Income Countries (LMICs), their 18.5 per cent tax revenue/GDP ratio is accounted for by a lower share for foreign trade (3.4 per cent), and a higher share of excises (2.3 per cent), general sales tax (4.9 per cent), and social security (3.7 per cent).

For Upper Middle-Income Countries (UMICs), their 23 per cent tax/GDP ratio has even lower shares for foreign trade taxes (3.1 per cent), and even higher shares for excise (2.5 per cent), general sales tax (5.9 per cent) and social security (6.4 per cent) (IMF 2004).

10. Other important fiscal issues, such as the role of public expenditure and democracy or tax evasion, are not taken up for lack of space. See, for instance, Hausmanna and Purfield (2004) and Sandmo (2004).

11. It could be argued that the opportunity cost of time for wealthier people is higher than that of the poorest, making self-provision a progressive tax. However, in practice, it is poor women who end up doing the work, while richer people 'avoid' this tax. Thus, we classify it as the most regressive of them all.

12. Although it was eventually truncated, some earlier steps were taken in the United States. On the one hand there was universalization (at least among the white population) of schooling since the early 1800s and, on the other hand, after the Civil War (1861–65) there was provision of pensions for widows and orphans (Skocpol 1995).

13. There are also geographical and (often associated with geographical differences) ethnic/linguistic disparities.

14. The lack of solidarity can be seen in the similarity between user fees and privatization. See, among others, Mackintosh and Koivusalo (2005); Prasad (2006); Reddy and Vandemoortele (1996); Webster and Sansom (1999).

15. Examples include Malawi since 1994, Uganda since 1996, as well as Kenya, Tanzania and Lesotho during the first decade of the twenty-first century.

16. For the health sector, a similar argument is often made in relation to the World Health Organization–United Nations Children's Fund (WHO–UNICEF) initiative called the Bamako Initiative. However, the argument is made in the context of community pooling of resources to meet a variety of costs, and involves, among other things, improvements in quality of service and local retention of funds. User charges in health, when they flow to the treasury, account for only a minuscule proportion of total funds available to the health ministry; thus, without contributing much to resource mobilization, they end up denying services to the poor.

17. This does not mean that everything is well in such systems. First, there is an issue of stigmatization, even in the presence of the sliding scale. Second, the user fees could be a barrier to access some services (for example, some specialized tests or treatments). Third, the introduction of the fees could be a first step to unravel the social contract and the society-wide understanding that the components of social policy are a right to which every citizen is entitled.

18. Barnum and Kutzin (1993); Creese and Kutzin (1997); Arhin-Tenkorang (2000).

19. Also for pensions.

20. By the late 1990s value added tax (VAT) had been introduced in over 30 developing countries in Asia, Africa, Latin America and Eastern Europe. India is about to introduce VAT over the financial year 2003–04.

21. Gemmell and Morrissey (2005) assert that VAT is not as bad as it is usually assumed to be, due to the fact that most of the poor purchase in informal markets where the VAT is not collected. However, were it to be collected properly, it would be regressive. Moreover, the authors clearly and honestly caution about the reliability of the evidence in the studies they reviewed.

22. Annuality means the budget is prepared every year, covering only one year; voted and executed every year, even though most Organisation for Economic Co-operation and Development (OECD) and some developing countries now develop the annual budget within a multiyear perspective, through the preparation of medium-term revenue and expenditure framework.

23. Unity means that revenue and expenditure (and borrowing constraints) are considered together to determine annual budget targets.

24. Curiously, the IMF does not seem to define what 'too many' means. We found little in the literature, which might suggest that a certain percentage of public expenditure would be deemed too high for allocation to extrabudgetary funds.
25. This may not be the case with 'sin' taxes (for example, on tobacco).
26. See Ramsey (1927), Mirrlees (1976), and Diamond and Mirrlees (1971a, 1971b).
27. Thus in 1989–90 the personal income tax generated less income than the entire amount spent on the fertilizer subsidy that year (Das-Gupta and Mookerjee 2000).
28. Peru managed to increase tax revenues as a whole from 5.4 per cent of GDP in 1990 to 9 per cent of GDP in 1991. Mookerjee (1997) notes that it is difficult to say whether these changes were caused entirely by the tax reform, since other administrative reforms were implemented at the same time.
29. In developing countries, outside of agriculture, a large proportion of those not in formal, organized manufacturing activities are in the so-called informal sector. However, the tax administration in many countries is either unable to cope with this sector of largely untaxed incomes, or is unwilling, having been co-opted in a web of corruption. Mookerjee (1997) and Dasgupta and Mookerjee (1998) spell out other reforms on the basis of the international experience. They mention the need for motivating high-level officials to evaluate the performance of their subordinates. This is encouraged by autonomy over budgets, personnel and control, which were increased in tax administration reforms in Argentina, Colombia, Ghana, Jamaica and Peru. In some cases budgets were linked to revenues collected. Some countries liberalized the rules for contracting out operations to the private sector.
30. These conditions are: ownership of house, cars and credit cards; membership of a club; undertaking foreign travel; and being subscribed to a telephone connection.
31. Some suggestions have been made to deal with these problems, based on the following principles. First, withholding taxes on interest, dividends, royalties and management fees, if these payments are to cross borders, would be collected universally at a set of uniform rates which are agreed internationally. Second, there should be a single international code system for identifying payers of individual payers of individual and corporate income tax, so that tax authorities can share information about taxpayers without revealing it to others. Third, a tax-return to any tax authority of the income of a corporation or other enterprise would be required to give information relating to the total world income of the firm (Clunies-Ross 1999).
32. Tax havens provide the possibility of avoidance by forming holding companies and shifting ostensible residence (see Tanzi 1995).
33. Budlender and Hewitt (2002); Çagatay et al. (2000); Judd (2002).
34. This is due to culturally imposed restrictions which imply different linkages and interactions with the market and marketing opportunities.
35. The answer is obvious too: because other growth-oriented policies (such as technological change to induce productivity increase, macroeconomic stability) are not present.
36. Our framework could be considered a 'magnifying lens' view of the Transformational Growth matrices developed in Nell (2005), whereby we introduce less elements (for example, we do not include youth socialization), but we attempt to provide more detail to the interactions we do explore.
37. Thus, no single element can be specified as the main cause (or 'development magic bullet') for success in all areas. Pritchett (2003) and Levine and Renelet (1992) discuss various shortcomings of econometric estimates that attempt (and fail) to establish these relationships.
38. It should be noted, in order to distinguish from the static influence of multiple factors in traditional economic analysis (for example, Cobb–Douglas production functions), that the synergies take place in terms of rates of change, not levels of activity.

39. A widely recognized simple example, and one often mentioned even within the Washington consensus literature, is that economic growth will be more successful in reducing income poverty, that is, the elasticity of poverty reduction will be higher, when human capital is more equitably distributed. We do not deny this. We only stress that this is only one of the many interactions among various interventions. A classic application in economics is Goodwin (1967).

40. 'The liberal reward of labour, therefore, as it is the necessary effect, so it is the natural symptom of increasing national wealth. The scanty maintenance of the labouring poor, on the other hand, is the natural symptom that things are at a stand' (Smith 1776: Book I, chapter 8).

41. See, for instance, Bleaney (1996) and Sirimaneetham and Temple (2006).

42. Further, the focus on freeing up financial markets in the Washington consensus may have had the adverse effect of contributing to macroeconomic instability by weakening the financial sector (UNCTAD 1999; Grabel 2003).

43. Abramovitz (1989); Chakravarty (1982); Schumpeter (1934); Solow (1997).

44. Anderson et al. (1988); Lesourne and Orléan (1998); Pack (1992); Verspagen (1992); Nell (1992, 1998a, 1998b).

45. For instance, see Rowthorn (1977) and Nell (1992) on relative bargaining and full employment.

46. In all of these issues, of course, there are great variations across countries.

47. Devereux and Sabates-Wheeler (2004); ILO (2001); Kannan (2004); Mkandawire (2004); Townsend (2004).

48. In addition, it must be remembered (see equation 4.1) that social development influences poverty reduction and economic growth, for example, as adult women in the household use less of their time to fetch water, their ability to earn incomes (and thus contribute to buying school supplies and books) or help children to study also increases.

49. The fees, paradoxically, could be introduced in order to finance the building of a school.

References

Abramovitz, M. (1989) *Thinking about Growth* (Cambridge: Cambridge University Press).

Agarwal, Bina (1994) *A Field of One's Own: Gender and Land Rights in South Asia*, South Asian Studies No. 58 (Cambridge: Cambridge University Press).

Agbeyegbe, T., J. Stotsky and A. Woldemariam (2004) *Trade Liberalisation, Exchange Rate Changes, and Tax Revenues in Sub Saharan Africa*, IMF Working Paper No. WP/04/178 (Washington, DC: IMF). www.imf.org/external/pubs/ft/wp/2004/wp04178.pdf, accessed on 15 June 2006.

Akin, J., N. Birsdall and D. de Ferranti (1987) *Financing Health Services in Developing Countries: An Agenda for Reform* (Washington, DC: World Bank).

Alfonso, J.R.R. and L. de Mello (2000) *Brazil: An Evolving Federation* (Washington, DC: IMF).

Anderson, P.W., K.J. Arrow and D. Pines (eds.) (1988) *The Economy as an Evolving Complex System: The Proceedings of the Evolutionary Paths of the Global Economy Workshop* (Reading, MA: Addison-Wesley Publishing Company).

Arhin-Tenkorang, D. (2000) *Mobilizing Resources for Health: The Case for User Fees Revisited*, Working Paper Series No. WG3:6 (Geneva: WHO Commission on Macroeconomics and Health).

Atkinson, A.B. (1999) 'Macroeconomics and the social dimension.' In Division for Social Policy and Development (ed.), *Experts Discuss Some Critical Social Development Issues* (New York: United Nations).

—— (1989) *Poverty and Social Security* (Brighton: Harvester Wheatsheaf).

Barnum, H. and J. Kutzin (1993) *Public Hospitals in Developing Countries: Resource Use, Cost, Financing* (Baltimore, MD and London: Johns Hopkins University Press).

Bleaney, M. (1996) 'Macroeconomic stability, investment and growth in developing countries', *Journal of Development Economics*, Vol. 48, No. 2, 461–77.

Budlender, D. and G. Hewitt (eds.) (2002) *Gender Budgets Make More Cents: Country Studies and Good Practice* (London: Commonwealth Secretariat).

Burgess, R. (1997) 'Fiscal reform and the extension of basic health and education coverage.' In C. Colclough (ed.), *Marketizing Education and Health in Developing Countries: Miracle or Mirage?* (Oxford: Clarendon Press).

Burgess, R. and N. Stern (1993) 'Taxation and development', *Journal of Economic Literature*, Vol. 31, No. 2, 762–830.

Çagatay, N., M. Keklik, R. Lal and J. Lang (2000) *Budgets As If People Mattered: Democratising Macroeconomic Policies*, UNDP Conference Paper Series (New York: UNDP).

Carciofi, R. and O. Cetrángolo (1994) *Tax Reforms and Equity in Latin America: A Review of the 1980s and Proposals for the 1990s*, Innocenti Occasional Paper No. 39 (Florence: UNICEF Innocenti Research Centre).

Chakravarty, S. (1982) *Alternative Approaches to a Theory of Economic Growth: Marx, Marshall and Schumpeter* (New Delhi: Oriental Longman).

Chang, H. and I. Grabel (2004) *Reclaiming Development: An Alternative Economic Policy Manual* (London: Zed).

Clunies-Ross, A. (1999) *Sustaining Revenue for Social Purposes in the Face of Globalization* (New York: United Nations).

Colclough, C. (1997) *Marketizing Education and Health in Developing Countries: Miracle or Mirage?* (Oxford: Clarendon Press).

Creese, A. and J. Kutzin (1997) 'Lessons from cost recovery in health.' In C. Colclough (ed.), *Marketizing Education and Health in Developing Countries: Miracle or Mirage?* (Oxford: Clarendon Press).

Das-Gupta, A. and D. Mookerjee (2000) 'Reforming Indian income-tax enforcement.' In S. Kähkonen and A. Lanyi (eds.), *Institutions, Incentives and Economic Reforms in India* (Thousand Oaks, CA: Sage Publishers).

—— (1998) *Incentives and Institutional Reform in Tax Enforcement: An Analysis of Developing Country Experience* (New Delhi: Oxford University Press).

Devereux, S. and R. Sabates-Wheeler (2004) *Transformative Social Protection*, IDS Working Paper No. 232 (Brighton: IDS).

Diamond, P. (2002) 'Public finance theory – Then and now', *Journal of Public Economics*, Vol. 86, No. 3 (December) 311–17.

Diamond, P, and J. Mirrlees (1971) 'Optimal taxation and public production: I–Production efficiency', *American Economic Review*, Vol. 61, No. 1, 8–27; and 'Optimal taxation and public production: II–Tax rules', Vol. 61, No. 3, 261–78.

ECA (UN Economic Commission for Africa), UNICEF (United Nations Children's Fund) and the World Bank (1998) *Addis Ababa Consensus on Principles of Cost Sharing in Education and Health in Sub-Saharan Africa*, report on an international forum, Addis Ababa, 18–20 June 1997 (New York: UNICEF).

Gemmell, N. and O. Morrissey (2005) 'Distribution and poverty impacts of tax structure reform in developing countries: How little we know', *Development Policy Review*, Vol. 23, No. 2 (March) 131–44.

Goodwin, R. (1967) 'A growth cycle.' In C.H. Feinstein (ed.), *Socialism, Capitalism and Economic Growth* (Cambridge: Cambridge University Press).

Grabel, I. (2003) 'International private capital flows and developing countries.' In H.J. Chang (ed.), *Rethinking Development Economics* (London: Anthem Press).

Gwilliams, K.M. and Z.M. Shalizi (1997) *Road Funds, User Charges and Taxes*, World Bank Discussion Paper, April (Washington, DC: World Bank).

Haken, H. (1977) *Synergetics: An Introduction* (Berlin and New York: Springer Verlag).

Hausmann, R. and C. Purfield (2004) *The Challenge of Fiscal Adjustment in a Democracy*, IMF Working Paper No. WP/04/168, September (Washington, DC: IMF). www.imf.org/external/pubs/ft/wp/2004/wp04168.pdf, accessed on 15 June 2006.

Hirschman, A.O. (1958) *The Strategy of Economic Development* (New Haven, CT: Yale University Press).

IEO (Independent Evaluation Office) (2004) *Evaluation of PRSPs and PRGFs* (Washington, DC: IMF).

ILO (International Labour Organization) (2001) *Social Security: A New Consensus* (Geneva: ILO).

IMF (International Monetary Fund) (2004) *Global Monitoring Report 2004* (Washington, DC: IMF). www.imf.org/external/np/pdr/gmr/eng/2004/041604.pdf, accessed on 12 March 2008.

Judd, K. (ed.) (2002) *Gender Budget Initiatives: Strategies, Concepts and Experiences – Papers from a High Level International Conference 'Strengthening Economic and Financial Governance through Gender Responsive Budgeting', Brussels, 16–18 October 2001* (New York: UNIFEM).

Kannan, K. (2004) *Social Security, Poverty Reduction and Development: Arguments for Enlarging the Concept and Coverage of Social Security in a Globalizing World*, ESS Paper No. 21, Global Campaign on Social Security and Coverage for All (Geneva: ILO).

Laffont, J.J. (2002) 'Public economics yesterday, today and tomorrow', *Journal of Public Economics*, Vol. 86, No. 3, 327–34.

Lesourne, J. and A. Orlean (eds.) (1998) *Advances in Self-Organization and Evolutionary Economics* (Paris: Economica).

Levine, R. and D. Renelet (1992) 'A sensitivity analysis of cross-country growth regressions', *American Economic Review*, Vol. 82, No. 4, 942–63.

Lindert, P.H. (2004) *Growing Public Social Spending and Economic Growth since the Eighteenth Century* (Cambridge: Cambridge University Press).

Lockheed, M., A. Verspoor and Associates (1991) *Improving Primary Education in Developing Countries* (Oxford: Oxford University Press).

Mackintosh, M. and M. Koivusalo (eds.) (2005) *Commercialization of Health Care: Global and Local Dynamics and Policy Responses*, Social Policy in a Development Context Series (Basingstoke: UNRISD/Palgrave Macmillan).

Mehrotra, S. (ed.) (2005) *The Economics of Elementary Education in India: The Challenge of Public Finance, Private Provision and Household Costs* (New Delhi: Sage Publishers).

—— (1996) 'Domestic liberalization policies and public finance: Poverty implications.' In UNCTAD, *Globalization and Liberalization: Effects of International Economic Relations on Poverty* (Geneva and New York: UNCTAD).

Mehrotra, S. and E. Delamonica (2007) *Eliminating Human Poverty: Macroeconomic and Social Policies for Equitable Growth* (London: Zed).

Mirrlees, J. (1976) 'Optimal tax theory: A synthesis', *Journal of Public Economics*, Vol. 6, No. 4, 327–58.

Mkandawire, T. (2004) 'Social policy in a development context: Introduction.' In T. Mkandawire (ed.), *Social Policy in a Development Context* (Basingstoke: UNRISD/Palgrave Macmillan).

Mookherjee, D. (1997) *Incentive Reforms in Developing Country Bureaucracies: Lessons from Tax Administration*, paper published for the Annual World Bank Conference on Development Economics (Washington, DC: IBRD/World Bank).

Nell, E. (2005) *Humanizing Globalization*, mimeo (New York: Graduate Faculty, New School for Social Research).

—— (1998a) *Transformational Growth and the Business Cycle* (London and New York: Routledge).

—— (1998b) *The General Theory of Transformational Growth: Keynes after Sraffa* (Cambridge: Cambridge University Press).

—— (1992) *Transformational Growth and Effective Demand* (New York: New York University Press).

Nelson, R. and S. Winter (1982) *An Evolutionary Theory of Economic Change* (Cambridge: Harvard University Press).

Pack, H. (1992) 'Endogenous growth theory: Intellectual appeal and empirical shortcomings', *Journal of Economic Perspectives*, Vol. 8, No. 1, 55–72.

Paternostro, S., A. Rajaram and E.R. Tiongson (2007) 'How does the composition of public spending matter?', *Oxford Development Studies*, Vol. 35, No. 1, 47–82.

Potter, B. and J. Diamond (1999) *Guidelines for Public Expenditure Management* (Washington, DC: IMF). www.imf.org/external/pubs/ft/expend/index.htm, accessed on 15 June 2006.

Prasad, N. (2006) 'Privatisation results: Private sector participation in water services after 15 years', *Development Policy Review*, Vol. 24, No. 6, 669–92.

Pritchett, L. (2003) 'A conclusion to cross national growth research: Foreword "To the countries themselves".' In Gary McMahon and Lyn Squire (eds.), *Explaining Growth: A Global Research Project* (Basingstoke: Palgrave Macmillan).

Ramsey, F. (1927) 'A contribution to the theory of taxation', *Economic Journal*, No. 37, 47–61.

Rao, Govinda (2005) *Fiscal Decentralization in Indian Federalism*, mimeo (Bangalore: Institute of Economic and Social Change).

Reddy, S. and J. Vandemoortele (1996) *User Financing of Basic Social Services: A Review of Theoretical Arguments and Empirical Evidence*, Evaluation, Policy and Planning Working Paper No. 6 (New York: UNICEF).

Rohde, J.E. and H. Vishwanathan (1995) *The Rural Private Practitioner* (New Delhi: Oxford University Press).

Rowthorn, R.E. (1977) 'Conflict, inflation and money', *Cambridge Journal of Economics*, Vol. 1, No. 3, 215–39.

Sandmo, A. (2004) *The Theory of Tax Evasion: A Retrospective View*, Discussion Paper 31/04, paper prepared for the Nordic Workshop on Tax Policy and Public Economies, Helsinki, November (Bergen: Norwegian School of Economics and Business Administration).

Schumpeter, J. (1934) *The Theory of Economic Development* (Cambridge, MA: Harvard University Press).

Sen, A. (1985) *Commodities and Capabilities* (Oxford: Oxford University Press).

Sirimaneetham, V. and J. Temple (2006) *Macroeconomic Policy and the Distribution of Growth Rates*, Bristol Economics Discussion Paper 06/584 (Bristol: University of Bristol, Department of Economics).

Skocpol, T. (1995) *Protecting Soldiers and Mothers: The Political Origins of Social Policy in the United States* (Cambridge, MA: Harvard University Press).

Smith, A. (1776) *Wealth of Nations* (1937 reprint) (London: Random House).

Solow, R. (1997) *Learning from 'Learning by Doing': Lessons for Economic Growth* (Stanford: Stanford University Press).

Stiglitz, Joseph E. (2000) *Economics of the Public Sector* (New York and London: Norton and Company).

Tanzi, V. (1996) *Is There a Need for a World Tax Organization?*, paper presented at the International Institute of Public Finance, 52nd Congress, Tel Aviv, August.

—— (1995) *Taxation in an Integrating World* (Washington, DC: Brookings Institution).

Taylor, L. (2006) *Reconstructing Macroeconomics: Structuralist Proposals and Critiques of the Mainstream* (Cambridge, MA: Harvard University Press).

—— (1991) *Income Distribution, Inflation and Growth* (Cambridge, MA: MIT Press).

Tendler, J. (2004) 'Why social policy is condemned to a residual category of safety nets, and what to do about it.' In T. Mkandawire (ed.), *Social Policy in a Development Context* (Basingstoke: UNRISD/Palgrave Macmillan).

Townsend, P. (2004) 'The restoration of "universalism": The rise and fall of Keynesian influence on social development policies.' In T. Mkandawire (ed.), *Social Policy in a Development Context* (Basingstoke: UNRISD/Palgrave Macmillan).

UNCTAD (United Nations Conference on Trade and Development) (1999), *Trade and Development Report* (Geneva: UNCTAD).

Verspagen, B. (1992) 'Endogenous innovation in neo-classical growth models: A survey', *Journal of Macroeconomics*, Vol. 4, No. 14, 631–62.

Webster, M. and K. Sansom (1999) *Public–Private Partnership and the Poor: An Initial Review*, WELL Study (Loughborough: Loughborough University). www.lboro.ac.uk/well/, accessed in August 2007.

WHO (World Health Organization) (1999) *World Health Report* (Geneva: WHO).

Williamson, J. (1989) 'What Washington means by policy reform.' In J. Williamson (ed.), *Latin American Adjustment: How Much Has Happened?* (Washington, DC: Institute of International Economics).

World Bank (1999) *Public Expenditure Management Handbook* (Washington, DC: World Bank).

—— (1993) *World Development Report: Investing in Health* (Oxford: Oxford University Press).

5
Financing Developmental Social Policies in Low-Income Countries: Conditions and Constraints

Alice Sindzingre

Introduction[1]

The consolidation of states cannot be dissociated from the structure of taxation and expenditure, which constitutes a major problem in low-income countries. Taxation systems are institutions, which need credibility in order to be effective, and revenues and spending are crucial in building this credibility. The economic literature has likewise highlighted the difficulty in financing social policies, in particular in the poorest countries, which are often caught in vicious circles where citizens and states do not feel bound by mutual 'contractual' obligations. This situation therefore weakens the justifications for the citizens to pay taxes and for governments to provide public goods, further weakening state credibility and capacity.

This chapter analyses the options and constraints for financing social policies in low-income countries, in particular those situated in sub-Saharan Africa. The key constraints that limit the financing of social policies in these countries are those stemming from the structure of taxation, in particular, its reliance on trade. The nature of resources and the prevalence of informal activities generate additional constraints as well. Further constraints are created by external causalities, such as foreign aid or the economic reforms that most low-income countries have had to adopt since the 1980s in exchange for access to external finance. Economic reforms, particularly trade liberalization, had the potential to impact negatively on revenues, and foreign aid, especially aid dependence, had the potential to impact negatively on domestic taxation and institutions.

Such constraints limit the types of social protection that low-income countries can conduct, whether they are provided at the domestic level by public social policies or via individual transfers, or at the external level by foreign aid. In particular, these constraints limit the capacity of governments to implement universal social policies and explain why social policies mostly take the form of targeted safety nets.

Key lessons may be drawn from the Asian 'developmental states', their structure of taxation and ways of financing social policy. These states have been built due not to high tax ratios recycled in large social expenditures and ownership of large shares of economies, but rather to a mode of state intervention that relies on policies committed to growth (for example, tax subsidies or exemptions conditional to export performance). Political economy has played a key role: the ingredients were strong institutions, policy credibility, coalition building between the state and interest groups, redistributive policies and access to education, all of which were oriented towards growth while growth was at the same time instrumental to political legitimacy.

The chapter is structured as follows. The first section examines the constraints that ensue from the nature of taxation, commodity and export dependence and the negative effects of volatility that stem from trade-based taxation. The second section analyses the consequences on tax systems of the reforms associated with the programmes of international financial institutions – trade liberalization and poverty reduction – as well as aid dependence. The third section explores the theoretical issues involved in social policies, the political economy dimensions of redistributive policies, the consequences of aid dependence in terms of fostering targeted projects instead of universal social policies and the ambiguous impact of the 'informal' mechanisms of social protection. The final section concludes by underscoring the lessons for low-income countries of the Asian developmental states, which were based more on growth-oriented policies than on high levels of taxation, a key lesson being the importance for low-income countries of triggering processes where growth and redistributive policies can mutually strengthen their legitimacy.

Financing social policies in low-income countries: The constraints stemming from the tax structure

The financing of social policies in low-income countries faces a series of constraints, in particular those arising from the nature of taxation as both an economic and a political institution, as well as from the structure of taxation, that is, the dependence on the exports of a handful of primary products and the reliance of taxation on external trade and natural resources, which therefore have a low value-added and exhibit high price volatility. These constraints are compounded by the existence of large informal sectors, which are both a cause and a consequence of the fragile credibility of states and narrowness of tax bases.

Taxation as an intrinsic dimension of the state

Taxation may be defined according to its functions: raising revenue to finance public goods and services, and redistributing income, with other additional objectives, such as correcting externalities or stabilizing the economy. The concept of fiscal policy includes both sides of the budget: tax or revenues, and public spending (Kaplow 2006; Tanzi 2004a). Taxation cannot be dissociated from the existence of a state; it is the mechanism that allows a state to exist and persist, and it has an intrinsic extractive dimension (Tilly 1990). As famously coined by Olson (1993), rulers have two alternative options – predation and taxation – which depend upon their time horizon. The 'roving bandits' have a short frame and the 'stationary bandits' a long one. The incentives for autocrats to build institutions stem from their interest in future tax collections and national income, which increases with their time frame and time in power.

Modes of taxation cannot be precisely dissociated from political institutions. In Europe they have been part of the emergence of European democracies since medieval times, as outcomes of a political equilibrium between kings and parliaments. The relationship between kings and the other social groups was based on the provision to the aristocracy of services in return for property rights in land and people and the provision by the aristocrats to the peasants of a protection of property rights in return for taxes and labour services (Sussman 2006). Taxation shapes the relationship between the state and its citizens, involving the credibility of commitments, reciprocity and trust. Otherwise, citizens may respond with exit strategies, as often occurs in developing countries.

As is well known, there is a relationship between the level of development and the tax ratio (taxation/gross domestic product [GDP]) – the so-called 'Wagner law' (Tanzi and Schuknecht 2000). Democracy has been a key determinant in the formation of modern welfare states. The rise of social spending, which represented over 30 per cent of GDP in the Nordic countries in 2000, had a positive effect on growth because welfare states used a set of taxes that minimized distortions (for example, by favouring savings and health, which fostered productivity). This was made possible by the checks and balances that democracy could achieve vis-à-vis social spending (Lindert 2004; Piketty 2005).

As defined in the World Bank World Development Indicators, government revenue includes not only taxes, but also social contributions (social security), grants and other revenue, while government expenditures include the compensation of employees, interest and subsidies, and grants and social benefits. In developing countries, in contrast with developed ones, revenue is mostly made up of taxes. Social contributions represent a small percentage of revenue (for example, in South Africa, 2 per cent of total revenue in 2003, versus 40 per cent in the United States or Sweden, or 42 per cent in France).

The tax ratio varies widely in low-income countries, from 7 to 10 per cent in Bangladesh and Rwanda to 30 per cent in Guyana. In the past decade it rose by only 0.5 per cent in low-income countries, to around 15 per cent (IMF 2005a). During the period 1980–96, it was also 15 per cent on average in sub-Saharan Africa, of which tax on income, profit and capital gains represented 4.06 per cent, domestic taxes on goods and services represented 4.61 per cent, and taxes on international trade 5.44 per cent (Agbeyegbe et al. 2004). For Gupta et al. (2005), tax revenues in sub-Saharan Africa represented 16.3 per cent of GDP in the early 1990s and 15.9 per cent in the early 2000s.

The traps created by commodity dependence and informality

Most low-income countries, especially in sub-Saharan Africa, have never escaped the model of the 'small open colonial economy' (Hopkins 1973), which is based on importing manufactures from the colonizing country while exporting primary commodities. Despite the reforms they have implemented since the 1980s under the pressure of the international financial institutions (IFIs), sub-Saharan African countries remain caught in this export structure and have not diversified their exports. Sub-Saharan African exports still consist mainly of fuels (38 per cent of total exports in 2004), ores and metals (10 per cent of total exports in 2004) and agricultural raw materials (5 per cent in 2004).[2] According to the United Nations Conference on Trade and Development (UNCTAD), the share of non-petroleum primary commodities has even increased during the 1980s and 1990s (26.6 per cent in 1997 versus 19.7 per cent in 1980[3]). These products are furthermore very limited in number. A case in point is Senegal, which at the beginning of the twentieth century produced 141,000 tons of groundnuts: in 1929 the latter represented 68 per cent of its exports, in 1960, 80 per cent and at the end of the twentieth century is still Senegal's principal export (Freud 1988).

Because of this dependence on commodity exports, many low-income countries experienced deterioration in their terms of trade. If fixed at 100 in 1990, the price index of agricultural commodities was 208 in 1960 and 90 in 2000 (99 in 2004).[4] Above all, commodity prices have been characterized more by high volatility (with petroleum prices being an obvious example) than by a decline, which is a matter of debate. As emphasized in numerous UNCTAD studies, the lack of diversification and the resilience of the commodity export model express the path dependence which entraps many low-income countries even if prices increase, as is the case since the late 1990s owing to demand from China and other emerging countries.

Commodity dependence has been analysed not only from the perspective of the terms of trade, price volatility and the Prebisch–Singer theses, or that of the Dutch disease, but also from the perspective of the 'resource curse', popularized by Sachs and Warner (2001). A large literature now identifies the negative effects of this 'curse' not only on growth but also on other variables, for example, on political stability and institutional consolidation. The resource becomes the main source of revenue and tends to crowd out other types of taxation – as in oil-producing countries. As emphasized by Auty (2001), Asian developmental states became developmental precisely because they had no natural resources. For Auty, commodity dependence is likely to lead to kleptocracy and predation when a country does not have strong institutions that can channel the resources equitably and prevent competition over these resources. Indeed, some countries that had such institutions have triggered a virtuous path to growth from natural resources, for example, the Scandinavian countries.

In addition, most developing countries are characterized by important 'informal' sectors, which are both a cause and an effect of difficulties in tax collection and contribute to the low levels of revenue. Large informal sectors typically generate a taxation trap (weak states, limited public goods, poverty). In some countries informal activities represent the majority – for instance, 93 per cent of non-agricultural employment in Benin was informal (ILO 2003). Informal employment represent between one-half and three-quarters of non-agricultural employment in developing countries (72 per cent in sub-Saharan Africa), with higher figures if informal employment in agriculture is included. The informal sector as a percentage of non-agricultural GDP is estimated at 41 per cent in sub-Saharan Africa (ILO 2002).

A recurrent explanation has been the excess of government regulation and bureaucratic corruption. It may also be, however, that taxation implies some degree of trust between the citizen and the state. More generally, the term of informality is often misleading. The 'informal' sector is linked to the 'formal' one through multiple links; moreover, workers in the informal sector often pay taxes (Sindzingre 2006).

Trade-based taxation and the volatility of revenues

Low-income countries are characterized by a trade-based taxation, which stems from their specific history. The richer the country, the more the extractive capacities of the state will be based on taxes on income, property and services, and on social security contributions. In the mid-1990s tariff revenue exceeded 30 per cent of the government's total tax revenue in more than 25 developing countries – and less than 2 per cent in high-income countries (Bacchetta and Jansen 2003).

As underscored by Aizenman and Jinjarak (2006), tax bases vary according to the level of development, and developing countries tend to rely on 'easy to collect' taxes (tariff, seignorage) while more developed countries shift towards 'hard to collect' taxes (value added tax, or 'VAT', and income tax). In contexts of low literacy, flexible land rights, low demographic ratios, and hence possibilities of exit options which undermined the capacity of the state to control and tax its citizens, governments have had difficulties implementing individualized taxes as, for example, on income. Governments in poor countries typically face enforcement problems. They have difficulties monitoring the taxable activities, and governments can enforce taxes only from those firms that use the financial sector. This explains why low-income countries make less use of broad-based taxes than rich countries, why they rely on tariffs and seignorage and why their revenue/GDP ratio is lower than in developed countries (Gordon and Li 2005).

Traditionally, it was generally easier to tax the import as well as the production, marketing (for example, via marketing boards and stabilization funds) and export of commodities. Marketing and stabilization boards were supposed to smooth the volatility of exports revenues: a share of earnings would be transferred to producers in the case of negative price shocks. Local political economy and other priorities, however, made it so that governments tended to keep the windfall gains and producers rarely benefited from the redistributive aspects of stabilization funds. The IFIs viewed these devices as inefficient and as opportunities for rent seeking, and their dismantling has been placed at the core of their programmes from their very beginning in the 1980s. For the World Bank the effects of price volatility may be mitigated though market instruments such as risk management, insurance and hedging.

Sub-Saharan African countries indeed rely heavily on trade taxes as a source of revenue: these taxes account for an average of a quarter of government revenue (Baunsgaard and Keen 2005), or one-third, according to other calculations (Agbeyegbe et al. 2004). Despite a declining trend, trade taxes still accounted for some 5.5 per cent of GDP on average in sub-Saharan Africa in 1995 (Ebrill et al.

1999). An obvious consequence of the reliance of revenues on external trade is revenue volatility and unpredictability. As underscored by UNCTAD (2003, quoting the IMF), sub-Saharan African exports experienced twice the volatility in terms of trade that East Asia's exports did from the 1970s until the 1990s, and about four times the volatility experienced by industrial countries. Moreover, in addition to potential Dutch disease effects, shocks appear to be asymmetrical: the gains from booms are short-lived while price declines entail high costs, which in turn exhibit a longer duration (Cashin et al. 2002). Furthermore, start–stop cycles have detrimental effects on the economy (Jones and Olken 2005). This represents a key difference in regard to revenue between commodity-dependent countries and Asian states, as Asian developmental states integrated into the world economy through export-led growth and specialization in specific sectors of manufactured goods.

There have been various attempts to solve the fiscal problems created by taxation based on volatile revenues, mechanisms of restraint such as rules-based 'cash budgets' and escrow accounts (as has been tried in some oil-exporting countries). In low-income countries the imperatives of state building and the complexities of the local political economy made these policies difficult to implement.

Such taxation systems fully benefited from the 'windfall' profits from commodity exports of the 1970s, but they incited governments to conduct expansionary fiscal policies. When price shocks hit commodity-exporting countries in the late 1970s, the fiscal deficits thus created have been a key justification for the IFIs for obliging governments to 'tie their hands' and commit to stabilization programmes (Schuknecht 1999).

The consequences on tax systems of external determinants: Liberalization reforms and foreign aid

Taxation systems and financing capacities have been subjected to further constraints, which arise from external determinants. Most low-income countries are complying with the reform programmes that are associated with IFI lending. Two key external factors impact on tax institutions and revenues: the economic reforms that are part of IFI conditionalities and international agreements, in particular trade liberalization; and foreign aid, as many low-income countries are characterized by aid dependence.

The consequences of trade liberalization

Trade liberalization, in particular tariff reduction, has been one of the key reforms recommended by the IFIs since the first stabilization and adjustment programmes that started in the early 1980s following the drop in commodity prices. Membership in the World Trade Organization (WTO) and other regional arrangements is also conditioned on measures of trade liberalization. Given the narrowness of industrial bases, export dependence on commodities and trade-based fiscal revenues, trade liberalization entails risks of further erosion of fiscal resources – directly via the drop in tariffs and indirectly via the disappearance of domestic firms that are not internationally competitive (or cannot compete with imported products that are subsidized in their country of origin). The problems created by this erosion of revenue are compounded by the fact that there may be a relationship between the size of government and trade openness, as governments need to have the capacity to address social conflicts and the political economic effects of trade openness as well as compensate losers (Rodrik 2000).

There has been a decrease in trade taxes in sub-Saharan Africa between the early 1990s and the early 2000s: from 4.9 per cent to 3.5 per cent of the GDP for the import duties, and from 1 per cent to 0.4 per cent of the GDP for export duties. In the early 1990s tax revenues in sub-Saharan Africa represented 16.3 per cent of GDP and 15.9 per cent in the early 2000s (Gupta et al. 2005). In countries eligible for the Poverty Reduction and Growth Facility (PRGF) programmes, tax revenue decreased from 15.2 per cent of GDP in the early 1990s to 14.8 per cent of GDP in the early 2000s.

The analysis of Glenday (2006) of tax revenues for 123 countries over the period 1975–2000 shows that most low-income countries have had difficulties in raising non-trade taxes in order to replace the decline in trade tax revenues resulting from trade liberalization: 101 countries experienced declines in their trade tax yields, of which 54 raised non-trade taxes to fully offset the loss in trade tax revenues, and 23 partially compensated these losses. Of 39 low-income countries, 28 suffered from trade tax yield declines, but only six fully replaced these losses and ten partially replaced the trade tax losses with non-trade taxes. Much of the loss of tax revenues ensued from cuts in tariffs as a consequence of regional trade agreements.

Aizenman and Jinjarak (2006) confirm this negative effect of trade liberalization with a sample of 86 developing and developed countries over the period 1980–99. Trade liberalization and financial integration have a positive relationship with 'hard to collect' taxes, and a negative relationship with the 'easy to collect' taxes. The revenue/GDP ratio of the 'easy to collect' taxes declined by about 20 per cent in developing countries, while the revenue/GDP ratio of the 'hard to collect' taxes increased by 9 per cent. As developing countries had a small initial base of 'hard to collect' taxes, total tax revenue/GDP dropped by 7 per cent. The high-income and middle-income countries more than compensated for the revenue decline of the 'easy to collect' taxes and increased the total tax/GDP ratio. This ratio, however, exhibited a substantial decline in low-income countries, which struggled to replace the 'easy to collect' sources of revenue with the 'hard to collect' ones.

Studies conducted within the International Monetary Fund (IMF) find mixed effects of trade liberalization on tax revenue. Using a panel of 22 countries in SSA over the period 1980–96, Agbeyegbe et al. (2004) do not find a strong link between trade liberalization and aggregate tax revenues. The revenue implications of trade liberalization are uncertain for Ebrill et al. (1999), but negative for Keen and Lighthart (2005).

The negative effects of dependence on trade taxes explain the recurrent IMF recommendations as part of most stabilization programmes that developing countries rely more on VAT, the VAT being for the IMF a more developmental and neutral tax. The adverse effects of trade liberalization indeed make tax replacement crucial. For the IMF, revenue losses may be recouped from the domestic tax system, especially through the strengthening of domestic indirect taxes, such as VAT. Some countries have recovered from other sources the revenues they have lost from trade liberalization, but it has been more the case in high- and middle-income countries (about 45–60 per cent of the lost trade tax revenue) than in low-income countries, which are those most dependent on trade tax revenues (only about 30 per cent of losses) (Baunsgaard and Keen 2005). Devising tax compensation mechanisms for trade liberalization – for example, establishing an appropriate VAT rate that would have the desired distributional effects – is indeed difficult (Del Ninno and Alderman 1999 on South Africa). A badly implemented VAT may even have worsening effects on poverty (Emini et al. 2005 on Cameroon).

The introduction of the VAT has been problematic in low-income countries and especially in sub-Saharan Africa, as the result of difficulties in the functioning of the refund and credit mechanisms (Ebrill et al. 2001; Harrison and Krelove 2005). The presence of large informal sectors, which are caused both by informational problems and deliberate underpaying, is a significant constraint. Moreover, the same transaction may include a formal as well an informal segment. For the IMF the usual instruments devised in order to tax the informal sector are indirect taxation (VAT) of the inputs that it uses, import tariff and direct presumptive taxes. Constraints on feasibility, however, remain significant. The 'flat taxes' recommended by the IMF improved compliance to a certain extent, but the results have been mixed (Keen et al. 2006).

The impact of poverty reduction programmes

The reforms that were part of the IFI programmes from the early 1980s – the stabilization (IMF) and adjustment (the World Bank) programmes – had an obvious impact on tax systems as they aimed at reducing fiscal deficits. IMF stabilization programmes had recessive aspects, as they were focused on the reduction of 'absorption'. They often led to significant cuts in expenditure, which in some cases dramatically reduced the capacity to provide elementary basic services or pay the wages of civil servants, which was compounded by the instability of the revenues from commodities exports. The IFIs supported the theory that large deficits impede growth. Studies now suggest, however, that the deficit–growth nexus may be nonlinear, and in particular the level at which deficit reduction no longer boosts growth is now subject to considerable uncertainty (Adam and Bevan 2004, 2005). The IMF recognizes that the experience with tax policy during the 1990s was mixed: revenue has been stagnant in the poorest countries and has even decreased (Keen and Simone 2004).

After 1999 these programmes were continued by the PRGF and Poverty Reduction Strategy Papers (PRSPs) programmes, which focus on poverty reduction via conditionalities prescribing the allocation of some share of expenditure to the social sectors. These conditionalities, however, still constitute constraints on the 'fiscal space' of low-income countries. The IFIs insist on the importance for growth of the composition and efficiency of public spending, which may be more important than its levels. IMF studies confirm the effectiveness of increased public expenditure on education and health care (Gupta et al. 2001, 2002).

The priority earmarking of resources by PRSPs to social sectors implies a trade-off, as these resources are not being earmarked directly for productive activities. The positive effects of social policy, however, depend not only on the volume of spending, but also on its design. These positive effects ensue both from its microeconomic impact (on human capital, health and education) and its macroeconomic impact (via the enhancing of economic, political and social stability) (Mkandawire 2004). Since the mid-1980s, sub-Saharan African countries have increased their public spending on education and health, both as a ratio of GDP and as a share of total government spending, with positive effects on growth (Pattillo et al. 2005; Baldacci et al. 2004).

The negative effects of aid dependence on tax systems

The negative effects of aid are increasingly acknowledged, both in the academic literature (for example, Easterly 2006) and within the IMF. Particularly detrimental effects of aid on taxation systems and growth stem from its volatility and unpredictability. Aid has a temporary component; it typically provides little insurance against other sources of volatility in public spending (Adam et al. 2006). In developing countries aid volatility is even larger than the fiscal volatility generated by commodity booms and busts, and adds to the latter's negative effects. The relative volatility of aid increased in the late 1990s, and the average volatility of aid is about 40 and 20 times higher, respectively, than that of revenue when expressed in per cent of GDP and constant US dollars per capita. The relative volatility of aid is the highest in the least and most aid-dependent countries, defined as having aid-to-revenue ratios of less than 25 per cent and more than 50 per cent respectively. Aid is also unpredictable; on average, aid delivery falls short of pledges by more than 40 per cent, especially for the poorest countries (Bulír and Hamann 2003, 2006).

Another negative effect is that aid can be a disincentive to tax collection: if states rely on donors for finance, 'Why bother to tax your own citizens'? (Moss and Subramanian 2005). As famously asked by Nicholas Kaldor: 'Will underdeveloped countries learn to tax?', incentives for collecting taxes might be undermined by an overreliance on external resources (Kaldor 1963, quoted by Moss and Subramanian 2005). The composition of aid may matter for assessing the likely pressures on revenue effort. The need to repay loans leads to increased domestic revenues, and grants have the opposite effect (Gupta et al. 2003). These problems may be compounded by the fungibility of aid. Aid includes loans that prescribe the allocation to social sectors. There is an ongoing debate as to whether loans or grants would be the optimal means of providing aid. Projects may in fact aggravate fiscal deficits when aid finances projects that have high social value but uncertain returns, particularly education and health, which may lead to deficits unless financing is achieved through grants (Daseking and Joshi 2005).

In contrast, there are studies that do not find this negative fiscal effect of aid, as is the case in Ghana (Osei et al. 2005). The review of the literature by McGillivray and Morrissey (2001) shows mixed and complex results. Their analysis of various fiscal response models reveals that aid may either discourage or increase tax efforts and, similarly, that it may either increase or reduce borrowing. These mixed – though often negative – results on how aid flows affect domestic revenues are confirmed by Gupta et al. (2005). The IMF warns that the scaling up of aid has a negative impact on revenue mobilization as governments may view aid as a substitute for domestic revenues.

A major issue in low-income countries is aid dependence, as this dependence exacerbates all of the problems attached to aid (volatility, fiscal disincentives), and may even create traps in the case of threshold effects. Between 1970–75 and 1991–95, aid as a share of GDP in low-income countries increased from 6 per cent to almost 15 per cent. During the same period private capital inflows (including foreign direct investment/FDI) fell from 2 to 1 per cent of GDP (Morrissey 2004). Aid dependence ratios may be much higher for particular countries. Many low-income countries' central government expenditures depend on aid for more than 50 per cent of the amount, and some countries are almost entirely dependent on aid for gross capital formation.[5]

Aid surges oblige governments to fine-tune their fiscal and monetary management. Such surges may create problems of absorption of newly available foreign exchange,[6] which must be absorbed by the economy and not generate spending[7] in excess of absorption with its inflationary effects.[8] As underscored by Bourguignon and Sundberg (2006) in the case of Ethiopia, large aid flows entail costs (for example, regarding the sector of tradable goods) rather than benefits when aid is not absorbed and if governments are not able to achieve a careful sequencing of public investment across sectors, which is facilitated by the quality of governance and institutional structures. Aid may induce 'Dutch disease' effects, with aid surges impacting on the real exchange rate and eroding competitiveness (Rajan and Subramanian 2005a, 2005b). The prospects for aid surges for sub-Saharan Africa entail genuine risks for fiscal sustainability as well as the risk of aggravating aid dependence. The scaling-up of aid makes it difficult for governments to maintain credible commitments to fiscal prudence and entails fiscal policy risks, for example, coordination with monetary policy. It therefore requires institutional changes (Heller et al. 2006).

Aid is less destabilizing for fiscal structures when it is supported by sound public institutions. Aid, however, may have a detrimental impact on these very public institutions. Aid surges affect the credibility of local institutions, especially political institutions, as aid dependence weakens the credibility of governments and their policies, and therefore weakens political institutions and their legitimacy. Since policies are evaluated by these donors, government policies are perceived as having been decided outside the country, and governments are perceived as being accountable towards donors and not towards domestic parliaments and constituencies. Aid dependence transforms the relationship between the state and its citizens: if governments raise their revenues from aid, they become more accountable to donors than to their own citizens. Governments in turn are not pressed to strengthen their legitimacy or to devise credible policies and effective institutions (Moss et al. 2006). This feature is a key difference with Asian developmental states, where growth has been a common interest between governments and segments of the society.

Social policies in low-income countries

This series of constraints regarding financing obviously have a deep impact on the feasibility and developmental capacity of social policies that low-income countries can implement, as highlighted by Mkandawire (2001). An additional constraint is that in most low-income countries social protection is not only achieved by domestic agents, such as government (via social policies) or individuals (via 'informal' protection devices), but is also implemented by external entities, via foreign aid. In the later case, they take the form of targeted projects rather than universal social policies.

The inequality, growth and social policy nexus

Social protection may be achieved by public programmes supported by public spending, 'tax expenditures' (or targeted provisions of the tax system) and regulation (Tanzi 2004b). Redistributive policies entail a cost; this is why the literature traditionally argues that there is a trade-off between equity and efficiency. One question that has long been debated in development economics is whether spending in developing countries is efficient, in the context of tight budget constraints and consequently tight trade-offs, as the allocation of public resources to social spending may reduce what is allocated to other determinants of growth (for example, to investment). In economic theory inequality has long been considered to have a positive effect on growth (for example, Kaldor 1961). Several studies later cast doubt on this relationship. They showed that inequality may be harmful for growth (reviewed in World Bank 2006b; UNRISD 2005) and that a low level of inequality is associated with more growth (Alesina and La Ferrara 1999). The channels through which this positive association is made possible include a greater degree of access to credit and education, a higher participation of individuals in the activities of the society and a low degree of polarization or social fragmentation.

A key theoretical debate refers to the capacity of growth to be sufficient to reduce poverty, which would make social policies secondary vis-à-vis the objective of growth. There is now a consensus that, for a given country, the relationship is mediated by the profile of the distribution, and that the poor receive lesser benefits from growth in the presence of high inequality. This growth–poverty–inequality nexus shows that the traditional trade-off between equity and efficiency should no longer constrain social policies (Bourguignon 2002, 2003; Nissanke and Thorbecke 2006).

Public social policies therefore play a crucial role in regard to the impact of growth on poverty, as they have the capacity to level inequality. Market forces in themselves may not reduce levels of absolute poverty or inequality and this market failure justifies state intervention and redistributive policies. It is indeed the social protection policies that were implemented in Europe, in contrast with the United States, which allowed European countries to achieve lower levels of inequality than occurred in the United States, although they remain criticized across the Atlantic (Alesina et al. 2001). Key channels of causality are the impact of growth on the evolution of the distribution and the categories of the population that capture a share of growth, not to mention the size of this share. Certain groups, for example, earners of non-farm income in rural settings, benefit more from growth than others (Ravallion and Datt 2002 on India). Some IMF studies also found an elasticity of poverty to growth that is less than one (Tsangarides et al. 2002).

The political economy dimensions of social and redistributive policies

Redistribution by the state is justified as poverty and poverty traps may be perpetuated by typical market failures stemming from local political economy. In particular, it is more difficult for the poor to form coalitions than it is for the rich, who are more able to form interest groups (Bowles 2006). An attribute such as poverty does not build a group, and the poor have heterogeneous preferences.

Developing countries may be characterized by processes of state formation that are less consolidated than centuries-old Western democracies, which makes the issues of state existence and credibility more central than in these democracies. The capacity to achieve redistributive functions is essential, as it is a foundation of state credibility. The credibility of states and their political legitimacy are strongly tied to taxes, their levels, the sectors subject to taxation and the pattern of redistribution. Redistribution reduces inequalities, consolidates the middle classes and prevents social conflict. Social policies and the reduction of inequalities enhanced the credibility of welfare states in developed countries, especially in Europe, such as in France and Great Britain (Atkinson 1999). A recurrent feature in low-income countries, however, is the low level of social protection provided by the state, usually limited to the formal sector. The 'taxation trap' therefore has a devastating effect, with the lack of credibility resulting in a low taxation level and weak redistributive capacity.

Highly polarized societies seem to induce a biased allocation of budgets and lower growth (Alesina et al. 1999), and social fragmentation may bias social spending. In developing countries this fractionalization is often analysed through the prism of 'ethnicity': a high level of ethnic diversity is associated in many studies with low levels of public goods provision, as it hinders collective action and makes free riding easier (Alesina et al. 2003; Habyarimana et al. 2006). As underscored by Fearon and Laitin (2003), however, 'ethnicity' is a loose concept: civil wars and conflicts are not correlated with ethnicity but rather with the level of development. Polarization appears to be one of the reasons behind the historical absence of developmental states in Latin American countries, which are affected by a high level of inequality and where oligarchies have tended to prevent social mobility and access to education (Bourguignon and Verdier 2000).

In sub-Saharan Africa a number of governments are characterized by personal rule and their legitimacy is linked to their capacity to redistribute, whereby redistributive policies are entrusted to a group of clients. Their choices in terms of allocation of resources do not reinforce the credibility of the state as a provider of public goods. For example, in 2003 public expenditure on health represented 2.4 per cent of GDP (compared with 6.7 per cent of GDP in high-income countries[9]) and public expenditure on education 3.3 per cent of GDP in the period 2002–03 (compared with 5.5 per cent in high-income countries[10]). The technocrats who entered into politics following the wave of democratization in the 1990s were confronted with the challenge of reduced redistributive capacities due to IFI conditionalities and the frequent earmarking of spending, while expectations of redistribution remained the main motive of the choice of voters (Wantchekon 2003 on Benin). This has generated political vicious circles, in which clientelism maintained itself under the institutional form of democracy.

The consequence of aid dependence on social policies: The role of donors

Public social policies are usually justified by economic theory because of pervasive market failure and information problems; they also have an intrinsic and instrumental value (Mkandawire 2004). They are even more necessary in low-income countries, where the majority of people are close to the subsistence level and more vulnerable to shocks (climatic, epidemic and the like) (Dercon 2002). When shocks are collective, 'informal' mechanisms, traditional risk pooling and insurance are inefficient. Moreover, the strategies of individuals for coping with them may have long-term costly effects: individuals indeed often reduce their investment in human capital (Chetty and Looney 2006 on Indonesia).

In low-income countries, public social policies and expenditure have difficulty achieving universal coverage. The question is how to implement them in those countries that are commodity-dependent and exhibit volatile revenues and low tax ratios. Dualistic structures that are typical of low-income countries may also necessitate the building of distinct social protection systems for rural and urban areas, as Hussain (1994) noticed in the case of China. Social protection is also constrained by the age structure, which in low-income countries is characterized by a greater number of young people but retirement schemes that are reserved for very narrow categories of the population (usually the formal sector, with the exception of South Africa).

A series of studies, typically elaborated within the IFIs, has viewed public social policies in developing countries as inefficient, costly for budgets, unable to reach the appropriate targeted groups, affected by leakages and absenteeism and with subsidies said to benefit the richest deciles.[11] Corruption is an additional factor of inefficiency of public redistribution.[12]

Against these arguments, however, it may be shown that liberalization, and leaving social insurance to the private sector, entail several detrimental effects in terms of equity and the exclusion of the poorest segments of the population, and still more in low-income countries, which are affected by high transaction and information costs. As shown by the case of China, but applying to most low-income countries, the shift to a market-based health care sector and private insurance generated inequity and exclusion of the poor. The majority of the population is not insured, health care is unaffordable and the incentives structure leads the medical personnel to care more for the wealthiest (Van Dalen 2006). Poverty also prevents access to profit-based private entities, as revealed by the recurrent failure of policies of cost recovery and transmitting costs to consumers (Cook and White 2001).

These debates on social spending cannot be dissociated from those on the role of the state. After the Second World War, state intervention was seen as necessary for correcting market and coordination failures and reallocating factors in order to trigger the catching-up process. In the 1970s, development economics, backed by the IFIs, viewed the state as the 'problem' and no longer the 'solution'. During the period of structural adjustment the IFIs considered universal redistributive public policies to benefit the supposedly privileged urban populations more than the poor. Given that budgets were limited, the IFIs thus justified the targeting of safety nets (for example, through public works programmes or food subsidies) to identified categories, the 'losers' of the reforms or the vulnerable groups. IFIs therefore dismissed the possibility of a universal system of social security. The state has been rehabilitated in the 1990s, although its role remains restricted to the provision of public goods, for example, macroeconomic stability, regulation and infrastructure (Stiglitz 1997). Within the IFIs, with the rise of the paradigm of poverty reduction in the late 1990s, the issue of access by the poor to social services has become an instrument of growth strategies that are based on 'inclusion'. The state has a 'responsibility' to secure the effective provision of public services like health, education, water and electricity, among others.

The IFIs view social protection since the late 1990s as a mix of market and state intervention, which often take the form of transfer programmes, such as 'social funds' or 'social safety nets', which are either permanent or temporary. These programmes are usually targeted at specific categories of individuals: the poorest decile, the population of a particular region, particular individuals within households such as the children or the elderly, or those deemed less able to work on account of age, household structure or disability. This process has been described as an 'ability-based taxation' (Kaplow 2006). These transfer programmes exhibit various forms: targeted subsidies and cash transfers, which may be unconditional (household, child and family allowances), social pensions (for older or disabled people) or conditional (cash for work, cash for human development); they also include fee waivers for health and education, near-cash transfers, food-based transfers input grants or community funds (Barrientos and Smith 2005). For the IFIs, targeted transfers may be efficient (Ravallion 2003).

The measurement of the effectiveness of targeting, however, remains a delicate task and the efficiency of targeted projects is often uncertain, for example, in regard to chronic poverty (Kakwani and Son 2006; Barrientos et al. 2005). A key point is that these projects are often driven and financed by aid. In this case, donors bypass existing public institutions, thus maintaining a minimal role for the state, but in a vicious circle preventing it from achieving learning processes and improving its capacity. This contributes to the negative effects of dependence on external assistance and the substitution of aid to state core functions. Many functions of redistribution, provision of social security and redressing market failures that are assigned to the state in developed countries are transferred to projects and private entities. Donor social assistance and projects, moreover, are exposed to the well-known problems affecting aid. As underscored by Mkandawire (2006), targeting should not be opposed to universal protection, and targeted projects and transfers should be steps towards general social security.

'Informal' social protection: An ambiguous efficiency

In developing countries individuals often rely on non-state social protection, 'traditional' institutions, and insurance devices, which allow for the mitigating and pooling of risks. In the absence of social protection provided by a third party – the state – individuals provide this protection via the social norms that govern exchanges. In sub-Saharan Africa, in contexts where social security is often very limited (for example, to employees in the formal sector), the possession of a stock of 'claims' on other individuals is an insurance against risks (sickness, unemployment), in environments marked by uncertainty (Berry 1993). Local norms institute mechanisms whereby group members are included in circuits of mutual rights and obligations, exchanging time, goods and money. Norms of redistribution may be asymmetric or be delayed to future generations. Individuals insure themselves against risks by investing in these circuits, creating debts and hoping for a return, although this anticipation is itself risky.

Membership groups relying on various criteria (for example, kinship, territory or occupation) provide social insurance and allow the smoothing of consumption to their members not only in village settings but also in urban and 'modern' ones. These traditional devices of insurance are efficient and can correct market failures. The norms of rights and obligations that are associated with group membership reduce transaction costs, such as informational costs; they foster trust, prevent opportunistic behaviour via reputational effects and provide insurance and even quasi-credit (Fafchamps and Lund 2003; Platteau 1991). They are flexible and mitigate risks (for example, those related to climate, such as drought) and inequity in agricultural contexts (Lavigne-Delville et al. 2001).

These institutions, however, are context-dependent. The content of these institutions and their functions in fact result from the combination of these institutions with other institutions and the broader environment (Sindzingre 2007a, 2008). The same traditional institutions, when combined with different institutions and contexts, may become inefficient. The instruments for risk coverage and insurance are inefficient when provided by individuals who are vulnerable to the same collective shock. Likewise, traditional institutions may perpetuate poverty by hindering demographic transition and creating intergenerational poverty traps, as descendants provide parents with insurance for their old age. Intergenerational poverty traps transmit poverty, poor health and limited education (Dasgupta 1997). This sets in motion a vicious circle in which the state remains incapable of providing transfers and social security, with demographic growth contributing to pushing countries deeper into poverty. These traditional insurance mechanisms are moreover fragile and erode with the expansion of markets (Platteau 2002). When members migrate or even marry outside the group, they lose the benefits of these protection mechanisms. As shown by Munshi and Rosenzweig (2005) in the case of caste in India, in contexts where alternative insurance devices or credit markets are lacking, such traditional arrangements hinder social mobility.

These risk-pooling and insurance devices apply to group members and therefore exclude non-members. Sub-Saharan African societies are characterized by 'institutional discontinuities', particularly between formal state institutions and 'informal' ones. In the absence of a credible state that institutes a broader 'public' sphere via the provision of public goods, affiliations to multiple membership groups offer coordination and protection devices, but with divisive norms and social fragmentation as recurrent consequences (Nissanke and Sindzingre 2006). In a vicious circle, the multiplicity of local memberships groups weakens the state and hence its redistributive capacity, while this weakness justifies the reliance of individuals on a variety of membership groups (Sindzingre 2003). When associated with specific spatial locations, these processes are self-reinforcing: groups strengthen via shared norms but segregate from others, which induces poverty traps in particular areas (Durlauf and Young 2001).

The multiplicity of membership groups limits the application of trust and reputational effects to particular groups. Trust reduces transaction costs, and market failures (for example, in credit markets) may be corrected through network effects, but these networks by definition exclude all other individuals. Reputation helps enforce norms of reciprocal exchange and protection, but it is ineffective outside the group and in broader settings, where opportunistic behaviour is a rational option. Networks in sub-Saharan Africa are often fragmented; they are efficient within small exchange circuits, which limit the domains of transactions.[13] These constraints have been contrasted with the 'productive' dimensions of networks in Asia and their specific arrangements allowing accumulation and preventing free-riding effects.

Agrarian societies are characterized by the existence of 'interlocking contracts' that function simultaneously in the markets for labour, credit and insurance, sharecropping being a classical example, where the contract made in the product market 'locks in' the tenant in regard to other markets. Both social insurance and credit are provided by the landlords and the contract therefore becomes one that simultaneously operates in the insurance and credit markets. These markets are therefore 'missing', or are segmented, which represents a crucial market failure and an impediment to growth (Bardhan 1989). Depending on contexts and their combination with other institutions, these types of contracts have encouraged the emergence of family firms in the case of Asia, but they may become lock-in devices and keep individuals in poverty, as has happened in sub-Saharan Africa.

Lessons from the 'developmental states' for social policies in low-income countries: The key role of political economy

Important lessons may be drawn from those few states – that is, the East-Asian 'developmental' states – that experienced spectacular growth from the mid-twentieth century, even though they began with low levels of development. Their structure of taxation was based more on credible policies oriented towards growth than high levels of taxation, and their financing of social policy was based less on social spending than on 'productivist' policies, relying on a mix of public and private sources. Asian developmental states confirm that the feasibility of models of taxation and social policies cannot be dissociated from political economy mechanisms.

Developmental states versus low-income countries: Key contrasts

The concept of the developmental state has explained the growth performances of the late industrializers in East Asia (for example, Japan, the Republic of Korea and Taiwan Province of China).[14] In these countries, state intervention took the form of economic incentives, targeted taxation and subsidies, and selective protection (Knowles and Gerces-Ozanne 2003). Asian developmental states exhibit low tax ratios. The ratio of revenue to GDP (including non-tax revenues) in the low- and middle-income countries in the East Asia-Pacific region averaged 12 per cent in 1990 and 11 per cent in 2003, which is close to that recorded in low-income countries (14 and 12 per cent).[15] This ratio was 17 per cent in the Republic of Korea in 1980 and 1990, and 23 per cent in 2004.[16]

Indeed, the success of Asian developmental states did not come from owning large shares of the economy and recycling national wealth as in Western welfare states, but rather from the effective use of incentives that were conditioned on growth and export performance. In contrast with sub-Saharan Africa, they exhibited high savings rates. Developmental states were not endowed with natural resources and over the course of time managed to place limits on their reliance on foreign aid. The credibility of policies relied on a mix of flexible policies (but rigid in the short term), of authoritarianism and coalition building, where politicians and the private sector forged a common interest in growth (Sindzingre 2007b).

Asian developmental states have implemented social policies that involved non-state entities and have spent little on welfare directly.[17] In the Republic of Korea, for example, in the 1980–97 period, before the financial crisis, the average level of government spending was around 20 per cent of GDP (Boix 2001). Social policies are subordinate to objectives of growth and are based on 'productivism, selective social investment and authoritarianism' (Kwon 2005).

A key point is that policies in the Asian developmental states have been oriented towards education and equality (Bourguignon et al. 1998 on Taiwan) – except, however, gender equality and women's access to education and wages. In contrast, the illiteracy rate remains high in sub-Saharan Africa.[18] Many low-income countries are characterized by high after-tax inequality (Chu et al. 2000; Sahn and Younger 1998). Sub-Saharan African countries display high income inequality, with an average Gini coefficient of 0.52 for the region. This inequality also involves access to health and education and is compounded by the dualistic structure of labour markets and skills.

A related point is that Asian developmental states reduced inequality not through massive redistributive transfers stemming from high levels of taxation but via policies such as land reform and the promotion of primary education that redistributed assets and reallocated factors. In the Republic of Korea, high-yielding varieties were introduced in the agricultural sector, and education fostered upward mobility and consolidated middle classes (World Bank 2004a; Kim 2006). A virtuous circle could therefore be triggered, as the more inequality was reduced, the more the model of the developmental state was legitimated.

Feasibility of developmental policies in low-income countries: Shared growth as a common political interest

Economics cannot be dissociated from political economy: budget structures express as much political as economic objectives, and there is now a consensus about the endogeneity between economic institutions and political conflicts over redistribution (Acemoglu and Robinson 2006).

In many low-income countries the historical processes of state formation has induced types of rulers and local political economy that have been more predatory than developmental (Evans 1989). In contrast with the authoritarian rule and strong institutions that characterized the Asian developmental states, states in low-income countries may be analysed as being 'weak' states – in the sense that they are still more affected than other states by the commitment problem (Acemoglu 2005). That is, there is no supra-entity that provides credibility to their policies – credibility being classically defined as the ability to commit (Kydland and Prescott 1977). Policies therefore suffer from low levels of credibility and trust in the eyes of their own citizens as well as external investors. This is why the IFIs have claimed that international agreements fill this deficit in credibility, as these agreements constitute hand-binding devices (Rodrik 1995). This has been ineffective, however, as confirmed by low levels of foreign investment and high capital flight that affect sub-Saharan Africa. These political economy processes dried up available resources and were fuelled by aid in a vicious circle (Ndikumana and Boyce 2002), which further eroded the effectiveness of taxation and social policies.

Political economy plays a key role in making policies effective and developmental. In Asia, social policies were never disconnected from political economy motives, and states built up social policy institutions not only because of the international context but also for domestic political motives, that is, the objective of governments to strengthen their legitimacy (Kwon 1999 on Korea). In sub-Saharan Africa, political regimes have been often unstable, which has not incited post-colonial leaders to focus on the improvement of long-term outcomes such as better equity, education and health. In the case of predatory rulers, development – in particular that of an industrial private sector – may even have been against their interests, as it implies autonomous wealth accumulation and therefore a potential political threat.

Developmental states were built on linkages between the state and the private sector, even if these linkages have sometimes been of a collusive nature (Kang 2002a; an 'alliance capitalism', Wade 2000). These states were built on common interests towards growth as a political objective; the increase of resources would be shared and be therefore in the interests of all. In the Republic of Korea corruption could be kept under control because political and economic groups were in a 'mutual-hostage' situation (Kang 2002b). Coalescence (among state, society and generations) has characterized institutions in the developmental states, which contrasts with the economic and institutional discontinuities prevailing in sub-Saharan Africa.

This highlights the limitations to the feasibility of developmental policies in low-income countries. The specific political economy, characterized by unfavourable market structures and commodity dependence, trade reforms and aid dependence, did not help in building effective taxation systems and social policies in most low-income countries, which furthermore remain exposed to threshold effects, such as the vicious circles of taxation traps and poverty traps.

Certain lessons from developmental states do stand out, however: in particular, the effectiveness of asset redistribution in contexts of tight constraints on public spending, income taxation and income redistribution (as well as on the taxation of firms' profits); and the importance of building common political interests and incentives to growth and redistribution in contexts of weak and fragmented states and institutions.

Conclusion

The constraints that limit the financing of social policies in low-income countries have been explored here, in particular with regard to taxation systems. With a focus on sub-Saharan Africa, it has been revealed that commodity dependence and the associated price volatility, together with a trade-based tax structure, constitute key obstacles to the effectiveness of taxation systems, which therefore limit the room for manoeuvre in the case of both social expenditure and policies. This is compounded by the existence of large informal sectors, which are both a cause and an effect of the fragility of state capacity and taxation systems and may therefore generate taxation traps.

Constraints on revenues have been intensified by the reforms that were conditional to IFI lending, that is, the reducing of budget deficits and trade liberalization. Foreign aid may similarly destabilize local taxation systems as well as the credibility of public institutions, although the latter are crucial for a developmental taxation.

Social policies in low-income countries are constrained by aid dependence and the pre-eminence of targeted projects over universalism in donors' assistance. 'Informal' mechanisms of social protection and insurance may be efficient complementary devices when public policies are limited. In contexts of social fragmentation, inequality and widespread poverty, however, their impact is ambiguous.

The Asian developmental states were not affected by the detrimental effects of dependence on natural resources and on foreign aid. The lessons from their taxation systems and social policies suggest that more so than high levels of tax rates, policies and political economy matter, especially common interests in regard to policies oriented towards growth and asset redistribution.

Notes

1. This chapter is based on a longer paper presented at the UNRISD Workshop on Financing Social Policy, Geneva, 1–2 March 2007. The author thanks the participants in the

workshop, in particular Thandika Mkandawire and Katja Hujo, as well as an anonymous referee, for their very relevant comments.
2.　World Bank (2006a: table 4.4).
3.　UNCTAD (2001: table 9).
4.　World Bank (2001) and (2006a: table 6.6).
5.　This is the case of Rwanda, Malawi, or Eritrea, among others (World Bank 2007: table 6.11).
6.　Absorption is defined as the widening of the current account deficit due to incremental aid.
7.　Spending is defined as the widening of the fiscal deficit due to incremental aid.
8.　IMF (2005b); Aiyar et al. (2005); Berg et al. (2006).
9.　World Bank (2006a: table 2.14).
10.　World Bank (2005b: table 2.9).
11.　Devarajan (2006); Coady et al. (2006); Reinikka and Svensson (2004).
12.　See Olken (2006) for a discussion of a government anti-poverty programme in Indonesia.
13.　Fafchamps (1992); Platteau (1994a, 1994b); Greif (1994); Sindzingre (2002).
14.　Johnson (1982); White (1988); Wade (1990); Amsden (1989).
15.　World Bank (2005a: table 4.11; 2004b). The 2005 and 2006 World Development Indicators do not provide data regarding current revenue in sub-Saharan Africa.
16.　World Bank (2006a: table 4.10; 2004b: table 4.11; 1998: table 4.12).
17.　Goodman et al. (1998); Gough (2000); Mwabu et al. (2001).
18.　The adult literacy rate in 2002 was 65 (World Bank 2005a: table 13.14).

References

Acemoglu, Daron (2005) *Politics and Economics in Weak and Strong States* (Cambridge, MA: MIT Press).

Acemoglu, Daron and James Robinson (2006) *Economic Origins of Dictatorship and Democracy* (Cambridge: Cambridge University Press).

Adam, Christopher S. and David L. Bevan (2005) 'Fiscal deficits and growth in developing countries', *Journal of Public Economics*, Vol. 89, No. 4, 571–97.

—— (2004) 'Fiscal policy design in low-income countries.' In Tony Addison and Alan Roe (eds.), *Fiscal Policy for Development* (Basingstoke: Palgrave Macmillan).

Adam, Christopher, Stephen O'Connell, Edward Buffie and Catherine Pattillo (2006) *Monetary Policy Responses to Aid Surges in Africa*. Paper presented at the WIDER Conference on Aid: Principles, Policies and Performance, Helsinki, 16–17 June.

Agbeyegbe, Terence, Janet G. Stotsky and Asegedech Woldemariam (2004) *Trade Liberalization, Exchange Rates, and Tax Revenue in Sub-Saharan Africa*, IMF Working Paper No. WP/04/178 (Washington, DC: IMF).

Aiyar, Shekhar, Andrew Berg and Mumtaz Hussain (2005) 'The macroeconomic challenge of more aid', *Finance and Development*, Vol. 42, No. 3, 28–31.

Aizenman, Joshua and Yothin Jinjarak (2006) *Globalization and Developing Countries: A Shrinking Tax Base?* NBER Working Paper No. 11933 (Cambridge, MA: NBER).

Alesina, Alberto, Reza Baqir and William Easterly (1999) 'Public goods and ethnic divisions', *Quarterly Journal of Economics*, Vol. CXIV, No. 4, 1243–84.

Alesina, Alberto, Arnaud Devleeschauwer, William Easterly, Sergio Kurlat and Romain T. Wacziarg (2003) 'Fractionalization', *Journal of Economic Growth*. Vol. 8, 155–94.

Alesina, Alberto, Edward Glaeser and Bruce Sacerdote (2001) *Why Doesn't the United States Have a European-Style Welfare System?*, NBER Working Paper No. 8524 (Cambridge, MA: NBER).

Alesina, Alberto and Eliana La Ferrara (1999) *Participation in Heterogeneous Communities*, mimeo, Harvard University and Bocconi University, Cambridge, MA, May.

Amsden, Alice H. (1989) *Asia's Next Giant: South Korea and Late Industrialization* (New York: Oxford University Press).

Atkinson, Anthony (1999) *Is Rising Income Inequality Inevitable? A Critique of the Transatlantic Consensus*, WIDER Annual Lectures No. 3 (Helsinki: UNU-WIDER).

Auty, Richard M. (ed.) (2001) *Resource Abundance and Economic Development* (Oxford: Oxford University Press).

Bacchetta, Marc and Marion Jansen (2003) *Adjusting to Trade Liberalization: The Role of Policy, Institutions and WTO Disciplines*, WTO Special Studies No. 7 (Geneva: WTO).

Baldacci, Emanuele, Benedict Clements, Sanjeev Gupta and Qiang Cui (2004) *Social Spending, Human Capital, and Growth in Developing Countries: Implications for Achieving the MDGs*, IMF Working Paper No. WP/04/217 (Washington, DC: IMF).

Bardhan, Pranab (ed.) (1989) *The Economic Theory of Agrarian Institutions* (Oxford: Clarendon Press).

Barrientos, Armando and Roger Smith (2005) *Social Assistance in Low Income Countries Database* (London: DFID).

Barrientos, Armando, David Hulme and Andrew Shepherd (2005) 'Can social protection tackle chronic poverty?', *European Journal of Development Research*, Vol. 17, No. 1, 8–23.

Baunsgaard, Thomas and Michael Keen (2005) *Tax Revenue and (or?) Trade Liberalization*, IMF Working Paper No. WP/05/112 (Washington, DC: IMF).

Berg, Andrew, Mumtaz Hussain, Shekhar Aiyar, Shaun Roache, Tokhir Mirzoev and Amber Mahone (2006) *The Macroeconomics of Managing Increased Aid Inflows: Experiences of Low-Income Countries and Policy Implications*, paper presented at the WIDER Conference on Aid: Principles, Policies and Performance, Helsinki, 16–17 June.

Berry, Sara (1993) *No Condition is Permanent: The Social Dynamics of Agrarian Change in Sub-Saharan Africa* (Madison, WI: University of Wisconsin Press).

Boix, Carles (2001) *The Public Sector in East Asia*, paper presented at the Conference on East Asia's Future Economy, University of Chicago, World Bank, Cambridge, MA, 1–2 October.

Bourguignon, François (2003) *The Poverty–Growth–Inequality Triangle*, paper presented at the Conference on Poverty, Inequality and Growth, Agence Française de Développement/EU Development Network, Paris.

—— (2002) *The Growth Elasticity of Poverty Reduction: Explaining Heterogeneity across Countries and Time-Periods*, DELTA Working Paper 2002–03 (Paris: DELTA).

Bourguignon, François and Mark Sundberg (2006) *Absorptive Capacity and Achieving the MDGs*, WIDER Research Paper No. 2006/47 (Helsinki: UNU-WIDER).

Bourguignon, François and Thierry Verdier (2000) *Globalization and Endogenous Educational Responses: The Main Economic Transmission Channels*, OECD Development Centre, Policy Dialogue on Poverty and Inequality in Developing Countries: The Effects of Globalisation (Paris: OECD).

Bourguignon, François, Martin Fournier and Marc Gurgand (1998) *Fast Development with a Stable Income Distribution: Taiwan, 1979–1994*, mimeo (Paris: DELTA).

Bowles, Samuel (2006) 'Institutional poverty traps.' In Samuel Bowles, Steven N. Durlauf and Karla Hoff (eds.), *Poverty Traps* (Princeton: Princeton University Press).

Bulír, Aleš and A. Javier Hamann (2006) *Volatility of Development Aid: From the Frying Pan into the Fire?*, IMF Working Paper No. WP/06/65 (Washington, DC: IMF).

—— (2003) 'Aid volatility: An empirical assessment', *IMF Staff Papers*, Vol. 50, No. 1, 64–89.

Cashin, Paul, C. John McDermott and Alasdair Scott (2002), 'Booms and slumps in world commodity prices', *Journal of Development Economics*, Vol. 69, No. 1, 277–96.

Chetty, Raj and Adam Looney (2006) 'Income risk and the benefits of social insurance: Evidence from Indonesia and the United States.' In Takatoshi Ito and Andrew Rose (eds.), *Fiscal Policy and Management: East Asia Seminar on Economics 16* (Chicago, IL: University of Chicago Press).

Chu, Ke-young, Hamid Davoodi and Sanjeev Gupta (2000) *Income Distribution and Tax and Government Social Spending Policies in Developing Countries*, IMF Working Paper No. WP/00/62 (Washington, DC: IMF).

Coady, David, Moataz El-Said, Robert Gillingham, Kangni Kpodar, Paulo Medas and David Newhouse (2006) *The Magnitude and Distribution of Fuel Subsidies: Evidence from Bolivia,*

Ghana, Jordan, Mali, and Sri Lanka, IMF Working Paper No. WP/06/247 (Washington DC: IMF).

Cook, Sarah and Gordon White (2001) 'New approaches to welfare provision: New institutional economics, politics and political economy.' In Germano Mwabu, Cecilia Ugaz and Gordon White (eds.), *New Models of Provision and Financing of Public Goods* (Oxford: Clarendon Press/UNU-WIDER).

Daseking, Christina and Bikas Joshi (2005) *Debt and New Financing in Low-Income Countries* (Washington, DC: IMF).

Dasgupta, Partha (1997) 'Nutritional status, the capacity for work, and poverty traps', *Journal of Econometrics*, Vol. 77, 5–37.

Del Ninno, C. and Harold Alderman (1999) 'Poverty issues for zero rating VAT in South Africa', *Journal of African Economies*, Vol. 8, No. 2 (July) 182–208.

Dercon, Stefan (2002) *Income Risk, Coping Strategies and Safety Nets*, WIDER Discussion Paper No. DP2002/22 (Helsinki: UNU-WIDER).

Devarajan, Shanta (2006) *Analyzing the Impact of Fiscal Policy on Poverty: Seven Stories*, South Asia Region (Washington, DC: World Bank).

Durlauf, Steven N. and Henry Peyton Young (2001) 'The new social economics.' In Steven N. Durlauf and Henry Peyton Young (eds.), *Social Dynamics* (Cambridge, MA: MIT Press).

Easterly, William (2006) *The White Man's Burden: Why the West's Efforts to Aid the Rest Have Done So Much Ill and So Little Good* (New York: Penguin Press).

Ebrill, Liam, Michael Keen, Jean-Paul Bodin and Victoria Summers (2001) *The Modern VAT* (Washington, DC: IMF).

Ebrill, Liam, Janet Stotsky and Reint Gropp (1999) *Revenue Implications of Trade Liberalization*, IMF Occasional Paper No. 180 (Washington, DC: IMF).

Emini, Christian Arnault, John Cockburn and Bernard Decaluwe (2005) *The Poverty Impacts of the Doha Round in Cameroon: The Role of Tax Policy*, Policy Research Working Paper No. 3746 (Washington, DC: World Bank).

Evans, Peter (1989) 'Predatory, developmental and other apparatuses: A comparative political economy perspective on the third world state.' *Sociological Forum*, Vol. 4, No. 4, 561–87.

Fafchamps, Marcel (1992) 'Solidarity networks in preindustrial societies: Rational peasants with a moral economy', *Economic Development and Cultural Change*, Vol. 41, No. 1, 147–74.

Fafchamps, Marcel and Susan Lund (2003) 'Risk-sharing networks in rural Philippines', *Journal of Development Economics*, Vol. 71, No. 2, 261–87.

Fearon, James D. and David D. Laitin (2003) 'Ethnicity, insurgency, and civil war', *American Political Science Review*, Vol. 97, No. 1, 75–90.

Freud, Claude (1988) *Quelle coopération? Un bilan de l'aide au développement* (Paris: Karthala).

Glenday, Graham (2006) *Towards Fiscally Feasible and Efficient Trade Liberalization* (Washington, DC: USAID).

Goodman, Roger, Gordon White and Huck-ju Kwon (eds.) (1998) *The East Asian Welfare Model: Welfare Orientalism and the State* (London: Routledge).

Gordon, Roger and Wei Li (2005) *Tax Structure in Developing Countries: Many Puzzles and a Possible Explanation*, NBER Working Paper No. 11267 (Cambridge, MA: NBER).

Gough, Ian (2000) *Welfare Regimes in East Asia and Europe: Comparisons and Lessons*, mimeo, workshop ABCDE-Europe 2000 on Towards the New Social Policy Agenda in East Asia, Paris, 26 June.

Greif, Avner (1994) 'Cultural beliefs and the organization of society: A historical and theoretical reflection on collectivist and individualist societies', *Journal of Political Economy*, Vol. 102, 912–50.

Gupta, Sanjeev, Marijn Verhoeven and Erwin H. Tiongson (2002) 'The effectiveness of government spending on education and health care in developing and transition economies', *European Journal of Political Economy*, Vol. 18, No. 4, 717–37. Also in Sanjeev Gupta, Benedict Clements and Gabriela Inchauste (eds.) (2004) op. cit.

—— (2001) *Public Spending on Health Care and the Poor*, IMF Working Paper No. WP/01/127 (Washington, DC: IMF). Also in Sanjeev Gupta, Benedict Clements and Gabriela Inchauste (eds.) (2004) *Helping Countries Develop: The Role of Fiscal Policy* (Washington, DC: IMF).

Gupta, Sanjeev, Robert Powell and Yongzheng Yang (2005) *The Macroeconomic Challenges of Scaling Up Aid to Africa*, IMF Working Paper No. WP/05/179 (Washington, DC: IMF).

Gupta, Sanjeev, Benedict Clemens, Alexander Pivovarsky and Erwin R. Tiongson (2003) *Foreign Aid and Revenue Response: Does the Composition of Aid Matter?*, IMF Working Paper No. WP/03/176 (Washington, DC: IMF). Also in Sanjeev Gupta, Benedict Clements, and Gabriela Inchauste (eds.) (2004) op. cit.

Habyarimana, James, Macartan Humphreys, Daniel N. Posner and Jeremy Weinstein (2006) *Why Does Ethnic Diversity Undermine Public Goods Provision? An Experimental Approach*, IZA Discussion Paper No. 2272 (Bonn: Institute for the Study of Labour).

Harrison, Graham and Russell Krelove (2005) *VAT Refunds: A Review of Country Experience*, IMF Working Paper No. WP/05/218 (Washington, DC: IMF).

Heller, Peter S., Menachem Katz, Xavier Debrun, Theo Thomas, Taline Koranchelian and Isabell Adenauer (2006) *Making Fiscal Space Happen! Managing Fiscal Policy in a World of Scaled-Up Aid*, WIDER Research Paper No. 2006/125 (Helsinki: UNU-WIDER).

Hopkins, A.G. (1973) *An Economic History of West Africa* (London: Longman).

Hussain, Athar (1994) 'Social security in present-day China and its reform', *American Economic Review*, Vol. 84, No. 2, 276–80.

ILO (International Labour Organization) (2003) *Global Employment Trends* (Geneva: ILO).

—— (2002) *Women and Men in the Informal Economy: a Statistical Picture* (Geneva: ILO).

IMF (International Monetary Fund) (2005a) *Monetary and Fiscal Policy Design Issues in Low-Income Countries* (Washington, DC: IMF Policy Development and Review Department, and the Fiscal Affairs Department).

—— (2005b) *The Macroeconomics of Managing Increased Aid Inflows: Experiences of Low-Income Countries and Policy Implications* (Washington, DC: IMF).

Johnson, Chalmers (1982) *MITI and the Japanese Miracle* (Stanford: Stanford University Press).

Jones, Benjamin A. and Benjamin A. Olken (2005) *The Anatomy of Start–Stop Growth*, NBER Working Paper No. 11528 (Cambridge, MA: NBER).

Kakwani, Nanak and Hyun H. Son (2006) *Evaluating Targeting Efficiency of Government Programmes: International Comparisons*, WIDER Research Paper No. 2006/55 (Helsinki: UNU-WIDER).

Kaldor, Nicholas (1963) 'Will underdeveloped countries learn to tax?', *Foreign Affairs*, Vol. 41, 410–19.

—— (1961) 'Capital accumulation and economic growth.' In Friedrich August Lutz and Douglas C. Hague (eds.), *The Theory of Capital* (New York: St. Martin's Press).

Kang, David C. (2002a) *Crony Capitalism: Corruption and Development in South Korea and the Philippines* (Cambridge: Cambridge University Press).

—— (2002b) 'Bad loans to good friends: Money politics and the developmental state in South Korea', *International Organization*, Vol. 56, No. 1, 177–207.

Kaplow, Louis (2006) *Taxation*, NBER Working Paper No. 12061 (Cambridge, MA: NBER).

Keen, Michael and Jenny E. Lighthart (2005) 'Coordinating tariff reduction and domestic tax reform under imperfect competition', *Review of International Economics*, Vol. 13, No. 2, 385–90.

Keen, Michael and Alejandro Simone (2004) 'Tax policy in developing countries: Some lessons from the 1990s, and some challenges ahead.' In Sanjeev Gupta, Benedict Clements and Gabriela Inchauste (eds.), *Helping Countries Develop: The Role of the Fiscal Policy* (Washington, DC: IMF).

Keen, Michael, Yi Tae Kim and Recard Varsano (2006) *The 'Flat Tax(es)': Principles and Evidence*, IMF Working Paper No. WP/06/218 (Washington, DC: IMF).

Kim, Ji-Hong (2006) *Korean Experience and African Economic Development*, paper presented at the African Development Bank Economic Conference Accelerating Africa's Development – Five Years into the Twenty-First Century, Tunis, 22–4 November.

Knowles, Stephen and Arlene Garces-Ozanne (2003) 'Government intervention and economic performance in East Asia', *Economic Development and Cultural Change*, Vol. 51, No. 2, 451–77.

Kwon, Huck-ju (2005) 'Transforming the developmental welfare state in East Asia', *Development and Change*, Vol. 36, No. 3, 477–97.

—— (1999) *The Welfare State in Korea: The Politics of Legitimation* (London: Macmillan).

Kydland, Finn and Edward Prescott (1977) 'Rules rather than discretion: The inconsistency of optimal plans', *Journal of Political Economy*, Vol. 85, No. 3, 473–91.

Lavigne-Delville, Philippe, Camilla Toulmin, Jean-Philippe Colin and Jean-Pierre Chauveau (2001) *Securing Secondary Rights to Land in West Africa* (London: IIED).

Lindert, Peter H. (2004) *Growing Public. Volume 1: The Story: Social Spending and Economic Growth Since the Eighteenth Century* (Cambridge: Cambridge University Press).

McGillivray, Mark and Oliver Morrissey (2001) *A Review of Evidence on the Fiscal Effects of Aid*, CREDIT Research Paper No. 01/13 (Nottingham: University of Nottingham).

Mkandawire, Thandika (2006) 'Targeting vs. universal protection', *Poverty in Focus (Special Issue: Social Protection: The Role of Cash Transfers)* (Brasilia: International Poverty Centre, UNDP).

—— (2004) 'Social policy in a development context: Introduction.' In Thandika Mkandawire (ed.), *Social Policy in a Development Context* (Basingstoke: UNRISD/Palgrave Macmillan).

—— (2001) *Social Policy in a Development Context*, Programme on Social Policy and Development, Paper No. 7 (Geneva: UNRISD).

Morrissey, Oliver (2004) 'Conditionality and aid effectiveness re-evaluated', *World Economy*, Vol. 27, No. 2, 153–71.

Moss, Todd and Arvind Subramanian (2005) *After the Big Push: The Fiscal Implications of Large Aid Increases*, Working Paper No. 71 (Washington, DC: Center for Global Development).

Moss, Todd, Gunilla Pettersson and Nicolas van de Walle (2006) *A Review Essay on Aid Dependency and State Building in Sub-Saharan Africa: An Aid-Institution's Paradox?*, Working Paper No. 74 (Washington, DC: Center for Global Development).

Munshi, Kaivan and Mark Rosenzweig (2005) *Why is Mobility in India so Low? Social Insurance, Inequality and Growth*, CID Working Paper No. 121 (Cambridge, MA: Harvard University).

Mwabu, Germano, Cecilia Ugaz and Gordon White (eds.) (2001) *Social Provision in Low-Income Countries: New Patterns and Emerging Trends* (Oxford: Oxford University Press and UNU-WIDER).

Ndikumana, Leonce and James K. Boyce (2002) *Public Debts and Private Assets: Explaining Capital Flight from Sub-Saharan Countries*, PERI Working Paper No. 32 (Amherst, MA: University of Massachusetts Amherst).

Nissanke, Machiko and Alice Sindzingre (2006) 'Institutional foundations for shared growth in sub-Saharan Africa', *African Development Review*, Vol. 18, No. 3, 353–91.

Nissanke, Machiko and Erik Thorbecke (2006) 'Channels and policy debate in the globalization-inequality-poverty nexus.' In Machiko Nissanke and Erik Thorbecke (eds.), *The Impact of Globalization on the World's Poor: Transmission Mechanisms*, UN-WIDER Discussing Paper No. 2005/08 (Helsinki: UNU-WIDER; and Basingstoke: Palgrave Macmillan).

Olken, Benjamin A. (2006) 'Corruption and the costs of redistribution: Micro evidence from Indonesia', *Journal of Public Economics*, Vol. 90, Nos. 4–5, 853–70.

Olson, Mancur (1993) 'Dictatorship, democracy and development', *American Political Science Review*, Vol. 87, No. 3, 567–76.

Osei, Robert, Oliver Morrissey and Tim Lloyd (2005) *The Fiscal Effects of Aid in Ghana*, WIDER Research Paper No. 2005/61 (Helsinki: UNU-WIDER).

Pattillo, Catherine, Sanjeev Gupta and Kevin Carey (2005) *Sustaining Growth Accelerations and Pro-Poor Growth in Africa*, IMF Working Paper No. WP/05/195 (Washington, DC: IMF).

Piketty, Thomas (2005) 'Taxation with representation', *Science*, Vol. 310, No. 5756, 1906–7.

Platteau, Jean-Philippe (2002) *The Gradual Erosion of the Social Security Function of Customary Land Tenure Arrangements in Lineage-Based Societies*, WIDER Discussion Paper No. DP/2002/26 (Helsinki: UNU-WIDER).

—— (1994a) 'Behind the market stage where real societies exist. Part 1: The role of public and private order institutions', *Journal of Development Studies*, Vol. 30, No. 3, 533–77.

—— (1994b) 'Behind the market stage where real societies exist. Part 2: The role of moral norms', *Journal of Development Studies*, Vol. 30, No. 4, 753–817.

—— (1991) 'Traditional systems of social security and hunger insurance: Past achievements and modern challenges.' In Ehtisham Ahmad, Jean Drèze, John Hills and Amartya Sen (eds.), *Social Security in Developing Countries* (Oxford: Clarendon Press).

Rajan, Raghuram G. and Arvind Subramanian (2005a) *What Undermines Aid's Impact on Growth?*, IMF Working Paper No. WP/05/126 (Washington, DC: IMF).

—— (2005b) *Aid and Growth: What Does the Cross-Country Evidence Really Show?*, IMF Working Paper No. WP/05/127 (Washington, DC: IMF).

Ravallion, Martin (2003) *Targeted Transfers in Poor Countries: Revisiting the Tradeoffs and Policy Options*, Policy Research Working Paper No. 3048 (Washington, DC: World Bank).

Ravallion, Martin and Gaurav Datt (2002) 'Why has economic growth been more pro-poor in some states of India than others?', *Journal of Development Economics*, Vol. 68, No. 2, 381–400.

Reinikka, Ritva and Jakob Svensson (2004) 'Local capture: Evidence from a central government transfer program in Uganda', *Quarterly Journal of Economics*, Vol. 119, No. 2, 678–704.

Rodrik, Dani (2000) 'Why do more open economies have bigger governments?', *Journal of Political Economy*, Vol. 106, No. 5, 997–1032.

—— (1995) 'Why is there multilateral lending?' In Michael Bruno and Boris Pleskovic (eds.), *Annual World Bank Conference on Development Economics* (Washington, DC: World Bank).

Sachs, Jeffrey D. and Andrew M. Warner (2001) 'The curse of natural resources', *European Economic Review*, Vol. 45, Nos. 4–6, 827–38.

Sahn, David E. and Stephen D. Younger (1998) *Fiscal Incidence in Africa: Microeconomic Evidence*, AERC Paper No. CR-2-5 (Nairobi: African Economic Research Consortium).

Schuknecht, Ludger (1999) 'Tying governments' hands in commodity taxation', *Journal of African Economies*, Vol. 8, No. 2, 152–81.

Sindzingre, Alice (2008) 'The multidimensionality of poverty: An institutionalist perspective.' In Nanak Kakwani and Jacques Silber (eds.), *The Many Dimensions of Poverty* (London: Palgrave Macmillan).

—— (2007a) 'Explaining threshold effects of globalisation on poverty: An institutional perspective.' In Machiko Nissanke and Erik Thorbecke (eds.), *The Impact of Globalization on the World's Poor: Transmission Mechanisms* (London: Palgrave Macmillan).

—— (2007b) 'Financing the developmental state: Tax and revenue issues', *Development Policy Review*, Vol. 25, No. 5, 615–32.

—— (2006) 'The relevance of the concepts of formality and informality: A theoretical appraisal.' In Basudeb Guha-Khasnobis, Ravi Kanbur and Elinor Ostrom (eds.), *Linking the Formal and Informal Economy: Concepts and Policies* (Oxford: Oxford University Press and UNU-WIDER).

—— (2003) 'Contracts, norms, and political economy: Sub-Saharan state credibility and the microeconomic foundations of developmental taxation', *Cambridge Review of International Affairs*, Vol. 16, No. 1, 89–103.

—— (2002) 'African corruptions: Elements for a comparative analysis with East Asia.' In Arnold J. Heidenheimer and Michael Johnston (eds.), *Political Corruption: Concepts and Contexts* (New York: Transaction Publishers).

Stiglitz, Joseph E. (1997) 'The role of government in economic development.' In Michael Bruno and Boris Pleskovic (eds.), *Annual Bank Conference on Development Economics 1996* (Washington, DC: World Bank).

Sussman, Nathan (2006) *Medieval Public Finances: The Case of Seignorage in France*, mimeo (Jerusalem: Hebrew University, Department of Economics). http://economics.huji.ac.il/facultye/sussman/Medieval%20public%20finances.pdf, accessed on 15 January 2007.

Tanzi, Vito (2004a) *Fiscal Policy: When Theory Collides With Reality*, paper presented at the Congress of the International Institute of Public Finance, Bocconi University, Milan, 25 August.

—— (2004b), *Social Protection in a Globalizing World*, Honorary Lecture given at the Conference on Managing the Future through Pension Schemes, University Tor Vergata, Rome, 22–23 April.

Tanzi, Vito and Ludger Schuknecht (2000) *Public Spending in the 20th Century: A Global Perspective* (Cambridge: Cambridge University Press).

Tilly, Charles (1990) *Coercion, Capital, and European States: A.D. 990–1992* (London: Basil Blackwell).

Tsangarides, Charalambos G., Dhaneshwar Ghura and Carlos A. Leite (2002) *Is Growth Enough? Macroeconomic Policy and Poverty Reduction* (Washington, DC: IMF).

UNCTAD (United Nations Conference on Trade and Development) (2003) *Economic Development in Africa: Trade Performance and Commodity Dependence* (Geneva: UNCTAD).

—— (2001) *Economic Development in Africa: Performance, Prospects and Policy Issues* (Geneva: UNCTAD).

UNRISD (United Nations Research Institute for Social Development) (2005) *Gender Equality: Striving for Justice in an Unequal World* (Geneva: UNRISD).

Van Dalen, Hendrik P. (2006) *When Health Care Insurance Does Not Make a Difference: The Case of Health Care 'Made in China'*, Tinbergen Institute Discussion Paper (Rotterdam: Erasmus Universiteit).

Wade, Robert (2000) *Governing the Market: A Decade Later*, Development Studies Institute Working Paper No. 00-03 (London: London School of Economics).

—— (1990) *Governing the Market: Economic Theory and the Role of Government in East Asian Industrialization* (Princeton, NJ: Princeton University Press).

Wantchekon, Leonard (2003) 'Clientelism and voting behavior: Evidence from a field experiment in Benin', *World Politics*, Vol. 55, 399–422.

White, Gordon (ed.) (1988) *Developmental States in East Asia* (London: Macmillan).

World Bank (2007) *World Development Indicators 2007* (Washington, DC: World Bank).

World Bank (2006a) *World Development Indicators 2006* (Washington, DC: World Bank).

—— (2006b) *World Development Report: Equity and Development* (Washington, DC: World Bank).

—— (2005a) *African Development Indicators 2005* (Washington, DC: World Bank).

—— (2005b) *World Development Indicators 2005* (Washington, DC: World Bank).

—— (2004a) *Republic of Korea: Four Decades of Equitable Growth: A Case Study from Reducing Poverty, Sustaining Growth, What Works, What Doesn't, and Why: A Global Exchange for Scaling Up Success*, paper presented at the Shanghai Conference Scaling Up Poverty Reduction (Washington, DC: World Bank).

—— (2004b) *World Development Indicators 2004* (Washington, DC: World Bank).

—— (2001) *World Development Indicators 2001* (Washington, DC: World Bank).

—— (1998) *World Development Indicators 1998* (Washington, DC: World Bank).

6
Aid and the Financing of Public Social Sector Spending

Oliver Morrissey[1]

Introduction

In the poorest developing countries that are major recipients of aid, and for which aid finances a large proportion of government expenditure, it is inevitable that aid receipts influence public social sector spending. In general, one would expect the level of social spending to be higher in countries that receive more aid, *ceteris paribus*, especially to the extent that aid is increasingly targeted on supporting social sectors (for example, as part of a poverty reduction strategy). This effect may be direct, if aid finances additional social spending, or indirect, if aid supports growth so that over time social sector spending (as a share of total spending and/or of gross domestic product/GDP) increases. A more interesting question may be on the effect of aid on the efficacy of social spending, that is, on the effectiveness of spending in delivering improved human development (or increasing welfare). This is a more difficult issue to address as available data are quite limited and aid receipts tend to be highest in those countries (the poorest) where human development is lowest, hence where the efficacy of spending appears to be lowest. Recent literature on the effect of aid on welfare and poverty indicators can shed some light on these issues.

Most of the literature on aid effectiveness is concerned with the impact of aid on growth. The current debate has been characterized by Morrissey (2006a) as between those who view the glass as half empty and those who view the glass as half full: there are credible arguments for and against the proposition that aid has been effective in promoting growth and the available empirical evidence can be read in different ways. A reasonable balanced view of the literature is that aid has had a positive effect on growth, but the effect has been small and far from universal. However, even if one is predisposed to the view that aid has not been, on balance, effective, it does not follow that one would oppose an argument that certain types of aid could usefully be increased. An implicit argument in this chapter is that some increase in aid to finance the provision of social services in poor countries is warranted. White (2007) cites examples of how aid-financed immunization has contributed to reducing child mortality and the important role of aid in the remarkable health improvements in Bangladesh (a country with a very poor growth record).

A number of recent papers have examined the impact of aid on indicators of welfare or poverty, reflecting the increasing emphasis being placed on poverty reduction in policy debates, in particular arguments that the objective of reducing poverty requires an increase in aid to poor countries (for example, Commission for Africa 2005). In this context, while there is still concern that aid should promote growth (as sustained growth is seen as vital for sustained poverty reduction), there is additional concern that aid should help to address the needs of the poor. As it is at least difficult for donors to target aid on poor households, the emphasis is on allocating aid to increase spending on social sectors as being the most likely to benefit the poor. This is the aspect of aid and social development on which this chapter concentrates: allocating aid to finance the provision of social services and, more importantly, broader measures to improve the effectiveness of the public sector in delivering such services.

There are two general arguments for (increasing) spending on social sectors (taken here to cover health, education and sanitation). First, it finances the provision of public goods, which would be underprovided in the absence of public support, and contributes to human development (improves the quality of human capital), and this contributes to growth. Second, there are equity arguments as spending on social sectors is the type of government expenditure most likely to increase aggregate welfare and to benefit the poor. Some writers like to use the term 'pro-poor' spending to capture this tendency (Mosley et al. 2004), but others advocate the more general notion of 'pro-public expenditures' as the poor may not actually benefit (Gomanee et al. 2005a). Higher levels of social sector spending do not ensure that the poor are better off, as the incidence of benefits from spending may be unequally distributed. For example, although Madagascar and Tanzania did improve access to health and education services, the benefits were least for the poor (Morrisson 2002). However, even if the incidence of spending is regressive (the poor derive least benefit), spending on social sectors tends to provide some benefit to the poor and are the areas of public spending most likely to contribute to welfare indicators, especially health and education (Gupta et al. 2002; Dabla-Norris et al. 2004). Although the focus of this chapter is on social sector spending, we acknowledge that this is only one element of social policy (albeit one that is especially important for delivering social development).

Social sector expenditures are not the only categories of government spending that might be pro-public or pro-poor – providing microfinance, agricultural extension services and technology, and financing (rural) infrastructure may also be beneficial to the poor, and should benefit the public at large (Morrissey 2004). However, as discussed below, the empirical evidence on aid and welfare or poverty concentrates on social spending. Furthermore, as aid financing has the potential to leverage upwards the level of social spending, the potential to benefit the poor may be enhanced. Lanjouw and Ravallion (1999) argue that the poor are more likely to benefit as public spending increases, both because the share of social in total spending rises and the distribution of spending improves.

The remainder of the chapter begins, in the second section, with the discussion of social sector services as public goods that benefit the international community in addition to benefiting each country, so there is a case for aid financing. The third section addresses evidence on the effect of aid on the level of social spending, and specifically considers the ability of donors to target aid on social sectors (addressing fungibility concerns). Note that we are not specifically concerned with aid that is used directly to finance donor-managed social sector projects, even if using aid in this way is quite common, as our focus is on aid financing of government social spending. The fourth section reviews existing evidence on aid and the efficacy of social spending. It examines whether aid delivered through public social spending is an effective way to deliver improved welfare outcomes? Often it is not the aid finance itself that is important, but the policies supported and promoted by donors. The fifth section reviews the influence of donors on social sector policy as reflected by pro-poor spending under Poverty Reduction Strategy Papers (PRSPs) and recent initiatives in expenditure monitoring and tracking. The conclusions and policy implications are in the final section, which also considers possible adverse effects of significantly increasing aid (to finance social services), although a core argument of the chapter is to focus on using aid more effectively rather than aiming to increase the amount granted.

Social services as public goods

The classic economic definition of a public good is one 'which all enjoy in common in the sense that each individual's consumption of such a good leads to no subtraction from any other individual's consumption of that good' (Samuelson 1954: 387). There are two characteristics intrinsic to the definition of a (pure) public good. A good is *non-excludable* if once it has been provided the benefits can be enjoyed by everybody in the relevant population. A good is *non-rival* if one individual's consumption does not diminish the amount available to others. The former implies that the market mechanism would undersupply a public good, while the latter implies that society benefits by increasing provision. Because exclusion is difficult or costly the market cannot force all beneficiaries to pay a price (due to free riding) so public provision, or a public contribution to the cost of provision, is necessary to ensure the socially optimal level of a public good is provided. In the case of non-rival benefits 'it is inefficient to exclude anyone who derives a positive benefit, because extending consumption to more users creates benefits that cost society nothing' (Kanbur et al. 1999: 61). For example, while it is possible to exclude somebody from education, it is not desirable because provision is non-rival (at least up to some level of congestion) and everybody can benefit from a more educated society (a positive externality).

Goods are rarely purely non-excludable or non-rival, and often they are one but not the other. For example, if a vaccine is given to one person the same vaccine cannot be administered to another person (it is rival in consumption), but the other person still benefits from the general reduction in the probability of contracting the disease (an external benefit that is non-excludable). There may also be scale benefits by vaccinating many people at the same time. As another example, while improved sanitation or access to clean water in a village is rival and excludable from the perspective of other villages, the population in other villages can still benefit from the reduction in water-borne disease. This is a useful example of weakest link – the villages without clean water increase the risk of disease to all (a negative externality), so the socially optimum provision is to provide clean water to all. The public benefit of providing health care is the reduction in disease in society (reducing or eliminating a negative externality), even though the provision of health care or sanitation may be rival (and may even be excludable). Similarly, the public benefit of education is knowledge even if the provision of the education may be to some extent rival and excludable. The essence of 'publicness' is the desirability and possibility of preventing people from benefiting once the good is provided.

Social sector services, specifically health, education and sanitation, are good examples of (impure) public goods. What is most important is not the intrinsic public good nature, but the importance of externalities. Poor sanitation, lack of access to clean water or health care all increase the incidence of disease and ill health in society; the external bad (or public bad) is that the risk of disease is greater for all in society. The public good is reducing this risk, and it is provided by investing in health and sanitation. As the market would underprovide, public social sector spending is necessary (it does not have to be public provision, although it is generally helpful). There is also a positive externality associated with a healthier society, at least in the sense of higher productivity which contributes to growth, but the essential argument is reducing the public bad. In the case of education the essence is provision of the public good, the positive externalities associated with greater knowledge and an enhanced ability of society to use that knowledge. Education provides both the knowledge and the ability to use it, so again there is justification for public provision, or at least a public contribution to the cost.

Social public goods also have a cross-border dimension – the 'spillover ranges' of the externalities (negative or positive) are regional or international, and may even be global. Eradication of a disease such as malaria or smallpox or avian flu provides non-excludable benefits at a global level. Everybody benefits from the reduced risk of contracting the disease. There is a large literature on global or international public goods[2] but from our perspective the relevance is in justifying aid to finance the provision of social sector services. Two arguments are involved: certain externalities are international by nature (the spillover range) and provision of the national public good may be necessary (complementary) to ensure the international benefit is provided (Morrissey et al. 2002). We consider these in respect of health (including sanitation, clean water) and education (knowledge).

- *Health*: The public good is to eliminate negative externalities (the risk of disease) and improve health status, and this is cross-border by nature. Eradicating contagious disease is the essence of the international public good, and requires each afflicted country to be able to contribute to the control and reduction of disease. Thus each country must have a functioning health service, and it is in the interests of the international community to ensure that the national health care provision is effective. Furthermore, an effective health care (and water, sanitation) system facilitates consumption of the public good, that is, increases the ability of individuals to avail of the benefit.

- *Knowledge*: The (international) public good element is that promulgating ideas and ways of doing things provides non-excludable and non-rival benefits that can increase productivity and well-being. The provision of education (a national public good) both contributes to the creation of knowledge and facilitates the ability of individuals to use the knowledge. Again, as the benefits extend across borders, the international community can benefit from better provision in each and every country.

Thus, there are inherent efficiency and equity arguments for aid financing of public goods (social services) in developing countries. The efficiency argument relates to increased (global) provision of the benefits and enhanced capacity to produce goods (which may be public or private), where the enhanced capacity is also a benefit available to all. 'Education enhances national capacity, and is therefore a national public good. Education also enhances the capacity to produce global knowledge, and is therefore an activity complementary to providing [international public goods]' (Morrissey et al. 2002: 38). The equity argument arises because achieving the socially optimal level of provision permits all to benefit from the public good, and this increases the well-being of the poor in addition to the efficiency gains.

The cost of providing universal social services is high and although the benefits (private and social) may exceed total global costs, this is not necessarily true for all countries. In poor countries the initial levels of provision tend to be very low, implying a high cost for achieving universal effective provision, so the benefits to the individual country could be less than the cost. For example, African countries, even collectively, may be unable to afford the cost of eradicating HIV/AIDS or malaria. As the international community derives a benefit, it should contribute to the cost, and aid is an appropriate way of doing so. Obviously, aid is used to finance the provision of public goods: te Velde et al. (2002) provide a conservative estimate that over 1996–98 donors allocated almost 10 per cent of aid to international public goods (some 70 per cent of this was on the environment) and about 30 per cent to national public goods (almost half on environment, with health and knowledge each about 15 per cent). Using broader definitions for less conservative estimates would raise these figures to maximums of 20 per cent and 50 per cent, respectively.

Aid and the level of social spending

We begin by reporting some results from Gomanee et al. (2005a: Appendix) to assess if the level of social spending is determined by aid. Social sector spending (Gs) is measured as spending on health, education and sanitation expressed as a share of GDP. This is specified as a function of aid flows (A) measured as a percentage of GDP (and lagged to avoid possible spurious estimates), tax revenue as a share of GDP (TR) and period average GDP per capita ($GDPPC$) (subscripts designating country *i* in period *t*):

$$Gs_{it} = a_0 + a_1 GDPPC_{it} + a_2 A_{it} + a_3 TR_{it} + u_{it} \tag{6.1}$$

As *Gs* is a component of government spending, one can interpret (6.1) as a rough test of whether the explanatory variables influence the allocation of spending to social sectors. Although aid may affect the level of total spending the test is whether, *ceteris paribus*, countries with higher aid revenue allocate a greater share of GDP to expenditure on social sectors. A similar interpretation applies to tax revenue. Income is included to capture the possibility that, for given levels of revenue, richer countries spend more on social services.

The results are reported in Table 6.1. Tax revenue and income per capita are significant determinants of social spending, as would be expected. Aid appears as a significant determinant of *Gs* for the full sample (All), but this is driven by aid being significant for low-income countries, but not significant for middle-income countries. Thus, we have some evidence that aid does finance social spending in the poorer countries. Mosley et al. (2004: F226) also find that aid has a positive and significant effect on the level of social sector spending (although they find no evidence that aid has a significant effect on health spending alone).

As the coefficients are elasticities, a 10 per cent increase in aid would increase *Gs* by 1.7 per cent, implying quite a small effect. One can infer that tax revenue has a greater impact on *Gs* than aid, although the coefficients cannot be directly compared (the impact depends on the aid/GDP and tax/GDP values). For poor countries, as long as tax/GDP is more than half aid/GDP, an increase in tax would

Table 6.1   Determinants of social sector spending

	Country groups (by income)		
	All	Low	Middle
AID_{t-1}	0.091	0.166	−0.162
	(2.03)*	(3.93)**	(1.61)
TR	0.312	0.322	0.290
	(3.97)**	(2.19)*	(3.14)**
GDPPC	0.001	0.009	0.001
	(3.69)**	(2.46)*	(2.97)**
Constant	−0.399	−4.591	1.619
	(0.26)	(2.10)*	(0.80)
N	300	103	197
R^2	0.16	0.36	0.16

Note: The data cover an unbalanced panel of four four-year and one five-year period averages over 1980–2000 for a sample of 104 countries. All variables measured in logs; estimates are fixed effects. Absolute values of t-ratios in parentheses; *, **, indicate significance at 5 per cent and 1 per cent levels, respectively. Explanatory power for fixed effect estimates reported by R^2 rather than adjusted R^2.
Source: Adapted from Gomanee et al. (2005a: tables B1 and B2).

have a greater impact. The Appendix (Table A6.1) reports some summary statistics and, on average for low-income countries, aid/GDP and tax/GDP are similar – at about 14 per cent. As countries get richer, aid becomes less significant (7 per cent on average for middle-income countries) but tax/GDP rises (to 20 per cent on average), implying that the impact on Gs is increasing. On average (over 1980–2000), while Gs is 8 per cent in middle-income countries it is only just above 5 per cent in low-income countries (Table A6.1). It is also worth noting that spending on water and sanitation, which Gomanee et al. (2005a) find to have the greatest impact on welfare, is the smallest component of Gs in low-income countries (1.5 per cent of GDP on average) but the largest in middle-income countries (4.9 per cent of GDP on average).

The low impact of aid on the level of social spending may be due to fungibility, where aid intended for social spending is used for a different purpose. Alternatively, the aid may not be additional: even if the aid is all allocated to social spending, tax revenues previously allocated to social spending may be reallocated elsewhere. The effect is that social spending does not increase by the full amount of the aid allocated to social spending. Note that, at least in the data used above (but in general for empirical studies of fungibility), we do not actually know how much aid was intended to finance social spending. McGillivray and Morrissey (2004) argue that fungibility tends to be overstated as a concern: even if spending on specific areas does not increase in line with aid immediately, over time the spending allocation to areas favoured by donors has increased. In simple terms, aid is an important reason why the level of social sector spending in poor countries is increasing (and in the poorest countries is probably the only way of maintaining any reasonable level of social spending). This is confirmed for the low-income group in Table 6.1, whereas the results for middle-income countries shows that as countries get richer aid becomes an unimportant source of finance for social spending (aid to richer countries is more likely to be for capital projects).

Concern about fungibility is one reason why many donors are reluctant to support providing aid in the form of General Budget Support (GBS), and try to impose conditionality on the allocation of resources. The use of ring-fenced funds, such as Poverty Action Funds (PAFs) associated with PRSPs, is one example of how donors try to restrict the way in which aid can be used. Although this may be effective in preventing fungibility in the sense that the aid is all allocated to the intended (social sector) use, it does not guarantee that the aid is fully additional (it remains possible that the government's own revenue is reallocated). There are costs associated with imposing conditions on the use of aid, and it may not be necessary to do so. The results in Table 6.1, acknowledging the simplicity of the exercise, suggest that government's own funds are at least as likely, and probably more likely, to be allocated to social spending. This suggests that GBS, where aid goes into the pot and is allocated in line with the government's priorities, may be equally effective in increasing social spending. Indeed, one interpretation of the low elasticity on aid in Table 6.1 may be that, for the time period considered, donors were more likely to target aid on spending other than for social sectors (perhaps addressing social needs through sector projects).

Morrissey (2006b) argues that concerns about fungibility are not a convincing reason not to adopt GBS. Donors will only grant GBS if they believe that the recipient's allocation of spending is broadly desirable, that is, in line with what the donor desires. This implies that donor and recipient preferences on allocation are aligned, so fungibility is not an issue by implication: recipients allocate aid more or less in the way donors' desire. In such cases GBS is appropriate and spending on social sectors is likely to increase if more aid is given. Furthermore, even if preferences are not aligned, fungibility is not likely to undermine GBS provided aid is a *large* share of the budget (because recipients have fewer own resources to reallocate). Fungibility may not be particularly germane to the issue of aid financing of increased levels of social spending.

It seems quite likely that as aid is increased social spending can rise more than proportionally. It is not necessary to attach conditions to the use of aid in order to achieve this, as long as recipients have identified a strategy for social sector spending. As discussed below, this is in place, albeit imperfectly, where there is a PRSP. While it may not be particularly difficult to increase the level of social spending, ensuring it is effective in delivering public goods and human development outcomes are greater challenges.

Aid and the efficacy of social spending

The notion of the efficacy of public spending relates to evaluating how effective spending is in delivering the intended outcomes: to what extent does spending on primary health reduce infant mortality, or does spending on primary education deliver increased educational attainment? The available evidence suggests that the efficiency of spending is quite low in poor countries. In simple terms, controlling for various country characteristics, in the poorest countries expenditures are only achieving 60–80 per cent of the outcome levels that could potentially be achieved, with rates below 50 per cent for many countries in sub-Saharan Africa (Rayp and Van de Sijpe 2007). Administrative and institutional weaknesses, and no doubt corruption and staff with low skills, mean that public spending is simply not delivering the benefits that could be expected.

We are not aware of any studies that specifically look at the effect of aid on the effectiveness of public spending in general, or of social sector spending in particular. However, there are a few studies that examine the effect of aid on indicators of human development (aggregate welfare measures) or poverty, and that include a measure of social sector spending. If the efficacy of social spending in delivering public goods is interpreted as the effect of such spending on indicators of welfare, then one can draw inferences from these studies. The studies we consider use any of three welfare indicators: the human development index (HDI), infant mortality and poverty headcount. The HDI is an index (between zero and one) of measures of different dimensions of quality of life, notably longevity, education and access to resources (measured as real per capita GDP in purchasing power parity dollars). The infant mortality rate (IMR) is the number of deaths in infancy per 1,000 live births, and tends to be a good proxy for average household welfare that is highly correlated with poverty. The headcount poverty measure is the percentage of the population deemed to be living below some established poverty line.

Although these studies are concerned with the effect of aid on poverty, data on the headcount index are sparse so other indicators are used. At the aggregate (country) levels, indicators of human welfare such as the HDI or IMR tend to be correlated with indicators of poverty. Furthermore, the headcount ratio is a monetary poverty measure, based on income, whereas non-monetary indicators of welfare, such as infant mortality, may be preferable to capture the material hardship aspect of being poor. Improvements in aggregate welfare (better health and education for example) may benefit the lives of the poor just as much as reductions in income poverty. As our principal concern is with social sector spending, welfare indicators may be the appropriate focus. For example, if health spending is not associated with reductions in infant mortality it is unlikely to contribute to poverty reduction (or at least to improving the well-being of the poor).

There are a number of ways in which aid can affect poverty or household welfare, only some of which include a link through social spending. Aid that generates income-earning opportunities (such as provision of microfinance) or that directly provides social services, such as donor-funded projects in health or sanitation, can increase welfare. These effects do not operate through social sector spending. Although it is difficult to target such aid on the poor, donor projects may be more effective at including the poor than government projects, and especially than general social spending. Aid that contributes to economic growth should lead to long-run increases in aggregate welfare, in part because of a general effect through growth and in part because growth tends to increase government revenue and social sector spending increases (see above).

As much aid is directed through government spending, aid can increase welfare by increasing expenditures towards those social services that contribute to welfare. This is the particular link of most concern here. Is there any evidence that the (increased) social sector spending financed by aid is associated with improvements in welfare or reductions in poverty? The answer is yes, although the evidence is not especially strong. Before considering some evidence, it is worth noting that aid, or the relationship between donors and recipients, may encourage recipient governments to place poverty reduction and the welfare of the poor higher on their policy agenda. An example would include PRSPs, discussed in the next section.

Gomanee et al. (2005a) use the term pro-public expenditures (PPE) for what we refer to as social sector spending (Gs) so we here alter their notation. They explore the relationship (subscripts designating country i in period t):

$$W_{it} = \beta_0 + \beta_1 Y_{it} + \beta_2 Gs_{it} + \beta_3 A_{it} + \varepsilon_{it} \qquad (6.2)$$

where W is a measure of aggregate human welfare.
       Y is a measure of income.
       Gs is social sector spending.
       A is a measure of aid.

In (6.2), the proposition is that aid affects welfare either through donor projects that deliver income or welfare-enhancing services (the aid targets welfare directly) or also, if lagged values of aid are used, indirectly through growth. The coefficient β_3 captures these effects of aid on welfare (and there is no basis on which to distinguish the effects). As mentioned above, and of primary concern here, aid can also affect welfare via the level of social spending. The coefficient β_2 can be interpreted as a measure of the effectiveness of spending in delivering the particular welfare outcome.

As shown in the previous section, some aid directly finances Gs, so aid and Gs should not be included together in the same regression (that would be double counting and would bias the estimated coefficients). To address this concern, Gomanee et al. (2005a) use a constructed regressor ($Gres$), measured as the proportion of social spending not financed by aid. They then estimate (all variables in logs):

$$W_{it} = \delta_0 + \delta_1 GDP0 + \delta_2 Gres_{it} + \delta_3 G_{m,it} + \delta_4 A_{it-1} + \varepsilon_{it} \tag{6.3}$$

In this specification, the coefficient on *Gres* (δ_2) captures the efficacy of spending (although this measure is of spending not financed by aid, the coefficient also applies to any spending that is financed by aid). The coefficient on aid (δ_4) captures the effects of aid other than through public spending. As lagged *Aid* (total aid flows as a share of GDP) is used, this allows for the fact that aid may take time to affect welfare, especially indirect effects via growth, and also addresses endogeneity concerns (the current allocation of aid across countries respond to their relative welfare levels). Government military expenditure as a fraction of GDP (G_m) is intended to capture spending diverted from productive or pro-public uses, and may also capture high levels of (political) instability in a country, so we expect a negative sign. The sign could be positive if such spending represents efforts to achieve or maintain security. Initial income (*GDP0*) is measured as real GDP per capita (in constant dollars) in the year preceding each period of the panel data. The data is a panel of four four-year and one five-year period averages over 1980 to 2000 for 104 countries (not all variables are available for all countries in all periods so the actual sample in regressions is smaller). Two measures of welfare (HDI and IMR) are tested as dependent variables.

Tables 6.2 and 6.3 present the results for HDI and IMR, respectively. Three explanatory variables are reported. Initial GDP controls for the tendency of richer countries to have higher levels of welfare. The *Gres* variable captures the efficacy of public spending at increasing welfare; a positive and significant coefficient implies that public spending (and aid that finances such spending) contributes to increasing welfare. The coefficient on the Aid variable captures the effects of aid, as mentioned above. Gomanee et al. (2005a) report additional results using different measures of spending and alternative specifications but the results are broadly similar to those reported here.

Considering Table 6.2, there is fairly robust evidence that aid does increase welfare measured by HDI, and this effect (the coefficient) appears to be greater for low-income than for middle-income countries. As income is a major component

Table 6.2 HDI, aid and social spending

Dependent variable log (HDI)

	Country groups (by income)		
	All	Low	Middle
GDPO	0.137	0.185	0.096
	(4.57)**	(3.15)**	(3.58)**
Gres	−0.005	−0.017	0.027
	(0.57)	(1.35)	(2.01)*
Aid_{t-1}	0.021	0.031	0.021
	(2.93)**	(2.33)*	(3.13)**
G_M	−0.034	0.007	−0.066
	(2.30)*	(0.28)	(4.75)**
Constant	−1.454	−1.942	−1.070
	(7.01)**	(5.44)**	(5.23)**
N	289	128	161
R-squared	0.17	0.17	0.35
F-Stat	8.65	3.58	12.65

Notes: As for Table 6.1. The F-statistic tests the joint significance of all coefficients (rejects the null that all are jointly zero).
Source: Adapted from Gomanee et al. (2005a).

Table 6.3 Infant mortality, aid and social spending

Dependent variable log (IMR)

	Country groups (by income)		
	All	Low	Middle
GDPO	−0.327	−0.187	−0.420
	(4.03)**	(2.20)*	(3.30)**
Gres	−0.018	−0.005	−0.096
	(0.73)	(0.27)	(1.55)
Aid_{t-1}	−0.049	−0.037	−0.068
	(2.65)**	(2.03)*	(2.21)*
G_M	0.123	0.047	0.215
	(3.31)**	(1.39)	(3.27)**
Constant	6.021	5.513	6.598
	(10.71)**	(10.56)**	(6.82)**
N	311	138	173
R-squared	0.17	0.11	0.25
F-Stat	9.23	2.53	8.35

Notes: As for Table 6.2, IMR is infant mortality rate.
Source: Adapted from Gomanee et al. (2005a).

of the HDI, and the correlation between HDI and GDP across countries is high (although not perfect), this is largely evidence for an effect of aid on or through growth. The coefficient on spending is insignificant overall and for low-income countries: in such countries we find no evidence that public social spending (and aid that finances such spending) contributes to increasing welfare. Public social spending does seem to increase welfare in middle-income countries. As expected, the coefficient on initial income is positive and significant; countries with higher incomes tend to have higher subsequent HDI (overall and within the two income groups). The coefficient on military spending is negative and significant but this only holds for middle-income countries. As fixed effects estimation is used country-specific effects (such as conflict) are accounted for, so this result suggests that middle-income countries that divert relatively more spending to the military have lower HDI (that is, it captures anti-public spending).

Considering Table 6.3, there is again fairly robust evidence that aid does increase welfare (the negative coefficient means a beneficial effect of reducing infant mortality), although in this case the effect appears to be greater for middle-income countries. The coefficient on spending is insignificant in all cases. One possible explanation for this is that overall, and especially for low-income countries, education is the largest component of social spending (Table A6.1) but this would have the least impact on infant mortality compared to sanitation and health spending. As expected, the coefficient on initial income is negative and significant; countries with higher incomes tend to have lower subsequent IMR (overall and within the two income groups, although the effect is weaker for low-income countries). The coefficient on military spending is positive and significant, again driven by middle-income countries (so it appears to capture anti-public spending).

Overall, the evidence is that aid does contribute to welfare (more so for HDI than IMR). In the case of HDI, the effect seems to be greater for low-income countries, whereas for IMR the effect seems to be greater for middle-income countries. In general, public social spending does not impact on welfare (except for HDI in middle-income countries, but aid is not a significant determinant of Gs in these countries). We note that spending on sanitation (especially) and health are significantly higher in middle-income compared to lower income countries (Table A6.1). This suggests that the effect of aid on welfare is not through government spending, but either through donor projects or growth. This issue is returned to below, but policy implications are that it may be more useful to address the ineffectiveness of public spending rather than trying to increase aid or, if additional aid is provided, channels other than through government spending may be most effective.

Two other papers adopt a similar methodology but, using different samples and alternative econometric approaches, find that aid is associated with higher welfare or lower poverty through the effect of aid increasing public social spending. Mosley et al. (2004), using data for some 46 countries in the 1990s, estimate simultaneously the effect of aid on social spending (or only health spending) and the effect of total (health) spending on poverty (infant mortality). They find that aid is associated with higher levels of social spending, and this is associated with lower levels of headcount poverty. Although higher health spending is associated with lower infant mortality, they find no evidence that aid is associated with higher health spending. Thus, in contrast to Gomanee et al. (2005a) who only find effects of aid directly or via growth, they only find effects of aid operating through public spending. The difference can to some extent be attributed to different samples and approaches, although it is notable that both studies had weaker results for infant mortality (that is, cross-country variations in IMR are difficult to explain adequately in these models).

Gomanee et al. (2005b) use quantile regressions for a sample of 38 countries, and again find that aid is associated with higher social sector spending, and this spending is associated with higher welfare. The novelty of the quantile regressions is that they allow one to consider differences in the effect of aid for countries at different parts of the welfare distribution. Gomanee et al. (2005b) find that the marginal impact of aid (via spending) appears to be greater for countries with lower levels of the welfare indicator (the poorer countries). Although they do not find that aid impacts on welfare directly or through growth, in line with Gomanee et al. (2005a) they do find that aid can have a greater impact in poorer countries.

While the results from different studies are not entirely consistent, there is robust evidence that aid improves welfare indicators, HDI and IMR, and tends to reduce poverty. The evidence is less conclusive on whether the effect is predominantly through direct impacts (aid provides incomes or social services) and growth, or through aid-financed social spending. The beneficial effect of aid is present for low-income and middle-income countries. In the case of middle-income countries, although social spending is associated with increased welfare (for the HDI measure), aid is not a significant determinant of public social spending. If anything, the marginal impact of aid is greater in the poorer countries, but this is not attributable to public social spending (which has a low or no impact). In the poorest countries there is evidence to support a policy of aid delivered through donor-managed projects, but the evidence suggests a major concern is the efficacy of public spending. Donors influence policy and practice on social sector spending and service delivery, and this can improve the effectiveness of spending (whether aid-financed or not), the issue we consider in the next section.

Aid and policy on social service provision

The results reviewed above suggest that aid is effective in increasing welfare, but public spending (on social services) does not appear to be effective (except perhaps in middle-income countries), or at least is not consistently so when country characteristics are accounted for. An underlying reason is the low quality of public services (that is, health clinics that do not have adequate staff or medicines, schools that have too few teachers or books). This is an endemic problem in the poorest countries and while it reflects in part a low level of social spending, a major concern is misallocation or misuse of spending. We here consider each of these issues briefly. By allocation, we refer to how central government spending is spread across social sectors and that is addressed below in the context of policy considerations. First we consider use and misuse – are public funds allocated to a particular service, such as primary schools or vaccination programmes, all actually spent on delivering the intended service?

In a frequently cited paper, Svensson and Reinikka (2004) provide evidence that in the early 1990s over 80 per cent of the central government allocation intended for non-wage spending in primary schools in Uganda was never spent in the schools. They provide a model of local capture to explain why such a large proportion of the government funds leak from the process of decentralized spending. What is perhaps more interesting, although it receives less attention in citations, is that by the late 1990s following the implementation of expenditure tracking surveys and improved expenditure monitoring, the figures were reversed such that less than 20 per cent of the funds leaked. In other words, techniques exist to ensure that most of the government spending allocated to a particular (decentralized) purpose are actually spent on the intended purpose. While there is no doubt that the efficiency of service delivery is limited, especially in getting to the poor, new techniques for monitoring expenditure and delivering services offer potential for improvement (Devarajan and Reinikka 2004; Reinikka and Svensson 2004). We merely observe that this is the case – misuse can be limited – and turn attention to policy links between aid and donors on the one hand, and recipients and social sector spending on the other (the allocation issue).

Traditionally, donors' concerns about allocation of spending, and in particular aid-financing of public spending, were with fungibility (discussed above). To address this, donors attach conditions to the use of the funds. McGillivray and Morrissey (2001) address this issue in a broad and conceptual manner, identifying limitations in donors' ability to ensure that funds are used as interpreted but concluding that general expenditure monitoring is often sufficient to ensure that desired spending does increase. In other words, as in the case of the use of funds, methods do exist to help ensure that aid, and government spending more generally, is allocated towards the areas favoured by donors. Put another way, social sector spending allocations have been increased and can be further increased and made more effective. This is an important conclusion as many donor policy developments, notably the Millennium Development Goals (MDGs) and Commission for Africa (2005), over the past decade have included increasing aid, especially to increase delivery of social services. A particular example of this is in the context of debt relief, where the resources saved are to be allocated to spending on poverty reduction initiatives, of which social sector spending is an important component.

In most respects debt relief is equivalent to aid and can be treated accordingly; donors account for debt relief as part of their aid budget, while for recipients both represent an increase in resources at the disposal of governments. The conditions associated with debt relief target increasing social sector spending as part of the poverty reduction strategy, and a brief discussion is therefore relevant to aid financing as, through conditionality, donors influence policy. Under the heavily indebted poor countries (HIPC) initiative, countries seeking debt relief are required to establish a good record of implementing economic and social policy reform and prepare a PRSP indicating how they will tackle poverty reduction. The funds made available by debt relief would then be channelled into poverty reduction, typically through a PAF that identifies pro-poor expenditures. In this sense the PRSP has a similar emphasis to *Gs* as discussed above, and spending on sanitation, health and education figure prominently in PRSPs.

To qualify for debt relief under HIPC, countries must demonstrate their ability for sound economic management through implementation of policy reforms over three years under International Monetary Fund (IMF) and World Bank programmes. If this is deemed satisfactory they pass the decision point and must then implement a PRSP for at least a year to reach the completion point, after which debt relief is provided. Morrissey (2004) argues that the inherent defect with this approach is that the resources to fund social sector expenditures are not released fully until the end of the process (which could take as long as six years). On the face of it, PRSPs are about listing the policy areas of specific concern to the poor and providing a list of proposed actions in these areas. Among the essential policies in PRSPs are those relating to the provision of, and increasing access to, public services (social service delivery) and those relating primarily to the rural sector (where most of the poor live). Increased public spending on the provision of social services is a central element of PRSPs, hence the debt relief process and conditionality is at the core of social sector policy in many of the poorest countries. The role of debt relief itself is then to provide increased government resources to finance these pro-poor policies.

Morrissey (2004) argues that it is generally easier to identify and implement pro-poor expenditures than it is to implement an economic reform programme that includes pro-poor policies. This is so because, although it is relatively easy to identify appropriate social sector spending needs, even if ensuring effective delivery is a major challenge, it is very difficult to design a coherent and feasible policy strategy that will be pro-poor in its effects (assuming it can be properly implemented). If the primary objective is poverty reduction, and this is what the donors emphasize, the primary policy instrument is pro-poor expenditures; a poverty reduction strategy is desirable, but identifying and providing the resources for social sector spending is essential.

Illustrating these issues with a case study of Uganda, Morrissey and Verschoor (2006) argue that the nature of the policy environment in developing countries, and how donors interact with this, is central to the potential for implementing poverty reduction policies. Donors can and do influence government preferences for pro-poor policies, in particular spending for the poor (directly or indirectly). Donors also promote a pro-poor agenda and help to establish commitment to poverty reduction strategies. Implementing the strategy requires increased spending in certain sectors, especially the social sectors. Aid can finance these expenditures, and debt relief can release resources to allocate to pro-poor expenditures (in this sense aid and debt relief financing are equivalent). However, the funds released through debt relief are insufficient in themselves, as HIPC debt was highly concessional (even if it was being serviced, the interest payments were relatively low). To achieve the required levels of pro-poor spending, the funds freed by relief must be combined with increased aid and matching government funds (to ensure spending is additional). The funds should also be delivered as part of a coherent policy strategy. Donors have begun to play a constructive role in providing the funds and supporting the development of a strategy for their effective use, but much needs to be done.

Conclusions and implications

The empirical evidence reviewed above shows that one can try and account for the channels through which aid affects welfare by including government social spending in addition to aid as explanatory variables for explaining welfare outcomes. One has to be careful to avoid double counting, as some of the government social spending is directly financed by aid. The results presented in this chapter control for this and measure social sector expenditures – on health, education and sanitation – that are not financed by aid. The research findings therefore allow for various channels: aid can affect welfare directly, through growth or through the level and allocation of public social spending. Although some studies do use data on poverty, comparative cross-country data on poverty over time is extremely scarce, and such data as exist are based on income measures of poverty (which do not capture all dimensions of poverty and are not fully comparable across countries). As there is a strong correlation between levels of poverty and levels of aggregate human welfare across countries, researchers often use welfare as measured by the HDI and the IMR. If there is evidence that aid is associated with higher welfare (higher HDI or lower IMR), then it is likely that aid benefits the poor (at least by improving access to public services).

The evidence suggests that aid can and does contribute to poverty reduction, by contributing to growth, by providing direct benefits to the poor, and by supporting and financing increased social sector spending. In the poorest countries, where the effect of aid on welfare appears to be greatest, the effect seems to operate primarily either directly through donor projects or indirectly via growth. There is no solid evidence that aid improves welfare by financing social spending, as government social spending in low-income countries does not appear to impact on welfare (implying that it is not effective in delivering social services). This is not an argument against aid but rather suggests that measures need to be implemented to improve the effectiveness of government spending before donors shift from directly managed projects (in health or education sectors for example) to providing aid-financing for social services through the budget. In middle-income countries, where social sector spending appears to be effective, aid is not a significant source of financing for such spending.

This suggests an issue of concern, as government spending does not appear to be very efficient in low-income countries. This is due in part to low levels of social spending in the poorest countries, in part due to poor allocation (too little on sanitation, too low a share for primary health care and primary education), but primarily because public service delivery is very inefficient (given corruption, misuse of funds, relatively low levels of skilled personnel and weak administrative structures). Aid effectiveness could be enhanced if the efficacy of public spending is increased, which involves analysis and intervention at the country level, applying the techniques that exist to improve the use and allocation of public spending and improve the efficiency of service delivery. Attempts to increase the targeting of expenditure in areas that are more likely to benefit the poor could yield a high pay-off if combined with improvements in social service delivery. The use of aid to guide the allocation of government spending offers a way to increase the leverage of aid on poverty reduction policies. Increasingly, aid is being used in this way, for example to support public spending as part of a Poverty Reduction Strategy or under the HIPC initiative.

It is evident that more can be done, especially in improving the effectiveness of public spending in delivering improvements in welfare, especially of the poor. Aid and donors will continue to play an important role. It is also evident that greater coherence is needed – debt relief should be aligned with aid, in terms of funds and policy, in tackling poverty, and this means that the emphasis should be on pro-poor spending and providing services. Although we argue that the major gains may come from improving the allocation and effectiveness of social sector spending, some increase in funds will be required. Aid is the obvious source of increased funding, and many donor initiatives are committed to significant increases in aid, but there may be adverse effects associated with the difficulties of absorbing the aid.

Concerns regarding the implications of doubling or significantly scaling-up aid tend to be of three major types: disbursement difficulties, effects on prices and effects on competitiveness. The first relates to limited administrative capacity, and can easily be illustrated with some examples. Funding may be available for a major vaccination scheme, but often this means only that the vaccines are provided (and financed through aid). For the scheme to be effective it is important to vaccinate all vulnerable members of the population, as this is a weakest link technology; the public good of eliminating the risk of infection is not delivered if some of the population are not vaccinated. To ensure full coverage of the population requires delivery capacity in the health care system, and such capacity may be inadequate. Even if donors recognize this and support capacity, it takes time to train staff and is difficult, even with donor personnel, to reach remote areas if they have no public health infrastructure. As another example, even if funding is available it is difficult to achieve universal primary education because one has to ensure that the schools exist with equipment and that there are sufficient teachers, and at least this takes time. If universal primary education is achieved, demands for secondary education increase.

Disbursement is an important concern in poor countries with very weak social sector capacity, but it is not an insurmountable problem. The social service delivery strategy must address and finance the needs for equipment, infrastructure and staff in addition to the capacity of the relevant ministry (including the Finance Ministry which will have to undertake expenditure planning and management). In fact, it is the need to support the whole social service infrastructure, rather than simply providing medicines or school books for example, that generates the need for significant funding. In this sense increased aid is needed, although the actual amounts may be considerably less than a doubling of aid. For example, increasing the level of social spending in low-income countries to the level in middle-income countries on average would be equivalent to an additional 3 per cent of GDP, about a 20 per cent increase in aid on average (see Table A6.1).

The two other concerns relate to macroeconomic effects of aid, and both have been addressed in the context of Dutch disease models. A useful distinction can be made between absorbing the increased spending (of local currency) in the economy, and absorbing the increased foreign exchange (as aid is received in foreign currency, typically US dollars). Taking the first of these, the aid increases the level of public spending and this increases the price of non-tradables relative to tradables. The essential argument is that government services become relatively more expensive, which can be interpreted as an increase in public sector wages, and in particular construction costs increase (the initial literature was concerned with aid-financing for infrastructure projects, and this was associated with a construction boom). In principle, this reduces the profits or competitiveness of the tradables sector, which must pay more for labour, land or construction, for example. In practice, if the extra aid goes to social services, there may be no adverse impact: poor economies are characterized by excess supply of labour, especially unskilled (which would be used in construction of schools or health clinics for example), so there is unlikely to be a significant impact on wages. They are also characterized by an undersupply of public goods, so increased provision of social services could enhance human capital and contribute to productivity improvements, offsetting any adverse price effects. Furthermore, any increase in public wage payments represents increases in incomes, and this increase in private demand is an injection to the economy. If the increase in aid was modest (less than 50 per cent) and targeted at needed social sectors, the adverse impacts are unlikely to be noticeable.

Absorbing the foreign exchange associated with aid is a more serious problem. Increased aid flows imply an increased inflow of foreign exchange and this must be accommodated (by the Central Bank). One possibility is that the aid is used to increase reserves of foreign exchange; this may be a viable short-term strategy but implies that no real resources are transferred from abroad (the foreign exchange is not spent on increased imports). Furthermore, the Central Bank still has to provide domestic currency (the equivalent of the aid) to the government for public spending. If the foreign exchange is banked in reserves (not cashed in for local currency), the Central Bank must either print money or increase lending to the government, either of which would have an inflationary effect. It is preferable that some or all of the foreign exchange is spent.

If the Central Bank simply sold the foreign exchange on the market, the supply of foreign currency increases so the price of local currency falls. To prevent such a nominal exchange rate appreciation, which would reduce competitiveness (imports become cheaper and the return to exports falls, in local currency), the increased supply of foreign exchange needs to be matched by increased demand. This requires increased imports to absorb the foreign exchange (Commission for Africa 2005). This is a potential constraint on increasing aid flows to sub-Saharan Africa as imports are already relatively high (large trade deficits financed by aid are how the foreign exchange of aid is accommodated), and a further increase in imports implies increased competition for import-competing sectors (Morrissey 2005). This problem is also not insurmountable, but requires that attention is paid to what goods are imported to use any increases in aid. Some imports may be necessary, such as medicines, vaccines and textbooks, while others can benefit local producers, such as intermediate inputs or technology goods.

One other broader potential effect of (increased) aid, on domestic tax revenue, also warrants some consideration. This issue has been addressed in the literature on the fiscal effects of aid, and there is no general evidence that aid is associated with reduction in domestic tax revenue (McGillivray and Morrissey 2004). A related concern is whether the form of aid matters as it is argued that grants (where there is no obligation to repay) are more likely to discourage domestic tax effort than loans (as these must be repaid they encourage better fiscal management). As the poorest countries tend to receive aid in the form of grants and also tend to have low tax/GDP ratios (because they are poor, the tax base is small), there is inevitably a strong cross-country correlation between the share of grants in aid and the tax/GDP ratio. To demonstrate that grants discourage tax effort one needs to control for this and show that, over time, grants are associated with reductions in tax effort. Allowing for this, the evidence that grants cause lower tax effort is far from compelling (Morrissey et al. 2006). It is desirable to encourage countries to increase domestic resource mobilization so as to reduce dependency on aid, but for the poorest countries this process takes time. The sustainable way to increase tax effort is to expand the tax base, and this requires economic growth, especially private sector growth. It should not be assumed that aid in general, or grants in particular, actually retard this process; most poor countries would like growth.

The macroeconomic effects of increased aid can be adverse effects, so this should be monitored by governments and donors. However, increased aid support for the provision of social services does not mean significantly increased volumes of aid – it is more important that aid is used more effectively and in particular that the efficiency of public social service delivery is improved. The poorest countries do need and can use increased aid, but a modest increase may be sufficient and is more easily accommodated, both in terms of disbursement and macroeconomic effects. Aid effectiveness in benefiting the poor could be enhanced if the efficacy of public spending is increased, while targeting public expenditure in areas that are more likely to benefit the poor could increase effectiveness.

The final point to note is that we have only addressed one specific aspect of social development, spending on public social services (and within this the role of aid). It is important that countries have a coherent social development strategy, and indeed that donors act in a manner consistent with this strategy (something they do not always do). Initiatives such as PRSPs, although proposed as owned by the government, are at best only in part consistent with such a strategy and often the details of the PRSP owe more to donors than to the governments. Social development, as distinct from poverty reduction or social protection, rarely receives prominence in donor discourse or rhetoric, and redistributive policies are rarely explicitly acknowledged. Indeed, the redistributive effect of the fiscal system (that is, tax-benefit incidence) is the broader context within which social sector spending delivers social development outcomes. It is entirely conceivable that the benefits of expenditures on the poor are offset by taxes that bear disproportionately on the poor. Such concerns should not be exaggerated, however; the tax reforms implemented in developing countries over the past decade or so have in general been more likely to make the tax system more progressive than more regressive (Gemmell and Morrissey 2005). Aid-financing of delivery of social services has an important role to play in increasing access to public goods in poor countries (which is one element of social development), and will continue to do so until these countries reach the levels of income that allow them to reduce aid dependency.

Appendix A6.1: Data and Summary Statistics

Gomanee et al. (2005a) compile a data set for 104 low- and middle-income countries for 1980–83, 1984–87, 1988–91, 1992–95 and 1996–2000. We report briefly on the data used here. The measure of government social sector spending (Gs) is in effect the *World Development Report*'s category of 'social services' (post-1993 definition), and includes housing, water and sanitation (P_s), health (P_h) and education (P_e). Thus, Gs is defined as the sum of these three components. The variables of interest to us are:

HDI	The Human Development Index for 1980, 1985, 1990, 1995 and 2000.
IM	Infant mortality rate; the number of infants (0–1 year), per 1,000 live births in a given year.

Table A6.1   Some summary statistics

Variable % GDP	N	Mean	Min	Max
		Full sample		
Gs	626	7.092	0.019	38.519
P_S	277	3.622	0.028	19.492
P_E	539	4.324	0.019	36.161
P_H	394	2.806	0.313	13.730
Aid	625	9.866	−0.035	178.292
TR	424	17.712	3.461	91.858
		Low-income countries		
Gs	254	5.371	0.019	38.519
P_S	105	1.532	0.028	8.678
P_E	213	4.077	0.019	36.161
P_H	159	2.107	0.313	8.567
Aid	259	14.382	0.002	143.508
TR	159	14.523	3.461	91.858
		Middle-income countries		
Gs	372	8.266	0.390	31.776
P_S	172	4.898	0.039	19.492
P_E	326	4.484	1.244	10.727
P_H	235	3.280	0.390	13.730
Aid	366	6.670	−0.035	178.292
TR	265	19.626	3.797	47.467

Note: Based on period-averaged data.

P_S Spending on housing, water and sanitation (share of GDP).
P_E Public expenditure on education (share of GDP).
P_H Public expenditure on health (share of GDP).
Gm   Public expenditure on the military (share of GDP).
GDPpc   Real GDP per capita (constant 1995 US$).
Aid   Aid (expressed as a share of GDP).
TR   Tax revenue (expressed as a share of GDP).

Notes

1. Helpful comments were received from UNRISD and participants at the Geneva workshop, but the usual disclaimer applies.
2. Kanbur et al. (1999); Kaul et al. (1999); Morrissey et al. (2002).

References

Commission for Africa (2005) *Our Common Interest: Report of the Commission for Africa* (London: Commission for Africa).

Dabla-Norris, Era, John Matovu and Paul Wade (2004) 'Debt relief, demand for education and poverty.' In Tony Addison, Henrik Hansen and Finn Tarp (eds.), *Debt Relief for Poor Countries* (Basingstoke: Palgrave Macmillan/UNU-WIDER).

Devarajan, Shantayanan and Ritva Reinikka (2004) 'Making services work for the poor', *Journal of African Economies*, Vol. 13, Supplement 1, 142–66.

Gemmell, Norman and Oliver Morrissey (2005) 'Distribution and poverty impacts of tax structure reform in developing countries: How Little We Know', *Development Policy Review*, Vol. 23, No. 2, 131–44.

Gomanee, Karuna, Oliver Morrissey, Paul Mosley and Arjan Verschoor (2005a) 'Aid, government expenditure and aggregate welfare', *World Development*, Vol. 33, No. 3, 355–70.

Gomanee, Karuna, Sourafel Girma and Oliver Morrissey (2005b) 'Aid, public spending and human welfare: Evidence from quantile regressions', *Journal of International Development*, Vol. 17, No. 3, 299–309.

Gupta, Sanjeev, Marijn Verhoeven and Erwin Tiongson (2002) 'The effectiveness of government spending on education and health care in developing and transition economies', *European Journal of Political Economy*, Vol. 18, No. 4, 717–38.

Kanbur, Ravi, Todd Sandler, with Kevin Morrison (1999) *The Future of Development Assistance: Common Pools and International Public Goods*, Policy Essay No. 25 (Washington, DC: Overseas Development Council).

Kaul, Inge, Isabelle Grunberg and Marc Stern (eds.) (1999) *Global Public Goods: International Cooperation in the 21st Century* (New York and Oxford: Oxford University Press).

Lanjouw, Peter and Martin Ravallion (1999) 'Benefit incidence, public spending reforms and the timing of program capture', *The World Bank Economic Review*, Vol. 13, No. 2, 257–74.

McGillivray, Mark and Oliver Morrissey (2004) 'Fiscal effects of aid.' In Tony Addison and Alan Roe (eds.), *Fiscal Policy for Development: Poverty, Reconstruction and Growth* (Basingstoke: Palgrave Macmillan/UNU-WIDER).

McGillivray, Mark and Oliver Morrissey (2001) 'Aid illusion and public sector fiscal behaviour', *Journal of Development Studies*, Vol. 37, No. 6, 118–36.

Morrissey, Oliver (2006a) 'Aid or trade, or aid and trade?', *The Australian Economic Review*, Vol. 39, No. 1, 78–88.

Morrissey, Oliver (2006b) 'Fungibility, prior actions, and eligibility for budget support.' In Stefan Koeberle, Zoran Stavreski and J. Wallister (eds.), *Budget Support as More Effective Aid? Recent Experiences and Emerging Lessons* (Washington, DC: World Bank).

Morrissey, Oliver (2005) 'Imports and implementation: Neglected aspects of trade in the Report of the Commission for Africa', *Journal of Development Studies*, Vol. 41, No. 4, 1133–53.

Morrissey, Oliver (2004) 'Making debt-relief conditionality pro-poor.' In Tony Addison, Henrik Hansen and Finn Tarp (eds.), *Debt Relief for Poor Countries* (Basingstoke: Palgrave Macmillan/UNU-WIDER).

Morrissey, Oliver, Olaf Islei and Daniel M'Amanja (2006) *Aid Loans versus Aid Grants: Are the Effects Different?*, CREDIT Research Paper No. 06/07 (Nottingham: University of Nottingham). www.nottingham.ac.uk/economics/credit/, accessed on 26 March 2007.

Morrissey, Oliver, Dirk Willem te Velde and Adrian Hewitt (2002) 'Defining international public goods: Conceptual issues.' In Marco Ferroni and Ashok Mody (eds.), *International Public Goods: Incentives, Measurement and Financing* (Dordrecht: Kluwer Academic Publishing, and (Washington, DC: World Bank).

Morrissey, Oliver and Arjan Verschoor (2006) 'What does ownership mean in practice? Policy learning and the evolution of pro-poor policies in Uganda.' In Alberto Paloni and Maurizio Zinardi (eds.), *The IMF, World Bank and Policy Reform* (London: Routledge).

Morrisson, Christian (ed.) (2002) *Education and Health Expenditure and Poverty Reduction in East Africa: Madagascar and Tanzania* (Paris: OECD Development Centre Studies).

Mosley, Paul, John Hudson and Arjan Verschoor (2004) 'Aid, poverty reduction and the new conditionality', *The Economic Journal*, Vol. 114, F217–F243.

Rayp, Glenn and Nicolas Van de Sijpe (2007) 'Measuring and explaining government efficiency in developing countries', *Journal of Development Studies*, Vol. 43, No. 2, 360–81.

Reinikka, Ritva and Jacob Svensson (2004) 'Efficiency of public spending: New microeconomic tools to assess service delivery.' In Tony Addison and Alan Roe (eds.), *Fiscal Policy for Development: Poverty, Reconstruction and Growth* (Basingstoke: Palgrave Macmillan/UNU-WIDER).

Samuelson, Paul (1954) 'The pure theory of public expenditure', *Review of Economics and Statistics*, Vol. 36, No. 4, 387–9.

Svensson, Jacob and Ritva Reinikka (2004) 'Local capture: Evidence from a central government transfer program in Uganda', *The Quarterly Journal of Economics*, Vol. 119, No. 2, 679–705.

te Velde, Dirk Willem, Oliver Morrissey and Adrian Hewitt (2002) 'Allocating aid to international public goods.' In Marco Ferroni and Ashok Mody (eds.), *International Public Goods: Incentives, Measurement and Financing* (Dordrecht: Kluwer Academic Publishing, and Washington, DC: World Bank).

White, Howard (2007) 'Book review of "The White Man's Burden" by William Easterly', *Journal of Development Studies*, Vol. 43, No. 3, 589–91.

Part III
Mineral Rents

7
Natural Resource Wealth, Development and Social Policy: Evidence and Issues

Andrew Rosser

Introduction

Natural resource wealth potentially provides a source of funds for governments to invest in development. But several recent studies have suggested that countries rich in natural resources have in fact performed poorly in developmental terms. Prior to the late 1980s, natural resource wealth was widely seen as a blessing for developing countries. In the 1960s, for instance, the prominent development theorist Walter Rostow (1961) argued that natural resource endowments would enable developing countries to make the transition from underdevelopment to industrial 'take-off', just as they had done for developed countries such as Australia, the United States and the United Kingdom (UK). In the 1970s and 1980s, neoliberal economists such as Bela Balassa (1980), Anne Krueger (1980) and P.J. Drake (1972) put forward similar arguments, with the former, for instance, arguing that natural resources could facilitate a country's 'industrial development by providing domestic markets and investible funds' (Balassa 1980: 2). But now natural resource wealth is widely seen as a curse. Rather than promoting development, it is argued, natural resource wealth in fact reduces economic growth, increases poverty, impairs health and education outcomes, impedes democracy, lowers the status of women, and increases the incidence, duration and intensity of civil war.

This chapter critically examines the developmental effects of natural resource wealth and, to the extent that these have been negative, explores the conditions under which they can be overcome. I argue that there is considerable evidence that natural resource wealth impedes development but that this is not conclusive. At the same time, it is clear that the relationship between natural resource wealth and development is not a deterministic one. In other words, countries that are rich in natural resource wealth can experience development, in some cases even rapid development, given the right conditions. After reviewing debates surrounding what these conditions are, I suggest that a broad consensus has emerged that political and social factors are the key to determining whether or not resource-rich countries overcome the resource curse, even if there is some disagreement about which political and social factors are most important in this regard. This in turn suggests that development in resource-rich countries requires not just change in resource-rich countries' economic policies – the focus of much of the economics literature on the resource curse – but also changes in the nature of broader political and social features.

In presenting this argument, I begin by reviewing the evidence that has emerged so far on the effects of natural resource wealth on various aspects of development. In the following section of the chapter, I then examine debates surrounding the conditions under which resource-rich countries have overcome the resource curse. In the final part, I explore the implications of the argument for social policy in resource-rich countries.

Are natural resources a curse?

A large number of academic studies has presented evidence to suggest that natural resource abundance, or at least an abundance of particular natural resources, has negative effects with regards to economic growth. Wheeler (1984), for instance, found that within sub-Saharan Africa, countries that were rich in minerals grew more slowly than those that were not rich in minerals during the 1970s. Similarly, Gelb and Associates (1988) found that mineral economies experienced a more serious deterioration in the efficiency of domestic capital formation during the boom period of 1971–83 than non-mineral economies, leading to negative growth in hard mineral economies and dramatically reduced growth in oil-exporting economies (see also Auty 1993). Sachs and Warner (1995) examined the experiences of a large and diverse set of natural resource economies between 1970 and 1989 and found that natural resource abundance was negatively correlated with economic growth. Leite and Weidmann (1999) and Gylfason et al. (1999) produced similar results, also using large datasets. Auty (2001) found that the per capita incomes of resource-poor countries grew at rates two to three times higher than resource-abundant countries between 1960 and 1990. Neumayer (2004) examined whether natural resource abundance had a negative effect on economic growth if one measured growth in terms of 'genuine' income – that is, gross domestic product (GDP) minus the depreciation of produced and natural capital – rather than GDP. He found that it did.

A number of academic studies has also suggested that natural resource wealth has negative effects with regards to poverty. UNCTAD (2002) and Ross (2003a), for instance, found that mineral wealth is associated with relatively high poverty rates, measured in terms of the World Bank's benchmark of income below $1 or $2[1] per day (in the case of the United Nations Conference on Trade and Development/UNCTAD) and countries' respective national poverty lines (in the case of Ross). Ross also examined the effect of mineral wealth on poverty as measured using proxy variables such as life expectancy, infant mortality and prevalence of child malnutrition. He found that mineral wealth had a small negative effect on these variables.

Many scholars have also suggested that natural resource wealth is associated with the onset, duration and intensity of civil war – that is, the number of battle-related deaths. After examining the experiences of 98 countries and 27 civil wars, Collier and Hoeffler (1998), for instance, found that natural resource wealth, defined in terms of the ratio of primary exports to GDP, is a strong and significant determinant of the onset of civil war, although they also found that the relationship between these variables was curvilinear: initially, natural resource wealth increased the risk of civil war, but above a certain level of exports, it reduced this risk. In a subsequent study, they confirmed this finding using a better dataset (Collier and Hoeffler 2000). In a third study, they examined the effect of natural resource wealth on different types of civil wars. They found that natural resources increased the risk of both secessionist and non-secessionist civil wars, but that the former were three times more likely to be associated with natural resources than the latter (Collier and Hoeffler 2002). Reynal-Querol (2002) conducted a similar study, focused on the association between natural resources and the onset of ethnic and non-ethnic civil wars. Using data from a sample of 138 countries between 1960 and 1995, she found that natural resource abundance was an important variable in explaining the incidence of non-ethnic civil wars and other forms of political violence, but not the incidence of ethnic civil wars. In their most recent paper, Collier and Hoeffler (2005) report on work showing that natural resource wealth continues to exhibit a curvilinear relationship with the onset of civil war even if a rent-based measure of natural resource abundance is substituted for their original export-based measure. However, they note that this result is less significant than their earlier finding and that the rent-based measure of natural resource wealth becomes insignificant, when the original measure of natural resource wealth is included in the regression analysis as well.

Some scholars have suggested that natural resource abundance may also lengthen the duration of civil wars. Collier and Hoeffler (1998), for instance, found that natural resource abundance and the duration of civil wars also had a curvilinear relationship. Similarly, Doyle and Sambanis (2000) found that natural resource wealth was significantly and negatively correlated with the success of peace-building initiatives. As Ross (2004b: 341) has noted, in so far as there is a link between the failure of such initiatives and the duration of civil wars, this finding suggests that natural resource wealth is associated with longer wars. Fearon (2004) found that countries that are rich in contraband resources such as opium, diamonds, or coca tend to experience longer civil wars and Ballentine (2003) found that natural resources served to prolong civil wars in a selection of resource-rich developing countries. Finally, as Ross (2004a: 45) has noted, several observers of Africa's civil wars, have suggested that natural resources worsen the intensity of civil wars 'by causing combatants to fight for territory that would otherwise have little value.' Ross (2004a) himself found only very modest support for this idea: of the 13 cases of civil war he examined, natural resources only clearly increased the intensity of conflict in two cases; in the 11 others, natural resources either had no effect or a mixed effect on civil war intensity.

Several scholars have suggested that natural resource abundance is also associated with low levels of democracy. Wantchekon (1999), for instance, examined data related to 141 countries between 1950 and 1990 and found that a 1 per cent increase in natural resource dependence, as measured by the ratio of primary exports to GDP, increased the probability of authoritarian government by nearly 8 per cent. He also found that countries that were rich in natural resources were more likely to experience failed or slow transitions to democracy. Jensen and Wantchekon (2004) presented similar findings in relation to Africa, concluding that resource-abundant countries in this region were more likely to be authoritarian and experience breakdowns in democracy after the democratic transition. Ross (2001a) investigated whether there was any variation in regime outcomes across different types of resource economy and different regions. After examining data from 113 states between 1971 and 1997, he concluded that 'a state's reliance on oil or mineral exports tends to make it less democratic; that this effect is not caused by other types of primary exports; that it is not limited to the Arabian peninsula, to the Middle East, or to sub-Saharan Africa; and that it is not limited to small states' (Ross 2001a: 346).

Finally, Ross (2006) has found that oil wealth is associated with relatively low status for women measured in terms of women's participation in the labour force and the number of women who hold seats in parliament or positions in government cabinets. Natural resource wealth, he argues, reduces women's participation in the workforce by 'crowding out' labour-intensive manufacturing activities that often employ women and by increasing women's access to unearned income, thus reducing their incentive to work. Low participation in the workforce, in turn, he argues, reduces the likelihood that women will organize and engage in collective action aimed at improving the status of women.

But while there is considerable evidence to support the idea that natural resource wealth has a wide range of negative developmental effects, there are several reasons to treat this evidence with caution. First, some scholars have suggested that the findings of studies such as those cited above may not be robust to differences in the measurement of natural resource abundance. In general, researchers have measured natural resource abundance in terms of either the ratio of countries' natural resource exports to GDP or the ratio of countries' natural resource exports to total exports. When they have used different measures of natural resource abundance, their results have been less clearly supportive of the notion of a resource curse. Stijns (2001), for instance, found that when natural resource abundance was measured in terms of levels of production and reserves rather than exports, it did not have a significant influence on economic growth. Similarly, Herb (2003) found that when natural resource abundance was measured in terms of the percentage of rents in government revenues rather than the levels of natural resource exports, there is little support for the idea that there is a negative relationship between natural resource abundance and the occurrence of democracy. De Soysa (2000) found that when natural resource abundance was measured in terms of the level of natural resource stock per capita, there was no relationship between the incidence of civil war and the overall level of natural resource abundance. Auty (2001: 5) has pointed out that a number of studies have used non-export-based measures of natural resource abundance including Gylfason et al. (1999) (who used labour force in the primary sector) and Auty (2001) (who used crop land per head), suggesting that the findings of these studies may be more robust than critics of the resource curse hypothesis have suggested. But the question of whether these findings are robust to broader changes in the measure of natural resource abundance remains unresolved.

Second, it is not clear that the ratio of natural resource exports to GDP or the ratio of natural resource exports to total exports are appropriate measures of natural resource wealth. Most studies that attempt to explain the resource curse – particularly those conducted by political scientists – suggest that the main problem with natural resource wealth is not that it leads to economic dependence on natural resources or a skewed export structure *per se* but that it creates rents – that is, excess earnings above normal profits.[2] The existence of these rents is, in turn, variously seen as contributing to negative development outcomes by encouraging myopia and overexuberance on the part of political elites, promoting damaging rent-seeking behaviour by political elites and/or social actors, weakening state capacity to regulate and supervise the economy, empowering social elements that are opposed to growth-promoting policies, or encouraging foreign intervention (Rosser 2006b). As such, it could be argued that rent-based measures of natural resource abundance provide a more useful basis for making judgements about the existence or non-existence of a resource curse. Yet studies that have used such measures – such as Herb (2003) and Collier and Hoeffler (2005) – have so far provided only mixed support for the notion of a resource curse.

Third, the finding that there is a strong relationship between natural resource wealth and the onset and duration of civil war seems to be contingent on the use of a particular civil war database. As Ross (2004b: 347–8) has pointed out, the studies that have presented this finding have all used Collier and Hoeffler's list of civil wars, yet scholars who have used alternative lists of civil wars have generally come to different conclusions. He suggests several reasons for this related to the way in which civil wars are coded and civil war duration is measured. In short, however, he suggests that Collier and Hoeffler's database 'may be biased in a way that overstates the impact of primary commodities' (2004b: 342).

Fourth, a number of scholars have presented evidence that suggests that the main problem vis-à-vis development outcomes in resource-abundant countries is not natural resource abundance per se – as many of the aforementioned studies suggest – but an abundance of particular types of natural resources. At the same time, there is some disagreement, at least in relation to civil war, about which natural resources are the main problem. Many researchers have pointed to 'point source' natural resources – for instance, oil, minerals, and plantation crops – as being particularly problematic. Isham et al. (2002), for instance, found that countries that are rich in point source natural resources grew much more slowly during the 1980s and 1990s than countries that are rich in 'diffuse' natural resources – for instance, wheat and rice – and countries that are rich in cocoa and coffee. Similarly, Sala-i-Martin and Subramanian (2004) found that an abundance of point source natural resources was significantly correlated with poor economic growth, but that an abundance of diffuse natural resources was not. Leite and Weidmann (1999) found that fuel and ores had a more negative effect on growth than agriculture (although a less significant negative effect than food production). Ross (2003a) found that oil wealth and non-fuel mineral wealth are associated with bad outcomes for the poor but not agricultural resources. De Soysa (2000) found that, while the incidence of civil wars was not related to total natural resource wealth, it *was* strongly related to the level of mineral wealth, suggesting that point source resources (specifically mineral resources) rather than natural resources in general are the main problem as far as the onset of civil war is concerned. In a subsequent study, he found that, among mineral-rich countries, oil exporters were particularly prone to civil war (De Soysa 2002). Fearon and Laitin (2002) have presented similar evidence on this point, showing that the size of countries' primary commodity exports is not a significant determinant of the onset of civil wars but that their level of oil wealth is. Fearon (2005) has provided further evidence to this effect. Finally, Ross' (2001a) findings on the relationship between oil wealth and democracy are also consistent with the emphasis on the negative effects of point source resources.

His findings in relation to civil war, however, are not. In Ross (2003b), he presents evidence to suggest that it is 'lootable' resources such as diamonds (particularly alluvial diamonds) and drugs (particularly opium and coca) rather than point source resources that are the most likely to produce civil war. After analysing 12 civil wars and three minor conflicts that occurred between 1990 and 2000, he found that, once income per capita was accounted for, there was little difference in civil war rates between resource-abundant countries in the four main categories of natural resources – oil and gas, minerals, food crops, and non-food crops. By contrast, he found that diamonds and drugs were strongly associated with the incidence of civil war. Humphreys (2005) has also presented evidence to suggest that point source resources are not the main problem vis-à-vis the onset of civil war, although his findings also challenge Ross's findings concerning lootable resources. According to his evidence, the main problem vis-à-vis the onset of civil war is the extent to which countries are dependent on agricultural production. This effect, he notes, is independent of a country's endowment of oil and diamonds, suggesting that the problem of resource dependence is not simply one of the availability of point source or lootable resources but also economic structure and how this shapes social relations (Humphreys 2005: 524–5). These findings stand in marked contrast to those of Fearon (2005), Fearon and Laitin (2002), and De Soysa (2000) and suggest that the issue of which types of natural resources are most likely to lead to the onset of civil war has not yet been resolved.

Fifth, there is some evidence, albeit limited, that natural resource wealth may in fact have a beneficial, or at least neutral, effect on development performance. Davis (1995), for instance, has shown that, by certain economic and social measures, mineral economies outperformed non-mineral economies between 1970 and 1991. These measures include average gross national product (GNP) per capita and improvement in various social indicators such as infant mortality, life expectancy, calorie supply per capita, and the United Nations' human development index. Stijns (2003) has presented similar evidence using more sophisticated statistical techniques. Such findings contrast with those of UNCTAD (2002) and Ross (2003a) in particular. In addition, some scholars have produced evidence to suggest that natural resource abundance may not have a negative effect on the onset, duration or intensity of civil war. In a study of the effects of oil dependence on regime failure and conflict in 107 developing countries between 1960 and 1999, Smith (2004), for instance, found that oil wealth is associated with lower levels of civil war and anti-state protest. Similarly, Sørli et al. (2005) found that oil dependence has not exercised a significant influence on the onset of civil war in the Middle East in recent decades. In respect of the duration of civil war, Humphreys (2005) has presented evidence to suggest that natural resource conflicts are more likely to end quickly while Ross (2003b) has presented evidence to suggest that while lootable resources may serve to prolong non-separatist conflicts, non-lootable resources serve to reduce non-separatist conflicts (see also Collier et al. 2004). In respect of the intensity of civil war, Ballentine (2003) has suggested that natural resource abundance has, in some cases, reduced the number of battle-related deaths during civil war.

Finally, while the studies above provide evidence that natural resource abundance – or at least an abundance of particular types of natural resources – and various development outcomes are *correlated* with one another, they do not prove that the former *causes* the latter. Those arguing in favour of the notion of a resource curse have merely inferred causality from the evidence of correlation. However, the direction of causation may in fact run the other way. That is, it may be that civil war, for instance, causes economic dependence on the natural resources sector by making it difficult for countries to attract manufacturing investment. As Schrank (2004) puts it, natural resource dependence may be a symptom of underdevelopment rather than the cause. Alternatively, the relationship between natural resource dependence and various development outcomes may be entirely spurious – that is, their correlation with one another may simply reflect the influence of an unidentified third variable. Just as ice cream sales and the number of sunburn cases are highly correlated because of changes in the seasons, rather than because ice cream consumption causes sunburn or vice versa, so it may be that natural resource abundance and civil war, for instance, are correlated because a third variable (say, the weak rule of law) both increases the risk of civil war and the difficulties countries face in attracting manufacturing investment (Ross 2004b: 338). It will only be by examining more closely the causal mechanisms surrounding the resource curse that scholars will adequately resolve these issues.

In sum, then, while there is strong evidence to support the notion that natural resource wealth is bad for development, it is by no means conclusive. First, there are a variety of factors related to the measurement of key variables – especially, natural resource abundance and civil war outcomes – that raise doubts about the findings of studies that are supportive of the 'resource curse' hypothesis. Second, it is unclear whether the resource curse (and its various dimensions) applies to all natural resource economies or just certain ones. Different studies point in different directions on this issue. In addition, there is ongoing debate among those who argue that particular natural resources are the main problem about which natural resources are most pernicious, especially in relation to civil war. Third, some studies report findings contrary to the resource curse hypothesis, even when they use the same measure of natural resource abundance as those that support this hypothesis (as is the case, for instance, with some studies on the link between natural resource abundance and the duration of civil war). Finally, these studies do not illustrate conclusively that the direction of causation runs from natural resource wealth to poor development outcomes rather than the other way around and that the relationship between the two does not reflect the influence of an independent third variable.

Overcoming the resource curse

At the same time that the aforementioned studies suggest that the relationship between natural resource wealth and development outcomes is negative, they also suggest that, to paraphrase Auty (1994: 24), the resource curse is a general tendency rather than an iron law. Indeed, many supporters of the notion of a resource curse acknowledge that, while resource-rich countries have in general performed poorly in developmental terms, there are a number of exceptions to this pattern including several developing countries, specifically Botswana, Indonesia, Malaysia and Chile (Stevens 2003). These countries have managed to achieve both rapid economic growth and at least moderate levels of social development. This, in turn, suggests that the relationship between natural resource wealth and the various development outcomes discussed above is mediated by one or more intervening variables. I now examine debates about the conditions under which resource-rich countries have overcome the resource curse and what this suggests about the strategies they should pursue in trying to promote economic and social development.

Much of the literature on the resource curse has focused either on trying to establish whether there is a resource curse or determine what causes the resource curse (Rosser 2006b). With respect to the latter, early work suggested that the causal mechanisms linking natural resource abundance and bad development outcomes were essentially economic in nature. Specifically, it was suggested that natural resource exporters suffered from declining terms of trade, volatile export earnings, an enclave economic structure, and/or the so-called 'Dutch disease' (a condition whereby a resource boom leads to appreciation of the real exchange rate and in turn damages manufacturing and other tradable sectors). Now, however, there seems to be broad agreement that the resource curse operates through causal mechanisms that are political in nature, although there is considerable disagreement about which political mechanisms are most important in this respect. While some scholars have suggested that natural resource abundance leads to emotional or irrational behaviour on the part of political actors (such as overexuberance or feelings of grievance), others have suggested that it increases the incentives for political actors to engage in damaging rational behaviour (such as rent seeking or looting). Others again have suggested that natural resource abundance leads to the emergence of 'rentier' states that lack the institutional capacity to regulate and supervise the economy, undermines social capital, strengthens social groups that have an interest in protectionist economic policies, and/or increases the likelihood that a country will be forcefully incorporated into the global economy (see Ross 1999 and Rosser 2006b for reviews of this literature).

However, a small number of scholars have focused on the question of why some resource-rich countries have done better than others in terms of promoting economic and social development. Many of these scholars have focused simply on the nature of economic policies in resource-rich countries and have suggested that their respective development performance depends on the extent to which they have adopted orthodox economic policies, particularly in the macroeconomic and fiscal realms. Sarraf and Jiwanji (2001: v), for instance, argue that Botswana was able to break the resource curse because its government adopted 'sound economic policies and [provided] good management of windfall gains'. More specifically, they argue that its government accumulated foreign reserves, ran budget surpluses to be spent only in leaner periods rather than deficits, and managed the nominal exchange rate in such a way as to avoid real appreciation of the national currency. By doing these things, they argue, the government ensured that the country avoided external debt, experienced stable rather than volatile economic growth, and developed a diversified economic structure.

But most scholars who have sought to explain why some resource-rich countries have done better than others have focused on political and social factors as well. Eifert et al. (2003), for instance, have argued that the economic performance of oil-exporting countries has depended on the respective type of political institutions that they have had. All oil-rich countries, they argue, have *rentier* states – that is, states that are funded mainly by natural resource rents rather than taxes on citizens. But the particular institutional form that these states have taken has varied from case to case with differing economic results. They suggest that rentier states come in five main types – 'mature democracies', such as Norway; 'factional democracies', such as Venezuela and Colombia; 'paternalistic autocracies', such as Saudi Arabia; 'reformist autocracies', such as Indonesia; and 'predatory autocracies', such as Nigeria. Each of these types of rentier state, they say, varies in terms of the extent to which their political frameworks and party systems are stable, the degree to which they exhibit social consensus, the ways in which governments obtain and maintain legitimacy, and the role that the state plays in the economy. These differences, in turn, translate into differences in policy horizons; levels of transparency, policy stability and policy quality; the political power of non-oil tradable sectors; the power of interests that are involved in activities directly attached to state spending; and ultimately the capacity of the state to address key policy challenges surrounding the resource curse.

Of these types of rentier state, Eifert et al. suggest that mature democracies and reformist autocracies have performed best in addressing these policy challenges. In the case of mature democracies, this is because their stable party systems, high level of social consensus, competent and insulated bureaucracies and judicial systems, and highly educated electorates, have translated into long policy horizons, policy stability and transparency, competitiveness and a coalitional structure in which pro-stabilization constituencies are politically stronger than pro-spending constituencies. In the case of 'reformist autocracies', it is because their stable governments; broad social consensus in favour of development; and autonomous, competent and politically insulated technocratic elites have translated into long decision horizons, policy stability and strong constituencies in favour of stabilization and fiscal restraint, even if they have also resulted in low levels of transparency. Factional democracies, paternalistic autocracies and predatory autocracies, by contrast, are seen as suffering from one or more problems in relation to these criteria, with predatory autocracies being by far the worst.

Snyder (2006) has similarly focused on the nature of domestic political institutions in his analysis of the relationship between natural resource wealth – specifically lootable natural resource wealth – and civil war. In his view, whether the existence of lootable natural resources leads to disorder depends on the extent to which rulers are able to create institutions of extraction that concentrate resource rents in their hands. Where they are able to do this, he suggests, the result is much more likely to be political order than if they are not able to (see also Snyder and Bhavnani 2005).

Weinthal and Jones Luong (2001), by contrast, have focused on the incentives facing political leaders in resource-rich countries in their work on the effects of the resource curse in five Soviet successor states – the Russian Federation, Kazakhstan, Turkmenistan, Uzbekistan and Azerbaijan (Weinthal and Hones Luong 2001; Jones Luong and Weinthal 2001). Like the first set of scholars mentioned above, Weinthal and Jones Luong emphasize the importance of policy in shaping economic outcomes in resource-rich states, although for them it is privatization policy rather than macroeconomic and fiscal policy that is the most important determinant of these outcomes. Countries that privatize their resources sectors, they argue, are more likely to avoid the resource curse than those that do not, but only if they sell these sectors to domestic interests. This is because domestic investors have greater bargaining power vis-à-vis the state than foreign investors: whereas the bargaining power of foreign investors declines once their capital and costs are sunk, domestic investors maintain their bargaining power vis-à-vis the state because 'both need the other in order to survive, enabling them to reach a compromise or find that their interests have converged over time' (Weinthal and Jones Luong 2001: 222). In this connection, they point to the different experiences of Russia and Kazakhstan, which sold their oil sectors to domestic and foreign interests respectively, in developing their taxation systems. Whereas 'domestic oil companies are helping to foster the development of an increasingly viable tax regime in Russia', Kazakhstan's tax regime 'has become increasingly volatile' and overly reliant on foreign businesses (Weinthal and Jones Luong 2001: 216).

But Weinthal and Jones Luong go beyond an analysis of the policy causes of economic success and failure in the five former Soviet states to examine the political dynamics that underlay these policies. The starting point for their analysis in this respect is the assumption that political leaders are rational and self-interested actors whose primary concern is to stay in power. More specifically, they argue that political leaders are primarily concerned about maximizing the difference between the resources they possess (R) and the costs they face in gaining support and appeasing or defeating opponents (C). At the same time, they argue that political leaders are constrained in their decision making by: (i) the availability of alternative sources of export revenue besides their natural resource reserves; and (ii) the level of political contestation over the basis for dispensing political power and economic patronage. The former, they say, determines the level of resources that political leaders have at their disposal (that is, R) while the latter determines the level of resources that leaders require to maintain their hold on power (that is, C). When R decreases relative to C or C increases relative to R, the ability of leaders to pursue their preferred development strategy for the resources sector – deemed to be nationalization with minimal foreign involvement – will be constrained 'because they must generate additional resources with which to appease or defeat their opponents' (Jones Luong and Weinthal 2001: 374).

In this context, political leaders will be willing to sell their country's resources sector to domestic business only if they have extensive access to alternative sources of export revenue and there is a high level of contestation over the basis for dispensing power and patronage.

> Under this scenario, leaders engage in extensive privatization as a means of maintaining support for their continued rule. By transferring ownership of these resources from the state to private domestic actors, they can bolster dominant patronage networks and appease the emerging rival one. They are able to minimize the role of international actors, however, because they can rely on revenue from their alternative exports. In fact, excluding foreign investors from the privatization process enables them to sell off these resources to domestic supporters and/or powerful rivals at below market value. (Jones Luong and Weinthal 2001: 376)

Finally, scholars such as Acemoglu et al. (2003), Bevan et al. (1999) and Rosser (2007) have focused on historical and structural factors in explaining why Botswana and Indonesia have done better than others in terms of promoting economic development. These scholars broadly accept the view of Sarraf, Jiwanji, Usui and others that orthodox macroeconomic policies and strong protection of property rights contributed to the economic success of these countries. However, they focus their analyses on the historical, political and social factors that facilitated the adoption of these policies and institutions in Botswana and Indonesia and impaired it in other countries. Acemoglu et al. (2003), for instance, suggest that Botswana adopted 'strong' institutions and 'good' policies in part because the dominant political elements in Botswana in the post-independence period – chiefs and cattle-owners – developed an interest in such institutions and policies – and, in particular, the strong protection of property rights – because of their involvement in ranching and other economic activities during that time. At the same time, they suggest that pre-colonial tribal institutions 'that encouraged broad-based participation and placed constraints on elites' survived the colonial period because Botswana was peripheral to the British Empire and hence had a relatively limited impact there. When the country later began to exploit its mineral wealth, they argue, it had already started to build democratic and efficient institutional structures and, consequently, its new mineral wealth 'likely reinforced' these structures (p. 105) rather than served to undermine them. Not entirely rejecting agency as a factor in shaping development outcomes, they add that Botswana's institutions also reflected sensible and far-sighted decisions on the part of post-independence political leaders.

Similarly, Bevan et al. (1999) argue that Indonesia outperformed Nigeria in economic terms between the 1960s and the late 1990s because differences in 'initial conditions' and 'the happenstance of events' in the two countries led their governments to make different economic policy choices. With respect to 'initial conditions', Bevan et al. emphasize a variety of factors related to these countries respective economic, political and social structures. The first is the fact that Indonesia was more vulnerable to fluctuations in world food prices than Nigeria during the period from the 1950s to the 1980s because it was a major importer of rice. This, they argue, made the Indonesian government more concerned about promoting agricultural development than the Nigerian government. The second is the fact that the Indonesian army, the main base of support for Suharto's New Order regime (1966–98), saw itself as having a 'dual function' – that is, a responsibility for sociopolitical as well as military tasks – whereas the Nigerian army did not. This, Bevan et al. suggest, made the Indonesian government more responsive to the poor than the Nigerian government, in turn contributing to a stronger emphasis on poverty alleviation. The third is the fact that Indonesia's commercial elite were predominantly ethnic Chinese, a factor that made them politically vulnerable, while Nigeria's commercial elite were from the south of the country, where the main opposition to the ruling elite was based. Bevan et al. suggest that this meant that the two countries' ruling elites had different incentives in relation to economic liberalization. While the ruling elite in Nigeria was concerned that economic liberalization would undermine their position by enriching southern business people and hence their political opponents in the south, the ruling elite in Indonesia had no similar concern about economic liberalization because of the political vulnerability of the ethnic Chinese. With respect to the happenstance of events, Bevan et al. emphasize the effects of three specific events: Indonesian President Sukarno's articulation of a clear vision of social cohesion during the 1950s and 1960s; the occurrence of hyperinflation in Indonesia in the mid-1960s; and rapid economic growth in the East Asian Newly Industrializing Countries (NICs) from the 1960s onwards. Bevan et al. argue that the first of these events created expectations among the Indonesian population relating to poverty alleviation that subsequent governments were unable to ignore. Because Nigeria did not have a leader as socially-committed as Sukarno, they argue, Nigerians did not have similar expectations. The second event, they say, caused the Indonesian population to attach a higher priority to the avoidance of inflation than the Nigerian population. Finally, the third event created greater trade and foreign investment opportunities for Indonesia than it did for Nigeria because of the former's greater geographical proximity and historical ties to the East Asian NICs.

My analysis of the Indonesian case (Rosser 2007) is similar but focuses more explicitly on contests for power between competing coalitions of interest and the economic consequences of the country's location in the global political economy. I argue that Indonesia's success in overcoming the resource curse during the 1970s and 1980s reflected two factors: (i) the political victory of counter-revolutionary social forces over communist and radical populist social forces during the mid-1960s; and (ii) the economic opportunities opened up by the country's geopolitical significance during the Cold War and its geographical proximity to Japan and the 'tiger' economies of East Asia. The first of these factors laid the political foundations for the Indonesian government to reorient its economic policies away from the radical economic nationalism of the 1950s and early 1960s and towards an economic policy agenda more favourable to capitalist economic development in the 1970s and 1980s. In particular, it laid the foundations for greater pragmatism in the macroeconomic and fiscal realms, greater investment in infrastructure and agricultural development, and the pursuit of an exchange rate policy conducive to the maintenance of international competitiveness in non-oil and gas sectors. The second of these factors opened up economic opportunities for Indonesia that other resource-abundant countries did not have. These included the receipt of generous levels of foreign aid, privileged access to lucrative Western export markets, access to important new technology (especially in the agricultural sector), and opportunities to attract large amounts of foreign direct investment in labour intensive manufacturing industries during the 1980s and 1990s. The combined effect of both of these factors was that Indonesia was able to keep a lid on foreign indebtedness, avoid a serious post-commodity-boom economic growth collapse, and successfully diversify its economy away from a reliance on natural resources – in short, it avoided the main economic problems associated with the resource curse.

In sum, then, these studies suggest that development outcomes in resource-abundant countries are primarily a function of political and social factors. There is some disagreement about exactly which political and social factors matter, with Eifert et al. and Snyder focusing on the character of political institutions in resource-rich countries, Weinthal and Jones Luong on the incentive structures facing elites, and Acemoglu et al., Bevan et al., and Rosser on historico-structural factors. But they nevertheless suggest that overcoming the resource curse requires more than simply voluntary economic policy choices on the part of state elites. It also requires fundamental change in the nature of political and social systems, particularly (but not necessarily only) at a domestic level.

The way forward

I have argued here that there is compelling (if not conclusive) evidence to support the notion of the resource curse. At the same time, I have also argued that the main causes of the resource curse – and the main hopes for overcoming it – lie in the political and social realms. The political and social obstacles to the resource curse are not insurmountable – as I have already noted, a number of resource-rich countries have done well in developmental terms over recent decades. But there is no easy fix for these obstacles. Overcoming the resource curse cannot be achieved through voluntary changes to government policy by policy makers but requires far-reaching political and social change.

In seeking strategies for promoting development in resource-abundant countries, then, we need to do three things. First, we need to gain a better understanding of the political and social conditions that are consistent with positive developmental outcomes in resource-rich countries. The work of Eifert et al., Weinthal and Jones Luong, Acemoglu et al., and so on, have initiated an interesting and important debate about the sorts of political and social conditions that facilitate successful management of the resource curse. But more work is needed (Rosser 2006a). Specifically, we need to determine whether change is required at the level of incentives, institutions or structures – or, indeed, all three – in order to create political and social conditions conducive to overcoming the resource curse; and what sort of change is required. Secondly, we need to improve our understanding of how changes in these variables occur in resource-rich countries. To use the phrase employed by the UK's Department for International Development, we need to know what the 'drivers of change' are. If we understand what these drivers are, it will be much easier to precipitate the required changes. Finally, we need to know more about how such changes might be consolidated once they have occurred. Specifically, we need to know how to ensure that elements within society that have the potential to disrupt the political and social order produced by these changes develop or retain an interest in this order.

This argument has two main implications for the role of social policy in resource-rich countries. First, it suggests that the key challenge in relation to social policy in resource-rich countries is a political and social issue rather than a financial one. Resource windfalls mean that governments in resource-rich countries will very often have enough money to fund social policies adequately and promote social development. The problem is either that political elites in these countries choose not to invest in social development or that their investments are rendered ineffective by poor public management, poor economic performance, the effects of violent conflict, or other problems associated with the resource curse. Depending upon one's point of view, this, in turn, reflects the incentives facing political elites, the nature of state institutions, or the interests and agendas of the dominant political and social groups. One or possibly more of these variables will need to change before problems associated with the financing and effectiveness of social policy in resource-rich countries will be overcome. Given the emphasis on the role of social forces in shaping state action in resource-rich countries in my work on the resource curse, I would hypothesize that the main required change in this respect is the formation of a strong working class in resource-rich countries and, in particular, its development to the point where it is able to pose a serious political challenge to capital. It is only at this point that the sort of class compromise that led to the emergence of the welfare state (and a central role for social policy) in many developed countries following the Second World War will be possible in resource-rich countries.

Second, the analysis here suggests that social policy may potentially have an important role to play in consolidating the political and social changes that are required to bring an end to the resource curse. Social policy is not simply a means by which state elites seek to achieve broad social goals such as economic growth, social protection and equity. It is also a means by which elites reinforce the existing political and social order. In particular, social policies are useful in managing tensions within society over the distribution of economic resources. To the extent that they are effective in this respect, they can work to ensure that key political and social groups have a stake in the existing political and social order and hence that this order is preserved. Put differently, they can work to preserve the class compromise that ensures stability and prosperity.

The effectiveness of social policy in this respect is likely to, in turn, depend to a large extent on how it is applied. Much current social policy is geared towards ensuring that vulnerable groups – the poor, women and children – are not harmed by economic change, particularly neoliberal economic reform, an approach closely aligned with the Third Way ideology of New Labour in Britain (Jayasuriya and Rosser 2001). The focus is, accordingly, on providing social safety nets – in health and education in particular – at times of economic change. Yet in political terms this approach is probably defective to the extent that it fails to reward vulnerable groups for remaining loyal to the existing political and social order – they are simply protected from being made worse off. Despite being poor, such groups often have the capacity to organize and cause disruption – especially at times of elite division – and they may be motivated to do so, even if they are not made worse off as a result of economic change. It may be enough that they perceive that they have lost out relative to other groups in society. As the literature on civil war has shown, grievances surrounding political and economic inequalities have been a primary motivation for many such wars (Ballentine 2003). Such grievances were also an important factor in generating instability in some East Asian nations at the time of the Asian crisis. This suggests the need for social policy to be based on a strategy that addresses inequality and grievance.

In sum, then, addressing the resource curse requires political and social change that makes possible a social contract that ensures that all groups in society – or at least those with the potential to cause disruption – share in some way in the benefits produced by natural resource wealth. Social policy has a potentially important role to play in this respect.

Notes

1. All $ amounts refer to US dollars.
2. For example, Ross (2001b); Torvik (2002); Sala-i-Martin and Subramanian (2004); Robinson et al. (2002).

References

Acemoglu, Daron, Simon Johnson and James A. Robinson (2003) 'An African success story: Botswana.' In Dani Rodrik (ed.), *In Search of Prosperity: Analytic Narratives on Economic Growth* (Princeton, NJ: Princeton University Press).

Auty, Richard (2001) 'Introduction and overview.' In Richard Auty (ed.), *Resource Abundance and Economic Development* (Oxford: Oxford University Press).

—— (1994) 'Industrial policy reform in six large newly industrializing countries: The resource curse thesis', *World Development*, Vol. 22, No. 1, 11–26.

—— (1993) *Sustaining Development in Mineral Economies: The Resource Curse Thesis* (London: Routledge).

Balassa, Bela (1980) *The Process of Industrial Development and Alternative Development Strategies* (Princeton, NJ: Princeton University Press).

Ballentine, Karen (2003) 'Beyond greed and grievance: Reconsidering the economic dynamics of armed conflict.' In Karen Ballentine and Jake Sherman (eds.), *The Political Economy of Armed Conflict: Beyond Greed and Grievance* (Boulder, CO: Lynne Rienner Publishers).

Bevan, David, Paul Collier and Jan W. Gunning (1999) *The Political Economy of Poverty, Equity, and Growth* (Oxford: Oxford University Press).

Collier, Paul and Anke Hoeffler (2005) 'Resource rents, governance, and conflict', *Journal of Conflict Resolution*, Vol. 49, No. 4, 625–33.

—— (2002) *The Political Economy of Secession*. users.ox.ac.uk/~ball0144/self-det.pdf, accessed on 11 May 2007.

—— (2000) *Greed and Grievance in Civil War*. worldbank.org/research/conflict/papers/greedhtm, accessed on 1 February 2006.

—— (1998) 'On the economic causes of civil war', *Oxford Economic Papers*, No. 50, 563–73.

Collier, Paul, Anke Hoeffler and Mans Soderbom (2004) 'On the duration of civil war', *Journal of Peace Research*, Vol. 41, No. 3, 253–73.

Davis, Graham A. (1995) 'Learning to love the Dutch Disease: Evidence from mineral economies', *World Development*, Vol. 23, No. 10, 1765–80.

De Soysa, Indra (2002) 'Paradise is a bazaar? Greed, creed, and governance in civil war, 1989–99', *Journal of Peace Research*, Vol. 39, No. 4, 395–416.

—— (2000) 'The resource curse: Are civil wars driven by rapacity or paucity?' In Mats Berdal and David Malone (eds.), *Greed and Grievance: Economic Agendas in Civil Wars* (Boulder, CO: Lynne Rienner Publishers).

Doyle, Michael W. and Nicholas Sambanis (2000) 'International peacebuilding: A theoretical and quantitative analysis', *American Political Science Review*, Vol. 94, No. 4, 779–801.

Drake, Peter (1972) 'Natural resources versus foreign borrowing in economic development', *The Economic Journal*, Vol. 82, No. 327 (September) 951–62.

Eifert, Benn, Gelb, Alan and Nils B. Tallroth (2003) 'The political economy of fiscal policy and economic management in oil exporting countries.' In Jeffrey M. Davis, Rolando Ossowski and Annalisa Fedelino (eds.), *Fiscal Policy Formulation and Implementation in Oil-Producing Countries* (Washington, DC: IMF).

Fearon, James D. (2005) 'Primary commodity exports and civil war', *Journal of Conflict Resolution*, Vol. 49, No. 4, 483–507.

—— (2004) 'Why do some civil wars last so much longer than others?', *Journal of Peace Research*, Vol. 41, No. 3, 275–301.

Fearon, James D. and David D. Laitin (2002) *Ethnicity, Insurgency and Civil War*, mimeo.

Gelb, Alan and Associates (1988) *Oil Windfalls: Blessing or Curse* (New York: Oxford University Press).

Gylfason, Thorvaldur, Tryggvi T. Herbertsson and Gylfi Zoega (1999) 'A mixed blessing: Natural resources and economic growth', *Macroeconomic Dynamics*, Vol. 3, 204–25.

Herb, Michael (2003) *No Representation Without Taxation? Rents, Development and Democracy*. www.gsu.edu/~polmfh/herb_rentier_state.pdf, accessed on 11 May 2007.

Humphreys, Macartan (2005) 'Natural resources, conflict, and conflict resolution: Uncovering the mechanisms', *Journal of Conflict Resolution*, Vol. 49, No. 4, 508–37.

Isham, Jonathan, Michael Woolcock, Lant Pritchett and Gwen Busby (2002) *The Varieties of Rentier Experience: How Natural Resource Export Structures Affect the Political Economy of Economic Growth*. www.middlebury.edu/NR/rdonlyres/23035072-BFD1-43A1-923C-99CF11831F32/0/0308.pdf, accessed on 11 May 2007.

Jayasuriya, Kanishka and Andrew Rosser (2001) 'Economic orthodoxy and the East Asian crisis', *Third World Quarterly*, Vol. 22, No. 3, 381–96.

Jensen, Nathan and Leonard Wantchekon (2004) 'Resource wealth and political regimes in Africa', *Comparative Political Studies*, Vol. 37, No. 7, 816–41.

Jones Luong, Pauline and Erika Weinthal (2001) 'Prelude to the resource curse: Explaining oil and gas development strategies in the Soviet Successor States and beyond', *Comparative Political Studies*, Vol. 34, No. 4, 367–99.

Krueger, Anne (1980) 'Trade policy as an input to development', *American Economic Review*, Vol. 70, No. 2, 288–92.

Leite, Carlos and Jens Weidmann (1999) *Does Mother Nature Corrupt? Natural Resources, Corruption, and, Economic Growth*, IMF Working Paper No. WP/99/85 (Washington, DC: IMF).

Neumayer, Eric (2004) 'Does the "resource curse" hold for growth in genuine income as well?', *World Development*, Vol. 32, No. 10, 1627–40.

Reynal-Querol, Marta (2002) 'Ethnicity, political systems, and civil wars', *Journal of Conflict Resolution*, Vol. 46, No. 1, 29–54.

Robinson, James A., Ragnar Torvik and Thierry Verdier (2002) *Political Foundations of the Resource Curse*, www.sv.ntnu.no/iso/Ragnar.Torvik/bardhanjde.pdf, accessed on 11 May 2007.

Ross, Michael (2006) *Does Oil Hurt the Status of Women?*, mimeo.

—— (2004a) 'How do natural resources influence civil war? Evidence from 13 cases', *International Organization*, Vol. 58, No. 1, 35–68.

—— (2004b) 'What do we know about natural resources and civil war?', *Journal of Peace Research*, Vol. 41, No. 3, 337–56.

—— (2003a) *How Does Mineral Wealth Affect the Poor?*, mimeo.

—— (2003b) 'Oil, drugs and diamonds: The varying role of natural resources in civil war.' In Karen Ballentine and Jake Sherman (eds.), *The Political Economy of Armed Conflict: Beyond Greed and Grievance* (Boulder, CO: Lynne Rienner Publishers).

—— (2001a) 'Does oil hinder democracy?', *World Politics*, Vol. 53 (April) 325–61.

—— (2001b) *Timber Booms and Institutional Breakdown in Southeast Asia* (Ann Arbor, MI: University of Michigan).

—— (1999) 'The political economy of the resource curse', *World Politics*, Vol. 51, No. 2, 297–322.

Rosser, Andrew (2007) 'Escaping the resource curse: The case of Indonesia', *Journal of Contemporary Asia*, Vol. 37, No. 1, 38–58.

—— (2006a) 'Escaping the resource curse', *New Political Economy*, Vol. 11, No. 4, 557–70.

—— (2006b) *The Political Economy of the Resource Curse: A Literature Survey*, IDS Working Paper No. 268 (Brighton: Institute of Development Studies).

Rostow, Walter (1961) *The Stages of Economic Growth: A Non-Communist Manifesto* (Cambridge: Cambridge University Press).

Sachs, Jeffrey D. and Andrew M. Warner (1995) *Natural Resource Abundance and Economic Growth*, NBER Working Paper No. 6398 (Cambridge, MA: NBER).

Sala-i-Martin, Xavier and Arvind Subramanian (2004) 'Tackling the natural resource curse: An illustration from Nigeria', *IMF Survey*, 15 March, 78–80.

Sarraf, Maria and Moortaza Jiwanji (2001) *Beating the Resource Curse: The Case of Botswana*, World Bank Environment Department Papers, Environmental Economics Series (Washington, DC: World Bank).

Schrank, Andrew (2004) *Reconsidering the 'Resource Curse': Sociological Analysis versus Ecological Determinism* (New Haven, CT: Department of Sociology, Yale University).

Smith, Benjamin (2004) 'Oil wealth and regime survival in the developing world: 1960–1999', *American Journal of Political Science*, Vol. 28, No. 2, 232–47.

Snyder, Richard (2006) 'Does lootable wealth breed disorder? A political economy of extraction framework', *Comparative Political Studies*, Vol 39, No. 8, 943–68.

Snyder, Richard and Ravi Bhavnani (2005) 'Diamonds, blood and taxes: A revenue-centred framework for explaining political order', *Journal of Conflict Resolution*, Vol. 49, No. 4, 563–97.

Sørli, Mirjam E., Nils Gleditsch and Havard Strand (2005) 'Why is there so much conflict in the Middle East?', *Journal of Conflict Resolution*, Vol. 49, No. 1, 141–65.

Stevens, Paul (2003) *Resource Impact: A Curse or a Blessing.* http://psweb.sbs.ohio-state.edu/faculty/tfrye/stevens.pdf, accessed on 11 May 2007.

Stijns, Jean-Philippe (2003) *Natural Resource Abundance and Human Capital Accumulation*, mimeo.

—— (2001) *Natural Resource Abundance and Economic Growth Revisited* (Berkeley, CA: University of California).

Torvik, Ragnar (2002) 'Natural resources, rent seeking and welfare', *Journal of Development Economics*, Vol. 67, 455–70.

UNCTAD (United Nations Conference on Trade and Development) (2002) *The Least Developed Countries Report 2002: Escaping the Poverty Trap* (Geneva: UNCTAD).

Wantchekon, Leonard (1999) *Why Do Resource Dependent Countries Have Authoritarian Governments?* www.yale.edu/leitner/pdf/1999-11.pdf, accessed on 11 May 2007.

Weinthal, Erika and Jones Luong, Pauline (2001) 'Energy wealth and tax reform in Russia and Kazakhstan', *Resources Policy*, Vol. 27, No. 4, 215–23.

Wheeler, David (1984) 'Sources of stagnation in sub-Saharan Africa', *World Development*, Vol. 12, No. 1, 1–23.

8
Mineral Rents and Social Policy: The Case of the Norwegian Government Oil Fund

Erling Holmøy

Introduction: why look to Norway?

In terms of several economic dimensions, Norway offers a very particular case study. Following the discovery of substantial petroleum resources in 1969, it has grown to become one of the richest countries in the world measured in terms of per capita gross domestic product (GDP). This extraordinary growth performance may have a number of causes that have nothing to do with the expansion of the petroleum sector and the transformation of petroleum wealth into financial assets. However, the Norwegian experience is an exception to the standard gloomy story of resource-rich countries told by Sachs and Warner (2001).

Most of the petroleum revenues accrue to the government. Thus, the current fiscal stance in Norway looks impressive and radically different from that found in most other countries. However, comparable long-run projections suggest that the fiscal future for Norway is likely to be very different. The projected increase in government expenditures is much sharper after 2020. This is a result of the design of the generous welfare schemes in Norway. Specifically, increased longevity raises the growth trend of government old-age pension expenditures.

Few other governments have the kind of opportunities Norway does to pre-fund a large proportion of the future increase in expenditures in order to smooth tax rates, without the political cost associated with heavy taxation of current generations. At present the fiscal situation in most Organisation for Economic Co-operation and Development (OECD) countries is already strained, let alone the long-run projections. The assets accumulated in the Norwegian Central Government Pension Fund – Global (CPF)[1] increased rapidly and passed 82 per cent of GDP by the end of 2006.

The intertemporal consumption of the petroleum wealth has been discussed in Norway since the early 1970s. A new fiscal policy rule was adopted in 2001, which recognized that the petroleum revenues reflect a temporary transformation of wealth from natural resources to more liquid assets, rather than ordinary contributions to GDP. The government petroleum revenues are invested in the CPF, and only the expected real return of the fund should be used to finance non-petroleum government budget deficits.

The purpose of this chapter is to make a quantitative assessment of the extent to which the present social policy or welfare state is financially viable. In particular, it examines to what extent government petroleum wealth makes it unnecessary to raise tax rates in the future when the ageing of the population makes government expenditures grow faster than the tax bases. In this context I also discuss the motivations for, and the effects of, two major policy reforms in Norway: (i) the adoption of the fiscal policy rule in 2001; and (ii) the public pension reform proposed in 2006.

The chapter is organized as follows. The second section describes the remarkable macroeconomic growth performance in Norway in recent decades, emphasizing how the key elements of social policy – that is, the government provision of individual services and the social security system – affect the government budget. The section also discusses the role of petroleum wealth and reviews how fear of the 'resource curse', or Dutch disease, has influenced the policy debate in Norway. The third section assesses to what extent population ageing and normal economic growth challenge the long-run financial viability of the Norwegian welfare system. More precisely, the section draws on model-based projections to shed light on the following questions: (i) what tax rate adjustments and degree of pre-funding follows from the fiscal policy rule; and (ii) how robust are the fiscal sustainability assessments to determinants of the tax bases and government expenditures? The fourth section discusses the motivations for, and the effects of, the fiscal policy rule and the public pension reform. The fifth section provides some final remarks and a summary of policy relevant conclusions.

Background

Norway's remarkable growth performance

Over the past century Norway has grown from being one of the poorest countries in Europe to being ranked first in many international comparisons of material well-being. In 1870 GDP per capita was estimated to be about 70 per cent of the average for Western Europe. The gap relative to the EU-15 was almost closed over the next 100 years, with respect to per capita figures for both GDP and individual consumption (private consumption plus government consumption of individual services) (see Table 8.1). Most of this catching up took place during the First World War, when Norway stayed neutral. However, in 1970 per capita levels of both GDP and individual consumption were still only 72.8 and 78.4 per cent, respectively, of the Swedish and Danish levels.

The 1970s witnessed a much stronger growth performance in Norway than in other OECD countries, especially in the aftermath of the first oil price shock in 1973. In the period 1971–80 the purchasing power parity (PPP)-corrected GDP per capital grew by 4.2 per cent annually in Norway, more than two percentage points faster than in the United States (USA) and the other Scandinavian countries (see Table 8.3). The growth (from zero) in oil and gas production contributed significantly to GDP growth. Since oil and gas production implies a corresponding reduction of petroleum wealth, it should be deducted when GDP is used as

Table 8.1   GDP and individual consumption per capita measured in 2000 prices and by PPP in 2000 (OECD = 100)

	GDP			Consumption		
	1970	*1995*	*2005*	*1970*	*1995*	*2005*
Norway	91	118	157	97	106	116
US	139	136	139	143	143	144
EU15	96	101	101	99	102	103
Denmark	116	112	114	120	109	104
Sweden	125	106	107	137	101	103

Source: OECD (2007).

Table 8.2   GDP: volume indices, 2000 = 100, and average annual growth rates (in percentages)

	1970	*1995*	*2005*	*Growth 1971–2005*
Norway	34.4	83.8	110.7	3.4
US	38.1	81.6	112.6	3.1
EU15	46.6	86.9	108.2	2.4
Denmark	50.5	86.9	106.9	2.2
Sweden	54.7	85.3	112.3	2.1

Source: OECD (2007).

Table 8.3   GDP per capita measured in 2000 prices and PPP in 2000 (average annual growth rates in per cent)

	1971–80	*1981–90*	*1991–2000*
Norway	4.2	2.0	2.8
Mainland sector	3.1	1.1	2.7
US	2.1	2.2	1.9
EU15			
Denmark	1.8	1.9	2.2
Sweden	1.6	1.7	1.4

Source: Ministry of Finance (2004).

an income measure. The growth of the Norwegian Mainland sector[2] still averaged 3.1 per cent in the 1970s, significantly higher than in other OECD countries. In 2005 Norway was one of the richest countries in the world. Table 8.1 shows that in 2005 GDP per capita, measured in prices and purchasing power parities in 2000, exceeded the OECD average by 57 per cent and the US level by 13 per cent. Due to a relatively high savings ratio, individual per capita consumption in Norway was only 16 per cent above the OECD average in 2005.

Although the causality is unclear, it is widely believed that the oil price shock in 1973 was an important determinant of the difference in growth performance between Norway and other OECD countries in the 1970s. High oil prices pushed most OECD countries into a period of stagflation and relatively slow growth in productivity. They suffered severe terms-of-trade losses, which limited the scope for an expansionary fiscal policy stimulus. For Norway, higher petroleum prices implied a terms-of-trade gain, since the discovery of the oilfield Ekofisk in 1969 made it clear that Norway would soon become a large net exporter of petroleum. In addition, the social cost of investment in the new petroleum sector in the 1970s was probably significantly lower than the market price. The booming petroleum sector absorbed labour from primary industries, shipbuilding and other manufacturing industries, sectors which contracted as a result of the international recession. Norway was therefore able to avoid the dramatic increase in unemployment observed in other countries by employing a countercyclical policy that stimulated the traded goods sector.

Natural resources have always played a large role in the Norwegian economy. Forestry, mining and fisheries provided important foreign exchange to the country in the last century. The development of hydropower and the electrification of the country, based on the numerous waterfalls from the mountains, contributed significantly to Norway's industrialization, in particular the development of a substantial power-intensive industry. Almost all of the electricity production is based on hydropower. The discoveries and development of the large oil- and gasfields off the mainland of Norway have become another energy resource contributing substantially to Norway's wealth. Today, Norway is one of the world's greatest petroleum producers and exporters. The total production in 2006 was 248.8 million Sm^3o.e.,[3] of which 161.2 million was oil and 87.6 million gas. Thus, Norway is perhaps one of the best illustrations of the textbook model of a small open economy with a highly specialized industrial structure with respect to production of tradables. In addition to oil and gas, the main exporting industries include fisheries and energy- (hydropower-) intensive products such as metals, pulp, paper and chemicals.

In addition to the importance of natural resources, the Norwegian economy stands out in comparison to most other OECD countries by having a relatively large government sector and high tax rates. The distribution of income is relatively even. The labour force is relatively well-educated and labour market participation rates are high for both men and women, but Norwegians work relatively short hours (see Table 8.4).

Social policy: the Norwegian welfare state

As in the other Scandinavian countries, the Norwegian welfare state is extensive, involving relatively high government expenditures and taxes. Table 8.5 shows the development in key government budget components after 1980. The GDP share of government expenditures increased from about 25 per cent in 1960 to about 44 per cent around 1980 (see Figure 8.1). The sharp increase in the 1970s was caused by both extensions of welfare schemes and investments in the petroleum sector.

Table 8.4 Labour market participation for different age groups and hours of work in 2005

	15–64 years (per cent)			55–64 years (per cent)			Hours of work
	Total	Males	Females	Total	Males	Females	Average
Norway	78.9	82.3	75.4	68.8	74.6	62.9	1360
US	75.4	81.8	69.2	62.9	69.3	57.0	1804
EU15	71.3	79.1	63.5	46.7	56.6	37.2	–
Denmark	79.4	83.6	75.1	62.9	70.2	55.7	1551

Source: OECD (2006).

Table 8.5 Government expenditures and revenues in Norway (current prices/per cent of GDP)

	1980	1990	2000	2005
Total expenditures, of which	44.0	49.7	39.3	39.5
Consumption	18.7	20.8	19.3	19.9
Fixed capital investment	3.9	3.6	2.6	2.7
Transfers to the private sector, of which	17.8	21.8	16.4	16.5
Households	11.3	15.9	13.2	13.3
Total revenues, of which	49.4	52.3	54.7	54.6
Total tax revenues, of which	46.1	42.5	42.6	43.5
Petroleum taxes	7.3	3.9	6.7	9.7
Net financial investment	5.4	2.6	15.4	15.1
Net taxes (taxes – transfers to the private sector)	25.4	20.6	26.2	26.9

Source: Statistics Norway (2008).

The GDP share of government expenditures grew at a lower rate in the 1980s and has fallen by as much as ten percentage points over the last 15 years, to about 40 per cent in 2005. However, this negative trend is to a great extent due to the expansion of the petroleum sector. The United States and other European countries have witnessed a more stable GDP share of government expenditures after 1985.

The generosity of the Scandinavian welfare states is also reflected in relatively higher tax rates. According to Eurostat (2006), total tax revenue in 2004 averaged 40.7 per cent of GDP in the EU-25 and 51.2 and 49.9 per cent, respectively, in Sweden and Denmark. The corresponding ratio in Norway was 44.5 per cent (see Statistics Norway 2006). These average tax rates measure gross taxes, which include the tax revenue that is reimbursed to the taxpayers as cash transfers. Net taxes amounted to 27.2 per cent of GDP in Norway in 2005.

Welfare services

The share of government consumption in total consumption increased from about 24 per cent in 1970 to approximately 33 per cent in 2003 (see Figure 8.2). This trend is driven by the increase in individual services produced and financed by the government, including health and social care for the elderly and disabled (55 per cent

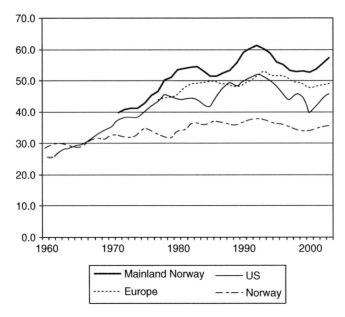

Figure 8.1   Government expenditures in per cent of GDP (current prices)
Source: Ministry of Finance (2004).

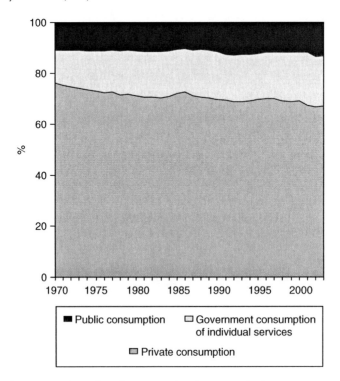

Figure 8.2   The composition of total consumption (current prices)
Source: Ministry of Finance (2004).

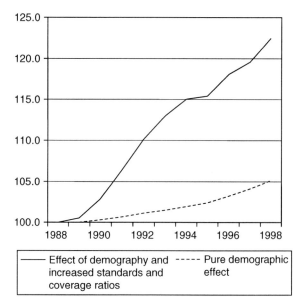

Figure 8.3 Decomposition of the growth in man-hours allocated to service provision by the local government sector. Index (1988 = 100)
Source: Ministry of Finance (2004).

in 2001); primary schools (17 per cent); and colleges, universities and other education (21 per cent). On the other hand, the share of public consumption (that is, infrastructure, public institutions and so on) has remained basically constant throughout the period.

The increase in the government consumption of individual services can be attributed to increases in both service standards (measured by man-hours per user) and coverage ratios (the number of users relative to the total number of individuals in specific age groups), as well as more rapid growth in the unit costs in service production compared to other prices. The latter effect rests on highly uncertain assumptions regarding productivity growth in government sectors. The local government sector provides most of the welfare in Norway. Figure 8.3 breaks the growth into man-hours allocated to service provision in this sector down into a demographic effect and the effect of increased service standards and coverage ratios. The demographic effect results from changes in the age composition as the average individual use of services varies with age. In the 1990s, the pure demographic effect played a minor role for employment growth in man-hours compared with the effect of increased standards and coverage ratios.

Figure 8.4 illustrates that the Scandinavian welfare states allocate a much larger share of their resources to government sectors producing individual services than is the case for either the United States or the countries of the European Union. This is particularly the case in respect of old-age care.

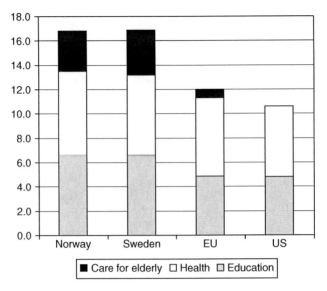

Figure 8.4   The composition of government consumption of individual services (per cent of GDP in 1999)
Source: Ministry of Finance (2004).

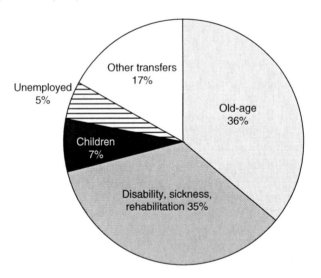

Figure 8.5   The composition of government social security expenditures in 2003
Source: Ministry of Finance (2004).

Social security

Turning to the 'transfer side' of the welfare state, old-age pensions and pensions to disabled and sick individuals dominate, amounting to more than 70 per cent of total government social security expenditures (see Figure 8.5).

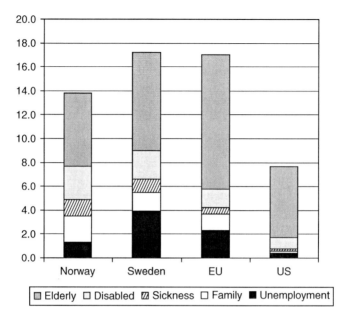

Figure 8.6 The composition of social security expenditures in different countries in 1999
Source: Ministry of Finance (2004).

The total levels of social security expenditure have been lower in Norway than in most other European countries, basically because the retirement age in Norway has been relatively high, but also because unemployment has been relatively low (see Figure 8.6). The public pension systems in Norway and in most European countries have historically provided a much higher replacement income, especially to low-income groups and groups with no attachment to the labour market, than does the 'minimum system' in the United States. This reflects a different mix between public provisions and private insurance and pension schemes.

The public old-age, disability and survivors' pensions in Norway are organized within the National Insurance Scheme (NIS), which was established in 1967. It replaced a general public pension system consisting of a flat pension benefit. The NIS benefit includes three elements: a basic benefit, a special supplement and a supplementary benefit. The basic benefit and the special supplement constitute the granted minimum benefit. The special supplement is means-tested against the supplementary pension, whereby pension benefit = basic benefit + Max (special supplement, supplementary benefit). The income basis for the supplementary benefit is the average labour market earnings over the 20 years with the highest earnings, after 1967. Full pension is reached after 40 years of labour force participation. The average benefit has grown and will continue to grow relative to the wage level until 2030 as the system matures. The growth in the minimum benefit and in female labour force participation also contributes to the growth in the average benefit.

The dependency between earnings and benefits is neither strong nor transparent. Simulations on a dynamic microsimulation model show that increasing labour market earnings by 1 NOK[4] raises the average present value of future pension benefits by 0.11 NOK (Fredriksen et al. 2006). Given the political intentions behind the wage indexation of both pension entitlements and individual benefits, the NIS benefits imply a pre-tax replacement ratio with respect to earnings in the final year of work, equal to about 50 per cent for a person with 40 years of labour market earnings and a steady and normal income level. Special tax rules for pensioners raise the average after-tax replacement ratio of NIS benefits to about 65 per cent. Replacement ratios with respect the average annual earnings over the whole working career are of course higher with normal age earnings profiles. Private pension schemes and special pension schemes for public employees may further increase the compensation level.

The formal retirement age in the NIS is 67 years. Both disability pensioners and early retirees obtain entitlements as if they were working until the age of 67. Roughly 40–50 per cent of the population is receiving a disability pension at retirement age, and about 60 per cent of the (still) employed are entitled to early retirement from the age of 62. Disability pension and early retirement imply that the present effective retirement age averages 59–60 years in Norway. Note that early retirement through these arrangements does not reduce future pension benefits at any point in time, neither due to a shorter period of labour market earnings, nor due to a longer period as a pensioner.

Population ageing in Norway is expected to be less pronounced than in most other OECD countries. Nevertheless, Antolin and Suyker (2001), as well as the Ministry of Finance (2004), conclude that the existing welfare state schemes imply that Norway will experience one of the sharpest increases in public expenditures as a share of GDP after 2010, mainly because old-age pension expenditures will increase faster in Norway than in other countries (see Figure 8.7). The three most important drivers are: (i) the Norwegian public pension system is still maturing; (ii) since there are no actuarial mechanisms in the public pension system, retirees receive their defined annual benefits over more years as they live longer; and (iii) the nominal value of public pension benefits is indexed to wage growth rather than to some average of wage and price growth.

The growth in the number of old-age retirees follows directly from demographic developments within the country. The growth in the number of social security beneficiaries in the working-age group is likely to be much more responsive to policy-based working incentives. This number has increased rather dramatically over recent decades (see Figure 8.8). Specifically, as unemployment has been reduced, the number of accumulated exits from the labour market due to health problems increased from 16 to 21 per cent of the labour force, which totalled 2.4 million in 2006. Today about 700,000 individuals of working age receive social security benefits. At the same time, longevity has increased by an average of about one year every tenth year, which indicates a general improvement in the overall health situation. Of the 200,000 exits from the labour market from 2000 to 2001, only 11 per cent were registered as unemployed. Of the 170,000 entrants to the

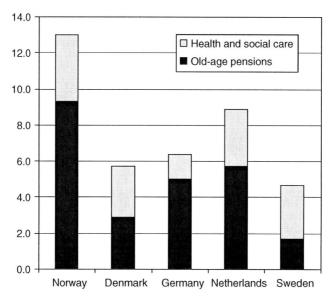

Figure 8.7 Projected growth in GDP shares of age-dependent government expenditures (Mainland sector GDP for Norway), 2000–50 (per cent)
Source: Ministry of Finance (2004).

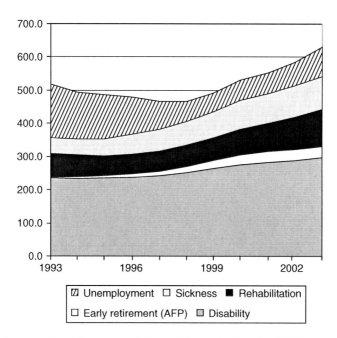

Figure 8.8 Persons of working age receiving social security benefits (1000 persons)
Source: Ministry of Finance (2004).

labour market, only 13 per cent exited due to unemployment (Røed 2007). Calculations by the same author suggest that employment would increase by 160,000 if, hypothetically, the shares of sick and disabled individuals in the potential labour force were reduced to 1995 levels.

Reduced labour market participation is a threat to the Scandinavian welfare state as the welfare state is highly employment-dependent. Generous individual welfare services and transfers are granted to all individuals, irrespective of their individual contributions to the system. The associated government expenditures are financed collectively, primarily via taxation on a 'pay-as-you-go' (PAYG) basis. Thus, individual entitlements are detached from individual financing. While young, the typical individual is a net beneficiary (as the result of childcare, education, and so on). He or she makes a net contribution during his or her working life, and becomes a beneficiary later in life (thanks to pensions, old-age care and so on). Accordingly, the PAYG-financed welfare state rests on an implicit social contract between generations.

The financial viability of a generous welfare state requires a combination of high employment rates and high tax rates. To be stable, such a combination rests on a high degree of confidence in the welfare system. *Ceteris paribus*, tax rates and labour supply are typically negatively related. Thus, individuals have to see some kind of returns to the high tax rates. If they do not, the common pool problem of the welfare state may erode its financial basis; individuals may replace work with leisure and generous social security compensation, without taking into account that their individual behaviour reduces the tax base.

As pointed out above, to date Norway has managed to combine high tax rates with high rates of labour market participation, especially for women, although Norwegians work few hours compared to other countries. To some extent, social policies have explicitly stimulated the female labour supply, particularly through a rapid expansion of highly subsidized daycare for children and flexible working arrangements. However, tax rates in the Scandinavian welfare states probably cannot be increased much further from the present levels. One reason is that doing so appears to be highly unpopular among the public, especially in Norway where the state accumulates petroleum revenues at a record high pace. Second, by distorting relative prices, taxes implies a loss in terms of the socially efficient allocation of economic resources, which increases progressively in the tax rates. For a person facing a 50 per cent marginal income tax, a 14 per cent payroll tax rate and an average indirect tax rate of 20 per cent, the effective marginal tax rate is $1.2 \times 1.14 - (1-0.5) = 0.87$. This means that if an individual *voluntarily* reduces his or her labour supply by a number of hours that corresponds to one dollar measured by the pre-tax wage rate, the decision implies a loss in both tax revenue and social efficiency equal to $0.87.[5]

The labour supply distortions are also magnified by several of the welfare transfers, since they are means-tested. The interplay between different means-tested benefits and tax rules is so complex that it has motivated several research projects that have attempted to calculate the total incentive effects on labour supply. Mogstad et al. (2006) find that several beneficiaries face effective tax rates above

90 per cent. According to Røed (2007), beneficiaries defined as completely disabled receive on average an income replacement of about 65 per cent of the labour income they can expect if they enter the labour market. However, social security benefits replace 86 per cent of expected labour income for 10 per cent of the beneficiaries. It is shown that 3 per cent of the labour force face effective tax rates that are above 100 per cent. For recipients of different kinds of social protection transfers, benefits replace on average 58 per cent of expected labour income, and 10 per cent face an 86 per cent effective tax rate. A particularly distortive arrangement is the present early retirement scheme, which is partly financed by the government (Holmøy 2002).

The role of petroleum revenues

The successful adjustment of the industry structure to the comparative advantages implied by relatively rich endowments of natural resources, especially of energy, has typically been regarded as important for the achievement of high living standards in Norway. However, as pointed out above, it is hard to identify such a positive effect until petroleum rents were phased into the economy in the 1970s. The performance of the Norwegian economy and economic policy since then has, of course, been discussed critically, based on more or less clear answers to the counterfactual question: What would Norway have looked like without oil? Nevertheless, several scholars conclude that petroleum wealth has been a blessing rather than a curse (for example, Torvik 2007 and Røed Larsen 2003). So far Norway seems to be an outlier compared to the poor growth performance of most other resource-rich countries (Sachs and Warner 2001). However, the terms 'resource curse' and 'Dutch disease' have been frequently used in the Norwegian policy debate after 1970.

Most of the petroleum revenues accrue to the state through the direct ownership or taxation, making the Norwegian government an international outlier with respect to financial wealth. The net financial government wealth is dominated by petroleum revenues accumulated in the CPF, which amounted to 82 per cent of GDP by the end of 2006.

The economics literature on the resource curse has given attention to three main reasons why petroleum wealth may turn out to be a curse rather than a blessing. First, there may be adverse 'learning by doing' effects associated with deindustrialization provided that dynamic learning by doing effects are stronger in manufacturing than in other industries.[6] However, there seems to be very little empirical support for this hypothesis.

Second, large government petroleum revenues are likely to stimulate socially unproductive rent seeking and magnify problems caused by politicians having effective discount rates that are too low. Specifically, a soft budget constraint may tempt politicians to expand public services and social welfare programmes beyond sustainable ambitions, whereas they postpone socially beneficial policy reforms characterized by short-run costs and long-run gains. This is probably one of the reasons why Norway has waited longer than other OECD countries with reforms of the social security system.

Third, spending the petroleum wealth may lead to an *excessive* real appreciation and deindustrialization. The adjective *excessive* is important here. Qualitatively, downsizing the traded goods sector is the rational equilibrium response to higher resource rents. However, deindustrialization processes and the expansion of welfare programmes may be hard to reverse once they have gathered momentum. The reasons for such irreversibility are not yet fully understood, but price rigidities, myopic behaviour and habit formation are likely elements in the story. Krugman (1991) and Venables (1996) give precise meaning to the concepts 'manufacturing base' and 'critical mass' suggesting that there may be activity levels below which further contraction of an industry is difficult to reverse.

The Norwegian policy debate has also pointed to the limited mobility of resources. If the petroleum wealth is too quickly phased into the economy through an expansionary fiscal policy, labour and other input factors may become unemployed rather than reallocated to the non-traded goods sector. This fear is partly motivated by the empirical evidence suggesting it is hard to re-employ unemployed individuals in Norway.

The international competitiveness of Norwegian industries has deteriorated in most of the years after 1974. In 2003 the average wage cost of blue-collar employees was estimated to be 30 per cent higher than the corresponding average in Norway's trading partners. Including white-collar employees reduces the difference to about 20 per cent. International comparisons of estimated productivity growth do not indicate that the cost effect of the extra wage growth in Norway is offset by a corresponding difference in productivity growth (see, for example, OECD 2008). Petroleum wealth is highly uncertain, and it is therefore hard to quantitatively assess whether the observed deterioration of international competitiveness and de-employment in manufacturing industries is a sustainable trend or is evidence of 'Dutch disease'.

Holmøy and Heide (2005) use an applied general equilibrium model to quantitatively assess the scope for a sustainable growth in Norwegian labour costs over the coming decades. Contingent on a 1.5 per cent annual growth in international prices and prolongation of historical productivity growth, and a real oil price of $25 per barrel, they find that manufacturing employment can on average be reduced by about 0.5 per cent per year without violating the national budget constraint related to foreign debt. There is room for a constant growth rate of nominal labour between 4 and 4.5 per cent. The observed wage growth over recent years is quite in line with this norm, whereas the real appreciation in 1998–2003 was much too strong. An overall conclusion is that the petroleum wealth is far from large enough to make the Norwegian economy immune to Dutch disease. There is a danger that the impressive current financial position of the government and for the economy as a whole may confuse the public with respect to long-run consumption possibilities. Basically, it reflects the pace of the temporary transformation of petroleum reserves into liquid foreign assets. Systematic use of numerical simulation models is one of the few possibilities for obtaining more adequate information about the sustainable possibilities for growth in real wages, consumption and reallocations.

Challenges to the Norwegian welfare state

The financial robustness of the Norwegian welfare state with respect to population ageing and economic growth has been examined in OECD (2001), and also in several white papers and reports by the Norwegian government, most notably the Ministry of Finance (2004), and in Heide et al. (2006). The latter two studies combine several models to build long-term scenarios that look beyond 2050, drawing on all of available relevant information. In the following I draw extensively on Heide et al. (2006).

Building a base scenario

One main building block is the most plausible demographic projection from Statistics Norway (2005). Here, the ratio of individuals of working age 20–66 to those 67 and older decreases from 4.7 in 2005 to 2.5 in 2050.[7] Over this period the labour force grows by 10 per cent. The demographic development enters a dynamic microsimulation model, which simulates the life courses of a cross-section of the Norwegian population, including labour market participation, earnings, individual pension entitlements and government pension expenditures, ex ante indexation.[8] The base scenario prolongs the present public pension system and other welfare schemes regulating government transfers to households. Most of these transfers are indexed to wages.

On the service side of the welfare state, the main share of government expenditures is allocated to the sectors *Education* and *Health and Social Care*. These costs are projected by decomposing cost changes into: (i) service standards, defined as man-hours and other resources per user; (ii) the price of the resources; (iii) the

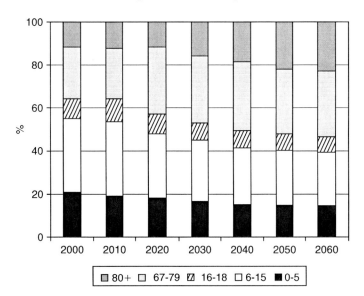

Figure 8.9 Projection of the age composition of the Norwegian population
Source: Figures derived from population forecasts by Statistics Norway (2005).

number of users, or the demand intensity, within different age groups; and (iv) the number of individuals in different age groups. The base scenario prolongs 2004 levels of, respectively, service standards and age-specific demand intensities, employment in the government sectors *Defence* and *Administration*, and the proportions of capital and intermediaries to labour in all government sectors.

The detailed calculations of the labour force, the number of various kinds of pensioners, average pension benefits *ex ante* indexation, and real government consumption, are exogenous inputs in a large-scale dynamic computable general equilibrium model called MSG6,[9] of the Norwegian economy.[10] The main role of MSG6 in this context is to capture the complex mechanisms that determine the tax bases as well as the wage rate and the unit costs of government consumption.

MSG6 describes the Norwegian economy as too small to affect world prices and the international interest rate. The exchange rate is fixed. All agents have access to international capital markets. The economy as a whole obeys an intertemporal budget constraint, which requires the present value of imports to be equal to the present value of exports plus initial foreign wealth. Goods and factors are perfectly mobile between industries. Supply equals demand in all markets in all periods. Consumers decide on labour supply and the composition of private consumption according to standard consumer theory. The parameters are calibrated so that the uncompensated wage elasticity equals 0.1.[11] Most imported products are close but imperfect substitutes for the corresponding domestic products. Firms are run by managers with model consistent expectations, who maximize present after-tax value of the net-of-tax cash flow to owners. All Norwegian firms face exogenous export prices, and most firms engage in monopolistic competition in the domestic market. It is costly to redirect output between these markets, and the production functions exhibit decreasing returns to scale.[12] In a long-term scenario nominal wage growth will be relatively close to the sum of the exogenous growth in world prices and the endogenous growth in labour productivity.

In addition to the assumptions in relation to demographic development and the prolongation of the present welfare schemes, the base scenario in Heide et al. (2006) rests on the following key assumptions:

(i) Total Factor Productivity (TFP) grows effectively by 1.1 per cent per year in private industries, which is in line with historical trends. Annual labour productivity growth in government sectors is 0.5 per cent.

(ii) The nominal interest rate stays constant at 5.5 per cent. World prices grow by 1.5 per cent annually.

(iii) Petroleum revenues contributed to 41 per cent of government revenues in 2005. If, hypothetically, the present production were kept constant the profitable resources would be depleted in 2038 (Ministry of Finance 2004). The real oil price is assumed to stay at $25 per barrel, in line with the International Energy Agency (IEA) forecast from 2004, but quite low compared to the prices observed after 2005 and recent forecasts. The price of natural gas follows the oil price.

(iv) All tax rates are maintained in real terms, with the exception of the payroll tax rate. Being a broad tax on labour income, the payroll tax rate adjusts annually

Table 8.6 Macroeconomic development in the base scenario (average annual growth rates/per cent)

	2004–25	*2026–50*
GDP	2.0	1.6
Employment	0.3	0.1
Wage cost per hour relative to world prices	4.1	4.1
Consumer real wage rate	2.5	1.7
Net foreign wealth relative to GDP	6.0	0.2
Private consumption	3.0	2.1
Government consumption	0.7	1.1

Source: Heide et al. (2006).

in order to meet the time path of the government budget constraint implied by the fiscal policy rule adopted in 2001.

(v) The base scenario assumes that the fiscal policy rule is followed strictly. Then the primary budget deficit, net of the cash flow from the petroleum sector accruing to the government (*P*), should be equal to the expected real rate of return on the assets accumulated in the Central Government Pension Fund (foreign) (CPF) at the beginning of the budget year. At present the expected real rate of return is set to 4 per cent. The fiscal rule is discussed in more detail below.

Table 8.6 summarizes the growth picture in our baseline scenario. Growth in GDP averages 1.7 per cent over the period 2004–50, mainly as a result of TFP growth and capital deepening. A more rapid growth in private consumption is feasible mainly because of the relatively slow growth in government consumption.

From an exceptionally solid to an exceptionally strained fiscal stance

Figure 8.10, taken from Heide et al. (2006), reveals that an evaluation of the financial robustness of the Norwegian welfare state would be strikingly misleading if the time perspective were confined to the first couple of decades. Under the baseline assumptions the fiscal stance would deteriorate dramatically after 2030 from the impressive current stance. The fiscal policy rule allows the payroll tax rate to be lower than the present rate of 13 per cent until 2030 in the baseline, but after 2020 it must be raised in every year, passing 31 per cent in 2050. And that is not the end. Population forecasts conclude that the demographic dependency ratio will continue to increase throughout the century. Recall in this context that the present effective tax on marginal labour income in Norway is already among the highest in the OECD area.[13] The dynamics of the payroll tax rate reflect more rapid growth in tax bases than expenditures until 2020, and that the 'permissible' spending 'oil money' finances a larger share of government expenditures in these years than in subsequent decades. Prolongation of the present welfare schemes and fiscal policy is far from sustainable. Note that if the strong fiscal stance until 2020 is used to expand government expenditures rather than cutting tax rates, the growth in the

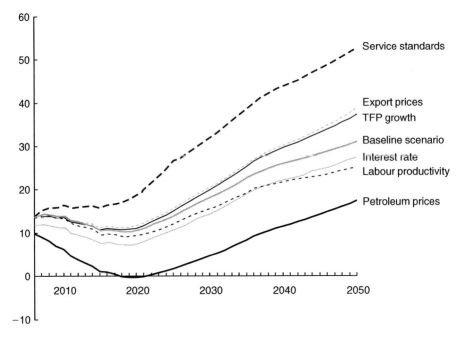

Figure 8.10   Projected payroll tax rate, given the fiscal policy rule (per cent)

TFP growth: TFP in private industries grow by 1.6 instead of 1.3 per cent per year.
Petroleum prices: Real world prices of oil and gas are increased from $25 to $50 per barrel in all years.
Export prices: World prices of all exports but oil and gas grow by 2 per cent rather than 1.5 per cent
per year.
Interest rate: World interest rate increased permanently from 5.5 per cent to 6.5 per cent.
Service standards: Prolongation until 2025 of the average growth in man-hours per user observed in the
1990s in the government sector Health and Social Care.
Labour productivity: Annual labour productivity growth in the government sector Health and Social Care
raised from 0.5 per cent to 1 per cent in all years.

Source: Heide et al. (2006).

tax burden will start from the present level, which is three percentage points above
the baseline level in 2020. Moreover, the growth in the tax burden may be accelerated if the additional expenditures are allocated towards the increased welfare of
the elderly.

Given the solid current fiscal situation, the large petroleum wealth, moderate
population ageing and the ambitious savings implied by the fiscal policy rule, it is
striking that the estimated necessary long-term tax burden turns out to be significantly higher in Norway than similar estimates for other countries. The Danish
Welfare Commission (2004) concludes that fiscal sustainability will be obtained
by increasing the base income tax rate permanently from 2011 by 8.7 percentage
points. OECD (2001) estimates that budgetary pressures from ageing on average
require a 7 per cent increase in the GDP share of taxes. This exceeds the corresponding estimates in Chauveau and Loufir (1995) for the seven major economies.

Table 8.7 GDP shares of government revenues and expenditures in the baseline scenario (per cent)

	2004	2025	2050
Total government revenues, of which	**69.5**	**57.5**	**60.5**
Net interest and other capital income	4.7	8.0	6.8
Total tax revenue, excl. petroleum revenues	47.8	44.1	52.0
Indirect taxes	17.8	13.9	12.7
Direct taxes, excl. petroleum revenues	30.0	30.2	39.3
Petroleum revenues	16.3	4.6	1.1
Total government expenditures, of which	**53.7**	**51.6**	**57.9**
Cash transfers to households, of which	19.5	24.3	27.3
Old-age pension expenditures	5.0	11.3	14.9
Government consumption, of which	27.3	22.0	26.0
Health and social care	10.5	12.4	16.6
Net financial investment	**15.8**	**5.9**	**2.6**
Capital in the Central Government Pension Fund – Global	47.7	128.9	116.5
Average payroll tax rate, per cent	13.1	13.8	31.0

Source: Heide et al. (2006).

According to Feldstein (2005), the actuaries of the United States Social Security Administration estimate that the payroll tax rate in that country must increase by about six percentage points from today to 2075 to finance the pension benefits specified in current law. Also accounting for other government expenditures and general equilibrium effects, Feldstein assesses that the payroll tax rate must be raised by is about nine percentage points. The corresponding estimate in Kotlikoff et al. (2001) is an increase by ten percentage points over the next three decades.

Growing pension expenditures is main determinant of the growth in the expenditures–GDP ratio in Norway (see Table 8.7). The GDP share of government old-age pension expenditures grows from 5 per cent in 2004 to 14.9 per cent in 2050. This is foremost caused by the combination of increased longevity and the non-actuarial design of the current public pension system. The total number of pensioners in 2050 will be more than doubled from the 2005 level (see Table 8.8) and annual individual benefits are independent of the number of years as a pensioner in the current Norwegian system. In addition, the GDP share of government old-age pension expenditures will increase due to growth in the average benefit, especially to women wage indexation of entitlements and benefits as well as increased use of early retirement schemes.

The projected increase in the tax burden is also driven by the growth in the already high number of disability pensioners and growth in the average disability benefit. In the period 2004–50 public disability pension expenditures will increase by nearly 50 per cent *ex ante* wage indexation. Over the same period, the GDP share of government spending on health and social care grows from 10.5 to 16.6 per cent. This reflects ageing and that the productivity growth in this sector is assumed to remain significantly lower than the wage growth.[14]

Table 8.8 Projected development in the number of pensioners, average annual benefits *ex ante* indexation and the labour force in the baseline scenario (thousand persons and thousand NOK, current prices)

	2004	2020	2050
Old age pensioners	639	873	1317
Average annual benefit	116	140	146
Disability pensioners	308	388	407
Average annual benefit	120	124	122
All pensioners (including widow pensioners)	971	1278	1734
Pensioners in per cent of labour force	40	50	65

Source: Heide et al. (2006).

Gloomy fiscal prospects – A robust assessment?

How robust is the conclusion that the apparently affluent Norwegian state faces severe problems of fiscal sustainability after 2020? What alternative trends would significantly change the gloomy fiscal prospects? Figure 8.10 summarizes the effects on the necessary payroll tax rate of alternative assumptions on the main determinants of tax bases and government expenditures. Below, I give a very brief explanation of the most striking results. Heide et al. (2006) provide more detailed explanations.

Doubling the real oil (and gas) price from the rather pessimistic base scenario level of $25/barrel allows for a long-run reduction of the payroll tax rate by 13–14 percentage points, also when production paths remain unchanged. This is a strong impact, but this model-based estimate is only half of a naïve estimate that ignores the positive equilibrium adjustments of the wage rate (Holmøy 2006b). The GDP ratio of the CPF becomes more than doubled, peaking at 2.7 around 2035, but even such a vast pre-funding would not eliminate the growth trend in the necessary tax burden after 2020. Terms-of-trade gains obtained by *higher non-petroleum export prices* highlight the adverse budget of accelerated wage growth. Compared to the base scenario, accelerating the growth in these prices from 1.5 to 2.0 per cent implies an additional increase in the payroll tax rate in 2050 of 7.6 percentage points. Since Norway, especially the government, is a creditor, an *increase in the world interest rate from 5.5 to 6 per cent* also represents a terms-of-trade gain, which allows for higher labour costs. Also accounting for an increase in the real rate of return used in fiscal policy rule from 4 to 4.5 per cent, the payroll tax rate can be somewhat reduced, in 2050 by 2.8 percentage points from the baseline level.

One perhaps counterintuitive result is that *accelerated Total Factor Productivity (TFP) growth in private industries* commands higher tax rates. Stronger TFP growth expands most tax bases, but it also raises the government wage bill and wage-indexed transfers, since growth in productivity and world prices are the driving forces of the nominal wage growth. Furthermore, in Norway, wage-dependent government expenditures exceed the wage-dependent tax bases. An important component of the difference is the use of petroleum wealth allowed by the fiscal policy rule. Thus, policy makers – at least in Norway – cannot rely on economic growth in the private sector as a source to finance the increase in government expenditure.[15]

The strongest payroll tax rate effect shown in Figure 8.10 comes from *prolonging the growth in service standards in public health and social care observed in the 1990s*, rather than prolonging the 2004 levels of service standards. It turns out that such a standard-growth scenario becomes completely unrealistic after a couple of decades, as the sector by then would absorb most of the total labour supply. The payroll tax rate would have to increase by 10.1 percentage points in 2025 compared to the baseline level. Even if the standard improvements were halted in 2025, the payroll tax rate would increase further, passing 50 per cent around 2050, due to the positive interaction effect between the increase in the number of elderly and the accumulated standard improvement.[16]

On the other hand, *accelerating the annual labour productivity growth in public health and social care in public health and social care from 0.5 to 1 per cent*, allows for a 4.5 per cent reduction of the payroll tax rate, if the productivity improvement is used to reduce employment. The base scenario assumes no changes in the age-specific demand for health and social care services despite an increase in life expectancy by more than seven years from 2005 to 2050. If, alternatively, *health among the elderly improves*, so that the individual use of these services on average remains constant over the individual lifetime, the payroll tax rate can be reduced from their baseline levels by 8.1 percentage points.

Policy responses to future fiscal sustainability problems

The demographic challenge to the financial viability of the Norwegian welfare state has long been recognized. The tradition for regularly carrying out long-term projections of the Norwegian economy plays an important role in this respect. The previous section demonstrates that the role of such long-term projections is likely to be more important for disciplining the policy debate in Norway than in other countries, since few other countries face such a dramatic deterioration of the fiscal stance when ageing sets in. In most other OECD countries the fiscal stance already commands unpopular policy actions. In Norway the impressive current financial position of the government and the current record high petroleum cash flows, may create a policy climate for even more generous welfare schemes, tax cuts and rent seeking. It is not difficult to find examples demonstrating that such pressures have had some success.

On the other hand, the political parties, with the exception of the liberal right-wing party ('Fremskrittspartiet'), have agreed on the fiscal policy rule adopted in 2001, which restricts the annual use of the petroleum wealth. In addition, a broad agreement on the main elements in a major cost-saving reform of the public pension system was achieved in 2006. The subsequent sections discuss the fiscal consequences of these policy reforms.

The fiscal policy rule and the government's pension fund

Until 2001 there was actually no plan for when and how quickly the petroleum wealth should be consumed. Rather, the policy implied that, on average, the structural non-petroleum deficit remained constant over time. Such a policy would not have remained credible for many years, especially not when the accumulation in the CPF rapidly made the wealth more visible and liquid. In 2001 there was a great need to clarify when the petroleum wealth should be consumed. If a policy rule had not been established, there would have been a great risk that the wealth could be used much too quickly.

The fiscal policy rule was motivated and described in Ministry of Finance (2001). The government budget constraint implied by the fiscal policy rule can be seen by decomposing the accumulation of the CPF, B, from year $t - 1$ to t:

$$B_t - B_{t-1} = iB_{t-1} + P_t - D_t, \tag{8.1}$$

where i is the international nominal interest rate, P is the cash flow from the petroleum sector to the government, and D is the non-petroleum primary budget deficit. As an average over the business cycle, the non-petroleum deficit should be equal to the real return on the financial assets, that is:

$$(i - \pi) B_{t-1} = D_t, \tag{8.2}$$

where π is a measure of inflation. The inflation measure in this context is not precise, but the common interpretation is that it measures the growth in world prices. Therefore, i-π is the expected real rate of return in terms of international purchasing power. So far, i-π has been set to 4 per cent. If the fiscal policy rule is followed, the stock of financial assets grows according to the following equation:

$$B_t - B_{t-1} = \pi B_{t-1} + P_t. \tag{8.3}$$

In a long-run perspective P is basically the result of exogenous oil and gas prices and the government regulation of the depletion of the profitable oil and gas fields. Contingent on P, the time path of B is determined purely by exogenous variables, which implies a constraint on the average *annual* non-petroleum primary budget deficit. However, the CPF was not established until 1990, and it did not have assets until 1995, when the rapid accumulation of government net financial wealth started.

The fiscal policy rule is not supposed to be realized strictly in each year. White Paper No. 29 states explicitly that fiscal policy should be used to stabilize the macroeconomic development. Thus, the rule should rather hold as an average over the cycle. So far, however, the use of petroleum wealth has exceeded the constraint implied by the rule in every year since its passage (see Table 8.9). The reasons include not only lack of discipline, but also macroeconomic stabilization (2002 and 2003), and appreciation of NOK (2003). The general view among most economists observing the Norwegian economy is that the rule so far has contributed to a reduction in the consumption of petroleum wealth compared to a no-rule scenario.

Table 8.9 Central Government Pension Fund – Global (CPF), expected real return and Structural Non-petroleum Budget Deficit (SNBD) (billions NOK, current prices)

	CPF, beginning of the year	Expected real return (4 per cent)	SNBD	Difference SNBD and expected real return, per cent	SNBD, per cent of trend-GDP of Mainland Norway
2001	386.6	–	23.0	–	2.0
2002	619.3	24.8	33.5	35.1	2.8
2003	604.6	24.2	43.6	80.2	3.5
2004	847.1	33.9	52.2	54.0	3.9
2005	1,011.5	40.5	52.4	29.4	3.8
2006	1,390.1	55.6	62.9	13.1	4.3
2007	1,756.0	70.2	71.0	1.1	4.6
2008	2,181.6	87.3	–	–	–
2009	2,623.4	104.9	–	–	–
2010	3,043.7	121.7	–	–	–

Source: Ministry of Finance (2006).

The fiscal policy rule has not been derived from explicit optimization, partly because there is no consensus on the criteria for such an approach. Moreover, formal optimization would have to be carried out within a highly simplified model of the economy, in which important concerns are ruled out by assumption. Rather, the fiscal policy rule should be interpreted as a practical, transparent and operational compromise among the following concerns:

(i) *Generational fairness*: The national petroleum wealth should not be consumed only by the generation that found and depleted it.
(ii) *Tax smoothing*: In order to avoid large increases in the future tax rates after 2020 (see also the discussion of the Norwegian welfare state, above), or dramatic reductions in public welfare, less than the permanent income associated with the total petroleum wealth (the CPF plus the value of undepleted resources) should be used in the nearest decades.
(iii) *Minimization of transition costs*: A stable macroeconomic development calls for a gradual increase in the use of the petroleum wealth. When adopted in 2001, the rule and the policy followed until then implied about the same non-petroleum deficit.
(iv) *Avoid 'Dutch disease'*: As pointed out above in the discussion of petroleum revenues, fear of 'Dutch disease' has been a recurring issue in the Norwegian policy debate. The crowding out of the exposed sector may go too far, and it has been a common view that reversing the process most likely would involve severe unemployment and other real losses.
(v) *Risk aversion*: Oil and gas prices are highly uncertain. Risk aversion implies that the sustainable annual consumption reflects a downward correction of the expected value of the undepleted resources.
(vi) *Operationality*: The policy rule should be easy to operate and to communicate to politicians and to the public.

The fiscal policy rule has often been contrasted with consuming the so-called permanent income rule, according to which the annuity associated with the total petroleum wealth is consumed annually. Compared with the permanent income rule, the fiscal policy rule implies lower consumption during depletion of the resources and more pre-funding. But as the petroleum resources are converted to financial assets, the fiscal policy rule converges from below to a permanent income rule based on financial assets. The fiscal policy rule can be interpreted as a consequence of extreme risk aversion, since only the liquid part of the total petroleum wealth is included in the base for calculating the annual consumption. Moreover, the fiscal policy rule makes the current non-petroleum deficit less sensitive to fluctuations in petroleum prices compared to the permanent income rule. Finally, implementation of the permanent income rule in 2001 would have raised the annual consumption of petroleum wealth quite dramatically from the trend in preceding years.

The discussion on the Norwegian welfare state above showed that the degree of pre-funding of government expenditures is far from sufficient to ensure tax smoothing. However, the accumulation of liquid assets in the CPF is quite ambitious. Under the baseline scenario the ratio between the CPF and GDP peaks in 2037 at about 1.3 (see Figure 8.11). If the oil and gas prices are doubled, the ratio peaks at about 2.7. It remains to be seen whether the Norwegian democracy will have the discipline to consume only the expected real return of such a vast liquid and visible wealth. A general lack of trust in fiscal discipline has been used both to motivate fiscal policy rule and as an argument against the rule, especially when this type of rule was first suggested in a report to the government in 1983. Some have argued that the fiscal discipline problems associated with a vast and highly liquid petroleum wealth were, and are, so severe that the intended saving of the petroleum wealth for future generations can be achieved only by reducing the annual production of oil and gas.

One may criticize the 'expected real rate of return' estimate of 4.0 per cent for being inconsistent with the intention of the fiscal policy rule. This estimate uses the growth in world prices as a deflator. However, most of the government expenditures are allocated to wages of civil servants and wage-indexed transfers to households. In the baseline scenario the nominal wage rate grows by about 4 per cent per year, whereas world prices grow by 1.5 per cent, and the nominal interest rate is 5.5 per cent. Consequently, if the effective return on the CPF capital is supposed to neutralize the contribution from the pure price effect of wage growth on the required increases in the tax burden, the relevant real return for the government would be 5.5–4.0 = 1.5 per cent, rather than 4.0 per cent. Obviously, reducing the real rate of return from 4.0 to 1.5 per cent would imply a dramatic fiscal policy contraction and a much stronger increase in the CPF.

Reform of the public pension system[17]

In order to improve the degree of fiscal sustainability, labour market efficiency and transparency, in 2004 the government proposed a reform of the public pension system. The new system is supposed to be phased in from 2010 over a 15-year

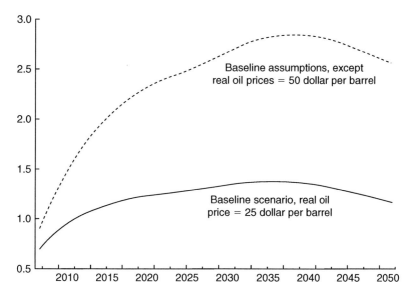

Figure 8.11   The Central Government Pension Fund (foreign) relative to GDP in current prices
Source: Heide et al. (2006).

period. The most important reform elements include:

(i) The pension benefit continues to include a granted minimum benefit and an income-based benefit. The level of the minimum benefit follows the same development as the minimum benefit in the present system. Contrary to the present system, it is means-tested against the income-based pension benefit.

(ii) Stronger dependency between earnings and pension benefits. In the present system the pension entitlement depends on the earnings in the 20 best years. In the proposed system the income-based benefit is based on *lifetime* earnings with a few restrictions.

(iii) In the present system annual pension benefit is independent of life expectancy and age of retirement. The reform implies that the annual benefit is adjusted so that the *total* value of the future pension benefits remains roughly invariant to life expectancy and age of retirement.

(iv) The income-dependent *entitlements* continue to be indexed by wage growth until retirement. On the other hand, benefits will after the reform be indexed to the average of growth rates of wages and consumer prices, rather than the wage growth alone. Over time this implies lower annual benefits than in the present system.

The macroeconomic and fiscal effects of the proposed reform is analysed in Fredriksen et al. (2006). They find that the reform allows an incremental cut in the payroll tax rate over time as longevity increases. In 2050 the payroll tax rate is as much as 14 percentage points below the baseline scenario. This is possible due to both reduced government pension expenditures and expansion of tax bases through higher employment. The most important cost saving element is the adjustment of the annual average benefit to changes in the average number of years as a pensioner (the third element in the list above). Employment is estimated to increase by as much as 10 per cent in the long run, basically due to (i) the increase in the private cost of early retirement; (ii) the stronger relationship between earnings and pension entitlements; and (iii) the reduction in the payroll tax rate made possible by the direct fiscal effects of the reform.

Final remarks

The findings of large oil and gas resources have probably been the main reason why GDP per capita in Norway has grown to become one of the highest in the world after 1970. The remarkable growth performance has been combined with an ambitious policy with respect intertemporal allocation of the expanded consumption possibilities associated with the petroleum wealth. Most of the petroleum revenues accrue to the government, and the Norwegian state has become a fiscal outlier compared to other OECD countries. So far the petroleum wealth seems to have been a blessing – not a curse – for Norwegians.

The literature relating to the 'resource curse' has identified five factors that are felt to be of crucial importance in determining whether resource abundance becomes a curse or a blessing. Torvik (2007) concludes that Norway scores high on all of them: (i) The savings ratio is relatively high, even after correcting for depletion of resources; (ii) Norway has strong institutions; the government protects property rights, corruption is low, and the bureaucracy is competent and accountable. Rent seeking takes place, but the social losses have been limited, partly due to democratic transparency; (iii) Petroleum resources have been found to stimulate growth to a greater extent than other natural resources. One reason may be that exploitation of the oil and gas stimulates research and development with positive spin-off effects. Learning-by-doing in the petroleum sector has replaced learning-by-doing in manufacturing industries that were crowded out; (iv) Norway has parliamentarianism, and the 'resource curse' is more frequently found in countries governed by presidency; and (v) Norway was industrialized relatively early, and such countries have been less vulnerable to the 'resource curse' than countries industrialized after the Second World War.

The first point deserves some comments. Government savings of the petroleum rents in the CPF have been institutionalized by the fiscal policy rule adopted in 2001. The rule is well motivated, and it has proved to be operational. Although the budget constraint implied by a strict interpretation of the rule has been violated in every year, savings have probably been greater than if no such rule existed. The rule implies that petroleum wealth is converted to highly liquid and visible financial assets. It remains to be seen whether the Norwegian parliamentary democracy will have the necessary discipline to obey the rule when, or if, the fund becomes twice as large as the GDP. Defining purposes of the savings is probably important in order to keep fiscal discipline, although they may be regarded as costly constraints in the future. Changing the name of the fund from the *Petroleum fund* to the *Pension fund* is a step in this direction. Distributing the fund by establishing individual pension accounts would be a much greater step. Moreover, it is important to keep long-run perspectives high on the policy agenda. Systematic quantitative projections of the economy and the budget components is one of the few ways to call attention to the long-run consequences of decisions made today. The use of model-based economic projections has a solid tradition in Norway.

The institutional set-up of the CPF has probably prevented rent seeking. There is a clear distinction between the fund's account and the state budget. The CPF is prohibited from being invested domestically, a decision that has been quite controversial. Exclusion from Norwegian assets is not likely to reduce the aggregate returns, since the returns in the international capital markets span the returns that can be obtained in Norway. Moreover, profitable Norwegian projects can be realized through international borrowing. The industry policy includes instruments that correct well-known market failures in the credit markets. If parts of the fund were channelled to domestic projects via political decisions, rent seeking would be stimulated, and the aggregate returns would probably fall.

Although the petroleum wealth is large and the present fiscal stance looks quite impressive, Norway faces severe problems of fiscal sustainability in the long run when ageing generates rapid growth in government expenditures. Maintaining the present policy, and assuming that the real price of oil averages $25 per barrel, such a broad-based tax rate as the payroll tax rate must be increased in every year after 2020, passing twice the present level between 2045 and 2050. This scenario is optimistic by assuming no improvements of the standards of the services provided by the government sector. Continuation of the observed growth in the standard of individual welfare service will be prohibitively costly after a few decades, unless productivity accelerates in government service sectors. The fiscal prospects look much less gloomy if instead the real oil price averages $50 per barrel, but such a shift does not eliminate the deviation between the *growth rates* of government expenditures and the tax bases.

The quite strong egalitarian traditions in Norway imply that productivity-based economic growth is spread quickly not only to workers in all sectors, including the public sector, but is also automatically distributed to recipients of pensions and other cash transfers through wage indexation. In Norway wage-dependent government expenditures tend to exceed the wage-dependent tax bases. Consequently, wage growth commands, ceteris paribus, higher tax rates. This implies that productivity growth in the private sector or improved terms-of-trade reinforces the fiscal sustainability problems in Norway.

The proposed reform of the public pension system is likely to be by far the most important single reform in Norway for decades. It implies a very long step towards a solution of the long-run fiscal sustainability problem. The most important reform element in this respect is the actuarial mechanism which, on average, makes the total value of individual old-age benefits received by the recipients over their lifetime much more invariant to both increased longevity and early retirement compared to the current system. This mechanism removes much of the difference between the respective growth rates of government pension expenditures and the tax bases, basically by stimulating labour supply.

If the real oil and gas prices continue to stay high, if the proposed pension reform becomes implemented, if the public accepts low or no growth in the standard of old-age care, and if governments obey the fiscal policy rule, it is reasonable to conclude that the somewhat downsized Norwegian welfare state is financially viable without unrealistic increases in tax rates. However, this should not be used as an argument for postponing reforms. In particular, it is important to redesign transfer schemes in order to increase working incentives of groups with a weak attachment to the labour market.

Notes

1. Until 2006, the fund was known as the 'Central Government Petroleum Fund'.
2. The Mainland sector is defined as the total economy less the off-shore petroleum sectors and Ocean Transport.
3. Standard cubic metres oil equivalents.
4. NOK: Norwegian krone.
5. All $ amounts refer to US dollars.
6. Van Wijnbergen (1984); Krugman (1987); Torvik (2001).
7. An important driving force behind the expected ageing is the increased longevity: Life expectancy for males increases from 77.5 years in 2004 to 84.7 years in 2050. The corresponding increase for females is from 82.1 to 88.9 years (Statistics Norway 2005).
8. Fredriksen (1998) describes this microsimulation model.
9. MSG6 is an abbreviation for the sixth version of the Multi Sectoral Growth model.
10. Heide et al. (2004) provide a detailed description of the model structure and its empirical characteristics.
11. This choice is consistent with the results in Aaberge et al. (1995).
12. The scale elasticities range from 0.85–1.00. Evidence of decreasing returns to scale at the firm level is presented in Klette (1999).
13. In addition to the payroll tax, its most important elements include an average marginal tax on personal labour income approximately equal to 40 per cent, compulsory social security premiums averaging 7 per cent of wages, and net indirect taxation of consumption (including value added tax/VAT) averaging about 20 per cent. In addition, the pension system, especially the early retirement scheme, magnifies the labour supply distortions at the extensive margin.
14. Such an increase in the relative prices of services provided by the government is often referred to as the *Baumol effect*.
15. This point has also been made in Ministry of Finance (2004). Holmøy (2006a) provides a more thorough analysis. The qualitative result also holds for Denmark (Andersen and Pedersen 2006).
16. The tax increase would have been larger if government consumption of individual goods entered the individual's utility functions in the model due to the income effect on labour supply.
17. The content of the reform has been somewhat revised since the proposal of 2004. However, the main elements have been maintained as described in this section.

References

Aaberge, R., J. Dagsvik and S. Strøm (1995) 'Labour supply effects of tax reforms', *Scandinavian Journal of Economics*, No. 97, 635–59.

Andersen, T.M. and L.H. Pedersen (2006) 'Financial restraints in a mature welfare state – the case of Denmark', *Oxford Review of Economic Policy*, Vol. 22, No. 3, 313–29.

Antolin, P. and W. Suyker (2001) *How Should Norway Respond to Ageing?*, OECD Economics Department Series Working Paper No. 296 (Paris: OECD).

Chauveau, T. and R. Loufir (1995) *The Future of Public Pensions in the Seven Major Economies*, OFCE Working Paper (Paris: Research Department-OFCE).

Danish Welfare Commission (2004) *Analyserapport – Fremtidens velfærd kommer ikke af sig selv.* www.velfaerd.dk (in Danish).

Eurostat (2006) *Tax Revenue in the EU, Statistics in Focus, Economy and Finance.* epp.eurostat.ec.europa.eu/portal/page?_pageid=1073,46587259&_dad=portal&_schema= PORTAL&p_product_code=KS-NJ-06-002, accessed in February 2006.

Feldstein, M. (2005) *Structural Reform of Social Security*, NBER Working Paper No. 11098 (Cambridge, MA: NBER).

Fredriksen, D. (1998) *Projections of Population, Education, Labour Supply and Public pension benefits: Analyses with the Dynamic Simulation Model MOSART*, Social and Economic Studies Paper No. 101 (Oslo: Statistics Norway).

Fredriksen, D., K.M. Heide, E. Holmøy and I.F. Solli (2006) 'Macroeconomic effects of proposed pension reforms in Norway.' In A. Harding, A. Gupta, R. Lloyd and K. Basu (eds.), *Population Ageing, Social Security and Taxation: Modelling Our Future, Vol. 1* (Amsterdam: North-Holland Publishing Company).

Heide, K.M., E. Holmøy, L. Lerskau and I.F. Solli (2004) *Macroeconomic Properties of the Norwegian Applied General Equilibrium Model MSG6*, Report No. 2004/18 (Oslo: Statistics Norway).

Heide, K.M., E. Holmøy, I.F. Solli and B. Strøm (2006) *A Welfare State Funded by Nature and OPEC: A Guided Tour on Norway's Path from an Exceptionally Impressive to an Exceptionally Strained Fiscal Position*, Discussion Paper No. 464 (Oslo: Statistics Norway).

Holmøy, E. (2006a) *Can Welfare States Outgrow Their Fiscal Sustainability Problems?*, Discussion Paper No. 487 (Oslo: Statistics Norway).

—— (2006b) *Real Appreciation as an Automatic Channel for Redistribution of Increased Government Non-tax Revenue*, Discussion Paper No. 471 (Oslo: Statistics Norway).

—— (2002) *Hva koster tidligpensjonering for samfunnet?* Økonomiske analyser No. 2/2002 (Oslo: Statistics Norway) (in Norwegian).

Holmøy, E. and K.M. Heide (2005) *Is Norway Immune to Dutch Disease? CGE Estimates of Sustainable Wage Growth and De-industrialisation*, Discussion Paper No. 413 (Oslo: Statistics Norway).

Klette, T.J. (1999) 'Market power, scale economies and productivity: Estimates from a panel of establishment data', *Journal of Industrial Economics*, No. 110, 451–75.

Kotlikoff, L., K. Smetters and J. Walliser (2001) *Finding a Way Out of America's Demographic Dilemma*, NBER Working Paper No. 8258 (Cambridge, MA: NBER).

Krugman, P. (1991) 'Increasing returns and economic geography', *Journal of Political Economy*, Vol. 99, No. 3, 483–99.

—— (1987) 'The narrow moving band, the Dutch disease, and the competitive consequences of Mrs. Thatcher', *Journal of Development Economics*, Vol. 27, Nos 1–2, 41–55.

Ministry of Finance (2006) National Budget 2007, White Paper (St.meld.), No. 1 (Oslo: Ministry of Finance) (in Norwegian).

—— (2004) *Perspektivmeldingen 2004 – Utfordringer og valgmuligheter for norsk økonomi*, White Paper (St.meld.), No. 8 (Oslo: Ministry of Finance) (in Norwegian).

—— (2001) White Paper (St.meld.), No. 29 (Oslo: Ministry of Finance) (in Norwegian).

Mogstad, M., I. Solli and A. Wist (2006) Lønner det seg å arbeide? Økonomisk Forum 7, 71–82 (Oslo) (in Norwegian).

OECD (Organisation for Economic Co-operation and Development) (2008) *Labour Productivity*. www.oecd.org/statistics/productivity, accessed on 15 February 2008.

—— (2007) *National Accounts and Historical Statistics 2007 – Vol. 1* (Paris: OECD).

—— (2006) *Employment Outlook 2006* (Paris: OECD).

—— (2001) 'Fiscal implications of ageing: Projections of age-related spending', *OECD Economic Outlook* No. 69, Ch. IV (Paris: OECD).

Røed, K. (2007) *Hele folket i arbeid*. Økonomisk forum No. 3, Oslo (in Norwegian).

Røed Larsen, E. (2003) *Are Rich Countries Immune to the Resource Curse? Evidence from Norway's Management of Its Oil Riches*, Discussion Paper No. 362 (Oslo: Statistics Norway).

Sachs, J.D and A.M. Warner (2001) 'The curse of natural resources', *European Economic Review*, Vol. 41, Nos. 4–6, 411–42.

Statistics Norway (2008) *General Government Fiscal Account: Revenue and Expenditure*. www.ssb.no/offinnut_en/tab-01-en.html, accessed on 29 April 2008.

—— (2006) *Economic Survey No. 1* (Oslo: Statistics Norway).

—— (2005) *Population Projections. National and Regional Figures, 2005–2060. Strong Population Growth Expected*. www.ssb.no/folkfram_en/, accessed on 10 January 2007.

Torvik, R. (2007) Rikdommens paradoks: Relevans for Norge, mimeo (Trondheim: NTNU).

—— (2001) 'Learning by doing and the Dutch disease', *European Economic Review*, Vol. 45, No. 2, 285–306.

Venables, A. (1996) 'Equilibrium locations of vertically linked industries', *International Economic Review*, Vol. 37, No. 2, 341–59.

Van Wijnbergen, S. (1984) 'The Dutch disease: A disease after all?', *Economic Journal*, Vol. 94, No. 373, 285–306.

Part IV

Social Insurance and Pension Funds

9
Social Insurance (Pensions and Health), Labour Markets and Coverage in Latin America

Carmelo Mesa-Lago[1]

Introduction

This chapter analyses the relationship between the labour market, social insurance pensions and health programmes, and the coverage of the labour force and the population in Latin America and is divided into four sections. The first section describes changes in the labour market which have led towards increasing informality and labour flexibilization and have resulted in jobs that lack social insurance coverage; examines the difficulties in the incorporation of the informal sector (self-employed, domestic servants, employees in microenterprises) and of the rural population and peasants; and identifies potential factors that could explain coverage differences between countries. The second section evaluates the impact of external factors and the system itself, as well as health and pension reforms, on various aspects of coverage, such as overall statistical coverage before and after the reforms, inequalities in coverage by income, gender, geographical areas and indigenous peoples, and coverage of the poor and the elderly. The third section outlines policies to extend coverage to the excluded sectors, compares divergent approaches of international and regional organizations and identifies common objectives, specifies policies to incorporate difficult groups and reduce inequalities by income, gender, geography and among indigenous peoples, and to protect the poor and the elderly. Finally, the fourth section draws policy lessons from the Latin American experience for other developing countries.

Labour force coverage by social insurance pensions in Latin America averaged 31 per cent in 2004; 66 per cent of contributors are in public systems and 34 per cent in private systems, but the 20 countries are equally divided between the two. Introduced by structural reforms in 1981–2003, private systems are characterized by defined contribution, fully-funded individual accounts and private administration. At the time of writing private systems were in place in Argentina, Bolivia, Chile, Colombia, Costa Rica, the Dominican Republic, El Salvador, Mexico, Peru and Uruguay; half of them had totally replaced the public system with a private one; three have mixed models that combine a public basic pillar with a private supplementary pension, and two had both systems in operation competing between them.[2] In terms of total coverage the private share ranges from 76 per cent to 100 per cent, with the exceptions of Colombia (53 per cent) and Uruguay (37 per cent). Conversely, public systems are characterized by defined benefit, pay-as-you-go or partial funding, and social insurance or state administration; several of them have undertaken parametric reforms. The division between the two types is somewhat arbitrary because private systems rely heavily on the state: they are mandatory instead of voluntary, and the government finances several important benefits such as minimum pensions, the value of insured contributions transferred from the public to the private system, and ongoing pensions during the transition (Hujo et al. 2004). Herein we deal with both systems as all are technically considered social insurance.

Most countries in Latin America have three health sectors: (i) public, which legally should protect the uninsured population (the majority in 12 countries), but in practice seldom does, hence making any estimation of the population with access extremely difficult; (ii) social insurance sickness-maternity (comprising a principal programme and separate schemes in most countries), which covers 41 per cent of the total population ranging from 8 per cent to 88 per cent and is the main provider in eight countries; and (iii) private (various types both for-profit and not-for-profit), which covers 11.5 per cent of the population stretching from 1 per cent to 25 per cent, hence the minority (a considerably lower proportion than in pensions). Two countries do not have social insurance, but rather have a public national system (Brazil and Cuba), whereas Chile combines public and social insurance. This chapter deals exclusively with coverage or affiliation to the social insurance health programme, including Chile.

The 20 countries are divided herein into three groups based on the time of inception of social insurance and its degree of development, as well as demographic variables: (i) pioneer-high (Argentina, Brazil, Chile, Costa Rica, Cuba and Uruguay); (ii) intermediate (Bolivia, Colombia, Ecuador, Mexico, Panama, Peru and Venezuela); and (iii) latecomer-low (the Dominican Republic, El Salvador, Guatemala, Haiti, Honduras, Nicaragua and Paraguay). Albeit with some exceptions in the characteristics, the pioneer-high group was the first in establishing social insurance in the region (1920s and 1930s), its systems are the most developed, have virtually universal coverage and the highest costs, usually face financial and actuarial disequilibria and their populations are the most aged with the longest life expectancy. The intermediate group introduced social insurance in the 1940s and 1950s, has medium levels of coverage and development of its systems, lower costs and better financial situations than the first group, although some suffer disequilibria, and its demographic variables rank between the two groups. The latecomer-low group was the last in implementing social insurance in the 1960s and 1970s, its systems are the least developed and have the lowest coverage, but usually have a better financial-actuarial situation than the other two groups, and their populations are the youngest but with the lowest life expectancy (Mesa-Lago 2008).

Social insurance, labour market and coverage

The transformation of the labour market in Latin America

Since the 1980s the urban formal labour sector has diminished in Latin America while the informal sector has grown, thus creating a formidable challenge to social insurance to maintain and expand its coverage because most informal workers are mostly legally excluded or have voluntary coverage. The informal sector is heterogenous, but normally involves unskilled manpower with low productivity, such as self-employed workers, domestic servants, employees in microenterprises, and so on; it augmented from a regional average of 43 per cent of urban employment in 1990 to 47 per cent in 2002, due to a reduction of formal public employment, growth of employment in large enterprises at a slower rhythm than the labour force, expansion of jobs in microenterprises, domestic service and self-employment, and an increase in labour 'flexibilization', that is, subcontracting, part-time work or jobs without contracts, all of which lack social insurance (ILO 2003).[3]

As a percentage of the employed urban labour force the informal sector averaged 47 per cent in 18 countries (data are not available for Cuba and Haiti) in 2001–04 and ranged (lower to higher) between 29 and 43 per cent in Chile, Costa Rica, Panama, Argentina, Brazil and Uruguay – countries in the pioneer-high group and one country in the intermediate group; and 50–63 per cent in El Salvador, Ecuador, Paraguay, Venezuela, Guatemala, Honduras, Nicaragua, Peru and Bolivia – countries in the latecomer-low group and the less developed intermediate group. Contrary to the urban informal sector, the rural percentage of the total labour force has diminished in the region, but still fluctuates between 29 per cent and 55 per cent in the latecomer-low group. Furthermore, self-employed and unpaid family workers average 56 per cent of the rural labour force and reach 69–86 per cent in three countries; the lowest percentages are in Costa Rica and Chile, with 26 per cent and 32 per cent, respectively (Table 9.1).

Legal and statistical coverage of difficult to incorporate groups

Argentina, Brazil, Chile, Costa Rica and Uruguay (all in the pioneer-high group) have the best legal mandatory coverage of the informal and rural sectors (with the exception of Chile's self-employed), while countries in the latecomer-low group have legal voluntary coverage or impose restrictions.[4] All salaried workers have mandatory legal coverage (including domestic servants and agricultural workers) in the pioneer-high group and five countries in the intermediate group. Conversely the latecomer-low group compulsorily covers only part of salaried workers, because either the insurance is not operative in all regions of the country, or it excludes domestic and agricultural workers, legally or in practice.[5]

Self-employed

Self-employment, the largest segment of the informal sector, averaged 30 per cent of the employed urban labour force in 2001–04, ranging from 15 per cent to 24 per cent in Chile, Argentina, Costa Rica, Mexico, Panama, Uruguay and Brazil, and from 32 per cent to 46 per cent in El Salvador Ecuador, Nicaragua,

Table 9.1 Population groups difficult to cover by social insurance in Latin America, 2001–04 (in percentages)

Countries[a]	Informal/ urban employed labour force[b]	Self-employed/ urban employed labour force	Self-employed and not salaried/rural labour force[c]	Poverty/total population
Argentina	37.0	17.1	n.a.	29.4[d]
Bolivia	62.8	45.7	86.0	62.4
Brazil	41.9	23.6	64.7	38.7
Chile	28.6	15.0	32.0	18.7
Colombia	44.4	38.5	54.8	50.6[d]
Costa Rica	31.4	18.1	26.4	20.3
Dominican Rep.	43.0	30.6	55.1	44.9
Ecuador	52.4	34.2	60.4	49.0[d]
El Salvador	49.5	32.4	40.5	48.9
Guatemala	54.1	36.0	62.3	60.2
Honduras	54.2	36.7	63.0	77.3
Mexico	41.4	19.0	35.4	37.0
Nicaragua	55.6	35.4	57.2	69.3
Panama	34.5	21.0	56.3	34.0
Paraguay	53.8	30.1	69.4	61.0
Peru	60.0	42.0	80.5	54.7
Uruguay	42.6	21.8	n.a.	15.4[d]
Venezuela	53.9	39.6	44.9	48.6
Regional average	46.7	29.8	55.6	41.7

Notes: [a] There are no statistics on Cuba and Haiti. [b] Percentage of the urban labour force employed that is either unskilled self-employed, domestic servant or employed in microenterprises (Colombia excludes the latter), all with low productivity. [c] Percentage of the rural labour force that is self-employed or unpaid family worker. [d] Only urban.
Sources: Based on ECLAC 2005; author's regional non-weighted averages, except poverty weighted by ECLAC.

Guatemala, Honduras, Colombia, Venezuela, Peru and Bolivia (Table 9.1). The proportion of self-employed is lower in the pioneer-high group, which have the highest overall social insurance coverage, and higher in the latecomer-low group, which have the lowest overall coverage. Although there is significant variety among the self-employed, a large majority are very difficult to cover because of the lack of employer, unstable and low-paid jobs, obligation to pay a contribution equal to the combined percentages charged to salaried workers and employers, and difficulties with enrolment and the collection of their contributions.

In 14 countries legal pension coverage of the self-employed is voluntary and two countries exclude them; legal compulsory coverage is only granted in Argentina, Brazil, Costa Rica and Uruguay, and laws in five countries stipulate such obligation but have not yet been enforced. Statistical coverage is higher in countries with mandatory affiliation (30 per cent, 29 per cent and 23 per cent in Argentina, Uruguay and Brazil, respectively) and lower in those with voluntary affiliation (0.2 per cent to 5 per cent in five countries), Costa Rica is an exception with 24 per cent, when affiliation was voluntary, and should have increased since 2006, when it became mandatory. In Chile coverage is voluntary and in the private system fell from 12 per cent to 5 per cent during the reform,[6] most of this group being high-income professionals. Compulsory legal affiliation helps but does not necessarily solve the coverage gap; incentives (particularly fiscal subsidies) and sanctions appear to have increased coverage in Argentina, Brazil, Costa Rica and Uruguay, but subsidies have not been entirely successful in Colombia.

The self-employed have mandatory legal coverage in the social insurance health programme only in Colombia and Costa Rica (since 2006); in Paraguay, the law is not enforced, whereas in Brazil and Cuba they are covered by the public system; they are excluded in three countries (El Salvador, Guatemala and Haiti), and have voluntary coverage in the remaining 12. Recent laws (not implemented) or legal drafts stipulate compulsory coverage in four countries. Statistical coverage of the self-employed as a proportion of total affiliates in the main social insurance programme ranged (lower to higher) from 0.4 per cent to 6 per cent in Nicaragua, Honduras, Mexico, Peru, Colombia, Ecuador and Argentina, considerably lower than the corresponding self-employed shares in the labour force. All of these countries have legal voluntary coverage, except for Colombia, but its goal of incorporating 80 per cent of the self-employed by 2000 (helped by a solidarity contribution) was not met. In Argentina only the tiny percentage of entrepreneurs who pay taxes are given compulsory coverage; the rest have optional affiliation, and only 15 per cent are covered compared with 30 per cent in pensions with mandatory coverage. In Chile, the level of coverage is optional, and only 1.7 per cent of the total insured in the private system is self-employed, however, all indigent self-employed are eligible for free care in social insurance (about 75 per cent of them). In Uruguay, 14 per cent of the self-employed is voluntary covered on health vis-à-vis 29 per cent which are mandatorily covered in pensions. Voluntary coverage of unskilled self-employed workers by social insurance in 2000–02 was 0.2 per cent in Paraguay, 1 per cent in Honduras and 5 per cent in Ecuador. Conversely, despite Costa Rica's voluntary coverage until 2006, 45 per cent of the self-employed were affiliated because the state provides a subsidy (in lieu of the employer's contribution) to those with low income.

Domestic servants

In 2001–04 domestic servants accounted for between 3 and 10 per cent of the urban employed labour force, a smaller proportion than the number of self-employed. These workers have an employer; however, many of them lack a labour contract and, where one does exist, it is either difficult for the employee to demand the employer's contribution, or the wage is very low and the worker collaborates with the employer to evade affiliation.

Domestic servants have legal compulsory (albeit difficult to enforce in practice) pension coverage in 12 countries, voluntary in only five and are excluded in three (non-enforced laws in four countries stipulate mandatory coverage). Brazil and Costa Rica, which have compulsory affiliation, cover 27 per cent and 39 per cent, respectively, of these workers, and data were not available from the other countries. In health care, domestic servants have legal mandatory coverage in

13 countries (although in three of them it is not very effective), voluntary in one and are excluded in six. Statistical coverage of domestic servants varies greatly: from 3 per cent in Paraguay, to 11 per cent in Panama, 13 per cent in Ecuador, 27 per cent in Colombia and 31 per cent in Uruguay.

Employees of microenterprises

Employees of microenterprises, excluding professionals and technicians, ranged from 7 to 16 per cent of the urban labour force in 2001–04 (ECLAC 2005). This figure is probably an underestimate because most microenterprises are informal and very hard and expensive to detect and control; for these reasons, social insurance usually gives priority to the enrollment and collection from large and middle enterprises, neglecting the smaller ones.

Employees of microenterprises, home, seasonal, part-time and unpaid family workers, as well as those without a labour contract are either excluded from social insurance coverage or included only optionally or under certain conditions in a few countries. In most countries the law determines the minimum number of employees in an enterprise (ranging between five and ten) required for mandatory affiliation. Data on the employed labour force by size of enterprises in 14 countries demonstrate that coverage in large enterprises is between three and 30 times higher that in small ones, supporting the hypothesis that larger establishments tend to be formal while the smaller ones are essentially informal (Rofman 2005). Employees of microenterprises are covered in pensions by 51 per cent in Argentina, but only by 4 per cent in Mexico; in Honduras health coverage according to the size of enterprises in 2000 decreased from 46 per cent among those with more than ten employees to 4 per cent among those with only three employees.

Rural sector and peasants

This segment is also very difficult to cover because the majority of people affected are peasants, seasonal workers, the self-employed, sharecroppers or squatters, all normally occupied in subsistence agriculture. They either lack an employer or have one only for a few months in the year, their income is meagre and their dispersion is a barrier to health care provision.

Five countries grant full legal pension coverage to agricultural workers, while the rest have special regimes or impose restrictions. The proportion of the agricultural labour force that is insured in pensions oscillates between 4 and 12 per cent in five countries, and the coverage of the rural population usually ranges between one-third and one-sixth that of the urban population. Only three countries have introduced special social insurance pensions for rural workers or peasants, covering 18 per cent of the rural labour force in Ecuador, 29 per cent in Mexico and 50 per cent in Brazil in 2004–05. In the first two countries coverage has declined in recent years, while in the third it has increased.

In half of the countries agricultural workers are legally excluded from health coverage; the other half covers mainly wage earners in large plantations and members of cooperatives in some countries. Self-employed peasants, sharecroppers, squatters and the like are excluded, with three important exceptions: the already noted peasant schemes of Ecuador and Mexico, and the agrarian insurance in Peru that covers self-employed rural workers. There are very few figures on coverage of agricultural workers: 1.5 per cent in Ecuador (but 18 per cent of the rural population covered by peasant insurance), 2 per cent in Honduras and 6 per cent in Mexico (but 29 per cent of the rural population covered by peasant insurance).

Factors that facilitate coverage among these groups

Table 9.2 summarizes all of the available comparable information related to pensions for three groups (self-employed, domestic servants and agricultural workers/peasants) for three dimensions: the proportional size of each in the employed labour force, the stipulated legal affiliation (obligatory, voluntary, and so on); and the percentage of each group covered by social insurance. Although data from more countries are needed, as well as more recent (for some) and standardized (for all) information, the following tentative conclusions can be induced: (i) the

Table 9.2 Proportional size of groups difficult to incorporate and legal and statistical pension coverage in selected countries, 2000–04

Groups/countries	Group/employed labour force[a] (%)	Legal coverage	% of the group covered
Self-employed			
Argentina	24	Obligatory	30
Brazil	26	Obligatory	23
Chile	15	Voluntary	5
Colombia	39	Voluntary[b]	10
Costa Rica	21	Voluntary[c]	24
Mexico	19	Voluntary	0.1[e]
Nicaragua	35	Voluntary	0.2
Paraguay	30	Voluntary[d]	0.2
Uruguay	22	Obligatory	29
Domestic servants			
Brazil	9	Obligatory	27[f]
Costa Rica	3	Obligatory	39
Paraguay	10	Voluntary	3[g]
Agricultural workers/peasants			
Brazil	65	Special regime	50
Chile	32	Obligatory	41
Costa Rica	26	Obligatory salaried	44
Ecuador	60	Special regime	18
El Salvador	41	Large farms only	6[h]
Honduras	63	Oblig. 10+ employees	2[h]
Mexico	35	Special regime	29

Notes: [a] Urban labour force for self-employed and domestic servants; rural self-employed and unpaid family workers in agriculture; data corresponds with the same year of coverage. [b] The reform stipulates obligatory coverage but it has not been implemented. [c] Until 2006 when it became obligatory. [d] Legally obligatory but not enforced in practice. [e] Percentage of informal sector covered. [f] Without a contract. Raises to 100 per cent with a contract. [g] In health programme. [h] Year 1997.
Sources: ECLAC 2005; legislation from the countries; Mesa-Lago (2008).

higher the proportional size of the group in the labour force, the more difficult it is to cover; (ii) countries that have legal obligatory affiliation have higher coverage than those with voluntary affiliation; (iii) fiscal subsidies to poor or low-income self-employed are incentives for coverage; and (d) special regimes for rural workers or peasants provide better coverage than voluntary or restricted regimes, but with diverse results (the best being in Brazil and the worst in Ecuador, due to different levels of government commitment and financial support).

Impact of the system, the reforms and other factors on coverage

Supporters of structural reforms have asserted that key elements of the private pension system provide stronger incentives for affiliation than the public system, leading to an expansion of coverage, for instance, enforcing equivalence between contributions and benefits, combined with targeting of fiscal resources on the poor and low-income populations (World Bank 1994). Recently, World Bank officials confirmed that increasing coverage is both an objective and a predicted result of implementing a private pension system, and Bank loans for structural reforms in several countries had the expansion of coverage as a main goal (Gill et al. 2005). Similarly, health reforms were expected to increase coverage and even reach universality in some countries because economic growth, the market and private enterprise would allegedly increase employment and income, thus creating conditions to enable individuals to satisfy their health needs with their own resources (Cifuentes 2000). Contrary to such assumptions, available data show the opposite results.

Overall coverage and trends

Pension programme

Private systems coverage based on affiliates averaged 60 per cent of the labour force in 2005, compared with 25 per cent based on contributors in the last month; the respective figures for Chile were 116 per cent and 60 per cent, demonstrating the noted overestimation (AIOS 2006). The gap between the two estimates results from the insured who are unemployed, or may have abandoned the labour force, or shifted from the formal to the informal sector, or who have been counted twice. Coverage based on contributors in turn may underestimate real coverage because some affiliates who did not pay in the last month could do so in the immediate future and retain effective coverage.

Coverage based on more reliable active contributors, before the reform and in 2004, declined in all ten private systems and their weighted average decreased from 38 per cent to 26 per cent (Table 9.3, first column). Comparisons in coverage between private and public systems are not precise, as a result of the different periods used to define the condition of active contributor. Table 9.3 (third column) estimates that in 2004 the weighted average in private systems was 26 per cent, which was lower than the corresponding average of 39 per cent in eight public systems (data on Cuba and Haiti were not available).[7] Standardized historical series based on active contributors in Chile, the country with the longest period of a

Table 9.3 Social insurance pension coverage of the labour force by private and public contributory systems, based on active contributors

Private systems	Coverage[a] (%) before structural reform	Coverage[a] (%) 2004	Coverage[b] (%) 2000–03 surveys
Argentina	50	24.3	34.6
Bolivia	12	10.5	9.9
Chile	64	57.3	58.2
Colombia	32	22.2	n.a.
Costa Rica	48	46.6	50.1
Dominican Republic	30	14.2	n.a.
El Salvador	26	20.1	29.7
Mexico	37	28.0	38.5
Peru	28	14.8	18.9
Uruguay	73	58.8	55.3
Average[c]	38	26.3	35.8
Public systems[d]	Non-applicable	Coverage[a] (%) 2004	
Brazil		45.2	45.1
Ecuador		19.4	21.9
Guatemala		20.2	19.6
Honduras		18.9	n.a.
Nicaragua		16.4	18.7
Panama		53.4	n.a.
Paraguay		8.5	13.9
Venezuela		20.5	35.1
Average[c]		39.0	41.0

Notes: [a] In private systems: percentage of the labour force covered by the public system before the structural reform and jointly by private and public systems in 2004; in public systems: percentage of the labour force covered in 2004 (except Brazil in 2003, Honduras 2001 and Paraguay in 2000); excludes insured persons with separate programmes: the armed forces in all countries, civil servants in some countries and other small groups. [b] Contributors in all systems, programmes and schemes as percentage of the labour force, based on household surveys. [c] Weighted: columns 2 and 3 based on total number of contributors and the total labour force (2004 for all private systems and 2000 to 2004 for public systems); last column weighted by labour force in 2000. Cuba and Haiti are excluded because they do not publish statistics on coverage.
Source: Mesa-Lago (2008).

reform in operation, show that coverage declined between 1973 and 1975 (before the reform) and 2000 (Arenas de Mesa and Mesa-Lago 2006). Estimates of coverage based on household surveys (last column of Table 9.3) have the advantage over the previous estimates that include the insured in separate schemes, albeit leaving out key countries, confirm that the weighted average of private systems (36 per cent) was smaller that the average of public systems (41 per cent). A rough estimate of the labour force covered by both public and private systems based on active contributors was 31 per cent circa 2004. All of these estimates are above the prescribed International Labour Organization (ILO) minimum coverage of 20 per cent of the labour force.

Regardless of whether the system is private or public, the older it is and the larger the formal labour sector, the higher its coverage, and vice versa. Hence countries in the pioneer-high group have the highest coverage and those in the latecomer-low group the lowest coverage, with few exceptions (Table 9.3, second column). Coverage based on active contributors in 2004 ranged from 45 per cent to 59 per cent: the highest in Uruguay, Chile and Panama, followed by Costa Rica and Brazil (Cuba does not publish statistics but gross estimates suggest that it belongs to this group), but only 24 per cent in Argentina. All of these countries are in the pioneer-high group, with the exception of Panama (intermediate group), which has noticeably improved its coverage and regional ranking in the past two decades; on the other hand, coverage in Argentina fell below the regional average as a result of the crisis. Coverage in the intermediate group ranged between 11 per cent and 28 per cent: the highest in Mexico, followed by Colombia, Venezuela, Ecuador, Peru and Bolivia; in the last two countries coverage fell sharply to 15 per cent and 10 per cent, respectively, the lowest rates with one exception. Finally, coverage in the latecomer-low group oscillated between 8 per cent and 20 per cent: the highest in Guatemala and El Salvador, followed by Honduras and Nicaragua (the last four superior to those of Bolivia and Peru), the Dominican Republic and Paraguay lagging behind (Haiti probably had the lowest coverage in the region). Public systems have kept their ranking in the region and some have improved it.

Health programme

Table 9.4 exhibits estimates of the percentage of the total population covered by the principal social insurance health programme in 17 countries (in 12 with two-year observations), excluding separate social insurance schemes existing in many countries for civil servants, the armed forces, oil workers, teachers and other groups. Estimates are based mainly on statistics provided by institutions and on household surveys from a few countries, but their accuracy is reduced because of the following problems: there are no historical series of statistical coverage in the region and only gross estimates are available in some countries; with few exceptions it is impossible to estimate coverage by separate schemes; there is an overestimation due to double coverage by social insurance in four countries; figures are from five to eleven years old in eight countries and are available for 2003–04 in only six countries; there are significant contradictions among divergent estimates in some countries, and surveys commonly lack standardized criteria to categorize the population protected by the three sectors, including social insurance (for details and analysis, see Mesa-Lago 2008).

In addition to the above stated reasons, the comparison of coverage before and after the reforms is difficult because only a one-year observation is available in the case of five of the countries surveyed; the first observation does not always correspond to the year prior to the reform or the latter has not been important; and due to changes in affiliation among health sectors before and after the reform (Colombia); or considerable multiplicity of social insurances prior to the reform (Chile). Rough estimates of the total population covered by social insurance in the region (weighted by the population of each country) indicate that it increased from 43 per cent in 1980 to 52 per cent in 1990 (before all of the reforms except Chile's) and decreased to 41 per cent in 2000–04 (Mesa-Lago 2008: table 4). These figures

Table 9.4 Social insurance health coverage of the total population and the labour force in Latin America, 1984–2004 (in percentages)

Countries[a]	Total population		Labour force	
	Years	Coverage	Years	Coverage
Argentina	1991	57.6	1997	63.9
	2001	54.4	2001	56.2
Bolivia	1997	25.8	1997	17.4
			2002	15.2
Chile	1984	83.4	1996	86.2
	2003	72.1	2000	87.3
Colombia	1993	23.7	n.a.	n.a.
	2002	53.3		
Costa Rica	1994	86.2	n.a.	n.a.
	2003	86.8		
Dominican Republic	2000	7.0	n.a.	n.a.
Ecuador	1994	18.0	1994	23.1
	2004	16.5	1998	33.2
El Salvador	2001	15.8	n.a.	n.a.
Guatemala	1995	16.6	2000	26.0
	2000	16.6		
Honduras	2000	11.7	n.a.	n.a.
Mexico	1985	41.8	n.a.	n.a.
	2002	45.3		
Nicaragua	1990	18.3	1998	14.8
	2001	7.9	2001	16.6
Panama	1996	61.1	n.a.	n.a.
	2004	64.6		
Paraguay	1999	12.4	n.a.	n.a.
	2001	12.4		
Peru	2002	26.0	1994	28.4
			2000	24.2
Uruguay	1987	15.8[c]	n.a.	n.a.
	2000	15.9[c]		
Venezuela	2000	38.4	n.a.	n.a.
	2004	38.3		
Regional average[b]	2000–04	41.0	n.a.	n.a.

Notes: [a] Brazil and Cuba do not have social insurance but a public health sector; Haiti rough estimates are 0.5 per cent in 1999. [b] Weighted by countries population (author's estimate). [c] Includes social insurance for maternity and collective sickness insurance in mutual-aid societies (IAMC), individual affiliation in IAMC is reported as private.
Sources: Mesa-Lago (2008); for the reliability of data in each country, see Mesa-Lago (2006).

exclude Brazil, which accounts for almost half of the total population protected in the region, which had social insurance until 1993 when it was integrated into its public sector.[8] All of these averages are below the ILO minimum coverage of 75 per cent of the resident population, but an undetermined part of it is protected by the public sector and, to a lesser extent, by the private sector and separate schemes. Social insurance coverage between two observation years in 12 countries mostly stagnated or declined: it was unchanged in five countries (Costa Rica, Guatemala, Paraguay, Uruguay and Venezuela), fell in four (Argentina, Chile, Ecuador and Nicaragua) and increased in only three (Colombia, Mexico and Panama).

The countries with the highest coverage in 2000–04 (53 per cent to 87 per cent) were three in the pioneer-high group (Argentina, Chile and Costa Rica – virtually universal), as well as Colombia and Panama in the intermediate group. Social insurance coverage in Uruguay was only 16 per cent because it is limited to the maternity branch and part of the sickness branch through mutual-aid societies (Instituciones de Asistencia Médica Colectiva/IAMC), and the rest is by IAMC and various types of private insurance. Coverage in the intermediate group ranged between 17 per cent and 45 per cent: Ecuador, Bolivia, Peru, Venezuela and Mexico. In the latecomer-low group coverage ranged from 0.5 per cent in Haiti to 17 per cent in Guatemala (Table 9.4).

According to household surveys, health care coverage of the labour force in 2000–02 was 56 per cent in Argentina and 87 per cent in Uruguay (pioneer-high group); 15 per cent to 33 per cent in Bolivia, Ecuador and Peru (intermediate group), 16 per cent in Nicaragua and 26 per cent in Guatemala (latecomer-low group). Changes in coverage between two points in time in six countries are inconclusive concerning the reform impact on coverage: decrease in three (Argentina, Bolivia and Peru) and increase in three (Chile, Ecuador and Nicaragua) (ILO 2003).[9]

Factors that influence coverage

The low levels of social insurance coverage in all of the countries in the latecomer-low group and the least advanced in the intermediate group is the result of external factors to the system but also to the system itself. External factors, in addition to the explained labour-market transformations are: underdevelopment, elevated poverty incidence, high unemployment and underemployment, political instability or crisis, lack of government commitment, cultural and ethnic barriers, gender inequality, large rural population, poorly developed regions, scarce fiscal resources and poor taxing capacity.

Concerning the system, social insurance pension programmes (particularly, but not exclusively in private systems) were originally designed for workers employed in the urban formal sector with stable jobs, medium-high salary, mostly males and with high density of contribution, but most of the labour force in the region is informal and/or agricultural, with unstable employment, low wages and poor density of contribution (especially among women), hence it is very difficult to extend coverage.

The health care system, rather than being neutral, can in fact determine the degree of exclusion. For instance, a segmented or highly segmented system without coordination, weak regulation and poor solidarity is typical of all countries with low coverage. In the latecomer-low group social insurance was introduced late, in some of them coverage has not yet been expanded to all geographical areas (health facilities and personnel are concentrated in the capital city and urban areas), and several of them have large rural and indigenous populations that are difficult to incorporate. Social insurance legally excludes the informal sector and the agricultural labour force and in some countries also restricts the coverage of dependent female spouses and children above a certain age. Furthermore, these countries endure a regressive distribution of health funds, allocating more to social insurance and private sectors than to the public sector that is legally in charge of the protection of the majority of the population, and the poor and low-income are burdened with out-of-pocket expenses. Several external factors, which are often combined, have also obstructed coverage expansion: economic crisis and persistent negative or low growth, high poverty incidence, a majority of the labour force informal and sizeable self-employment, high unemployment and underemployment, a large and dispersed rural population with a significant proportion of self-employed small farmers and peasants, political instability (civil war in three countries), and a considerable indigenous population.

In countries with high levels of coverage, both the system itself (integrated or well coordinated, for instance, in Costa Rica, Chile and Panama) played a key role in coverage and also specific policies. Examples of these policies include a strong public or social insurance sector that provides free coverage to the poor and either free or subsidized coverage to low-income groups, including the rural labour force as well as the self-employed in most countries; fiscal transfers targeted towards the poor; and continuous political and financial commitments to expand and preserve coverage. Most of these countries also benefited from external factors such as economic growth and stability, a low incidence of poverty, a relatively small informal sector and self-employment, a high rate of urbanization, low unemployment, political stability and the absence of physical and ethnic-cultural barriers to coverage.

The factors that impeded Colombia from meeting the 2001 target of 100 per cent health coverage were: the lack of political consensus; the economic recession and high unemployment partly caused by the civil war; the postponement of the start of the subsidized regime for the poor and low-income and delays to and cuts in the funding designated for it; an inadequate information system to identify the poor population eligible to receive subsidies; resources initially assigned to the poor being shifted to the salaries of medical personnel; and an increasingly exclusive contributory regime due to restrictions and that was afflicted by growing evasion, payment delays and the underdeclaration of wages (Mesa-Lago 2008).

Inequalities in coverage by income, gender, geography and ethnic groups

Coverage of the labour force by the contributory pension programmes increases with income, as is shown by data from 14 countries (with very few exceptions) distributed by income quintiles in 2000–03: from 0.1 per cent to 11 per cent covered in the poorest quintile; 1 per cent to 48 per cent in the second quintile; 6 per cent to 70 per cent in the third quintile; 12 per cent to 80 per cent in the fourth quintile; and 31 per cent to 90 per cent in the richest quintile. Countries with the lowest coverage in the poorest quintile included those with the highest poverty incidence and with a large indigenous population in most of them; all countries in the latecomer-low group; Bolivia, Ecuador and Peru in the intermediate group;

and Argentina in the pioneer-high group as a result of the crisis. Conversely, countries in the pioneer-high group, which also have the lowest poverty incidence, exhibited the highest coverage in the lowest quintile Brazil, Chile, Costa Rica and Uruguay (based on Rofman 2005). Statistics from 13 countries on the population covered by social insurance health programmes by income quintiles in 1996–2003 equally demonstrate that coverage increases with income and vice versa: the ratio of coverage between the wealthiest and the poorest quintile ranged from two to 54 times. In four countries this trend was accentuated in private insurance coverage; in Chile's private sector, coverage declined as age rose while public sector coverage increased. The comparison of the impact of the reform on coverage is feasible in only two countries: Bolivia's coverage fell in all quintiles in 1996–2000, and Colombia's increased significantly in all quintiles in 1993–97, but decreased across the board by 2000, although still at a higher level than in 1993 (Mesa-Lago 2008).

Separate social insurance schemes for powerful groups (civil servants, the armed forces, teachers, oil workers, and so on) cover upper-middle and high-income insured, have larger coverage (usually universal) of their members and better entitlement conditions than the rest of the insured population, and receive costly fiscal subsidies that absorb scarce public funds and hence have regressive effects on distribution. The reforms left these groups virtually untouched.

Data from 12 countries on geographical differences in health coverage show that inequality is lowest in the pioneer-high group and highest in the latecomer-low group. The ratio between the best- and worst-covered areas were virtually nil or very small in Costa Rica and Uruguay; 1.4 in Argentina and Chile, 2 in Colombia, 3 in Mexico and 4 in Ecuador (both with peasant insurance), 5 in Panama and Paraguay, 155 in Guatemala, 350 in Honduras and 400 in Nicaragua (PAHO 2005). The best-covered geographical areas are the most developed, urban and wealthy, while the worst covered or not covered at all are the least developed, rural and poor. The segmentation and lack of coordination of the health care system in more than half of the countries, which was not corrected by the reforms, intensifies geographical inequalities because of divergent coverage through public, social insurance and private providers. These last two (particularly private) are greatly concentrated in capital cities and other highly urbanized areas, whereas rural and poor areas are mostly protected by public services.

Gender inequities are the outcome of labour market factors and also those factors internal to the social insurance system. Among the former, women compared with men suffer from the following discriminations: more than 50 per cent do not participate in the salaried labour force; have a higher unemployment rate; are concentrated in low-paid jobs and overrepresented in occupations not covered by social insurance such as informal work; receive a lower salary for equal work; and suffer a higher poverty incidence when they are heads of households (Bertranou and Arenas de Mesa 2003). But the system also discriminates, for instance, against the spouse (usually female) and children who are economically dependent upon the insured are compulsorily covered (pre-dating the reforms) by the health programme in all countries but with important restrictions in the latecomer-low group.

The female spouse is covered in maternity, but not in the event of sickness (in El Salvador, Guatemala, Honduras and the Dominican Republic, while the opposite occurs in Ecuador), and these five countries and Nicaragua exclude children above ages ranging from one to 12. The reforms have not changed that situation, except for two individual policies which recently increased slightly the coverage ages for children.

Household surveys taken in 14 countries in 2000–03 show that, in eight of them, social insurance coverage of women in the labour force was lower than coverage of man. It was about equal in four countries and higher in only two. Costa Rican coverage of women was 84 per cent versus 77 per cent for men, which results from indirect insurance as a spouse dependent on the insured, and hence women had only 24 per cent of direct insurance versus 52 per cent for men. Uruguayan coverage of women was 96 per cent as compared with 94.5 per cent for men (Rofman 2005). In the Dominican Republic's private system only 42 per cent of affiliates were women, compared with 58 per cent of men in 2003, but the proportions in the closed social insurance system were 54 per cent and 46 per cent, respectively (Lizardo 2004). The pension coverage of women aged 65 and above was considerably lower than among men of the same age in 17 countries in 2000–05, except in Uruguay, where the opposite was true. The gender gap in coverage was threefold in the Dominican Republic and twofold in El Salvador and Peru, but was smaller in countries of the pioneer-high group, as well as in Panama (Table 9.5).

Additional gender inequalities related to the health system are numerous. Direct access to social insurance is affected by permanent exit from the labour force to raise children that results in a loss of coverage in sickness-maternity insurance; coverage of the dependent spouse of an insured male worker is often indirect and in some countries only partial (for instance, only on maternity but not in sickness); coverage is usually lost by abandonment, divorce or death of the insured; private providers often exclude women of a fertile age because of the higher costs of their care (during pregnancy and some peculiar pathologies) or alternatively charge higher fees to compensate for such costs; and user fees in the public sector particularly affect poor women because they use such services for themselves and their children more often than men.

According to data from 12 countries on coverage mainly by systems of social insurance, the extreme ratios between the best- and worst-covered geographical areas were: virtually nil or very small in Costa Rica, Cuba and Uruguay; 1.4 in Argentina and Chile, 2 in Colombia, 5 in Panama, 38 in Paraguay, 107 in Ecuador, 350 in Honduras and 400 in Nicaragua (inequality is lowest in the pioneer-high group and highest in the latecomer-low group). The best-covered geographical areas are the most developed, urban and wealthy, whereas the worst-covered, or those not covered at all, are the least developed, rural and poor (the segmentation without adequate coordination of the health care system in more than half of the countries contributes to that situation). Comparative data on the impact of the reforms on such differences were available only in the case of Colombia: the extreme ratio between the best- and worst-covered department decreased from 2.8 to two times in 1993–2003, while the ratio of urban–rural inequality declined from

Table 9.5   Social insurance pension coverage of the population age 65 and above in private and public systems, 2000–05 (in percentages)

Systems/countries	Total	Men	Women
Private systems			
Argentina	68.3	74.3	64.2
Bolivia	14.7	16.1	12.7
Chile	63.8[a]	72.6	57.2
Colombia	18.6	22.9	13.1
Costa Rica	62.0[b]	71.1[b]	54.2[b]
Dominican Republic	10.9	15.5	5.9
El Salvador	14.5	18.0	9.6
Mexico	19.2	17.8	18.0
Peru	23.2	27.7	14.6
Uruguay	87.1	76.9	78.9
Public systems			
Brazil	85.9	80.0	76.4
Ecuador	15.2	17.3	10.8
Guatemala	11.3	17.0	4.6
Nicaragua	4.7	n.a.	n.a.
Panama	45.0	52.0	48.2
Paraguay	19.6	18.9	14.5
Venezuela	23.9	26.7	18.0

Notes: [a] Coverage in Chile increases to 76 per cent adding non-contributory pensions. [b] Based on the household survey of 2005, Rofman gives 36.6 per cent, 48 per cent and 36.6 per cent, probably excluding non-contributory pensions.
Sources: Based on household surveys; data compiled by Rofman (2005), except Costa Rica from Mesa-Lago (2008); no data available for Cuba, Haiti and Honduras.

4.4 to 1.3 times. Nevertheless, there was an increment in the inequalities between urban and rural capitals, and the basic package in the subsidized regime that covers poor and low-income people was half of the package in the contributory regime.

In those countries that have a considerable indigenous population, they tend to be concentrated in the poorest, most rural and worst-covered areas, but there are no figures on specific coverage by ethnic group. Access by the indigenous population is worse than the rest of the population in four countries: is half the access to social insurance of the non-indigenous population, and between 30 and 90 per cent of indigenous persons use traditional medicine or self-medication. The reforms have not changed this situation.

Coverage of the poor by social assistance pensions

Poverty incidence in the region averages 42 per cent and ranges from 15 to 30 per cent in the pioneer-high group (except 39 per cent in Brazil), and from 32 to 77 per cent in the rest, the highest being in the latecomer-low group and Bolivia (Table 9.1). Countries with the lowest coverage of contributory pensions in the poorest quintile are those with the highest poverty, and vice versa. Before the reforms, social assistance pensions for the uninsured poor were established in four of the ten private systems (Argentina, Chile, Costa Rica and Uruguay), as well as in two of the ten public systems (Brazil and Cuba); all of them are supplementary means-tested schemes in the pioneer-high-group countries with the highest regional coverage in their contributory programmes and the lowest poverty incidence. Bolivia's scheme (*Bonosol*), the only one created by a structural reform, is not targeted at the poor but is granted regardless of income. Eighty-four per cent of beneficiaries are urban residents and 80 per cent also receive a contributory pension, whereas 75 per cent of the elderly do not get a pension.

The number of social assistance pensioners as a percentage of the total population in 2000–05 was: 1 per cent in Argentina, 2 per cent in Costa Rica, Cuba and Uruguay, 4 per cent in Chile, and 5 per cent in Bolivia and Brazil (including the rural programme and other aid schemes). Such coverage represents only a fraction of these countries' poverty incidence, which ranged from 15 to 39 per cent of the total population in five of those countries (62 per cent in Bolivia).[10] Furthermore these programmes are subjected to financial constraints and most have quotas and waiting lists. Despite their limitations, however, social assistance pensions have significantly reduced poverty by 19–31 per cent and extreme poverty by 21–96 per cent in five countries (Bertranou et al. 2002).

Thirteen countries have no social assistance pensions, and they endure the lowest coverage in the contributory programme and the highest poverty incidence. Structural reforms have emphasized the private mandatory savings pillar for pension systems but paid little or no attention to the poverty prevention pillar in countries that already had it in place, and even less so in countries lacking such a pillar. These priorities have now been reversed by World Bank officials (Gill et al. 2005). Reform laws in four countries (Colombia, the Dominican Republic, Ecuador and Venezuela) stipulate the creation of social assistance pensions for the poor, but they had not been implemented by the end of 2006. In 2006, a Chilean law extended coverage to all the indigents and a legal draft created a universal basic pension to that section of the population in the lowest 60 per cent of income. The structural reforms in El Salvador, Mexico and Peru (as well as the failed reform in Nicaragua) did not include a social assistance pension, and four poor countries with public systems are in the same situation. Often high costs are the alleged cause of the lack of social assistance but in reality fiscal transfers to this programme are a fraction of transfers to social insurance. Social insurance transfers are regressive because they are received mainly by employees in the formal sector and financed by general taxation, while the poor work mostly in the uninsured informal and rural sectors. Estimates of costs of supplementary means-tested schemes indicate that they are financially viable and would reduce poverty by about 18 percentage points (ECLAC 2006).

Coverage of the elderly by pensions and health care

In 2000–03 coverage of the population aged 65 and above ranged from 62 to 87 per cent in Argentina, Brazil, Chile, Costa Rica and Uruguay (all in the pioneer-high group); declined to 15–24 per cent in the intermediate group (Bolivia, Colombia, Ecuador, Mexico, Peru and Venezuela), except for Panama with 45 per cent; and was lowest (5–14 per cent) in four countries of the latecomer-low group (Table 9.5). The impact of structural reforms on coverage of the elderly is difficult to measure due to lack of historical series, but partial data from three countries indicate a decline: Chile's coverage increased slightly in 1992–2000 because of the expansion of social assistance pensions that compensated for the decline in coverage by contributory pensions, and by 2003 overall coverage had deteriorated below the 1992 level; Argentina's coverage fell at an annual average of almost one percentage point in 1994–99 and it is projected to continue declining by one percentage point over the period 2000–30; and Uruguay's coverage decreased in the period 1995–2002 (Mesa-Lago 2008). Such evidence is contrary to the World Bank's prediction that poverty among old people will decrease over time in the region (Gill et al. 2005). Actually the noted decline in coverage of the labour force in most countries is resulting in a decreasing protection of the elderly cohort of the population that is rapidly growing in the region.

Social insurance pensioners in all countries (except Haiti) are entitled to health coverage, but in Nicaragua they receive a mini package of benefits, considerably lower than the active insured.

Policies to extend social insurance coverage

Guidelines to expand overall coverage: International and regional organizations

In recent reports several international and regional organizations reach conclusions similar to those in this essay: social insurance coverage has stagnated or declined due to a shrinking formal sector and a growing informal sector, and it has failed to adapt to such changes in order to incorporate the self-employed and other excluded groups like informal and rural workers. Such organizations propose general approaches to extend coverage, some diverse but others reaching common ground.

The International Social Security Association (ISSA 2006) considers social insurance coverage to be stagnant or declining, particularly in developing countries because the formal sector has shrunk, while the informal sector, subsistence agriculture and migratory labour have expanded. Lacking or earning uncertain/irregular income, these groups cannot contribute to social security, hence the current contributory model is inadequate and many systems have not been designed to extend coverage to the excluded workers.[11] ISSA presents the following guidelines to cope with the above problems: (i) universal and inclusive coverage should be a priority for all nations; (ii) governments must guarantee the right of protection to the population, enact adequate legislation that includes a regulatory framework in order for the private system to function correctly, make political and financial commitments with continuity through future administrations, and properly inform the people of their social security rights and corresponding financial costs; and (iii) social security institutions take the lead in extending coverage, adapting to existing labour market conditions through two levels of coverage – the current contributory for formal salaried workers, and another of subsistence level for the rest of the labour force (directly or in cooperation with the state), with the ultimate goal being that the latter is gradually incorporated into the former.

The ILO recommends three complementary forms: social insurance and assistance as the conventional tools; the promotion of independent decentralized programmes based on local or community initiatives, self-financed and self-managed (especially microinsurance); and the design of mechanisms to connect all forms of social protection. In middle-income developing countries (the pioneer-high group and the most advanced in the intermediate group in Latin America), the state and social insurance play a central role, although the insurance must be adapted to incorporate groups of workers such as the self-employed and to provide grant subsidies to protect low-income groups that are uninsured. In low-income countries (the latecomer-low group and the least advanced in the intermediate group), where the capacity of the state and social insurance to extend coverage is limited, insurance must be restructured to improve the protection of the insured, but decentralized mechanisms have the greatest potential.[12]

In the area of pensions, the Economic Commission for Latin America and the Caribbean (ECLAC 2006) recommends that governments: (i) emphasize the inception and consolidation of non-contributory schemes capable of providing general access to basic pensions targeted on the elderly poor, a less costly approach than universal flat pensions but one which requires adequate targeting based on need instead of contributory history; (ii) fortify solidarity models geared towards low-income contributors; (iii) provide incentives to join contributory schemes to that part of the labour force with some contributory capacity but that is not affiliated;[13] and (iv) guarantee an adequate integration between the contributory and non-contributory schemes to avoid disincentives to join the former, permitting compatibility between both types of pensions (those who receive an insufficient contributory pension and are in need could supplement it with a targeted basic pension). ECLAC suggestions on health care include: (i) expansion of systems to insure mandatory universal coverage, independent of labour insertion, contributory capacity and risk level, to avoid that the need to disburse out-of-pocket expenses becomes an obstacle to access; (ii) specification of insurance coverage by defining packages of explicit guarantees that constitute a universal right for the entire population; (iii) fortification of the public sector, the expansion of primary care, the adequate coordination of services, and the integration of financing sources to guarantee equity and solidarity in the system and compensate gaps among regions.

In the area of pensions, the World Bank (1994) supported 'social-risk management', an essentially economic approach centred on the individual, household or group combining various means of protection – social insurance, private insurance and the market, and the state – in a subsidiary manner to provide or subsidize protection when the other two means fail. This is accomplished through targeting the most vulnerable households so that they are capable of confronting risks in an efficient way (poverty reduction), as well as creating and promoting a friendly environment that is conducive to the development of private protection mechanisms. Bank officials have recently changed the previous emphasis giving priority to the public pillar of poverty prevention but asserting that 'The only sustainable way for countries in Latin America to increase coverage is to focus on policies that increase economic growth rather than social security coverage' (Gill et al. 2005: 274). The World Bank's (1993) first worldwide report on health care endorsed a combination of diverse means to facilitate universal coverage similarly to that of pensions. A new Bank report, specific to health care in the region, warns that while the current focus on covering the formal salaried sector through risk-pooling mechanisms (social insurance) persists, it would be very difficult to ensure effective coverage beyond a comparatively well-off minority. To change that situation, the report proposes several policies, some ratifying previous ones but others new: (i) give priority to the extension of risk-pooling to the large and growing informal sector, inventing contributory means for households whose contributory capacity is above the average cost of basic benefits, so that they participate in risk-pooling mechanisms not linked to the work place or labour status; (ii) disconnect risk-pooling financing from labour status replacing salary contributions by general tax revenue; (iii) expand the participation of the private sector in the delivery of publicly financed health services as well as in contributory risk-pooling under an effective regulatory framework; (iv) define universal explicit rights to a specific benefit package; and (v) better target fiscal subsidies to public health goods (such as vaccinations) granted to the poor, the aged and other disadvantaged groups (Baeza and Packard 2005).

The Pan American Health Organization (PAHO 2002) advises health care authorities to guarantee universal basic protection to all the population, regardless of economic means, in order to reduce inequalities in access to needed services with adequate quality. For this purpose, effective coverage should be provided to excluded groups, especially those in the informal sector and the marginalized population, through five strategies practised in the region (sometimes combined), pinpointing their advantages and limitations: (i) non-contributory social assistance for the poor and low-income groups, which could be successful in the short run but lacks financial sustainability in the long run because often being financed with temporary external funds, not being properly integrated into the general health system and offering unequal care; (ii) voluntary insurance with fiscal subsidies for some population groups, which function if the government continues its support, but that could provide an inferior level of care compared to the general system;[14] (iii) community programmes administered by users in areas afflicted by significant exclusion and where conventional social insurance has been unsuccessful, whose advantages are the capacity to adapt to local needs and to be self-managed, but which require diverse and sustainable sources of financing and managerial capacity and proper coordination with public services; (iv) a public or social insurance system open to the entire population, usually combined with a supplementary private programme, with diverse financial sources, its principal limitation being the lack of guaranteed access to higher levels of care;[15] and (v) in all cases a shift in emphasis towards health promotion and primary care, guaranteeing referrals and continuity among levels and sectors of care.

The Inter-American Development Bank (IDB 2004) sets as priorities the inclusion of the poor, the lowest-income groups and others excluded such as indigenous peoples and communities neither ethnically nor culturally integrated and discriminated by gender, as well as the reduction of inequities in coverage and quality between low and high-income groups. To achieve such objectives it is essential to improve coverage in public health programmes. The IDB (2006) also argues that, with appropriate regulations, market solutions can be used to address health needs, including those of the poor. Public funding of private provision and private funding of private provision have the most potential for expanding coverage, if some essential conditions are met, such as ensuring flexibility in managing resources to make them free from traditional bureaucratic constrains.

Most organizations have reached a consensus on several crucial points: (i) give priority to the extension of coverage to excluded groups; (ii) combine in a coordinated fashion diverse forms of protection (public, social insurance and private, contributory and non-contributory); (iii) adapt the contributory programme to incorporate informal workers and provide fiscal and other incentives for their affiliation (avoiding disincentives for affiliation in the contributory); (iv) emphasize the non-contributory scheme with fiscal subsidies and efficiently targeted at the poor and low-income population; (v) introduce a universal package of explicit health benefits guaranteed to all the population regardless of the providing sector, labour status, income or risk; and (vi) give priority to the extension of prevention and primary care. There is no consensus, however, on the role that each sector should play. For instance, for the World Bank, the state should be subsidiary and promote a friendly environment for the expansion of private provision (the latter also endorsed by IDB), whereas the ILO and ISSA give a central role to the government and social insurance. Yet all organizations agree that the state should establish a proper regulatory role for all of the pension and health systems, including the private sector. It would be ideal if all these international and regional organizations cooperated in identified common policies to extend coverage, and discussed divergent approaches with the ultimate target of designing and financing joint programmes, eliminating duplications and financing research on unresolved problems and issues.[16]

Regardless of their model all pension systems and reforms should have as a first priority the prevention of old-age poverty; a second priority should be the universal coverage of all salaried workers, including domestic servants; and a third more complex target, depending upon a country's degree of development, should be the extension of coverage to those groups that are difficult to incorporate. In order to achieve the goal of universalization, a well-conceived plan ought to be drafted in each country by social insurance, or the government, or both, with an open public debate, participation of relevant social actors, support from a feasibility study and a timetable for the gradual implementation of the extension. Such a plan should be flexible in the means of incorporation (see below), as well as its contributions and benefits, adjusting them to the contributory capacity and needs of these workers and providing incentives for affiliation.

The segmentation of the health system in more than half of the countries contributes to low coverage and overlapping efforts, wasting scarce resources that should be employed in extending coverage, hence the integration, or at least high coordination, of those systems is essential. The separate schemes for powerful groups should be integrated into the general social insurance programme or become entirely financed by the insured, eliminating all fiscal subsidies that must be used for the extension of coverage. Furthermore, fiscal subsidies granted to some social insurance general programmes in the region that have a very low and stagnant coverage (basically concentrated in a middle-income minority) should also be shifted to expand the coverage of low-income workers, matching their contributions as an incentive for affiliation.

To cope with the crucial void in accurate data on coverage, all international and regional organizations involved in social security should join efforts in a coordinated manner in order to develop unified, standardized and reliable statistical series on population and labour force coverage, with pertinent information on direct insured and dependent relatives.[17] For that purpose, various mechanisms should be established: a modern integrated information system; a unified registry with data on all insured and their features, periodically revised and updated; and a single identity card for all insured containing basic information. Half of the countries in the region generate standardized statistics on coverage regarding private pensions, published biannually by a regional association (Asociación Internacional de Organismos de Supervisión de Fondos de Pensiones/AIOS), but such data are not available for public pensions and the private health care sector. Collecting such data should be mandatory for the information system in order to develop better control and supervision. Household surveys in the region should include standardized questions to identify the uninsured and their economic, social and health characteristics. This information is essential for designing policies of extension, estimating their costs and setting priorities (Chile has pioneered periodical social protection surveys with such information).

Coverage of difficult groups

With some notable exceptions, social security in the region has not adapted to the transformation of the labour market over the past quarter-century. Nevertheless, such adaptation is necessary since failing to do so will continue to affect coverage adversely. Pension and health systems, regardless of their model, should confront the obstacles to incorporating difficult groups such as the self-employed, domestic servants, employees of microenterprises and other informal workers, as well as rural-agricultural workers and indigenous peoples. In this sense, the pursuit of flexibility is essential. Examples of ways to do so include: weekly or quarterly payments (instead of only monthly) directly or through banks, postal offices, by electronic means, and so on; offering the option to join the social insurance branch of preference (pensions, health care) instead of forcing affiliation in all branches at once; voluntary insurance with alternative plans adjusted to the payment ability of the workers and their families; obliging enterprises that hire self-employed professionals to retain their contributions and add the employer's contribution, sanctioning transgressors (as done in Brazil); offering incentives to promote labour formalization; providing mechanisms for certifying self-employed income; simplifying tax declarations from small enterprises; offering tax deductions for contributions; granting to pension affiliates benefits not currently enjoyed, such as occupational-risk coverage and family allowances (the last two measures are included in Chile's law of 2008); ensuring the portability of contributions paid by these workers when performing salaried work; using the accumulated pension fund as collateral for loans to establish or expand a business, build a house, educate their children and so forth, but without compromising the minimum pension.

Mandatory coverage of the self-employed should also be considered, as it already exists in four countries in the area of pensions, and in two countries in the area of health, and is stipulated in the laws or legal drafts in other countries that should be enforced. Legal compulsory coverage might help but would not solve the problem by itself, hence the need to consider a state subsidy (as in Costa Rica and the still non-enforced laws of the Dominican Republic and Venezuela), or a solidarity contribution geared to low-income workers, especially those who have no employer, in order to stimulate their affiliation and reduce the proportion of the population that lacks insurance and is forced to pay out of pocket for private services. Colombia charged such solidarity contributions to relatively high-income insured persons in the contributory programme geared to increase coverage of the self-employed and other vulnerable groups. Although laudable and with progressive distribution effects, it has not fully achieved its purposes and should be fortified.

Domestic servants have low coverage despite the fact that their coverage is legally mandatory in around a dozen countries. This is essentially because inspection and enforcement are difficult and the additional risk of dismissal of the worker who denounces the employer for non-compliance. Such a situation demands a wide campaign of dissemination of information about the rights of domestic servants, combined with strict job security for those who report the evasion and fiscal incentives for affiliation to the low-income majority.

The special programmes to cover rural workers and peasants in Brazil, Ecuador and Mexico should be fortified and expanded. A comparative evaluation of the results of these three programmes, weighing their successes and weaknesses, is much needed in order to assess their potential replication elsewhere. Brazil's programme should develop a registry of active rural workers who are potential beneficiaries and include their income levels, purge the list of current beneficiaries to eliminate free riders, and detect those who are truly low-income workers (about half of the total) and do not receive a pension, even though they may qualify for one. Ecuador and Mexico ought to reverse the decrease in coverage of recent years. Ecuador has identified the potential population eligible and should expand coverage gradually, while Mexico has more abundant resources to accomplish that task. Countries in which the above recommendations are not feasible should stimulate and support the microinsurance of informal workers and peasants, granting the proper incentives and gradually coordinating or integrating them into social insurance, with actuarially adjusted packages of contributions and benefits. In the poorest countries, the only alternative would be to promote and support family help with some type of state incentive.

In the process of incorporating these groups, social insurance should promote and support associations, trade unions or cooperatives of self-employed, domestic servants, peasants, and so on, which could be placed in charge of the affiliation and collection of contributions from their members. If this approach is unsuccessful, then either social insurance or the government should create a public scheme with similar functions and adequate representation, financed through solidarity contributions and fiscal subsidies. Where social insurance is incapable of extending health coverage to the self-employed and similar groups, particularly in latecomer-low countries, the public sector should be fortified to protect them, as is already done in Brazil and Cuba. Previously suggested policies to extend coverage should be supported by financial and actuarial studies and the identification of new sources of financing to avoid the generation of a fiscal deficit. Nevertheless, some countries in the latecomer-low group have sufficient tax capacity to extend coverage, for instance, in El Salvador, the tax burden was 10 per cent in 2003, the lowest in Central America.

Reduction of inequalities in coverage by income, gender, geography and ethnic groups

Advisable policies to reduce inequality in health coverage by levels of income include: granting fiscal subsidies to the low-income groups (as in Chile), or to guarantee the basic package in the entire system regardless of age, gender or risk (as in Colombia and Argentina); make financing either proportional to income or progressive as income increases; eliminate fiscal subsidies awarded to non-poor (free riders); impede affiliates of private insurance firms from utilizing public or social insurance services (the proposed universal identity card should include a code with the owner's affiliation); and eradicate risk selection practised by insurers/providers through strict regulation to avoid discrimination and the extra financial burden imposed on the public sector.

In both private and public pension systems, policies to reduce gender inequality need to address both its external and its internal causes. Concerning external causes, policies include: promoting productive and stable employment for women; investing more in female training at the national and enterprise levels; rigorously enforcing the principle of equal salary for equal work; ensuring that paid maternity leave and unemployment insurance (in those countries where they exist) make contributions to pensions while beneficiaries are not working; and mandating nursery provision in large enterprises or establishing a public programme with low tariffs and fiscal subsidies. Regarding inequality derived from within the pension system, social insurance should incorporate those occupations in which women are concentrated (domestic service, self-employment, home work, and so on) and grant voluntary coverage to housewives. The latter is already done in a few countries, but should include paying a fiscal subsidy as an incentive to those on low incomes. Among important policies adopted or in process are: Brazil's coverage to low-income housewives; Costa Rica's new strategy to extend coverage to housewives who do not have their own pension coverage and are included in the husband's survivors insurance but who, if they divorce before the husband retires and he remarries, lose the right to the widow's pension; and Chile's law of reform in 2008 that includes an annual bonus to be granted to the mother (regardless of her socioeconomic status) for each child born alive, equivalent to 10 per cent of 18 minimum wages. Correction of gender inequalities in health demand other policies: extension to the spouse or companion of the insured the right to sickness care where only maternity care is provided, without discrimination with services provided to male insured (by the same token the male spouse or companion of an insured female should have the right to sickness care);[18] allocating at least equal health resources to women and men; making compulsory the basic health package throughout the entire health system, taking into account women's needs, and prohibiting risk selection based on gender by private insurers and providers.

Significant inequalities in coverage across geographical areas, particularly in countries of the latecomer-low group and at least two in the intermediate group, require a plan to reduce them through the use of proper targeting and financing. Only Brazil's public system has a compensation fund to reduce inequalities among regions, but even it is limited to highly complex and costly care, and a similar fund exists in Uruguay to reduce inequalities among income groups.[19] A national fund to mitigate inequalities in coverage among geographical areas targeted at the poorest should be established, financed from general taxes and, where feasible, by solidarity contributions paid for by the high-income insured and their employers. Several countries have gradually extended coverage of social insurance to all geographical areas (for instance, Mexico, although gaps subsist between the best and worst covered), but in others (for example, Guatemala, Honduras or Nicaragua), part of such areas or regions either lack coverage altogether, or it is very low and there are significant disparities in geographical coverage. In these cases it would be very difficult for social insurance to accomplish that task by itself and hence it is advisable to join forces with the public sector, as in Chile. The experience of Colombia, which was able to reduce such differences in just a few years, should be emulated, but this requires sustained effort and funds, combined with a campaign of information in the poorest areas.

The protection of the indigenous population demands targeting in the areas where they live: for pensions, through targeted social assistance and for health, through the expansion of the basic package and fiscal subsidies. In Chile, 80 per cent of the indigenous population is covered by public social insurance and half of the beneficiaries are extremely poor and pay no contributions. In Mexico 35 per cent of affiliates in the peasant programme are indigenous persons, and a significant proportion is also covered by Ecuador's peasant scheme. These cases represent three important models for the region. The incorporation of effective practices and practitioners from traditional medicine (herbal medicine, midwives), as well as personnel from indigenous communities, are positive policies with which to promote intercultural health, as carried out in Ecuador and Mexico, but they are no substitute in the long run for an adequate provision of health care, capable of eliminating current inequalities.

Pension coverage of the poor

The choice between a social assistance pension targeted towards the poor, and a means-tested or a flat universal pension, would depend largely on the level of development and social security of each country, but not even the most advanced can afford a universal flat pension. For instance, Argentina estimates that the universal flat pension would cost 2.7 per cent of gross domestic product (GDP) and the poor-targeted pension only between 0.4 per cent and 0.7 per cent of GDP. Furthermore, a universal flat pension would benefit the medium- and high-income strata with a longer life expectancy. The idea that these strata can be taxed to compensate for the received benefit will not work in the least developed countries that rely mostly on regressive consumer taxes and either lack a progressive income tax or have poor capacity to collect it.

The five countries of the pioneer-high group grant a means-tested targeted assistance pension, but despite significant progress, these countries still have to extend coverage to protect all the elderly, disabled and dependent relatives who are poor. Argentina should abolish pensions granted by Congress to non-poor persons. In Brazil, rural pensions cover an important segment of the poor and low-income population and they should be better coordinated with other social assistance benefits to avoid overlapping, save resources and extend protection to all the poor. Chile's law of 2008 provides a basic solidarity pension to 40 per cent of the households with the lowest income (to be expanded to 45 per cent in 2009); the beneficiary should be 65 years old; all quotas and waiting lists are eliminated Costa Rica's reform law of 2001 ordered that the social assistance targeted pension become universal, a mandate had not been implemented at the time of writing. Cuba increased the number of social assistance pensions in 2005, although a large majority of the poor still do not receive them. Better targeting of the poor and more effective means tests are needed to eliminate or reduce moral hazards in Costa Rica and other countries. A modest increase in the percentage of GDP assigned to these programmes (currently quite low) would fortify the current effect of poverty reduction in all these countries.

In the intermediate group, several countries lack social assistance pensions even though they have the resources to implement them: Colombia, Ecuador and Venezuela have reform laws which stipulate such pensions, but these have not been enforced; Mexico announced at the start of 2006 a new targeted assistance scheme for the elderly; Panama's ongoing reforms do not include such assistance pensions. Bolivia's *Bonosol* pension could be extended, or its amount increased, if targeted on the poor, rural and indigenous population, instead of being concentrated on the urban population regardless of income or even the reception of a contributory pension. In Ecuador, a targeted assistance pension equal to half the minimum wage would cost 1 per cent of GDP but only 0.25 per cent if granted at a lower level, and 0.16 per cent if implemented gradually, starting with the extreme poor. The 1 per cent cost is tantamount to current fiscal transfers to subsidize pensions of a minority currently insured, concentrated in the two highest income quintiles (World Bank 2005).

In the latecomer-low group the Dominican Republic reform law stipulating a social assistance pension for the poor should be implemented. Other countries in this group with high informality, low contributory coverage and high poverty incidence should consider a tax-financed public system of social assistance pensions targeted at the extreme poor. However, the cost of that system could compete for scarce resources needed for more urgent expenses, such as primary health care, nutrition, and so on. If resources are available for pensions, therefore, benefits should be small.

Social insurance is, to a significant extent, financed from taxation, resulting in competing claims from social assistance that require coordination and the setting of priorities. The separation in the administration of both programmes is advisable to avoid transfers from social insurance to assistance.

Coverage of the elderly

In view of the declining trend of protection of the elderly observed in three countries of the pioneer-high group and the low levels of coverage in most of the remaining countries, plus increasing numbers and proportions of the elderly population in the future, the policies suggested above are urgently needed to halt that decline and improve coverage of the elderly.

Lessons from Latin America for other developing countries

Social insurance systems have been in operation for more than 80 years in some Latin American pioneer countries, and rough estimates for 2004 indicate that 31 per cent of the labour force was covered in pensions and 41 per cent of the total population in health (the latter lower than in 1990). Coverage is higher in the pioneer-high group and inferior in the latecomer-low group, indicating that the age and development of the social insurance system influence coverage. Current low coverage and deteriorating trends are determined by three important factors: the transformation of the labour market, the lack of adaptation of social insurance to such change in most countries, and external variables.

The covered formal sector has shrunk, while the uncovered informal sector has expanded and averages 47 per cent of the urban labour force. About 30 per cent of the urban labour force is self-employed, has legal voluntary coverage or is excluded in 15–17 countries, and their statistical coverage stretches from 0.2 per cent to 15 per cent in health and to 30 per cent in pensions. A great barrier to the incorporation of the self-employed is the imposition of a contribution equal to the sum of the percentages paid by salaried workers and employers. Only Costa Rica, which had voluntary coverage until 2006, incorporated 45 per cent of the self-employed in pensions because the state pays the equivalent of the employer's contribution to the low-income self-employed. Domestic servants account for between 3 and 10 per cent of the urban labour force and have legal mandatory coverage in 12–13 countries, but their coverage ranges from 3 per cent to 39 per cent because many of them lack contracts, are unable to denounce evasion or conspire with the employer to evade the scheme. Employees in microenterprises oscillate from 7 per cent to 16 per cent of the urban labour force (probably underestimated because they are informal), and coverage in these enterprises is between one-third and one-thirtieth that of large enterprises. The rural percentage of the total labour force averages 56 per cent, exceeding it in most countries, particularly in the latecomer-low group, and is excluded from legal coverage in half of the countries. Statistical coverage is 1 to 6 per cent, but in Brazil, Ecuador and Mexico, which have special social insurance schemes for peasants, coverage increases to between 18 and 50 per cent of the rural population. In summary, the following conclusions stand out: the higher the proportional size of the group in the labour force, the more difficult to cover it; countries that have legal obligatory affiliation have higher coverage than those with voluntary affiliation; fiscal subsidies to the low-income self-employed and similar groups provide incentives for affiliation; special regimes for rural workers or peasants get better coverage than those with voluntary or restricted coverage, but with diverse results due to different levels of government commitment and financial support; a segmented health system without coordination among the three sectors, with weak regulation and low solidarity, is prevalent in half of the countries that have the lowest coverage, but conversely pioneer-high group countries have reached high coverage with different systems but integrated and with solidarity; external facilitators or obstructers of coverage are the degree of development, poverty incidence, cultural-ethnic integration, and sustained government commitment and taxing capacity. Social insurance must be adapted to a labour market in transition, infusing flexibility, creating special schemes for peasants, targeting fiscal subsidies to incorporate low-income self-employed, launching educational campaigns and better executing the compulsory affiliation of domestic servants. Segmented systems should be integrated or well coordinated (particularly between the public and social insurance sectors) to eliminate overlapping, to save resources and to be able to extend coverage to those excluded, thereby eliminating fiscal subsidies granted to separate schemes for powerful groups.

There is a positive correlation between income, degree of development, urban location, male gender and non-indigenous ethnicity on the one hand, and social insurance coverage on the other, while a negative correlation exists between age and coverage.[20] The impact of the reforms on coverage by income quintiles could be measured in two countries only: Bolivia's coverage diminished in all quintiles, whereas in Colombia it first improved in all quintiles but later declined. Gender inequalities in coverage result from external factors, but also the nature of the system itself: the female spouse is legally covered in maternity, but not sickness in four countries, and the opposite occurs in another one; in most countries the statistical coverage of women is lower than that of men, which results from indirect insurance as a spousal dependent of the insured; direct access is affected by women leaving the labour force to raise children; and pension coverage of women at age 65 and above is considerably lower than among men of the same age in 17 countries. The best-covered geographical areas are the most developed, urbanized and wealthier, whereas the worst covered are the least developed, rural and poor. Only two countries have compensation funds to reduce geographical inequalities, but these are limited to highly complex care. Indigenous populations are largely excluded from coverage because they are poor or have low incomes, work in the informal sector and/or live in rural areas. The three countries that have special programmes for rural populations and peasants have been able to cover part of the indigenous population. These inequalities could be reduced by pursuing the following policies: providing better allocation of resources, targeting and compensation funds; giving priority to the coverage of indigenous populations excluded or with very low coverage, suffering extreme poverty, through targeting in the geographical areas where they live; offering social assistance pensions and the extension of the basic package and fiscal subsidies; extending legal integral coverage to the spouse of the insured, granting optional insurance to housewives, and bonuses to women leaving the labour force to raise their children.

Poverty incidence averages 42 per cent in the region and reaches 60–77 per cent in four latecomer-low countries. Only the five countries in the pioneer-high group have targeted means-tested social assistance pensions (Bolivia has a non-targeted universal flat pension), although they do not cover all the poor and have significantly reduced poverty incidence. Coverage of the elderly population is lower in the latecomer-low group (5–14 per cent) and highest in the pioneer-high group (62–87 per cent), but is declining in three of these countries. For 25 years, structural pension reforms emphasized the compulsory saving (private) pillar and seriously neglected the poverty prevention public pillar that is now given priority by virtually all international/regional organizations.

Social security has not adapted to the transformations that have occurred in the labour market in the past quarter-century, and must do so in order to tackle these problems and extend coverage to the growing informal labour sector and the still significant rural sector in the least developed countries of the region. International and regional organizations that now agree on giving priority to the extension of coverage should coordinate their policies to achieve that objective.

Notes

1. This chapter is partly based on materials from the author's previous works (Mesa-Lago 2006, 2007, 2008), but integrates, restructures and summarizes those material around the UNRISD central themes of Financing Social Policy, and adds new tables and information. The author thanks an external reviewer for comments.
2. By late 2008 Argentina's private system was closed and integrated with the public system, while a mixed system has begun in Panama at the beginning of the year.
3. Based on household surveys between 1992 and 2002, the International Labour Organization (ILO) estimates diverse levels of social protection in the labour force of seven countries (Argentina, Bolivia, Chile, Ecuador, Guatemala, Nicaragua and Peru), according to the degree of vulnerability set by the worker's labour condition typified by three variables: kind of occupation (employer, salaried worker, self-employed, worker without a salary and unemployed), type of enterprise or sector (large, small and public), and skills (professional or non-professional).
4. In virtually all countries in the region political constitutions and social security laws establish the right to health care coverage and yet the seven countries in the latecomer-low group and the four least developed in the intermediate group have failed to implement said mandate.
5. The source for this section, unless specified is Mesa-Lago (2008).

6. A law in 2008 made coverage mandatory but gradually.
7. Subtracting Brazil that has the bulk of insured, the weighted average in public systems decreased to 20 per cent, lower than the 26 per cent average of private systems.
8. If those protected in Brazil are included in the regional estimate, coverage increase from 61 per cent in 1980 to 64 per cent in 1990 and decline to 53 per cent in 2000–04.
9. Health reforms have not expanded social insurance legal coverage in the informal and rural sectors, except for Colombia that extended mandatory coverage to the self-employed (albeit not implemented), the insured dependent family and the poor, most of whom where not previously covered. The Dominican Republic reform law of 2001 stipulates an extension of legal coverage but only one of its three regimes was operational and with limited coverage by the end of 2006.
10. A more appropriate indicator would be the population aged 65 and above who are poor and covered by social assistance pensions, but systematic data are not available.
11. The International Social Security Association (ISSA) notes, however, that Costa Rica, a developing country, accomplished wide health care coverage in 20 years and virtual universal coverage in 50 years, faster than many European countries.
12. ILO (2001); Reynaud (2002); Ginneken (2003).
13. For this purpose it is not sufficient to infuse a higher equivalence between contribution and level of benefit (because of the relatively low income of the labour force and other more urgent needs), but it is necessary to tie the contribution to other short-term benefits such as housing, health care services and loans.
14. Successful examples of the first two approaches are found in Costa Rica: a non-contributory health care scheme for the poor, financed with fiscal transfers and integrated to the unified social insurance programme, which does not discriminate in the treatment with those insured in the contributory programme; and fiscal subsidies granted to the self-employed, increasing as income decreases, which have been successful in expanding voluntary affiliation in social insurance to almost half of these workers and do not discriminate.
15. The system in Brazil is a good example of the mixed public and private-supplementary, and in Chile of the mixed public-social insurance and alternative private; Cuba's public system is open to all the population but without a private component.
16. ILO and the Pan American Health Organization (PAHO) have signed an agreement for a regional initiative to support member countries in their efforts to extend health care protection to excluded groups and guarantee universal access to services independent from people's contributory capacity.
17. ISSA (2003) conducted a study with estimates of coverage in 15 countries in the world, including Costa Rica, Mexico and Uruguay. The ILO (2001) has undertaken 20 studies of coverage (including various countries in Latin America) and the International Conference of 2001 gave maximum priority to the extension of coverage and compilation of statistics.
18. The six countries that restrict social insurance coverage by age to dependent children (1–12 years) should increase that coverage to 18 years of age. In Nicaragua all pensioners should be covered with the same benefits as the active insured.
19. Mexico has introduced a compensation fund to reduce inequalities among states but this is limited to the public popular health insurance (Seguro Popular de Salud/SPS) that provides basic services.
20. In Chile social insurance coverage increases with age, whereas private coverage decreases because of cream skimming, exclusion of chronic diseases and increases in premiums.

References

AIOS (Asociación Internacional de Organismos de Supervisión de Fondos de Pensiones) (2006) *Boletín Estadístico AIOS* (Buenos Aires), No. 14 (December).

Arenas de Mesa, Alberto and Carmelo Mesa-Lago (2006) 'The structural pension reform in Chile: Effects, comparisons with other Latin American reforms and lessons', *Oxford Review of Economic Policy*, Vol. 22, No. 1, 149–67.

Baeza, Cristian and Truman Packard (eds.) (2005) *Beyond Survival: Protecting Households from Impoverishing Effects of Health Shocks in Latin America* (Washington, DC: World Bank).

Bertranou, Fabio and Alberto Arenas de Mesa (eds.) (2003) *Protección Social y Género en Argentina, Brasil y Chile* (Santiago: ILO).

Bertranou, Fabio, Carmen Solorio and Wouter van Ginneken (eds.) (2002) *Pensiones no Contributivas y Asistenciales: Argentina, Brasil, Chile, Costa Rica y Uruguay* (Santiago: ILO).

Cifuentes, Mercedes (2000) 'El proceso de reforma del sector salud en Chile.' In Héctor Sánchez and Gustavo Zuleta (eds.), *La Hora de los Usuarios: Reflexiones sobre Economía Política de las Reformas de Salud* (Washington, DC: IDB and Centro de Estudios Salud y Futuro).

ECLAC (Economic Commission for Latin America and the Caribbean) (2006) *La Protección Social de Cara al Futuro: Acceso, Financiamiento y Solidaridad* (Montevideo:Trigésimo Período de Sesiones).

—— (2005) *Social Panorama of Latin America* (Santiago: ECLAC).

Gill, Indermit, Truman Packard and Juan Yermo (2005) *Keeping the Promise of Social Security in Latin America* (Washington, DC: Stanford University Press and World Bank).

Ginneken, Wouter van (2003) *Extending Social Security: Policies for Developing Countries*, ESS Paper No. 13 (Geneva: ILO).

Hujo, Katja, Carmelo Mesa-Lago and Manfred Nitsch (eds.) (2004) *¿Públicos o Privados? Los Sistemas de Pensiones en América Latina Después de Dos Décadas de Reformas* (Caracas: Nueva Sociedad).

IDB (Inter-American Development Bank) (2006) *Sustaining Development for All: Expanding Access to Economic Activity and Social Services* (Washington, DC: IDB).

—— (2004) *Estrategia de Salud (Marco para la Acción Sectorial del Banco) Perfil* (Washington, DC: IDB).

ILO (International Labour Organization) (2003) *Panorama Laboral 2003* (Geneva: ILO).

—— (2001) *Social Security: A New Consensus* (Geneva: ILO).

ISSA (International Social Security Association) (2006) *Towards a More Secure World: Results of the ISSA Initiative* (Geneva: ILO).

—— (2003) *Assessing the Coverage Gap: A World Report* (Cases of Costa Rica, Mexico and Uruguay), mimeo (Geneva: ILO).

Lizardo, Jeffrey (2004) *Dime de Cuánto Dispones y te Diré para Cuanto Alcanza: La Reforma de Salud y Seguridad Social en la República Dominicana* (Santo Domingo: Universidad INTEC and UNDP).

Mesa-Lago, Carmelo (2008) *Reassembling Social Security: A Survey of Pension and Health Care Reforms in Latin America* (Oxford: Oxford University Press).

—— (2007) 'The extension of healthcare coverage and protection in relation with the labour force: Problems and policies in Latin America', *International Social Security Review*, Vol. 60, No. 1, 3–31.

—— (2006) *Las Reformas de Salud en América Latina y el Caribe: Su Impacto en los Principios de la Seguridad Social*, Documentos de Proyectos (Santiago: ECLAC/GTZ).

PAHO (Pan American Health Organization) (2005) *Profiles of Health Systems of the Countries* (Washington, DC). http://www.lachsr.org, accessed in April 2008.

—— (2002) *Health in the Americas 2002* (Washington, DC: PAHO).

Reynaud, Emmanuel (2002) *The Extension of Social Security Coverage: The Approach of the International Labour Office*, ESS Papers No. 3 (Geneva: ILO).

Rofman, Rafael (2005) *Social Security Coverage in Latin America*, Social Protection Discussion Paper Series, No. 0523 (Washington, DC: World Bank).

World Bank (2005) *Ecuador: Expanding Social Insurance to Protect All*, Report 32771-EC (Washington, DC: Regional Office for Latin America and the Caribbean).

—— (1994) *Averting the Old-Age Crisis: Policies to Protect the Old and Promote Growth* (Washington, DC: World Bank and Oxford University Press).

—— (1993) *World Development Report: Investing in Health* (Oxford: Oxford University Press).

10
Pensions and Pension Funds in the Making of a Nation-State and a National Economy: The Case of Finland[1]

Olli E. Kangas

Introduction: 'Poor Is the Country and Poor It Will Be'

Finland has traditionally been highly agrarian and poor, a nation at the ultimate northern edge of the world. The country, situated around the Arctic Circle, did not offer particularly lucrative opportunities for making an easy livelihood. Farmers, who until the 1960s formed the biggest socioeconomic group, had to fight a constant battle against nature. During the short and rather cool summers, they had to try to gather stores to be used during the long and cold winters. Older Finnish literature tells many tales of frost that destroyed seeds and caused hunger, suffering and premature death. At the beginning of the nineteenth century, the Finnish gross domestic product (GDP) per capita was among the lowest in Europe; at times it was less than half of that of the United Kingdom and the United States (Maddison 1982). 'Poor is the country, and poor it will be if you look for gold!' stated the writer of the national anthem, which was first presented in 1848. The situation was not helped by the brutal civil war that broke out in 1918 (Alapuro 1988) or the wounds caused by the Second World War (Jussila et al. 1999; Pesonen and Riihinen 2002).

Much has changed since this time. At present, Finland lies in tenth place on the Human Development Index, with a GDP close to that of the United States and somewhat higher than that of the United Kingdom (UNDP 2002). Finland is classified as one of the leading telecommunications countries with the most widespread mobile telephone and Internet networks. It ranks, along with Denmark, the Netherlands, Sweden and the United States, among the top five countries on the Euro-Creativity Index (Florida and Tingali 2004).[2] According to the World Competitive Index, the leading countries in 2004 were Denmark, Finland, Sweden and the United States.[3] Finland also ranks highest in the Organisation for Economic Co-operation and Development Programme for International Student Assessment achievement survey of the knowledge and skills of 15-year-olds.[4] Considering the dismal starting point and harsh prerequisites, this is a commendable record. The million-dollar question to be addressed is how one of the most backward nations transformed itself into a high-tech society. Of course, there are several competing explanations; each contains some elements of truth but no single one is able to provide a comprehensive explanation.

However, one important aspect for this successful development has been the state's ability to implement reforms. This capacity, which has been the focus of many welfare state analyses,[5] is the result of interaction between various factors. First and foremost, the state itself must have a structure that facilitates reforms. Unilateral states with ethnically and culturally homogenous populations are easier to manage than federal states with highly diversified populations. The state must also have the bureaucratic ability and power to plan and execute reforms (Heclo 1974; Orloff and Skocpol 1984). Both of these factors were present in the case of Finland.

As long ago as the early 1500s, the founder of the Swedish kingdom, Gustaf Vasa (1496–1560), paid particular attention to the administration of his country in order to keep a record of the Swedish and Finnish population, although this was principally for the purposes of taxation and military conscription. Access to individual citizens – and, more importantly, to their income and assets – created a basis for effective taxation, which was a crucial precondition for the independence of the state vis-à-vis other societal actors. As the people were poor, the administrators had to develop quite a close relationship with their subordinates in order to accumulate the capital required by the state, since revenues consisted of small amounts in every location. These small amounts were democratically distributed across the whole of society and, in contrast to many other developing and poor countries, the Finnish state became powerful and independent enough not to be harnessed as merely a vehicle for pursuing specific interests. The state was able to make its own plans and decisions that sought to promote the collective or national good instead of simply promoting group-specific endeavours, something which was an important precondition for the rapid industrialization of this poor rural society (Vartiainen 1995).

The early foundation of Finnish statehood and nationhood was inspired by the Hegelian vision of society: in order to promote the well-being of the nation, the state should represent the common will of the people and merge various particularistic group-based needs into a single collective goal. In this respect, Finland has some similarities with the so-called developmental states, where the state plays a crucial role in promoting and coordinating private investments and maintaining the overall competitiveness of the country (Kosonen 1987).

The strongly collectivist, nationhood-based thinking is apparent in the development of Finnish social policy. The starting point, in contrast to the Bismarckian-style workers' insurance, was a people's or national insurance offering equal coverage to the entire population. The early programmes were designed to meet the needs of both the rural and urban sections of the population (Kangas and Palme 1992). These flat rate-based, universal national insurance schemes, supplemented later by income-related benefits, came to form the basis for the elimination of poverty.

However, it should be recalled that social policy amounts to much more than simply guaranteeing security against various social risks. Social policy creates and fortifies social bonds, and by pooling different groups of people together, it may enhance the creation of trust or 'social capital', which is beneficial for economic growth.[6] All of the international comparisons show that Finland, together with the other Nordic countries, is top of the league in terms of social trust (Mackie 2001), which may be a significant explanation for the country's highly successful development. People have faith in each other and in the honesty of the public bureaucracy.

Social policy may also be used to accumulate 'real' capital, particularly when it comes to the issue of pensions. Pension funds are an important source of capital accumulation that can be used for different purposes. A closer inspection of the Finnish case illustrates this point. In the 1950s, the National Pension funds (NP funds) were used to build up the basic national infrastructure, power stations and electric networks, for example, whereas the employment-related pension funds, which began to be accumulated at the beginning of the 1960s, were invested principally in the national industries and provided investment capital for the industrialization of society. The Finnish case provides an excellent example of how it was possible to unify social policy goals with the economic goals of building up modern industrial market economies – and this is precisely the focus of this chapter.

The aim is to analyse and describe the development of Finnish pension schemes. Special focus is given to the use of pension funds in national policy making. The Finnish case offers fruitful material for the study of two latent functions of social policy: (i) how to create a unified nation (after a harsh civil war); and (ii) how to invest pension funds in a way that makes national developmental projects possible. The study concentrates on the first national pension programme of 1937, which was fully funded and accumulated in individual accounts. Those funds were used to provide the country with electricity. There is also an assessment of role of employment-related pensions, implemented in 1961. The 1961 scheme funds were used to industrialize the country. The municipal pension scheme that was introduced in 1966 and is partially funded is also of particular interest. The communal pension funds were partially invested in the production of housing, which in turn helped the transformation from an agrarian to an industrial and urban society. Finally, the present-day situation, where such 'national meta-projects' no longer seem to be possible, are discussed. Nowadays, capital – including pension capital – is invested according to where the highest profits can be made without taking into consideration national goals, as was previously the case. Here, we come up against a classic collective action problem: pension funds are collected from Finnish employment, but they are increasingly being invested in projects outside the country. This in turn means fewer jobs in the country, which in turn squeezes the base for collecting pension premiums. Thus, the crucial question is whether or not this vicious circle can be broken; and if it can be broken, then how?

The Finnish experience serves as a good example of how social policy has been used successfully as a developmental strategy (Mkandawire 2001). In the history of the Finnish pension policy, there are a couple of issues that may serve as learning strategies for developing countries. First, the initial national pension scheme was introduced in predominantly agrarian and poor areas. Hence, the implementation of the scheme, in addition to the way in which problems related to the insurance premium collection were solved, may be something to learn from. Second, social policy programmes may create and fortify solidarity and a sense of belonging among the populace. The way in which social security is constructed has important ramifications for social solidarity (Rothstein 1998, 1989). Institutions, in particular, matter. Apparently, the Finns were successful in this area: they trust each other and their institutions. According to various surveys, Finland is the least corrupt country in the world.[7] Third, social policy may be used as a device to promote national economic goals, which is the main topic of this chapter. In this respect, the Finnish case is a telling example, both in a positive and negative sense.

The First National Pension Scheme of 1937: Investments in basic infrastructure

In comparison to most other European countries, until the 1960s Finland had an extremely agrarian social structure. This economic backwardness left its mark on Finnish social policy, not least as a result of the strong political impact of the independent peasantry. The farming population was the most populous social class until the mid-1960s (Alestalo 1986). The central position of the agrarian movement was also fortified by the civil war of 1918 where the independent peasantry was the nucleus of the victorious White army, which gave political and cultural hegemony to the agrarian vision of society. Correspondingly, the importance of the political left was circumscribed (Jussila et al. 1999; Pesonen and Riihinen 2002).

There were crucial differences in social policy priorities between the working-class movement and the agrarians. The former placed workers' insurance with protection against illness and unemployment at the top of their list, while pensions were of secondary importance. The agrarian party was more eager to carry through a pension scheme and demanded that any social insurance programme they supported be universal, thereby opposing Bismarckian-type solutions and only considering schemes that would also provide benefits for the agrarian population (Mannio 1967; Ahtokari 1988). Finnish history lends qualified support to Baldwin (1990), who argues that the universalistic characteristics of the Nordic welfare state were determined by the farmers' narrowly self-interested demands. More clearly than in the other Nordic countries, due to their leading position, Finnish farmers were able to block the implementation of workers' insurance schemes, and the pension issue was brought to the political agenda in the mid-1930s, with coverage expanded to the entire population.

In principle, there were two alternatives: (i) an insurance-based system; and (ii) a premium-financed, tax-based pay-as-you-go (PAYG) scheme. The conservatives, followed by the other bourgeois parties, wanted to have a savings-based and fully funded system. The PAYG system that was favoured by the Social Democratic Party (SDP) was regarded as too expensive by the non-socialists. After heated debates, the parties were finally able to agree on the basic principle of the scheme and carry through the first national pension in 1937. The resulting scheme was a hybrid, so full of compromises that it did not meet all the requirements of any of the parties. Yet the agrarians were able to introduce a national, nearly universal system, and the other bourgeois parties were satisfied with the premium-based and -funded insurance. The socialists managed to include tax-financed pension supplements for people with very low income. The accepted system was universal in the sense that everyone between the age of 18 and 55 was insured. However, the system was not wholly universal – those who were over 55 years of age when the law became effective were totally excluded. In addition, there was a transition period of 10 years when the scheme only accumulated funds and did not pay out any pensions (Niemelä 1994; Häggman 1997).

The programme was genuinely an obligatory savings scheme. Initially, every insured person contributed 1 per cent (which increased to 2 per cent in 1944) of their income and the employer paid half of the fee. In the case of those with no income, the state and municipalities paid a means-tested pension. Every insured person had an individual account with the National Pension Institution (NPI), a semi-public organization that was established to administer the scheme. The NPI occupied a rather independent position, which was regarded as necessary for the administration of the funds. A direct state-run institution was ruled out by the bourgeois parties that were concerned that the state, with the help of the pension funds, would buy up private companies and thereby 'socialize' the whole Finnish economy. The aim was to prevent the political misuse of funds.

At the age of 65, people who were covered by the insurance and who had accumulated savings in their accounts could start to receive benefits. The size of the pension was dependent on the capital that was accumulated in the claimants' accounts. This kind of system was based on individual accounts, and individual premiums were difficult to determine and administrate in an agrarian country as Finland was at that time. How was it possible to define pension premiums for peasants who were living partially in a subsistence economy? In principle, the insured person had to go to the post office to pay the premiums. A special receipt showing that the national pension premium had been paid was given in return, and all receipts had to be carefully preserved for future claims on pensions. In practice, there were variations depending upon the labour market status and the place of residence. In bigger towns, employers usually paid all of the premiums for their employees. This happened four times a year. Farmers paid their premiums retroactively, based on municipal taxes at the end of each year. According to statistics for 1945, about 60 per cent of the premiums was paid by the employers, about 25 per cent was paid through municipal taxes and about 15 per cent was never paid (Häggman 1997). All in all, the system was regarded as difficult, with many problems associated with the documentation of premiums paid and, consequently, there were numerous complaints.

In 1947, the tax system underwent a total reform and instead of retroactive taxation, a prospective taxation was introduced: instead of paying taxes retroactively at the end of the year for the annual income or at periodic intervals, taxes were paid simultaneously with the receipt of income; that is, when employees received their wages or salaries, both state and municipal taxes were automatically deducted from their income. The national pension premiums were made a part of municipal taxes,

Table 10.1 Investments from the NP funds, 1940–57 (per cent)

Year	State	Municipalities	Industry	Merchant/ transport	Power stations	Other
1940	38	15	10	1	7	29
1945	69	9	5	0	9	8
1950	10	11	10	2	57	10
1957	4	11	18	4	59	4

Note: In addition to power stations, some investments in electricity are included under Industry and Other.
Source: Häggman (1977).

which simplified the collection of payments and solved the problems associated with collecting the contributions (Häggman 1997).

The political aims of the 1937 scheme were apparent. First, following the Civil War and the right-wing radicalism of the early 1930s, the national insurance tried to unify the nation by placing all citizens under the same insurance. Therefore, the scheme was a universal *national* pension connoting nationhood and universalism. Second, the savings-based insurance accumulated huge capital stocks. One motivation for such a system was the beneficial consequences for the national economy. In a poor country like Finland, the rate of savings within households was low. The national pension programme presented a good opportunity to save collectively, with individuals surrendering a part of their household consumption for future pension purposes (Niemelä 1994).

According to the original investment rules, loans to the state were not to exceed 10 per cent of the total amount of investments. However, the Second World War changed the situation dramatically, and by the end of the war in 1945 the state loans corresponded to almost 70 per cent of all funds (see Table 10.1). Thus, national pension funds helped the country to heal the wounds of the war. After the war, state loans decreased rapidly and the NPI actively and deliberately invested in national infrastructure, especially in power stations and electricity. By 1957, more than half of all investments were targeted towards the development of electricity in power stations and electrical networks. Around 70 per cent of all power stations were de facto financed by the NP funds (Niemelä 1994; Häggman 1997).

Until 1946, it was also possible to invest NP funds in housing, which was an ongoing problem in Finland. As late as the early 1950s, for instance, many families in Helsinki lived in provisional housing in bomb shelters. However, instead of investing in housing – which was the recommendation of the Ministry of Social Affairs – the NPI decided to follow the recommendations made by the Treasury and concentrate on producing electricity. The country had lost one-third of its power stations in the war, hence the urgent need to replace them. It can be argued that the needs of industry (more electricity) were placed before the needs of the people (more houses) on the list of priorities (Häggman 1997).

In summary, the NP funds formed an important basis for building up the basic infrastructure that later provided a solid foundation for the rapid industrialization of the country. The role of the NP funds was to provide a common good – an infrastructure – that served the interests of the whole nation, including the private economy. However, the private sector was unwilling and unable to carry out the task that was successfully taken on by the NPI – a good example of the 'developmental state'.

The National Pension Reform of 1956: Universalism at the cost of funds

The problems of the strictly premium-based system soon became clearly apparent. There were three main shortcomings. First, in principle, the scheme was universal in its coverage, but due to the long maturation period (40 years), the majority of the elderly were excluded from receiving benefits. By 1950, only one-fifth of the elderly above the normal pension age of 65 years were entitled to national pensions (Kangas and Palme 1992). At the beginning, coverage was very slow in becoming universal. Reformation of the scheme was a question of social justice and safeguarding pensions for all citizens. The second problem was the low level of the benefits. With all available supplements, the full national pension amounted to no more than 15 per cent of the average industrial wage, which was one of the lowest replacement rates in the Western hemisphere (Kangas and Palme 1992). Thus, reform was needed to increase the level of benefits. The third problem was linked to the funds. After the Second World War, the value of funds was rapidly reduced by postwar inflation and the elderly ran the risk of totally losing their pensions. The funded individual scheme required a stable environment, and when the requirement was not met, the system collapsed and the state had to take over.

The national pension was completely revised in 1957. A coalition cabinet consisting of the SDP and the agrarians agreed on a system whereby the universal basic pension was complemented by income-related pensions for employees. However, in the final vote, the agrarians decided to abandon the income-related part. Previous funds, built up principally by employee and employer contributions, were distributed on a flat-rate basis to every citizen over 65 years of age. As there was a general strike at the same time that the bill was being discussed in the Finnish Parliament, the SDP and trade unions were more occupied with the strike than with the issue of pensions (Niemelä 1994). Therefore, the bill was accepted in the form preferred by the agrarians. Later, employee organizations criticized the 1957 law for confiscating the employee's pension funds collected on the basis of the 1937 law and distributing them to the agrarian elderly. This dissatisfaction and mistrust of the agrarians had important ramifications for social democratic and trade union strategies when employment-related pensions were at stake a few years later.

The new National Pension Act of 1956 established universalism, and everyone older than 65 de facto became automatically eligible for a national pension. The pension was divided into two separate parts: (i) a universal basic amount payable unconditionally to everybody over 65 years of age who had resided in the country for five years before their retirement; and (ii) an income-tested supplementary amount that was inversely related to the claimant's total remaining income.

The 1956 scheme abandoned the previous principle of financing and, instead of individual funds and a defined contribution principle, it implemented the PAYG and defined benefit principles. The pension contribution was distributed between the employer (1 per cent of payroll) and the employee (1 per cent of taxable income). By 2005, the contribution rates – including employer's illness insurance fees – were 3 per cent to 6 per cent, depending on the size of the payroll, and 2.5 per cent, respectively.

On one hand, the 1956 Act provided universalism and equality for all citizens, while simplifying the pension system and its administration. On the other hand, the reform nullified the NP funds, and the NPI rapidly lost its importance as a fundraiser for important common efforts such as projects related to the Finnish national economy.

Employment-related pensions in the 1960s: Bonds between social partners

Individual employers did provide some type of pension for their elderly workers as a gesture of gratitude for their long and faithful service. Despite the rapid growth of occupational schemes towards the end of the 1950s, the actual coverage of these programmes remained limited. Only about 20 per cent of private sector employees, mainly white-collar workers in big companies, were covered. An additional problem of these occupational schemes was that in most cases they were bound to a specific employer. If a person changed jobs, the right to a pension was lost. Many American enterprises offering company-based health insurance currently face the same situation. Needless to say, this is not good for labour mobility.

In order to guarantee portability and to extend the coverage to include all blue-collar workers, the trade unions – supported by the SDP – insisted on a legislated compulsory scheme. At first, the employers rejected the idea of legislated pensions as a whole, but their attitudes gradually changed when they realized that such reform was inevitable. In addition, the consultations between Finnish and Swedish employer organizations contributed to this change in attitudes. Swedish employers had lost their fight over pensions just a couple of years earlier. The Finnish employers concluded that it was better to steer than to be steered. The employers' federation proposed a legislated, but decentralized, scheme with private insurance companies as insurance carriers. The employment-related pension act for private sector employees (TEL) that was accepted in 1961 gave employers many concessions as they were paying the whole insurance premium, which amounted to 5 per cent at the beginning of the 1960s (Salminen 2003, 1987).

For the employees, the most important issue was adequate pension security, and the matter of organizational form was of less importance. Moreover, the trade unions and SDP were sceptical about a publicly administrated system or a scheme based on the NPI: they were afraid that the agrarians would once again be in a position to 'confiscate' employees' pension funds if the scheme remained in the domain of the public sector and open to political decision making (Ahtokari 1988).

The employment-related pension scheme for private sector employees was fully legislated and mandatory, but run by private insurance carriers. A special bipartite organization was established in order to coordinate the activities of these private companies. The labour market partners were centrally involved in the administration of the programme. This bipartite system offered employees and employers an institutional opportunity to resist the actions of Parliament should it attempt to radically change the scheme. In a way, markets were used against politics, whereas in the other Nordic countries politics were used against markets (Esping-Andersen 1985). Therefore, the representatives of the trade unions could, in the final instance, accept the pact proposed by the employers' federation, the Finnish Employers' Central Organization, rather easily. The former got their statutory pensions fully financed through employer contributions, and the latter got a decentralized system, mainly organized through private pension insurance companies. In Parliament, the agrarians and communists were against the proposals, while the social democrats and the conservatives backed them. The social democratic initiative was finally accepted in 1961 and private sector employees got their TEL scheme. A separate pension scheme was established for employees in the private sector with short-term employment contracts. In 1974, farmers and other self-employed people each acquired their own programmes. Thus, a certain degree of corporatism has influenced the Finnish pension design, where coverage follows sectoral and occupational lines. The target pension level was intended to be 60 per cent of the final wage after 40 years in employment.

The Finnish public sector workers at the state and municipal levels had had their own separate pension arrangements for almost a century, and the existing arrangements for these employees were neither financially nor administratively merged with the TEL scheme. Pensions for state employees were somewhat codified and homogenous; however, as a result of the independence of local administration, there was a plethora of municipal arrangements. The introduction of the TEL system accentuated the need to codify and homogenize the divergent public sector schemes. In the same way that the central organization of trade unions and the SDP feared leaving employment-related pensions in the hands of the public body, the representatives of municipalities rejected the suggestion of joining the TEL system. In agrarian municipalities there was a fear of a social democratic takeover since the SDP had the upper hand in state politics, even though a vast majority of municipalities were dominated by the agrarian/centre party. Thus, they wanted to build up a separate scheme run by representatives of the local authorities. The act for local sector pensions for the municipal employees (KVTEL), run by a special insurance body, the Municipal Pension Institution, was accepted in 1964. A separate state pension scheme for state employees (VEL) became effective two years later. In this respect, the Finnish pension design also has some Central European or corporatist traits (Blomster 2004).

Benefits in the public sector have traditionally been somewhat more generous than those to be found in the private sector. Both the KVTEL and VEL offered 66 per cent of the final salary after 30 years of employment. Hence, the occupational 'bonus' that was built into the legislated schemes for the public sector employees and separate occupational arrangements, common to many other countries, was not developed. The primary function of the Finnish public sector employees' scheme, however, is to provide income-related pensions in the same way as the TEL programme (Kangas and Palme 1996, 1992). This function became more evident in 1993 when the public sector schemes were homogenized with the TEL pensions and civil servants were deprived of their privileged position. Thus, all employees were guaranteed homogenous benefits regardless of their sector of employment.

The social commitments or bonds that the employment-related pension schemes created in Finland were different from those created by the national pension. The TEL scheme, devised jointly by employer and employee organizations, contributed to the creation of something that has been labelled social corporatism. By pooling their interests in social policy issues, the social partners initiated a tradition of mutual negotiation – a tradition that has lasted to the present.

The peculiar political pre-history of the introduction of the Finnish TEL system had important ramifications for the subsequent administration of pensions. The labour market-based system offered the social partners strong institutional veto points against the political decision making. Only after consent from the labour market partners have the political decision makers been able to change the existing legislation, and only then according to the guidelines agreed by the social partners. This is evident when considering the changes in pension programmes implemented in the 1990s and the early 2000s (Kangas and Palme 2005). In fact, the reformation of the Finnish pension system has many more similarities with the Central European so-called corporatist schemes than with pension systems in the other Nordic countries (Schludi 2001; Lundberg 2003). For example, in Sweden, the 1959 employment-related pensions were organized through a public insurance carrier and consequently the pension reform in the 1990s was a predominantly political process in which social partners played a minor role; whereas in Finland – and in Central Europe – the administration of the pensions was organized through the labour market, and the government had to negotiate with the social partners. Sometimes the politicians expressed their frustration at merely being rubber stamps for pacts decided on by labour market partners. In sum, the very structure of social policy programmes facilitated the creation of strong social bonds and a specific kind of social capital that has conditioned the overall policy-making process in Finland, and which serves as strong evidence that pension programmes exist not only to safeguard the livelihood of the elderly.

Funds: From national projects to foreign profits

The financing of the different pension schemes varied. Both of the self-employed schemes are PAYG schemes, and the revenues consist of pension contributions collected from the insured individuals and revenues from the state. The TEL scheme is partly funded and partly PAYG. The funded part aimed to mitigate the undesirable impact caused by changes in the size of successive age cohorts. In pace with the maturation of the scheme, the TEL funds rapidly replaced the decreasing NP funds in the national credit and investments markets. Both of the public sector programmes were initially financed totally on a PAYG basis, but in order to confront the challenges arising from the anticipated demographic changes, a substantial degree of funding was introduced in the municipal KVTEL scheme in 1988 and in

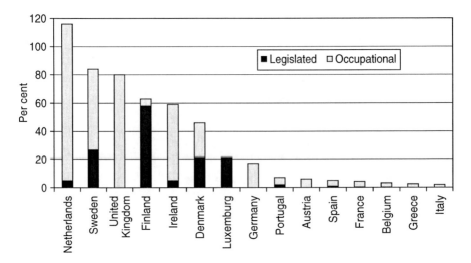

Figure 10.1   The percentage of pension funds in relation to GDP in the European Union, 2002
Source: www.tela.fi, accessed in June 2005.

the VEL state pension scheme in 1990. At present, the total pension fund – private plus public – constitutes about 70 per cent of GDP, which is one of the highest figures in the European Union, as indicated in Figure 10.1.

In Finland, the legislated pension insurance is responsible for funding. By contrast, in the three countries with the largest funds – the Netherlands, Sweden and, most notably, the United Kingdom – it is the occupational pensions that are the main source of funds. The same goes for Ireland and, to some extent, Denmark. In international terms, the funds accumulated by the Finnish legislated pensions are relatively large and, needless to say, an important factor in the Finish national economy. Therefore, the investment policy is of the utmost importance not only for safeguarding future pensions, but also in helping the national economy operate smoothly.

The opening paragraph in the law that governs investments made by pension insurance companies states that the 'funds must be invested profitably and safely'. In the beginning, the regulations also stipulated that priority for investment should be given to national projects. Until the 1980s, the vast majority of the investments were indeed directed at Finnish industry. In principle, these investments had two alternative routes. First, according to the TEL rules, it was possible for companies to loan a part of their pension contribution as funding. This was the most frequently used alternative. The second way was for pension insurance companies to make investments. In the 1970s and 1980s, about one-third of all of these investments was directed at industry. In addition to industry, funds were invested in the building sector (about 20 per cent) and real estate (about 15 per cent). The building sector has been an important means of investment for public sector pensions as well. This, in turn, helped to provide housing for those who had to move from the countryside to urban areas. In the municipal scheme, precisely as in the TEL

Table 10.2 Investment portfolio of the Finnish pension funds, 1997–2004 (per cent)

Year	Money market	Bonds	Shares and convertibles	Real estate	Loans to companies	Total
1997	11	42	13	8	26	100
2000	3	47	28	9	13	100
2004	4	48	32	9	7	100

Source: www.tela.fi, accessed in June 2005.

scheme, individual municipalities had the possibility to loan money on reasonable terms from their own centralized municipal pension institutes.

In sum, both the private and public sector employment-related pension funds were more or less deliberately used in national investment projects to promote the national common good. The rapid industrialization that took place in Finland from the 1960s was largely facilitated by employment-related funds, which provided capital for industrial growth.

However, the globalization of economies changed the situation and the under-pinning commitment to national projects. In addition, the investment policy adopted by the pension funds became more and more criticized as investments yielded dividends that were very low compared to the alternative options. Towards the end of the 1980s, credit markets were liberalized and pension insurance also had greater freedom to manoeuvre. In addition, in the hope for greater profits, greater risks were tolerated. Foreign investments seemed and still seem to offer larger profits and more lucrative projections. As a consequence, the share of national investments has fallen markedly. In 2000, almost 60 per cent of investments were still made in Finland. By 2004, the share was down to 34 per cent, while a little more – 40 per cent – was invested in the Euro zone, and the rest in countries outside Europe.[8]

When it comes to new methods of investment, by 2004 almost half were in bonds (see Table 10.2). The main debtors are the Finnish, French and German states, which have about 90 per cent of all bond investments. The more risky part of the portfolio consists of shares, representing a little more than 30 per cent of the investment portfolio. The shares are mostly foreign investments (see Table 10.3). The rest is divided between real estate and investment loans (about 10 per cent each).

Before allowing the possibility of making foreign investments, there was an active discussion of whether investing Finnish pension money abroad is a 'correct' procedure, which concluded that the main task of the pension scheme was to safeguard future pension promises, and as foreign investments appeared to give better dividends they were also regarded as safer investments. In addition, there were arguments that the risk should be divided into different pools: profits in some pools may balance deficits in other pools. As Finnish investors monitor various world indices for investments and the relative weight of the Finnish projects

Table 10.3 Investment portfolios by investment categories in Finland and abroad, 2000–04 ($ billion)

	2000			2004		
	Finland	*Abroad*	*All*	*Finland*	*Abroad*	*All*
Money market	2.0	0	2.0	3.6	1.6	5.2
Bonds	15.5	22.1	37.6	6.6	46.4	53.0
Shares and convertibles	11.5	10.5	22.1	9.7	23.6	33.3
Real estates	7.3	0	7.3	9.4	0.2	9.6
Loans	10.2	0	10.2	6.7	0	6.7
Total	*46.5*	*32.6*	*79.2*	*36.0*	*71.8*	*107.8*

Source: www.tela.fi/tela/telabri.nsf/alkusivu?Open, accessed in June 2005.

in these investments is marginal, more and more investments are targeted abroad (see Table 10.3).

At present, there are critics who demand the return to the original idea of investment policy, if only partially. Pension contributions are collected from the payroll of Finnish labour, but contributions are increasingly invested abroad. Compared to the previous situation where investments were made to fortify the national infrastructure and the basis for employment, the situation is quite different and will, in the long run, squeeze the basis of domestic employment, which in turn will lead to a squeezing of the basis for pension contributions and problems with the financing of future pensions.

Discussion: Social and monetary capital in the new situation

The initial point of this chapter is that social policy is not only a distributional issue – that is, who gets what and how much – but that it can also be used to build up social and physical capital. The history of the Finnish pension insurance was used to demonstrate this. When it comes to institutional set-ups, social policy programmes unify and divide people and social groups. According to Putnam (2000), who makes an important distinction that forms the overarching theme for the idea proposed here, there are two dimensions of social capital: *bridging* (or inclusive) and *bonding* (or exclusive) social capital (see also Granovetter's (1973) reference to 'weak' and 'strong' ties; Olson 1982, 1965).

The bridging form of social capital creates broader identities and brings larger sections of society together by unifying them with weak ties, whereas bonding social capital pertains to specific, group-based solidarity. The bonding form of social capital generates strong ties, yet as a result of its intragroup solidarity, it may create strong out-of-group antagonism. Therefore, there is a danger that the exclusion of social capital will turn out to be antisocial and detrimental for society as a whole. Throughout its history, social policy has had both bridging and bonding functions. In some countries, like Finland, the emphasis has been on the bridging side: the basic principle in social policy schemes has been universalism expressed through *people*'s insurance. This is what happened when Finland instituted national pensions: all of the people were put together under the same umbrella.

In some other countries – especially Central European, Asian and African nations – the schemes have been based on membership of a certain occupational group or category of people. These schemes have relied on bonding social capital and consequently they have created strong intragroup interests. This is evident if we look at the development of the Finnish employment-related pensions at the beginning of the 1960s. By putting social partners together to administrate pensions and pension funds, the schemes gave institutional power resources to social partners that could, to some extent, resist – or, if you like, counterbalance – the political decision-making machinery.

Here, we face a dilemma. How is it possible to find a fruitful balance between bridging and binding social capital? How can we strike a balance between obedience to the state – or society, community or, to put it more generally, 'wholeness' – and intragroup loyalty? How is it possible to preserve a sufficient level of group-based social capital – that is, essential for 'democracy to work' and for many other good things in society – without sacrificing more general, society-level goals? How can smaller interest groups with their strong bonding social ties be persuaded to make compromises that would cut group-specific benefits (for example, pensions or illness benefits), yet are essential for the maintenance of a collective level of goals (for example, the balance of national economy). In the Finnish case, the balance was in the sheer size of the schemes. The trade unions and employers' organizations knew that they were the big actors and that their decisions inevitably would have national economic consequences. Therefore, they were prepared to act in a reasonable manner and have 'wholeness' in mind when 'their' pension policy was at stake. From the social capital point of view, the Finnish pension system managed, in its developmental phase, to combine both the bridging and bonding forms of social capital and avoid the problem of special interests being attached to more scattered schemes, which is a problem that many other countries in the developmental phases are futilely wrestling with. This is perhaps the first of five learning points from the Finnish case.

The second lesson to be drawn is related to the history of the first national pension scheme of 1937, which was based on a system of individual savings accounts. The idea was perhaps brilliant: to accumulate investment capital in a country that was so poor that all of the income was used for consumption. The pension scheme was a kind of obligatory saving or a confiscation of consumption for investment purposes. To some extent it worked, and the NP funds were used to help the country through the turmoil of the Second World War and the period of its postwar reconstruction. These funds were used deliberately to establish the basic infrastructure of the country. In that sense, the savings-based, totally funded scheme was a success.

However, when it came to the other task of the pension scheme – safeguarding a decent livelihood for the elderly – the scheme did not fare that well. There were severe problems, and initially the bookkeeping for individual premiums in a country where a part of the population was still living in a subsistence economy was such an enormous task that it did not quite succeed in the beginning. These administrative problems caused much mistrust. However, after the taxation system was changed and premium collection was merged with taxation, these problems were solved and the legitimacy of the system was regained. In a developmental context, systems like the Finnish 1937 scheme are difficult to administer: the simpler, the better. This is our third learning point and it is exactly what happened with the national pension system of 1956: it simplified the premium collection and benefit calculation. The darker side, however, was that the NP funds were lost and possibilities for 'national projects' disappeared.

The long maturation period of the 1937 system caused many problems relating to equality or social justice, which undermined the legitimacy of the scheme. As a result of the maturation period, a great number of the elderly were excluded from the benefits. In addition, as the pension was dependent on individually accumulated capital, no one really knew what the actual size of the pension would amount to. This problem of predictability was not made any easier by postwar inflation that threatened to nullify the entire capital stock accumulated in those individual accounts. This is the fourth learning point: fully funded schemes need stable circumstances to function properly. Under turbulent circumstances, we must always rely on the public hand as the ultimate guarantor. PAYG is always lurking behind even the most decorative premium-based system.

As stated above, the shift to the simpler national pension system eradicated pension funds. The problem was to some extent relieved by the employment-related pension scheme that was based on partial funding. These funds, which are now among the highest in the European Union, were intended to accelerate the industrialization of the country. Therefore, an important part of the funds were loaned back to, or invested in, Finnish industry. Thus, where the NP funds were of the utmost importance in providing electricity for the country, the employment-related pension funds helped to create an industrial society. Against this background, the fifth developmental learning point is that it is in fact possible to unify social policy and economic development in such a way that a more or less just and stable society, decent social security and strong economic growth can be achieved simultaneously. These aspects are by no means mutually exclusive. In fact, this idea was strongly emphasized by social planners in the late 1950s and early 1960s. 'In the contemporary society, democracy, social equality and economic growth seem to be interdependent in a fortunate way' as one of the main ideological founders of the Finnish welfare state stated in 1961 (Kettunen 2001: 231).

However, as the current situation in Finland displays, there are new problems. We avoided a bear, but met a lion. The basic problem is a classical collective action problem. Pension insurance companies are profit-seeking entities. They try to maximize the dividends on their investments. Presently, the biggest dividends are not in Finland, but are highly scattered across the globe. To cite just some examples: hourly wage costs in industrial production are about \$31[9] in Germany, \$24 in Denmark, Finland and Norway, \$21 in Sweden, \$17 in the United States and \$14 in the United Kingdom. In the Republic of Korea, the costs are about \$8, while they are less than $0.30 in China and India (Collier and Dollar 2001). In the era of global production, this situation puts strong pressure not only on Finland, but also on all other high-cost countries since there is a tendency for industrial production to (re)locate in less expensive countries. Consequently, the most lucrative investments are somewhere other than in Finland. And it is here that we face the problem of collective action. From the viewpoint of the common good – national economy/future pensions – it would be advantageous if the funds that are collected from Finnish labour contributed to the expansion of that labour base and, consequently, the base for solid pension finances. However, capital, even pension capital, tends to seek out the highest short-term profits. In the long run, such a strategy may be detrimental to the maintenance of the national system that created general prerequisites. Of course, if such a boom in global investment leads to acceleration in the developmental processes in less developed countries, this will possibly forge a more balanced situation between the formerly rich and formerly poor countries, which from a global perspective is a most welcome process. Here, the Robin Hood principle (transfers from those who have to those who have not) is more justified than the older Matthew principle (transfers from those who have to those who have).

Notes

1. This chapter is an abridged version of Programme Paper No. 25, previously published with the same title under the UNRISD Programme on Social Policy and Development, March 2006.
2. See also www.demos.co.uk/media/creativeeurope_page373.aspx, accessed in June 2005.
3. See www.imd.ch/wcy/ranking/index.cfm, accessed in June 2005.
4. See www.pisa.oecd.org, accessed in June 2005.
5. See Evans et al. (1985); Immergut (1992); Orloff and Skocpol (1984); and Skocpol (1992).
6. See Fukuyama (1995); Putnam (1993); and Rothstein (2003, 1998).
7. See www.globalcorruptionreport.org and www.transparency.org/pressreleases_archive/2004/2004.10.20.cpi.en.html, both accessed in June 2005.
8. www.tela.fi, accessed in June 2005.
9. All $ amounts refer to US dollars.

References

Ahtokari, Reijo (1988) *Tuntematon vaikuttaja* (The Unknown Actor) (Porvoo: WSOY).
Alapuro, Risto (1988) *State and Revolution in Finland* (Berkeley, CA: University of California Press).
Alestalo, Matti (1986) *Structural Change, Classes and the State: Finland in a Historical Perspective*, Research Group for Comparative Sociology, Research Reports 33 (Helsinki: University of Helsinki).
Baldwin, Peter (1990) *The Politics of Social Solidarity: Class Bases of the European Welfare State 1875–1975* (Cambridge: Cambridge University Press).
Blomster, Peter (2004) *Kunnallisen eläkejärjestelmän historia* (The History of the Municipal Pension Scheme) (Helsinki: KEVA).
Collier, Paul and David Dollar (2001) *Globalization, Growth, and Poverty: Building an Inclusive World Economy* (Oxford: World Bank and Oxford University Press).

Esping-Andersen, Gøsta (1985) *Politics Against Markets* (Princeton, NJ: Princeton University Press).

Evans, Peter, Dietrich Rueschemeyer and Theda Skocpol (1985) *Bringing the State Back In* (Cambridge: Cambridge University Press).

Florida, Richard and Irene Tinagli (2004) *Europe in the Creative Age* (London: Carnegie Mellon and Demos).

Fukuyama, Francis (1995) *Trust: The Social Virtues and the Creation of Prosperity*. (London: Penguin Books).

Granovetter, Mark (1973) 'The strength of weak ties', *American Journal of Sociology*, Vol. 78, 1360–80.

Häggman, Kai (1997) *Suurten muutosten Suomessa. Kansaneläkelaitos 1937–1997* (Change in Finland – The Big Transformation: National Pension Institution 1937–1997) (Helsinki: KELA).

Heclo, Hugh (1974) *Modern Social Politics in Britain and Sweden* (New Haven, CT: Yale University Press).

Immergut, Ellen (1992) *The Political Construction of Interests: National Health Insurance Politics in Switzerland, France, and Sweden, 1930–1970* (New York: Cambridge University Press).

Jussila, Osmo, Seppo Hentilä and Jukka Nevakivi (1999) *From Grand Duchy to a Modern State: A Political History of Finland Since 1809* (London: Hurst and Company).

Kangas, Olli and Joakim Palme (2005) 'Does the most brilliant future of the "Nordic Model" have to be in the past?' In Olli Kangas and Joakim Palme (eds.), *Social Policy and Economic Development in the Nordic Countries* (Basingstoke: Palgrave Macmillan).

—— (1996) 'The development of occupational pensions in Finland and Sweden: Class politics and institutional feedbacks.' In Michael Shalev (ed.), *The Privatization of Social Policy: Occupational Welfare and the Welfare State in America, Scandinavia and Japan* (New York: Macmillan).

—— (1992) 'Public–private mix in old age pensions.' In Jon-Eivind Kolberg (ed.), *The Study of Welfare State Regimes* (New York: M.E. Sharpe).

Kettunen, Pauli (2001) 'The Nordic welfare state in Finland', *Scandinavian Journal of History*, Vol. 26, No. 3, 225–47.

Kosonen, Pekka (1987) *Hyvinvointivaltion haasteet ja pohjoismaiset mallit* (Challenges for the Welfare State and the Nordic Models) (Tampere: Vastapaino).

Lundberg, Urban (2003) *Juvelen i kronan. Socialdemokraterna och den almänna pensionen* (Jewels in the Crown: Social Democrats and the General Pension) (Stockholm: Hjalmarson & Högberg).

Mackie, Gerry (2001) 'Patterns of social trust in Western Europe and their genesis.' In Karen S. Cook (ed.), *Trust in Society* (New York: Russell Sage Foundation).

Maddison, Angus (1982) *Phases of Capitalist Development* (Cambridge: Cambridge University Press).

Mannio, Niilo (1967) *Sosiaalipolitiikon kokemuksia 50 itsenäisyysvuoden ajalta* (Experiences of a Social Politician During 50 Years of Independence) (Porvoo: WSOY).

Mkandawire, Thandika (2001) *Social Policy in a Development Context*. Programme on Social Policy and Development, Paper No. 7 (Geneva: UNRISD).

Niemelä, Heikki (1994) *Suomen kokonaiseläkejärjestelmän muotoutuminen* (Constructing the Pension System in Finland) (Helsinki: KELA).

Olson, Mancur (1982) *The Rise and Decline of Nations* (New Haven, CT: Yale University Press).

—— (1965) *The Logic of Collective Action: Public Goods and the Theory of Groups* (Cambridge, MA: Harvard University Press).

Orloff, Ann Shola and Theda Skocpol (1984) 'Why not equal protection? Explaining the politics of public spending in Britain, 1900–1911, and the United States, 1880s–1920', *American Sociological Review*, Vol. 49, No. 6, 726–50.

Pesonen, Pertti and Olavi Riihinen (2002) *Dynamic Finland: The Political System and the Welfare State* (Helsinki: Finnish Literature Society).

Putnam, Robert (2000) *Bowling Alone: The Collapse and Revival of American Community* (New York: Simon and Schuster).
—— (1993) *Making Democracy Work* (Princeton, NJ: Princeton University Press).
Rothstein, Bo (2003) 'Social capital, economic growth and quality of government', *New Political Economy*, Vol. 8, No. 1, 49–71.
—— (1998) *Just Institutions Matter: The Moral and Political Logic of the Universal Welfare State* (Cambridge: Cambridge University Press).
—— (1989) 'Marxism, institutional analysis, and working class power: The Swedish case', *Politics and Society*, Vol. 18, No. 3, 317–45.
Salminen, Kari (2003) *Pension Schemes in the Making: A Comparative Study of the Scandinavian Countries* (Helsinki: ETK).
—— (1987) *Yhteiskunnan rakenne, politiikka ja eläketurva* (Social Structure, Politics and Pension Security) (Helsinki: ETK).
Schludi, Martin (2001) *The Politics of Pensions in European Social Insurance Countries*, Max-Planck-Institut für Gesellschaftforchung, MPIfG Discussion Paper 01/11 (Cologne: MPIfG).
Skocpol, Theda (1992) *Protecting Soldiers and Mothers: The Political Origins of Social Policy in the United States* (Cambridge, MA: Harvard University Press).
UNDP (United Nations Development Programme) (2002) *Human Development Report 2002* (New York: Oxford University Press).
Vartiainen, Juhana (1995) 'The state and structural change: What can be learnt from the successful late industrializers?' In H.-J. Chang and R. Rowthorn (eds.), *The Role of the State in Economic Change* (Oxford: Clarendon Press).

11
Provident and Pension Funds and Economic Development in Selected Asian Countries

Mukul G. Asher[1]

Introduction

It is generally accepted that globalization has made social security arrangements essential for at least three reasons. First, for cushioning the burden of restructuring; secondly, for increasing the legitimacy of reforms; and thirdly, for enabling risk taking by individuals and firms by providing a floor-level income in case the rewards from risk taking do not materialize.

There has been considerable debate and experience with social security reform but no single idea, system or model has emerged even among Asian countries. There has, however, been appreciation that from a practical policy point of view, a multi-tier framework is better able to address various social security risks than reliance on a single tier (Holzmann and Hinz 2005).

This chapter analyses the role provident and pension funds could play in this phase of globalization in economic and social development for four middle-income Asian countries: Indonesia, Malaysia, Sri Lanka and Thailand. While Malaysia and Sri Lanka make extensive use of provident funds, the other two countries use a mixture of social insurance principles and mandatory savings to finance retirement.

A provident fund (PF) is a form of retirement savings. PFs are defined-contribution schemes in which individuals bear the investment risk, but allocations are determined by authorities. On retirement or under predetermined circumstances, members may be able to receive their contributions and interest accrued part in cash and part as an annuity. Most PFs require equal contributions from both the employer and employee.

This chapter is organized as follows. The next section provides an overview of the macroeconomic, demographic, human development, and competitiveness indicators of the four countries. This is followed by a brief summary of the provident and pension fund systems of the four countries. There then follows a discussion of the three channels through which provident and pension funds may impact upon a country's economic and social development. The final section provides the concluding observations.

The primary objective of provident and pension funds should be to permit smoothing of consumption over a lifetime, ensuring that retirement benefits last until death, preserve real income, and are sufficient to ensure that there is absence of high correlation between poverty and old age.

To the extent success is achieved in pursuing the primary objectives indicated above, there will be a positive impact on welfare of the elderly. Since the elderly will form an increasing proportion of the population (Table 11.2), provident and pension funds will be beneficial for society as a whole. Well-run and sustainable provident and pension systems also provide confidence in the future to the working population.

The first broad channel through which the contribution of provident and pension funds to economic and social development can be enhanced is through their competent management and broad access. Indeed, access issues are quite critical in ensuring that the vast majority of the population benefits from a measure of retirement income security.

The second broad channel involves the impact of provident and pension fund on the trend rate of economic growth. A sustained high rate of economic growth has the potential to provide economic security to both the young and the old in the long term (Barr 2006). The provident and pension funds can contribute to economic growth by having a positive impact on the level and composition of savings, and from efficient intermediation of savings into productive investment, including infrastructure.

The third channel involves using provident and pension funds to facilitate investments of the insured in the social sector like housing, health care and education. It should, however, be noted that there are opportunity costs of using provident and pension funds for these purposes which should be taken into account.

Social policy literature has paid considerable attention to public policies designed to provide opportunities to individuals to accumulate assets through savings and/or endowments instead of income or consumption transfers (Sherraden 2001). Experiments with asset-based social policies have been undertaken in North America, the United Kingdom (UK) and Europe. Thus, the Child Trust Fund (CTF) in the United Kingdom is a long-term savings and investment account in which the initial payment is made by the state, and then additions to the account are tax-advantaged. No withdrawals from the account are permitted until the child is 18 years old.

In the United States and Canada, under the sponsorship of SEDI (Social and Enterprise Development Innovations), there are experiments to 'top up' the savings of poor families (usually in the form of a generous match of $1^2 or $2 for every dollar saved) for particular uses – such as education and training, or home repair and purchase (Jackson 2004).

These policies have been targeted primarily at low-income welfare recipients and the working poor, and therefore towards poverty reduction. The main rationale has been that asset accumulation by the poor may provide them with a more sustainable basis for generating income, and may lead to a better balance between entitlements (or rights) and responsibilities (or duties) (Jackson 2004).

Macroeconomic, demographic and labour market trends

This section provides an overview of selected macroeconomic, demographic, and labour market trends in the sample countries. These are essential to appreciate the country context, the magnitude, and the nature of the old-age financing challenge facing the sample countries.

On the basis of macroeconomic indicators presented in Table 11.1, the following observations may be made.

(i)   The sample countries are at varying stages of development, as indicated by their per capita income status. Malaysia is a high middle-income country, while the others are middle-income countries.

(ii) The shares of the four sample countries in world GDP range from 0.05 to 0.8 per cent, in current dollar terms.

(iii) The GDP growth has been impressive in the sample countries, and has averaged around 5 per cent during the period 2000–06, above the world average of about 3 per cent. In Malaysia and Thailand, much of the growth has been due to an impressive growth in the services sector.

(iv) The share of GDP by sectors varies. The share of industry in GDP is especially high in Indonesia, Malaysia, and Thailand, reflecting their emphasis on manufacturing exports. The share of services in GDP is more than half in Sri Lanka, which is relatively high at its stage of economic development. Sri Lanka is attempting to increase the share of industry in GDP, while the others are attempting to become more internationally competitive in knowledge-intensive services.

(v)   The agricultural share of GDP ranges from a low of 8 per cent in Malaysia to 16 per cent in Sri Lanka. As the share of employment in agriculture is much higher, a shift in population from agriculture to other sectors is needed to raise per capita incomes generally as well as in agriculture.

(vi) Indonesia and Sri Lanka experienced high average annual inflation of 9.5 per cent and 8.8 per cent, respectively, during the 2000–06 period. Inflation rates in Malaysia and Thailand were moderate.

There are three demographic trends which are evident globally. First, fertility rates are dropping nearly everywhere. Second, life expectancy is rising in many – although not all – parts of the world. Third, developed countries are well advanced with respect to the above two trends – as reflected in their declining share in world population. The non-developed countries are further behind, though the variation among them is large. The combined impact of these trends has led to rapid ageing of the world's population.

These above trends are also reflected in the demographic data of the sample countries (Table 11.2). The following observations may be made from the data.

Table 11.1 Macroeconomic indicators of selected Asian countries, 2006

Countries	GDP (US$ bn.)	GDP growth 2000–06 (%)	Population (million)	Per capita GDP, PPP (current intl. $)	PPP GNI (current intl. $, bn)	Agriculture (% of GDP)	Industry (% of GDP)	Services (% of GDP)	Inflation (%) 2000–06
World	48,244.9	3.1	6,517.8	10,252	66,596	NA	NA	NA	4.6
Indonesia	364.5	4.9	223.0	4,130	881	13	47	40	9.5
Malaysia	148.9	5.3	25.8	11,674	291	8	49	43	2.0
Sri Lanka	26.9	4.8	19.8	5,081	99	16	27	57	8.8
Thailand	206.2	5.0	64.7	9,330	592	10	45	45	2.5

Source: Calculations based on data from World Bank (2007) and ADB (2007).

Table 11.2 Demographic indicators in selected Asian countries

Country	Total population median variant (millions)		Average annual rate of change of population		Total fertility rate		Median age		Life expectancy at birth		Percentage of total population aged 60 and above		Population aged 60 and above (millions)	
	2005	2050	2005	2050	2005	2050	2005	2050	2005	2050	2006	2050	2006	2050
World	6464.8	9075.9	1.21	0.3	2.6	2.0	28.1	37.8	65.4	75.1	11	22	687.9	1968.1
Indonesia	223.0	285.0	1.30	0.8	2.2	1.8	26.5	40.5	69.6	76.9	8	24	19.0	67.3
Malaysia	25.2	43.1	1.80	1.4	2.6	1.8	24.7	39.3	72.2	79.9	7	22	1.8	8.4
Sri Lanka	20.7	23.5	0.77	-0.2	1.9	1.8	29.6	43.5	75.1	80.5	11	29	2.2	6.9
Thailand	64.0	75.0	0.70	0.2	1.8	1.8	30.5	42.5	72.0	79.1	11	28	8.9	20.7

Source: Calculations based on data from UNDESA (2005).

(i) The total fertility rate (TFR) of Sri Lanka and Thailand is already below the replacement rate, which, unless it is reversed, will lead to a decline in population. The TFR in Indonesia is only slightly above the replacement rate, suggesting success in the family planning programmes. Malaysia has a TFR which is moderately higher than the replacement rate.

(ii) The median age in the sample countries is expected to rise rapidly, particularly in Sri Lanka, Thailand and Indonesia; and will be higher in all sample countries then the world average by 2050.

(iii) Among the sample countries, Sri Lanka exhibits the highest life expectancy at birth, followed by Malaysia and Thailand. For retirement financing purposes, it is the life expectancy at age 60 which is relevant as it determines the number of years for which financing needs will occur. The difference between life expectancy at age 60 in the sample countries and the OECD countries is much narrower than life expectancy at birth.

(iv) By 2050, the share of elderly will rise dramatically in the sample countries, by 11 to 18 percentage points from the current levels. The challenge will be not just the share of elderly but the pace of ageing. The rapid pace implies less time for the countries to put appropriate social security systems in place. For countries with large populations, such as Indonesia, the absolute numbers of elderly will be huge. Thus, in Indonesia the elderly will increase from 19 million to 67 million.

Table 11.3 provides the human development and competitiveness rankings of the sample countries. Malaysia ranks among high human development countries, while other sample countries are classified under medium human development (UNDP 2007). Indonesia and Sri Lanka have higher HDI rank than the GDP per capita (purchasing power parity/PPP US$), indicated by a positive value in column 4, while the opposite is true for Malaysia and Thailand.

Malaysia, with a ranking of 21 out of 131 countries (in both Global Competitiveness Index and Business Competitiveness Index), has the best ranking of the four countries under analysis (Table 11.3). The importance of these rankings is far higher for the externally dependent economies of Malaysia and Thailand. Sri Lanka needs to examine how it can improve its rankings.

On the basis of data on the labour market indicators provided in Table 11.4, the following observations are made.

(i) Except for Thailand, the total labour force to population ratio is relatively low in the sample countries. This is largely explained by the substantially lower level of female labour force participation in these countries.

(ii) The definition of informal sector is not uniform across sample countries. It is usually estimated as a residual – that is, whatever is not included in the formal sector. The term 'formal sector' is sometimes used interchangeably with the organized sector, that is, the sector to which formal labour laws apply. The estimates of the informal sector therefore vary widely among different sources.

Table 11.3   Human development and competitiveness rankings of selected Asian countries

Country	Human Development Index rank (2005)	Human Development Index value (trends)		GDP per capita (PPP US$) rank minus HDI rank (2005)	Global Competitiveness Index (GCI) (2007–08)	Business Competitiveness Index (2007–08)
		(2000)	(2005)			
Indonesia	107	0.692	0.728	6	54	36
Malaysia	63	0.790	0.811	−6	21	21
Sri Lanka	99	0.731	0.743	7	70	52
Thailand	78	0.761	0.781	−13	28	37

Source: UNDP (2007).

Table 11.4   Selected labour force indicators of sample countries, latest estimates

	Indonesia	Malaysia	Sri Lanka	Thailand
Labour Force[a] (million)	108.2 (44.1)	9.9 (40.4)	7.6 (40.2)	34.6 (54.5)
Male	NA	6.0	5.1	19.0
Female	NA	3.9	2.5	15.6
Share of the Informal Sector (%)	60.0	31.1	44.6	59.0
Labour Force Participation Rate (LFPR)[b] *(%)*	68.6	65.5	50.7	73.5
Male	NA	85.6	68.0	81.5
Female	NA	45.4	35.0	35.6

Notes: The definition for the informal sector is country-specific.
[a] The figures in brackets represent labour force as a percentage of total population.
[b] LFPR is defined as proportion of the total number of persons in the labour force to the total population 15 years old and over.
Source: Figures compiled from various official sources and are the latest available. Figures for Indonesia are obtained from ILO (2003) and *CIA World Factbook 2007*.

Given the above caveat, the size of the informal sector in the sample countries ranges from a low of 31 per cent of the labour force in Malaysia, to a high of around 60 per cent in Indonesia and Thailand. In Sri Lanka the informal sector is slightly above two-fifths.

A large informal sector increases the complexity and the magnitude of the tasks of providing retirement income security. This is because most social security arrangements are designed with the implicit or explicit assumption of a formal employer and employee relationship. Moreover, the income and education levels in the informal sector vary widely and therefore group-specific pension products and marketing strategies are essential.

An overview of provident and pension funds in the sample countries

Indonesia

Since independence in 1945, Indonesia has made significant progress in terms of economic and human development (Arifianto 2006). Indonesia has a complex set of social security arrangements, but the level of coverage remains low, and the professionalism with which provident and pension funds are managed could be greatly improved. Traditionally, the extended family has been relied upon for old-age support.

The private sector workers in Indonesia are covered under Jamsostek programmes which provide life insurance, work accident protection, provident fund, and health maintenance plans. Firms with ten or more employees are covered. Jamsostek is a state monopoly. Only about 20 per cent of the workers are covered by Jamsostek schemes (Arifianto 2006). However, in 2007, of the 23.1 million registered with the Jamsostek, only about a third were actual contributors. The compliance by eligible employers is also low at around 25 per cent.

The previous Indonesian Social Security law (law No. 3/1992) stipulated that except for provident fund contributions of 5.7 per cent of wages, which are shared by employer (3.7 per cent) and employee (2.0 per cent), premiums for other programmes are paid only by the employer. The total contribution varies between 9.24 and 13.74 per cent, of which workers pay only 2 per cent.

The provident fund system under Jamsostek is a defined contribution system paying a lump sum at retirement. In practice, the provident fund is not portable[3] as accumulated balances can be withdrawn at the termination of employment, under some conditions. The Jamsostek fund is invested mostly in banks, 86 per cent in 1999; and the rate of return has been below the inflation rate for many years. In 1999, the total assets of Jamsostek were only 0.9 per cent of GDP, while those of all provident and pension funds were around 4 per cent of GDP (Asher 2002). The assets of employers' funds have been the largest among the social security institutions, at around 2.5 per cent of GDP. The total pension assets are only around 4.5 per cent of GDP, of which Jamsostek accounts for about a quarter. For a mandatory national provident fund, this is quite low, suggesting severe design and implementation challenges.

Any employer can establish a private pension plan. In 2005 these plans had a membership of no more than two million persons. The plans for the employees of financial institutions, which have relatively high per member balances, are supervised by the Ministry of Finance.

The civil servants are covered under the Perseon Terbatas Taspen (PT Taspen), another state monopoly. Civil servants receive defined benefit pensions for life and death benefits paid to survivors. The retirement age is 56 years, quite low when compared to life expectancy. The contribution rate for employees is 4.75 per cent of the basic salary. This covers little less than a quarter of the total benefits, with the rest provided from the budget. The contributions of those who leave before retirement are not returned, reducing the levels of labour mobility. The pensions of civil servants are indexed to salary increases for active civil servants.

The military has a separate defined-benefit scheme, administered by Asabri (Asuransi Angkatan Bersenjata Republik Indonesia), the pension scheme for the armed forces. Its provisions are similar to those for PT Taspen.

Thus, in Indonesia, the civil servants and the armed forces are protected against longevity and inflation risks, but private sector employees are not. Lack of professionalism in performing functions by Jamsostek has prevented members from benefiting fully from the scheme. This and the inherent limitations of the provident fund scheme have meant a very low replacement rate.

On 28 September 2004, the Indonesian House of Representatives (Dewan Perwakilan Rakyat, or DPR) passed the law on the National Social Security System (Undang-Undang Sistem Jaminan Sosial Nasional, or SJSN). The law became a public law (Law No. 40/2004) on 19 October 2004 and will replace the current system based on the provident fund system of Jamostek, Taspen and Asabri with a compulsory social security system that would cover both formal and informal sector. All four state institutions will be involved in administering the law.

In addition, the SJSN law establishes the Social Security Council which will have a Secretariat. The powers of the council have been left undefined. It is also not clear to what extent the council will be permitted to be autonomous, and be able to pursue overall development of the social security sector in Indonesia. It is not clear to what extent the council has regulatory powers or autonomy. The SJSN Law aims to apply the social insurance principle on a comprehensive basis. It covers health insurance, work injuries, old age (provident fund), pensions and death benefits. The law further stipulates that the government will develop social assistance programmes. The mandatory savings component, and building up of pension reserves could reach between 10 and 20 per cent of GDP over time. The law aims to create a social fund for the informal sector for pensions and health insurance. Estimating the financial (and fiscal) implications of the device to reach the informal sector workers would be especially challenging.

The wage indexing envisaged in the law will enable workers to share in Indonesia's future economic growth. It may be worth estimating the projected pension costs if the price rather than wage indexing is used. The price indexation is increasingly more of a norm (for example, in the United Kingdom and the Philippines) than is wage indexation.

There are, however, concerns regarding a serious mismatch between the objectives of the law, on one the hand, and financial, institutional, organizational and regulatory capacities to implement the law, on the other. The impact of this law on employment growth also needs to be considered as any slowdown in job creation will adversely impact the flow of contributions.

Arifianto (2006) has estimated that a total contribution rate of between 22.54 and 23.75 per cent of wages will be required in order to achieve the objectives of the new law, but the law has identified contribution rates equivalent to 6.24–7.75 per cent of wages. It is not clear where the balance is likely to be obtained.

With the technical assistance of the Asian Development Bank (ADB), Indonesia has begun rigorous studies designed to estimate the financial and fiscal costs of the different schemes included in the SJSN law. These simulations will involve long time periods, as the pension and health care systems should be viable for at least 50 to 60 years. These studies are still at a preliminary stage, and the results have not yet been published. It is however expected that by the end of 2008, there will be progress in implementing the SJSN law.

In addition to the studies, which will help improve design parameters, the effective implementation of the law will require fixing the current system (particularly the low level of administrative and compliance efficiency, better interagency coordination, and more adequate morbidity and mortality database).

Malaysia

Malaysia essentially relies on a single mandatory savings pillar for retirement financing for private sector employees. The key institution is the Employees Provident Fund (EPF). The contribution rate is 23 per cent of wages with no ceiling (12 per cent by the employer and 11 per cent by the employees).[4] The contributions are channelled into three accounts. Account I is for retirement and can only be withdrawn when a member reaches 55 years of age. Savings in Account II can be used in housing, tertiary education, pre-retirement investments and withdrawal at age 50. Account III is for withdrawal for health expenditure. It is thus a medical savings account. Of the total contributions, 60 per cent are credited to Account I, 30 per cent to Account II, and 10 per cent to Account III.

In 2006, total contributions to the EPF were RM26.2 billion ($8.1 billion),[5] equivalent to 5.4 per cent of GDP. Pre-retirement withdrawals were RM15.05 billion, 57.5 per cent of contributions. In recent years, pre-retirement withdrawals to contributions ratio has averaged about 40 per cent.

Total membership at end-2006 was 11.4 million, of which 5.3 million (46.5 per cent) were actual contributors. The contributors to the labour force ratio have hovered around 50 per cent. As at end-2006, the accumulated balances with the EPF were $91.3 billion, equivalent to 51.5 per cent of GDP.

Under the current statutory provisions, nearly all of the EPF funds must be invested domestically. Figure 11.1 provides allocation of EPF funds among alternative asset classes for the period 1991–2006. There is a noticeable shift in asset allocation away from Malaysian government securities and from money market funds, towards debentures and loans and equities. This author's estimates suggest that the historical rates of return have been moderately high, averaging 3.36 per cent per year in real terms for the 1961–2006 period; and 3.44 per cent per year during the 1990–2006 period.

There are, however, indications that since 2005, the EPF has been investing in additional asset classes such as private equity and real estate. It also appears to have shed its inhibition relating to not becoming involved in the management of the companies and assets it owns.[6] Some analysts have suggested that the higher risk strategy may be linked to the new compensation structures for the EPF management. But this hypothesis cannot be confirmed by the empirical evidence.

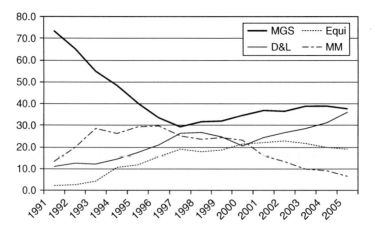

Figure 11.1   Malaysia: investment allocation of EPF, 1991–2005
Note: MGS – Malaysian Government Securities; D & L – Debentures and Loans; Equi – Equities;
MM – Money Market.
Source: Calculated from the Annual Reports of the Employees Provident Fund (EPF).

In contrast to the defined contribution scheme of the EPF, where longevity and inflation risks are borne by the individuals, the civil service pensions are of defined benefit type based on a formula incorporating years of service, salary level and other factors. There is however no automatic indexation. All civil servants are covered, but they do not have to contribute toward their pensions.

Malaysia has used past budget surpluses to set up a pension trust fund. This arrangement has meant secure funding for future pension liabilities, but the essential nature of the pensions being paid out of current revenue remains unaltered. The operations of the pension trust funds are not transparent. Therefore, its investment policies and performance are not publicly available. Malaysia has been considering requiring civil servants to contribute to their pensions, but no decisions have been announced as of early 2008.

The workman compensation, sickness, disability payments, invalidity and survivors' pension, and other such schemes are organized along social insurance principles in Malaysia. A separate organization, the Social Security Organization (SOCSO), set up in 1971, administers these schemes. Its membership is similar to that of the EPF, but the wage base and the contribution rates are much lower. Its total assets are around RM15 billion ($4.3 billion). Its balances are also invested domestically in a diversified portfolio, including equities and properties.

To summarize, Malaysia's pension system, established more than half a century ago, has remained essentially unchanged since then. Its main dilemma is that it is unable to make a transition from a national provident fund system, with no social risk pooling for longevity and inflation risks, to a system more commensurate with its high middle-income country status. For the formal sector workers, the adequacy of pensions and risk management will continue to be major issues.

Nearly 30 per cent of the domestic labour force (excluding foreign workers) are not members of any formal provident or pension fund scheme. This suggests a need for large well-funded social pension programmes aimed at mitigating old-age poverty. But Malaysia has not shown the requisite political commitment to institute such a programme. Without it, Malaysia will find it difficult to sustain the high degrees of social cohesion and support for globalization which is required by its externally dependent economy.

Sri Lanka

In Sri Lanka, the private sector employees rely primarily on mandatory savings defined-contribution schemes, while the public sector employees are covered by a non-contributory[7] defined-benefit 'pay-as-you-go' (PAYG) pension system. There is thus a different philosophy applied to private and public sectors.

For the private sector employees, the EPF, established in 1958, is the most important organization in terms of membership and asset size. Firms with one or more employees are covered by the EPF. Responsibilities for the EPF are divided between the Monetary Board of the Central Bank, which manages investments and the Department of Labour which undertakes non-investment functions. Somewhat unusually, the EPF income is subject to income tax. In 2006, the EPF was the largest taxpayer in the country, contributing Rs.2.8 billion ($26 million),[8] equivalent to 6 per cent of its total income.[9]

The total contribution is 20 per cent of total earnings of the employee (12 per cent from the employer, and 8 per cent from the employee) with no earnings ceiling. There are preretirement withdrawals, particularly for housing. In 2006, contributions were Rs.34.9 billion ($325 million), equivalent to 1.25 per cent of GDP. The total withdrawals, including for housing in 2006, were Rs.17.3 billion ($161 million), 49.5 per cent of total contributions. This ratio has been increasing since 1991 when it was 30 per cent.

The EPF members have been provided with a housing loan facility since 1988. In recent years between 15,000 and 20,000 members have been permitted to borrow up to a maximum of 75 per cent of their balances for housing from approved lenders. As at end-2006, however, 41 per cent of the members permitted to obtain housing loans had defaulted. As the defaulting members are penalized by the EPF, and are not permitted access to other subsidized housing loans, their retirement income security is adversely significantly affected.

In 2006, the total gross membership of the EPF was 10.8 million,[10] of which only 2 million (18.5 per cent) were active contributors. In 2006, active contributors formed 26 per cent of the total labour force. In 2004, the total number of employers registered with the EPF was 150,000 of which only about a third were actively contributing.

The above strongly indicates a low level of efficiency in recordkeeping. Three-quarters of the active contributors had balances below Rs.100,000 ($930). The total members' balances in 2006 were Rs.432.6 billion ($4 billion), equivalent to 15.4 per cent of GDP. The average balance per member was only Rs.382,790 ($356), equivalent to about 40 per cent of per capita income. This suggests that the average balance at the time of retirement will be quite low and inadequate to finance the complete retirement period.

The balances are wholly invested domestically. In 2005, 97 per cent of the balances were in Treasury bonds, a long-term marketable investment instrument (83 per cent), and in Government Rupee Securities, a long-term off-market instrument (14 per cent). The exposure to domestic equities is therefore small (Rs.2.3 billion), but gross realized return on this asset class was 40 per cent in 2004, and 39 per cent in 2005.

The returns credited to EPF members have been quite low. During the 1981 to 2006 period, the average annual real effective rate of return was only 1.15 per cent. This however reflects significant negative returns in the 1980s. The five-year moving average of real returns has been positive since 1995. The real value of the EPF balances remains vulnerable to even a one-time increase in the cost of living, as well as to inflation.

The Employees' Trust Fund (ETF)

The ETF, set up in 1981, is administered by the ETF Board and supervised by the Ministry of Labour. The original objective of the ETF was to promote employee ownership of equities, but it currently does not serve this purpose, duplicating the functions of the EPF.

The contribution rate is 3 per cent of the gross earnings, payable by the employer. Members can withdraw balances when they change jobs. This adds to administration costs, and results in multiple accounts. In May 2006, its total investments were Rs.64 billion ($595 million), equivalent to 2.3 per cent of GDP. The annual real returns on balances have been low, averaging only 0.30 per cent for the 1982–99 period. Nearly four-fifths of its invested balances are invested in government securities. More recent data are not available.

Approved Private Provident Funds (APPFs)

Under the EPF Act, the Commissioner of Labour has the power to approve private funds for specific firms. As these funds are an alternative to EPF, vesting regulatory powers under the agency which administers the EPF is not a good governance practice. The Labour Department also does not have the capacity to effectively supervise the APPFs.

The APPFs cannot have a lower rate of contribution than the EPF. They are more flexible than the EPF in investments. But like the EPF, the balances are withdrawn in a lump sum at retirement, exposing members to longevity and inflation risks. There is no centralized agency which collects data on APPFs. This gap must be filled.

Public Service Pension Schemes (PSPS)

The PSPS is an unfunded, non-contributory defined-benefit scheme financed from the government budget. The retirement age is 55 years. The employees are covered for survivor and disability benefits, but unlike pensions, these are contributory.

According to the 1996 pension formula, the maximum pension payable after 30 years of service is equal to 85–90 per cent of the last drawn salary. In addition, a lump sum of two years of the last drawn salary is payable upon retirement. There is no automatic inflation indexing for pensions, but ad hoc adjustments are made.

As these have lagged behind inflation and rising cost of living, real replacement rates are lower than the nominal rates (Karunarathne and Goswami 2002).

The fiscal impact of the PSPS is large. In 2000, pension expenditure was Rs.20.4 billion (equivalent to 1.62 per cent of the GDP) for 371,722 pensioners, suggesting an average annual pension of Rs.54,789 per member, equivalent to 80 per cent of per capita income.

Public Sector Provident Fund (PSPF)

The PSPF, established in 1942, is a mandatory defined contribution (DC) scheme for the non-pensionable government employees. The contribution rate is 12 per cent by the government and 8 per cent by the employee, for a total of 20 per cent. The accumulated balances are paid as a lump sum at retirement. This is fairly minor scheme in terms of membership (in 1999, only 59,000 persons were contributors). The PSPF invests only in government securities.

Sri Lanka faces the challenges of undertaking core functions, including record-keeping, and investment management in a more professional manner. It also needs to redesign its non-contributory civil service pension schemes. The regulatory and supervisory functions also need to be streamlined. The rationale for EPF and ETF as two separate organizations is quite weak. Attempts to amalgamate them have not been successful, primarily due to organizational and bureaucratic resistance. Relatively low coverage has meant that a large number of the workforce does not have access to provident and pension funds.

Thailand

Thailand has accepted the principle of social risk pooling for both public and private sector employees. It has also made some progress towards developing a multi-tier social security system. This is in contrast with Malaysia, the neighbouring high-middle-income country, which has consciously decided not to incorporate social risk pooling in its social security system. It is noteworthy that Thailand introduced social insurance in the Old Age Pension (OAP) scheme in 1998, in the midst of the East Asian financial crisis.

An overview of the main provident and pension fund schemes is provided below.

The Social Security Office (SSO) is responsible for administering social insurance programmes for private sector employees. These comprise:

- Short-term programmes. This includes benefits for sickness, disability and death.
- Long-term programmes. This includes the OAP pension programme and child-care allowances.
- Unemployment. Benefits are paid for a transition period for those who are looking for new employment.
- Workers' compensation. This programme pays benefits for death, illness and injuries incurred on the job. Employers pay the full cost of this programme.

Table 11.5 shows the current payroll tax burden imposed on Thailand's formal sector workers and their employers. The total burden is 5 per cent each on the

Table 11.5   Thailand: Contribution rates for the SSO schemes (per cent)

	Employer	Employee	Government	Total
SSO short-term benefit schemes	1.50	1.50	1.50	4.50
Old-age pension	3.00	3.00	0.00	6.00
Childcare allowances	0.00	0.00	1.00	1.00
Unemployment	0.50	0.50	0.25	1.25
Total	5.00	5.00	2.75	12.75

Note: Employers also pay an additional 0.2 per cent to 1 per cent to the workers' compensation fund.
Source: Social Security Office, Thailand. Website: www.sso.go.th.

employer and the employee, and 2.75 per cent for the government, for a total of 12.75 per cent.

The OAP has a total contribution rate of 6 per cent – 3 per cent each from the employer and the employee. The wage ceiling for contributions at 15,000 Baht[11] has remained unchanged since OAP became operational in 1999. Employers with one or more employees are required to participate in the system. The pension eligibility conditions require a minimum of 180 months of contributions. The retirement age is 55. Given Thailand's life expectancy, this age is quite low and must be raised for sustainability. There are no disability or survivor benefits.

A novel feature of the OAP is that the first pensions will begin only in 2014 since work history prior to 1999 is not recognized. This implies gradual phase-in. This feature is due to the OAP being introduced at the time of the 1997 economic crisis in East Asia, which severely impacted Thailand.

Currently while contributions are being received by the SSO, no pension benefits are being paid. There is therefore an accumulation of pension reserves. At the end of 2003, the OAP account of the SSO fund had estimated reserves of about 100 billion Baht. It is projected that this will continue to grow until around 2030, with peak accumulation of about 16 per cent of GDP. This assumes that the reserves are invested according to modern investment management practices, and that fiduciary responsibilities are not diluted.

The current contribution rate of 6 per cent is likely to be adequate until around 2030, but the current system will not be financially sustainable by around 2040. This suggests that within 25 years of first pension payments, the current system will be unsustainable. It therefore requires parametric reforms, such as increasing the contribution rate, and extending the retirement age. The replacement rate of the current system is likely to be low. In 2014, when the first pension starts, a person with a 30-year labour market participation can expect replacement rate in the teens, far lower than the two-thirds to three-quarters usually recommended. Even when a full 30-year work history is reflected in the OAP benefits, the replacement rate is unlikely to exceed 30 per cent.

The government of Thailand sponsors many pension programmes in addition to OAP. These pension programmes are outside of SSO and are controlled by the

Ministry of Finance and the Securities and Exchange Commission (SEC) rather than the Ministry of Labour. These systems are briefly summarized below.

Defined-benefit pension scheme for government workers

The benefits under this scheme are paid according to the Government Pension Act of 1951. The pension benefits under this scheme are paid directly from the state budget for retired government officials. The employees do not need to make any contribution. This system is not funded. Benefits are paid when due. There is provision for a lump-sum gratuity benefit under certain circumstances. The pension benefit is equal to the last drawn salary times 2 per cent accrual for every year of service. The government has set aside a reserve account to partly meet future pension liabilities (Kanjanaphoomin 2005). The investment policies and performance of the reserve fund are not known publicly.

Government Pension Fund (GPF)

The GPF covers government officials. This is a mandatory accumulation system funded by a 6 per cent contribution (3 per cent each from workers and employers).

Funds can be drawn from the GPF pool only in one lump sum and upon the termination of membership, which occurs upon retirement at the age of 60, leaving the government services or death. There is therefore an absence of portability. Lump-sum withdrawal at retirement is defensible in this case as the members will be drawing defined benefit pensions as government officials.

Each GPF member is entitled to an annual personal income tax exemption on the contributions paid to the GPF fund for the contribution amount not exceeding Baht 300,000. GPF membership in 2005 was more than one million, and the total assets were 317 billion Baht ($9.3 billion), equivalent to 5.3 per cent of GDP. Figure 11.2 provides asset allocation of GPF as at December 2005. The investment portfolio is well diversified among asset classes, and nearly one-tenth of the funds are invested internationally. Slightly more than two-thirds are in Thai fixed income and 14 per cent in Thai equities.[12]

The GPF is supervised by the Ministry of Finance. Thailand's GPF is becoming more sophisticated in diversifying investment risk, both domestically and abroad. Nevertheless, greater efforts are needed to ensure that it is not used for short-term political objectives of the government in power. As the assets of the GPF grow, the political risk (the risk that its assets may be used for political objectives rather than maximize investment returns to members consistent with its fiduciary responsibilities) may also grow. With the exception of 2004, the real rate of return earned by the GPF was positive between 2001 and 2005 (Figure 11.3). The GPF is making efforts to become a professional fund manager, with globally diversified portfolio.

Government Permanent Employees Provident Fund (GPEF)

This plan covers government employees who are not officials, and is a voluntary accumulation system with a 6 per cent contribution rate (3 per cent each from workers and employers).

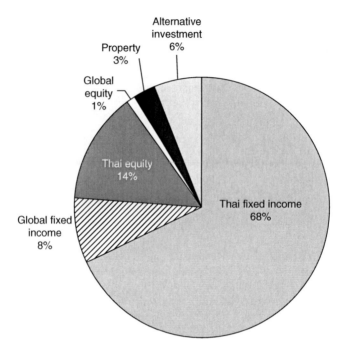

Figure 11.2   Thailand: asset allocation of GPF
Source: GPF Website, http://www.gpf.or.th.

State-Owned Enterprise Provident Funds (SOE Funds)

SOEs have been 'strongly encouraged' by the government to establish voluntary provident funds. Most have already done so. Features vary from plan to plan.

Employer Sponsored Provident Funds (PVD Funds)

These are voluntary defined contribution plans (mandatory for companies listed on the Thai stock exchange) sponsored by about 7,000 employers. Contribution rates vary, and employer contributions must be equal to or greater than employee contributions.

Retirement Mutual Funds (RMF)

This is an individual savings programme to allow workers to accumulate additional money for retirement. Each of these programmes serves different constituencies and they are not coordinated with each other. In fact, workers moving from one type of programme to another often face adverse tax consequences for retirement savings accumulated prior to changing employment. In addition, none of these programmes covers Thailand's 24 million informal sector workers.

Thailand is contemplating introducing a national mandatory provident fund, as well as reforming its OAP, with the two combined expected to provide adequate retirement income security. Even then, it will require a large social assistant or

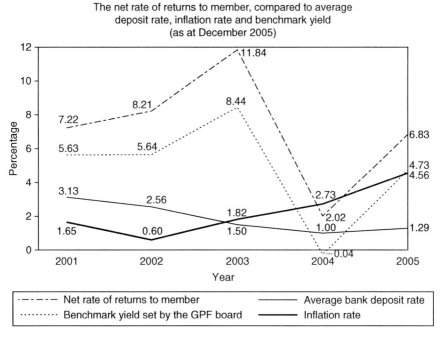

The net rate of returns to member, compared to average deposit rate, inflation rate and benchmark yield (as at December 2005)

Figure 11.3 Thailand: Rates of return from GPF, 2001–05
Source: GPF Website, http://www.gpf.or.th/.

social pension programme as the coverage of the formal system does not exceed one-third of the labour force.

The military coup in early 2007 and the continuing political uncertainties since then have stalled pension reform in Thailand. With increasing sophistication and growth of the provident and pensions fund sector there is a strong case to establish an independent pension regulator in Thailand with a view to ensuring internationally benchmarked professional practices and governance. The regulator would also be in a better position to help develop the provident and pensions sector as a whole in an integrated manner.

Channels impacting development

In the introduction, three channels through which provident and pension funds may impact economic and social development were identified. Each is discussed in turn.

Competent management

Competent management involves performing core functions of provident and pension funds well.[13] The discussion in the previous section strongly suggests that there is considerable scope for greater competency in performing the core functions (see endnote 10) in each of the sample countries. Thus, provident and pension fund organizations in Indonesia exhibit low levels of efficiency and high transaction costs in such record-keeping tasks as registering members, crediting contributions to appropriate individual accounts, ensuring portability to enable the labour mobility advantage of the national provident fund to be realized.

Based on Jamsostek's Annual Reports, the operating cost as a percentage of contributions for Jamsostek was 10 per cent in 2004, and 13 per cent in 2006. A similar calculation for Malaysia's Employee Provident Fund (EPF) suggests that the corresponding ratio was 1.7 per cent in 2004 as well as in 2006. For Sri Lanka's Employees' Provident Fund (EPF), the corresponding ratio was 1.5 per cent in 2005. There is therefore considerable scope for enhancing the administrative efficiency of the Jamsostek.

The laws and governing regulations, including provision for extensive pre-retirement withdrawals, have not been modernized. The organization and governance structures are rooted in the past, with inadequate investment in modern technology and in appropriate human resources. This is in spite of the fact that integration of these economies with the world economy has increased considerably, and the state–market mix has been undergoing reformulation in favour of a greater role of the market.

Key stakeholders in Indonesia and Sri Lanka currently view social schemes as essentially welfare schemes, requiring little or no analytical rigour or expertise in terms of their design, implementation, sustainability, or consistency with, and impact upon, the rest of the economy and society. The fact that social security results in foregone opportunity costs to spend on health, education, infrastructure and other areas is also not adequately reflected in the reform debates. As the coverage of provident and pension schemes ranges between a sixth and a quarter in these countries, the opportunity costs become of even greater importance.

Malaysia and Thailand have managed to perform well on non-investment-related core functions with a reasonable degree of effectiveness. Their challenge lies in investment management (discussed below) and in governance. Given the size of provident and pension fund assets in Malaysia (over 50 per cent of GDP), and in Thailand (20 per cent of GDP), good governance practices are particularly needed.

In all four countries, the absence of a pension regulator has had a particularly adverse impact on the reform of civil service pensions (Asher and Nandy 2006; Asher 2000). In Malaysia and Sri Lanka civil servants do not even contribute to their pensions, but their pension benefits are relatively generous. This results in a relatively small proportion of the labour force receiving a disproportionate share of society's income devoted to the elderly and providing an impetus to intra-elderly inequalities.

Coverage

The previous section has shown that, with the exception of Malaysia, the coverage offered by these formal social security systems does not exceed 25–30 per cent of the labour force. This suggests that in any employer–employee relationship-based systems, the level of formal sector employment acts as a constraint on coverage. Two implications emerge from this finding.

First, the formal sector employment needs to be increased through domestic reforms (for example, labour market reforms), and through increasing the employment elasticity with respect to GDP. Clear rules about who is covered are essential. Good management systems should be developed to ensure that the wages reported are consistent with actual wages paid to members. The formal sector coverage can also be expanded through improved administration and compliance. For this purpose, unique identification number for the members and strong information technology support are essential.

Secondly, the needs of the informal sector workers, which is substantial (Table 11.4), should be addressed. This, however, poses difficult challenges, particularly as such workers are found in both urban and rural areas, and the sector is very heterogeneous in terms of income levels, occupations, assets ownership, and so on. Therefore, it is more difficult to cover and has high administrative costs. So, evidence-based public policies to target particular types of persons for coverage, and designing specific schemes to reach them, are essential.

In most of the countries there are identifiable occupations which employ a large number of people. These may include fishermen from a particular area, small tobacco growers and handicraft workers concentrated in a small area. Specialized coverage schemes, including possible livelihood insurance, could be devised for such large, identifiable groups to sustain their incomes and to organize them in cooperative bodies. Micropensions represent another avenue through which increased coverage could take place.

The proportion of lifetime poor in the sample countries is high. Therefore, targeted social assistance[14] schemes should be an integral part of any strategy for increasing coverage. Its effectiveness will depend on fiscal reforms as budgetary expenditure will be the main constraining factor. The delivery mechanisms for government services will also need to be substantially improved, particularly in Indonesia.

The coverage of workers employed in foreign countries is also an important issue. Indonesia and Sri Lanka are major labour-exporting countries; Malaysia is a major importer of foreign labour; while Thailand imports as well as exports labour. A decentralized, multiple approach, which permits scalability and flexibility, will be better suited than the nationwide comprehensive social security systems to be implemented in Indonesia.

Addressing the social security needs of these workers therefore requires a regional agreement. The ASEAN Social Security Association (ASSA), formed in 1998, might be an appropriate forum to discuss the possibility of a regional agreement on minimum coverage standards and reciprocal arrangements for Southeast Asian countries.

Savings and investment

As indicated in the introduction, the provident and pension funds can contribute to economic growth through the level and composition of savings and efficient intermediation of savings into productive investments. Ideally, it is the net impact of provident and pension funds on the level of savings that is relevant. However this requires a full-fledged economic model of savings behaviour, which is not available for the sample countries. Mandatory savings are in part likely to be at the expense of voluntary savings. In the schemes where there are large pre-retirement withdrawals for consumption, the net impact on savings is likely to be much lower than that suggested by gross contributions plus investment income earnings.

Changes in total assets between the two periods are usually taken as an approximate measure of the gross savings impact of provident and pension funds. If this measure is adopted, in 2006 the contribution to gross savings as a proportion of GDP would be 2.4 per cent (14 per cent of Gross Domestic Savings) for Sri Lanka; 5.5 per cent (12.5 per cent of Gross National Savings) for Malaysia.[15] While the precise data for Indonesia and Thailand are not available, the qualitative picture is similar. Thus, from the overall level-of-savings perspective, the contributions of provident and pension funds are fairly modest.

The overall investment returns on the provident and pension funds portfolio vary considerably among the sample countries, and among organizations within the same country (section 11.3). The real returns in Indonesia and Sri Lanka are particularly low. The real returns in Malaysia's EPF (averaging 3.4 per cent per year for nearly two decades) are moderately high. Thailand's GPF has consistently outperformed the relevant bench marks, yielding a real annual return of 4.95 per cent during the 2001–05 period (Figure 11.3). These returns, in turn, impact the adequacy of retirement financing.[16]

The main issues in Malaysia and in Thailand (in the case of SSO) lie in geographical diversification as their provident and pension fund assets are wholly invested domestically. The global portfolio of Thailand's GPF suggests what could be possible. Too aggressive a diversification into exotic assets (such as derivatives) should, however, be undertaken cautiously; and so should departure from being a portfolio investor. Furthermore, provident and pension funds have little expertise in managing companies. Malaysia's EPF's fairly aggressive investment strategy in recent years could create significant fiscal risks as any adverse outcome will most likely be met through budgetary resources.

In Indonesia and Sri Lanka, asset diversification is wholly inadequate as aside from government bonds and bank deposits (in the case of Indonesia), other assets are absent. While Sri Lanka's EPF asset, managed by the country's Central Bank, does engage in trading in government securities, in Indonesia even the opportunities for such trading profits are not utilized.[17]

Some scholars have argued that national provident funds permit governments to make strategic investments in the national interest, contributing to development (Charlton and McKinnon 2001; Gill et al. 2005). The recent proliferation of sovereign funds, in part due to the commodity and resource boom, and in part due to higher accumulation of reserves through current account surpluses, has created greater interest in this line of reasoning. Some countries such as Canada, China and Norway have set up sovereign funds to help finance future pension liabilities (Truman 2007).

The mainstream view, however, is that provident and pension funds are a fiduciary responsibility of the board of trustees of provident and pension funds, in both public and private sectors. The main objective should therefore be to maximize returns for the members, subject to the risk tolerance level, which is set by the relevant authorities.[18] The provident and pension fund savings need to be intermediated through the financial and capital markets into productive investments, which have a positive impact on economic efficiency and on the trend rate of economic growth. It is in this context that the role of financial and capital markets becomes important.

The above two views are not necessarily mutually exclusive. In all of the sample countries, qualitative and quantitative expansion of physical infrastructure is given a high priority. The provident and pension balances could be used to partly finance such expansion provided appropriate financial instruments, such as long-term bonds, are developed, and that the decisions to invest are based on sound corporate governance and regulatory principles and practices. So, the focus should be not on whether these funds are invested in infrastructure projects of national priority, but rather on the quality of the decisions and regulatory environment under which such investments are made.

Empirical research suggest that only if the provident and pension fund savings are invested productively, which, in turn, raises the trend rate of economic growth, can national savings increase. Indeed, if mandatory provident funds are relied upon to finance current government expenditure and to postpone fiscal reforms, the national savings may even decline. Thus the use of savings is crucial.

Indonesia, in particular, needs to examine whether provident and pension savings are invested productively. The case of Sri Lanka is more complex. In the absence of provident funds purchasing government bonds, the overall taxation would have been much higher as the funds have been needed to finance long-running internal military conflicts. On the other hand, availability of provident and pension fund balances may have strengthened incentives to pursue military means for resolving the conflict.

Payout phase

There are two phases in mandatory saving schemes: the accumulation phase and the payout phase. In the accumulation phase the balances at retirement depend on the contribution rate, the wage base, the extent of pre-retirement withdrawals, and the real interest rate credited to members' accounts. At the time of retirement, arrangements must be made for a phased payout. This is because a lump-sum payment is not consistent with the primary rationale of mandating savings on the basis that people are myopic. As people grow older, they do not necessarily become wiser. The concepts used in the behavioural finance literature, such as lack of self-control, inadequate pension finance literacy, herd mentality and others, remain as valid for the elderly as they are for the young (Holzmann and Hinz 2005).

The payout phase has not received sufficient attention in the defined contribution systems in any of the sample countries. The annuity markets are not well developed. Because of severe informational constraints in pricing annuity risks, and lack of long-term assets, particularly government and private sector bonds, the annuities option is not very popular, nor is mandatory annuitization optimal for all members.

In Malaysia, the EPF did attempt to organize a deferred annuity scheme under which a member can purchase a desired amount of monthly annuity income any time during his working years. A member could make annuity purchases in small amounts throughout the working career. As Malaysia does not have long-term assets, such as bonds, in which insurance companies providing such annuities could invest, the insurance companies naturally took a very conservative view of the risks involved. As a result, the rate of return offered on the deferred annuities was significantly lower than the dividend paid by the EPF. Hence, this scheme was not successful. The government is, however, considering issuing special bonds for pensioners. Whether these help provide at least partial inflation protection will depend on the terms and conditions of such bonds.

It may therefore be useful to consider the phased withdrawal option under which there is no risk pooling as in annuities. An individual's balances are invested in government-guaranteed deposits or bonds; the principal amount plus interest are withdrawn over a specified period (between 10 and 20 years). As the property right on the accrued balances lies with the individual, this option is particularly suited for those with low balances. It also permits a degree of social solidarity in sharing of retirement risks through modest interest subsidies. This is because the interest subsidies will be financed out of general budgetary revenue obtained from the taxpayers. The social solidarity element could be further augmented by effective implementation of adequate social assistance or social pension to the poor elderly.

Physical and human capital enhancement

Provident and pension funds in all the four sample countries permit pre-retirement withdrawals for housing, health care, member investments,[19] education and other purposes. As noted, Sherraden (2001) and Jackson (2004) have argued for such asset enhancement schemes to assist the poor in developed countries. Housing equity can potentially be utilized for the smoothing of consumption over time, and is commonly regarded as a hedge against inflation. Health care and education are an important part of human capital accumulation, which is an important avenue for the poor to break the poverty cycle.

However, the sample countries only partially satisfy the conditions for the effectiveness of such schemes. The critical analytical consideration that schemes which usually increase demand should be structured in such a way that corresponding supply response is forthcoming. Thus, an increase in demand for health care or housing in the face of inelastic supply could only increase inflation in these sectors, adversely impacting on the intended beneficiaries.[20]

It does appear that in many of the schemes in the sample countries, the supply response has not been incorporated adequately. A more than 40 per cent default rate in housing loans in Sri Lanka (discussion above) also suggests that the implementation capabilities for such schemes are weak. Discussions with the officials of

Malaysia's EPF suggest that even in the otherwise well-administered national provident fund, their officials do not have sufficient skills to evaluate preretirement withdrawal applications for housing or health care. This in turn has lead to benefit diversion and ineffectiveness of the scheme.

Concluding remarks

This chapter has argued that there are three channels through which provident and pension funds in Indonesia, Malaysia, Sri Lanka and Thailand can contribute to economic and social development. The analysis strongly suggests that there is considerable scope in each country to reform the three channels – that is, competent management; savings and investment; and asset enhancement – in order for provident and pension funds to have a stronger impact on economic and social development. In the current phase of globalization, with high shorter production and policy cycles, and the inability of most countries (including the sample countries) to sustain international competitiveness in economic activities, strengthening the three channels identified above has become essential.

Notes

1. The excellent research assistance provided by Amarendu Nandy and Azad Bali is acknowledged; the usual caveats apply.
2. All $ amounts refer to US dollars.
3. Portability usually requires that throughout the working history of the individual, he/she has only one provident fund account number. If a person is permitted to withdraw the provident fund balances when there is unemployment, it is unlikely that the individual will redeposit the withdrawn balances when a new job is found. In Indonesia, as the result of fragmented recordkeeping, a person changing jobs often acquires a new provident fund account number. Thus, an individual may have several accounts with the provident fund organization, resulting in avoidable inefficiencies and discontinuities.
4. From 1 February 2008 the contribution rate has been reduced to 11.5 per cent for those between 55 and 75 years of age. The Employees Provident Fund (EPF) will not be paying dividends to those who are above 75 years of age, effective from August 2008. For those who do not claim the EPF by the age of 80 years, the EPF will transfer the savings to the Registrar of Unclaimed Monies. These changes are retrogressive, particularly from the viewpoint of social equity and development.
5. 1US$ = MYR3.23 (Malaysia ringgit) (exchange rate as at 8 February 2008).
6. The EPF owns 30 per cent in Rashid Hussain, Malaysia's fourth-largest financial group. It submitted a RM8.75 bid for a 33 per cent further stake, with a view to controlling it (Burton 2007). As the EPF has little experience in directly managing financial institutions, this bid, if successful, will fundamentally alter its role as the national provident fund, as well as increase state control of the banking sector.
7. For a brief period, civil servants were required to contribute to their pensions. But the current arrangement is once again non-contributory.
8. 1US$ = LKR107.52 (Sri Lanka rupees) (exchange rate as at 8 February 2008).
9. Unless otherwise noted, the EPF data are from its 2005 Annual Report, available at www.epf.lk.
10. The membership does not mean individuals, as cases of multiple accounts by the same individual with the EPF are quite frequent.

11. 1US$ = THB31.12 (Thailand baht) (exchange rate as at 8 February 2008).
12. See www.gpf.org.th.
13. Ross (2004) has identified the following five core functions. These are: (1) reliable collection of contributions, taxes and other receipts, including any loan payments; (2) payment of benefits for each of the schemes in a timely and correct way; (3) securing financial management and productive investment of provident and pension fund assets; (4) maintaining an effective communication network, including development of accurate data and recordkeeping mechanisms to support collection, payment and financial activities; and (5) production of financial statements and reports that are tied to providing effective and reliable governance, fiduciary responsibility, transparency and accountability.
14. Targeted social assistance refers to a system of income support on the principle of need, as determined by a means test, which is financed from general revenue.
15. Calculated from official annual reports of respective Central Banks.
16. Gill et al. (2005); Barr (2006); Asher (2002); Ramesh (2005).
17. An important fiduciary question concerns the responsibilities of the trustees of provident and pension funds who, due to their ignorance or dogma, adopt policies inimical to the financial interest of their members.
18. Holzmann and Hinz (2005); Barr (2006); Thillainathan (2004).
19. Malaysia's EPF for example permits members under certain conditions to invest in capital markets through approved external fund managers. As at end 2006, 235,000 members had invested RM2.2 billion under this scheme (EPF 2006: 104–5).
20. It is easier to increase demand for health care, education and housing relatively quickly (for example, through health insurance and housing and educational loan programmes). In each case, however, long lead time is needed to increase supply. Moreover, the market failure is inherent in health care, education and housing.

References

Arifianto, Alex (2006) 'The new Indonesian Social Security Law: A blessing or curse for Indonesians?', *ASEAN Economic Bulletin*, Vol. 23, No. 1, 57–74.

Asher, Mukul. G. (2002) 'Southeast Asia's social security systems: Need for a system-wide perspective and professionalism', *International Social Security Review*, Vol. 55, No. 4, 71–88.

—— (2000) *Reforming Civil Service Pensions in Selected Asian Countries*, paper prepared for the World Bank Social Security Workshop, March (Washington, DC: World Bank).

Asher, Mukul.G. and Amarendu Nandy (2006) 'Governance and regulation of provident and pension schemes in Asia. In M. Ramesh and M. Howlett (eds.), *De-regulation and Its Discontents: Rewriting the Rules in the Asia Pacific* (Cheltenham: Edward Elgar).

ADB (Asian Development Bank) (2007) *Key Indicators 2007* (Manila: ADB).

Barr, Nicholas (2006) 'Pensions: Overview of the issues', *Oxford Review of Economic Policy*, Vol. 22, No. 1, 1–14.

Burton, John (2007) 'EPF joins battle for Rashid Hussain', *Financial Times*, 8 March.

CIA (Central Intelligence Agency) (2007) *The World Factbook*. www.cia.gov/cia/publications/factbook/print/id.html, accessed on 15 December 2007.

Charlton, Roger and Roddy McKinnon (2001) *Pensions in Development* (Aldershot: Ashgate).

EPF (Employees Provident Fund) (2006) *Annual Report 2005* (Colombo: EPF). www.epf.lk, accessed on 15 December 2007.

EPF (Employees Provident Fund) Board (various years) *Annual Report* (Malaysia: EPF).

Gill, Indermit S., Truman Packard and Juan Yermo (2005) *Keeping the Promise of Old Age Income Security in Latin America* (Washington, DC: World Bank).

GPF (Government Pension Fund) Thailand. www.gpf.or.th.

Holzmann, Robert and Richard Hinz (2005) *Old Age Income Support in the 21st Century: An International Perspective on Pension Systems and Reform* (Washington, DC: World Bank).

ILO (International Labour Organization) (2003) *ILO: 2003–2004 Key Indicators of the Labour Market* (Geneva: ILO). www.ilo.org/kilm, accessed on 15 December 2007.

Jackson, Andew (2004) *Asset-Based Social Policies – A 'New Idea' Whose Time Has Come?* (March) (Ottawa: Caledon Institute of Social Policy).

Kanjanaphoomin, Niwat (2005) 'Pension fund, provident fund and social security system in Thailand.' In Noriyuki Takayama (ed.), *Pensions in Asia: Incentives, Compliance and Their Role in Retirement* (Tokyo: Maruzen Co., Ltd.).

Karunarathne, W. and Ranadev Goswami (2002) 'Reforming formal social security systems in India and Sri Lanka', *International Social Security Review*, Vol. 55, No. 4, 89–105.

Ramesh, Mishra (2005) 'One and a half cheers for provident funds in Malaysia and Singapore.' In Huck-Ju Kwon (ed.), *Transforming the Developmental Welfare State in East Asia* (Basingstoke: UNRISD and Palgrave Macmillan).

Ross, Stanford G. (2004) *Collection of Social Contributions: Current Practice and Critical Issues*, paper presented at the International Conference on Changes in the Structure and Organization of Social Security Administration, Cracow, Poland, 3–4 June.

Sherraden, Michael (2001) 'Asset-building policy and programs for the poor.' In T.M. Shapiro and E.N. Wolff (eds.), *Assets for the Poor: The Benefits of Spreading Asset Ownership* (New York: Russell Sage Foundation).

Social Security Organization, Thailand. www.sso.go.th, accessed on 15 December 2007.

Thillainathan, Ramasamy (2004) 'Malaysia: Pension and financial market reforms and key issues on governance.' In Noriyuki Takayama (ed.), *Pensions in Asia: Incentives, Compliance and Their Role in Retirement* (Tokyo: Maruzen Co., Ltd.).

Truman, Edward (2007) *Sovereign Wealth Funds: The Need for Greater Transparency and Accountability* (Washington, DC: Peterson Institute for International Economics).

UNDESA (United Nations Department of Economic and Social Affairs) (2005) *World Population Prospects: The 2004 Revision* (New York: UNDESA, Population Division). www.un.org/esa/population/publications/WPP2004/2004Highlights_finalrevised.pdf, accessed on 13 January 2006.

UNDP (United Nations Development Programme) (2007) *Global Competitiveness Report 2007–08* (New York: UNDP).

World Bank (2007) *World Development Indicators Online.* www.worldbank.org/data/onlinedatabases/onlinedatabases.html, accessed on 8 February 2008.

Part V
Remittances

12
Remittances and Social Development[1]

Hein de Haas

Introduction[2]

In the past few years there has been a remarkable renaissance of interest in remittances. This interest has undoubtedly been triggered by a striking increase in the levels of remittance flows. This often coincides with a certain perception that it concerns a 'new' issue. However, any suggestion that the topic is 'new' testifies to a striking level of amnesia of decades of prior research and policies on this issue. Lest we 'reinvent the wheel' (Russell 2003), we should therefore not lose sight of the findings of previous empirical work and policies on remittances, migration and development.

The issue of remittances and, more broadly, migration and development has been the subject of heated debate over at least the last four decades. It is possible to distinguish four periods in the post-Second World War thinking on migration and development (see Table 12.1). While 'developmentalist' optimism dominated in the 1950s and 1960s, large-scale pessimism prevailed in the 1970s and 1980s with the rise of structuralist and dependency theory, which considered migration a process draining countries of origin from their valuable human and financial resources. It was generally believed that remittances were mainly spent on conspicuous consumption and not invested productively. Migration would lead to the breakdown of traditional economies and a dangerous dependency on remittances.

This changed with the emergence of more nuanced views in the 1990s. This was under the influence of the emergence of the new economics of labour migration (NELM), which saw migration as the risk-sharing behaviour of households (Stark and Levhari 1982). Migration is perceived as a household response to income risks, since migrant remittances serve as income insurance for households of origin (Lucas and Stark 1985). NELM scholars also argue that migration plays a vital role in overcoming failing capital markets by providing a potential source of investment capital through remittances.

The debate on migration, remittances and development suffers from a number of shortcomings. First, there has been a unilateral focus on remittances and their direct economic consequences. Less systematic attention has been

Table 12.1   Main phases in migration and development research and policies

Period	Research community	Policy field
Before 1973	Development and migration optimism.	Developmentalist optimism; capital and knowledge transfers by migrants would help developing countries in development take-off.
1973–90	Development and migration pessimism (dependency, brain drain).	Growing scepticism; concerns on brain drain; after experiments with return migration policies focused on integration in receiving countries. Migration largely out of sight in development field.
1990–2001	Readjustment to more subtle views under influence of increasing empirical work.	Persistent scepticism; tightening of immigration policies.
After 2001	Boom in publications: mixed, but generally positive views.	Resurgence of migration and development optimism and a sudden turnaround of views: brain gain, remittances and diaspora involvement; further tightening of immigration policies but greater tolerance for high-skilled immigration.

paid to the non-pecuniary consequences of remittances. Secondly, the recent empirical and policy literature on remittances has been poorly embedded in more general theoretical frameworks on migration and development. Many empirical studies have not been designed to test hypotheses, and, even more importantly, make no reference to broader theoretical debates on migration and development at all. Finally, although migration research cuts across many academic disciplines, there is often very poor communication across disciplinary boundaries.

More fundamentally, and perhaps even more striking, is the almost total absence of a foundational debate in migration studies about what the concept of 'development' actually means. Most approaches towards migration and development tend to be based on notions of development that focus on (gross) income indicators. This conventional focus is arbitrary, since remittances and, more generally, migration, impact on a wide range of societal issues beyond income. These may include their impact on income risks (rather than levels alone), income inequality, investments in human capital (for example, education), gender inequality, birth and death rates, ethnic relations, political change, the environment and so on.

Therefore, evaluating 'the' impact of migration and remittances is far from straightforward, as this depends on which dimensions of socioeconomic change are considered as developmental and the relative weight attached to them. What is seen as developmental, moreover, depends upon the disciplinary, cultural and ideological perspectives of researchers and policy makers, who tend to project their own norms, preferences and expectations – for instance, on appropriate styles of consumption, housing and investments – onto the communities and societies that they study.

Sen (1999) offered a more comprehensive approach to development by conceiving it as the process of expanding the real freedoms that people enjoy. In order to operationalize these 'freedoms', Sen used the concept of human capability, which relates to the ability of human beings to lead lives they have reason to value and to enhance their substantive choices. The basic assumption here is that the expansion of human capabilities adds to the quality of people's lives. Sen's capabilities approach contrasts with narrower views of development that are largely, if not uniquely, restricted to income indicators (for example, gross national product per head) and material growth. His understanding of development includes elements such as social well-being, poverty alleviation, income inequality, gender equality and universal access to primary education, health care and meaningful employment. Sen (1999) argued that income growth itself should not be the litmus test for development theorists, but instead the question of whether the capabilities of people to control their own lives have expanded.

Applying such a broad view of human or social development[3] to the remittance debate evokes the necessity of looking beyond income indicators, and also studying the multifaceted ways in which migration and remittances affect the well-being and capabilities of people in migrant-sending societies. This also points to the importance of looking not only at how remittances affect migrants and their families, but also how they affect sending communities and societies as a whole. How do remittances affect equity and inequality in social and economic opportunities within communities? Do remittances increase people's capabilities to protect themselves from income shocks? How do remittances affect those people who do not receive them? Do some of the remittances indirectly accrue to them through investments and income multipliers, or do they instead deepen their poverty and exacerbate inequalities? How do remittances affect ethnic and gendered inequalities? What are the consequences for social reproduction and care regimes? And, finally, how do migration and remittances affect institutional change as well as the capabilities of people to participate in public debate in countries of origin?

This chapter aims to review the empirical literature on the relationship between international remittances and various dimensions of social development in the developing world.[4] Because the chapter looks at both the economic and noneconomic (social, cultural and political) impacts of remittances, it draws on the relevant economic, sociological, anthropological, geographical and demographic literature. The remittance focus of this chapter should not by any means suggest that migration does not affect development in ways other than through remittances. For instance, migration often has important effects on (transnational) identity, cultural change, social structures and political debate. In fact, the following analysis exemplifies the fact that remittance impacts are seldom isolated from other migration impacts.

The protective dimension of remittances: Co-insurance and risk spreading

Micro impacts

Most recent empirical research supports the view that labour migration, rather than being a response to destitution or absolute poverty (Hampshire 2002), is a livelihood strategy pursued by social groups (typically households) in reaction to relative deprivation (Stark and Taylor 1989; Quinn 2006) in order to spread livelihood risks, secure and increase income and acquire investment capital. Remittances are central elements of such household strategies to overcome local development constraints.

However, the extent to which households succeed in achieving these goals critically depends upon the specific circumstances under which such migration occurs. For instance, recent studies conducted in Burkina Faso (Hampshire 2002; Wouterse 2006) and Morocco (de Haas 2006) suggest that internal and international migration *within* the African continent should primarily be seen as a means to enhance livelihood security through income diversification because the welfare gains, if any, are relatively small. In both countries, it was mainly migration to Europe that allowed households to accumulate substantially more wealth. In these cases, intracontinental migration is difficult to explain from a neoclassical viewpoint, and rather seems to corroborate the risk-spreading argument.

The literature on the motivations to remit provides additional insight. The literature distinguishes two main motives for remitting money: altruism on the one hand, and self-interest to secure inheritance and to invest in home assets in the expectation to return on the other. The findings of empirical studies are often conflicting, with some finding support for altruism and others for self-interest (Agunias 2006: 21). However, Lucas and Stark (1985: 904) argued that the motives of altruism and self-interest are often inextricable, and that, in the end, one cannot probe whether the true motive is one of caring or more selfishly wishing to enhance prestige by being perceived as caring.

Therefore, they argued that instead of opposing these two motivations, one could develop a far richer model of 'tempered altruism or enlightened self-interest in which remittances are one element in a self-enforcing arrangement between migrant and home' (Lucas and Stark 1985: 901). In such a model, remittances can simultaneously be seen as the return to household investments in migration, as part of a household risk diversification strategy (co-insurance through risk spreading, securing inheritance claims) and as a source of investment capital that can be used for entrepreneurial activities, education or to facilitate the migration of other household members.

A growing number of studies indicate that economic and currency crises in origin countries tend to increase remittance transfers (see, for instance, Blue 2004). Such evidence further corroborates the risk-spreading and co-insurance hypotheses. Analysis of household data collected in the North-West Frontier Province in rural Pakistan indicated that the ability to cope with negative income shocks is lower for households that do not receive remittances regularly (Kurosaki 2006). Similarly, a recent study on Turkish remittances concluded that consumption smoothing is an important short-run motive for sending remittances to Turkey (Alper and Neyapti 2006). In Hargeisa, Somalia, Lindley (2006) equally found that migrants tend to send more remittances from abroad when the family experiences a decline in fortunes. Besides protecting against income shocks, a range of empirical studies have indicated the often very positive contribution of international remittances to household welfare, nutrition, food, health and living conditions in places and regions of origin.[5]

Macro impacts

In addition, at the national level, there is substantial evidence that remittances are an increasingly important and relatively stable source of external finance that often play a critical social insurance role in countries afflicted by economic and political crises (Kapur 2003). Remittances have proved to be less volatile, less procyclical and, therefore, a more reliable source of foreign currency than other capital flows to developing countries such as foreign direct investment and development aid.[6] It is claimed that remittances are nearly three times the value of the official development assistance provided to low-income countries, and that they comprise the second-largest source of external funding for developing countries after foreign direct investment (GCIM 2005).

Because many remittances are sent through informal channels, the actual importance of remittances is even higher than is shown by official figures. A recent review concluded that the economies of countries such as Fiji, Somalia and Surinam are in a much better state than official figures would imply thanks to highly developed informal remittance systems (Pieke et al. 2005). Remittances often cover an important part of developing countries' trade deficits.

Time dimensions: Are remittances an unreliable source of finance?

Remittances have often been seen as an unreliable source of external revenue for families, communities and states. This view was based on the assumption that remittances would rapidly decline with the settlement or return of migrants. Combined with the idea that remittances are rarely spent productively, it has often been thought that remittances would create an artificial and temporary improvement in livelihoods and establish a dangerous dependency on external revenues (Birks and Sinclair 1979). Bonds to the sending country would weaken and remittances would decline rapidly after migrants settle and integrate at the destination (Merkle and Zimmermann 1992; Ghosh 2006: 22).

Ultimately, this remittance decay hypothesis is based upon the assumption that remittances are primarily sent to pay back migration debts or out of altruistic feelings. It is also based on the assimilationist model of immigrant integration, which assumes a gradual weakening of transnational ties over time. Theoretically, this is in conflict with the new economics of labour migration (NELM) and other household approaches that see migration and remittances as a co-insurance and investment capital-generating strategy of households and families. However, Stark (1991: 223) has already argued that it is difficult to predict future remittances, because migrants are part of larger social units such as families and households. The inclination to remit strongly depends on contractual arrangements and bargaining powers within the family. Therefore, it is far from certain that remittances will decline rapidly over time.

At first sight hypothesis-testing empirical work on the issue of remittance decay is scarce and often conflicting. Whereas some studies show declining remittances over time (Agunias 2006: 12), others show much more stable or even increasing patterns. Yet it is possible to integrate such apparently conflicting findings by conceiving of a more dynamic model in which the relationship between the duration of stay, social and economic integration and remittances is not linear. Integration indicators such as employment and income tend to have a positive effect on migrants' capability to remit. This effect might partly or entirely counterbalance the remittance-decreasing effect of the weakening of ties with home countries over time. Even this weakening of transnational ties over time cannot be taken for granted, as such ties can often be sustained over very long periods.

This evidence casts doubts on the proposition that temporary migrants would be better and more reliable remitters than integrated and settled migrants. Several studies have suggested that migrant remittances sent by individuals tend to reach a peak approximately 15–20 years after migration.[7] There is also evidence that employed and migrants with higher earnings remit more (Taylor 1999; Fokkema and Groenewold 2003). Sustained migration and the often higher than previously expected durability of transnational bonds explain why remittance declines often occur in a much more delayed fashion, and are less steep, than once expected (de Haas and Plug 2006).

Remittances, poverty and inequality

Remittances and poverty

It has been argued that remittances are an important safety net for relatively poor people and poor regions (Jones 1998a). This 'private' foreign aid seems to flow directly to the people who really need it, does not require a costly bureaucracy on the sending side and 'far less of it is likely to be siphoned off into the pockets of corrupt government officials' (Kapur 2003: 10). While there is certainly an element of truth to this logic, there is also a clear danger of unrestrained optimism concerning the potential of remittances to reduce poverty and inequality.

First, there is a tendency to overestimate the magnitude of migration and remittances. In fact, international migrants comprise only about 3 per cent of the world's population and, in 2001, remittances represented only 1.3 per cent of total gross domestic product (GDP) of all developing countries (Ratha 2003: 10). These figures are enough to put the argument that remittances alone can generate take-off development into a more realistic perspective.

Second, the observation that remittances make a significant contribution to income stability and welfare in developing countries does not necessarily imply that they contribute to poverty alleviation. As migration tends to be a selective process, most direct benefits of remittances are also selective and tend not to flow to the poorest members of communities (CDR 2002: 2; Schiff 1994: 15), nor to the poorest countries (Kapur 2003: 7–8). However, it is important to realize that the specific patterns of migrant selectivity fundamentally affect poverty impacts.

Although middle-income countries receive most remittances, in relative terms remittances tend to be more important to small and sometimes very poor countries (such as Haiti, Lesotho, Moldova and Tonga), which often receive more than 10 per cent of their GDP as remittances (World Bank 2006: 89). Although most international remittances do not flow directly to the poorest people, remittances often make up an important share of the income of poor people and poor communities. Moreover, the non-migrant poor might be affected indirectly (positively or negatively) through the economy-wide effects of remittance expenditure on wages, prices and employment in migrant-sending communities (Taylor et al. 1996). Most studies conclude that international remittances have reduced poverty directly or indirectly (Adams and Page 2005).

Migration and inequality in a spatio-temporal perspective

One of the 'truths' advanced by structuralist and dependency perspectives has been that migration and remittances have a negative effect on income inequality within migrant-sending communities as well as between peripheral and central regions (Lipton 1980; Papademetriou 1985). However, recent research has provided enough evidence to reject this as a general hypothesis. Although inequality-increasing effects have been found in various studies at the regional (Adams 1989) and national (Mishra 2007) levels, this mechanism is not inevitable. It is more correct to say that the impacts of migration on income inequality in migrant-sending communities differ for different types of migration and for different periods in a community's migration history (Stark et al. 1988).

First, as in respect of its impacts on poverty, the effect of remittances on income distribution and other aspects of wealth is primarily a function of migration selectivity. If the majority of migrants originate from relatively wealthy households, migration is more likely to imply greater inequality in the community of origin, while the reverse seems likely if migrants come from relatively poor households. Pioneer migrants tend to be from relatively wealthy households, as early migration – analogous to the adoption and diffusion of a new technology through space and populations – often entails high costs and risks.

Second, migration selectivity tends to change over time. During the first stages of the evolution of a migration system, selectivity tends to decrease rapidly as a consequence of the development of social networks between migrants and people staying behind, which diminishes the risks and costs of migration (Bauer and Zimmermann 1998: 5). As a result of this diffusion process, the initially negative effect of remittances on income equality might, therefore, be dampened or even reversed in the long term.[8] However, Jones (1998b) demonstrated that inequality might again increase at the 'late adopters' stage of migration, when selectivity of migration, other things being equal, tends to increase again.

Third, differences in spatial scales of analysis may account for contradictory conclusions in relation to the effect of migration on income distribution (Jones 1998b; Taylor and Wyatt 1996). For instance, one might conclude that migration has contributed to increasing interhousehold income inequality within a certain community or region. However, when comparing this migrant-sending region as a whole with other more wealthy and centrally located regions in the same country (or between countries), one may find that inequality between the regions has actually *decreased* as a consequence of the developmental effects of migration and remittances (Taylor et al. 1996). The choice for either of the two scales is not obvious and might partly reflect value judgements.

Such evidence indicates that migration and remittances do not automatically lead to increased inequalities between the developed 'core' and the underdeveloped 'periphery', as predicted by dependency and structuralist views. However, the (neoclassical) assumption that migration leads to factor price equalization certainly should not also be taken as axiomatic.

Value judgements, ancient and new forms of inequality

Migration and remittances can have profound consequences for class, ethnic and other hierarchies. Traditional social hierarchies may be fundamentally upset if lower- or middle-status groups manage to migrate internationally and obtain access to international remittances. However, whether to judge such changes as 'positive' or 'negative' depends strongly on whether or not we adopt the viewpoints of the relative winners or losers of such community transformations. While older elites might view migration as a devastating process, lower- or middle-class groups may have a more mixed or positive opinion (Taylor et al. 2006; de Haas 2006). A recent overview of case studies on migration and inequality demonstrates how the mutual causality between migration and inequality varies both between and within regions (Black et al. 2005).

Hence, it is important to carefully consider the specific historical evolution of class or ethnic stratifications as well as the relative access of classes and ethnic groups to migration in order to assess the impact of migration and remittances upon inequalities. To a considerable extent, 'measuring' the impact of remittances on inequality is an ambiguous and normative affair. For instance, conclusions on the 'severity' of inequality partly depend on the weight attached to incomes of households at different points in the income distribution (Stark et al. 1988: 309). There is also no objective, scientific yardstick with which to judge a situation in which inequality has increased, but in which the majority of migrant and non-migrant households are better off and poverty has decreased. This scenario exemplifies the ambiguities involved in attaching relative weights to distributional versus absolute income objectives.

Remittance expenditure, investment and regional development

Migration, remittance expenditure and investments

Perhaps the most common reason for scepticism in relation to migration and development has been the widespread and persistent belief that migrants rarely invest their money in productive enterprises, but instead spend it on consumption or non-productive investments. Such views usually underpin ideas that governments should develop policies to 'channel' remittances into productive investment (Zarate-Hoyos 2004; European Commission 2005). However, the common idea that migrants do not use their money 'productively' tends to have rather weak empirical foundations. Since the 1990s, an increasing number of studies have emerged, which challenge the crude views that migrants would fritter away their remittance earnings on personal consumption (Adams 1991: 719; Taylor 1999). Several studies suggest that households receiving international remittances have a higher propensity to invest than non-migrant households when controlling for income and other relevant household variables.[9] Rapoport and Docquier (2005: 2) cite several studies indicating that there is considerable evidence that remittances promote access to self-employment and raise investment in small businesses.

As with poverty and inequality, the impact of remittances on investments and economic growth in migrant-sending communities tends to change over time. For instance, in a study of the effects of temporary labour migration from five African countries to South Africa's mines on agricultural production in the countries of origin, Lucas (1987: 313) concluded that migration diminishes domestic crop production in the short run, but enhances crop productivity and cattle accumulation through invested remittances and increased domestic plantation wages in the long run. Also, Taylor (1994: 100) found village economy-wide evidence that the combination of 'lost-labour' effects and positive remittances effects may negatively affect production in migrant-staging areas initially, but eventually have a positive effect. Activities, expenditure and investment patterns are likely to change over the course of migration and household lifecycles (Conway and Cohen 1998: 32; de Haas 2003).

The short-term effects of migration on livelihoods and household production in sending communities are often negative due to the immediate lost labour effect. It is often only at a later stage – when the migrant has more or less settled at the destination, and the most basic needs of the household 'back home' are fulfilled – that there is more room for investments. In the meantime, households and communities have had the chance to readjust local production systems to the absence of migrants. It is, therefore, unrealistic to expect that the full development effects of migration and remittance will materialize within the first one or two decades following the onset of large-scale migration. Table 12.2 summarizes this hypothesized relationship between the household migration stage (related to the family lifecycle) and consumption and investment patterns of households receiving remittances.

However, this is not to say that the 'migration optimists' are right, as there is no automatic mechanism through which migration and remittances lead to increased investment, employment creation and economic growth. The extent to which money is remitted, and how and where remittances are spent, depends fundamentally on the migrants' social and economic position at the destination[10] as well as the investment conditions in the countries of origin. Interestingly, internal migration is more often associated with rural and agricultural stagnation or even decline (Regmi and Tisdell 2002; de Haas 1998) than international migration to wealthy

Table 12.2   Relation between household migration stage, consumption, and investments

Stage	Migration	Consumption and investment patterns by migration households.
I	Migrant is in the process of settling	Most urgent needs are filled if possible: food, health, debt repayment, education of children.
II	Migrant is settled and has more or less stable work	Housing construction, land purchase, basic household amenities, continued education.
Three optional outcomes		
IIIa	Ongoing stay	(Higher) education of children. Diverse investments: commercial housing and land, shops, craft industries, agriculture. Magnitude, spatial and sectoral allocation depending on (i) household income, (ii) macro and (iii) local development/investment context.
IIIb	Return	Continuing investments (as IIIa) if the household has access to external income (for example, pensions, savings or creation of businesses).
IIIc	Family reunification	No significant investments, besides help to family/community members. This view is challenged by evidence that more and more migrants seem to adopt transnational lives and identities, which may be associated with continued home country engagement and/or investments.

countries, where much higher remittances enable households to substitute the lost labour and to actually invest in agricultural and other sectors.

The indirect economic effects of remittances on migrant-sending communities

Remittances may also have significant impacts on non-migrant households, and hence may reshape sending communities as a whole (Taylor 1999: 65). Such indirect effects are usually not captured by remittance-use studies. For instance, research has tended to negatively evaluate consumptive expenses as non-developmental. However, consumptive expenses, provided that they are done locally, can have positive impacts by providing non-migrants with labour and income. This is confirmed by empirical evidence that consumption by migrant households can lead, through multiplier effects, to higher incomes for non-migrant households (Adelman et al. 1988; Durand et al. 1996).

The same holds true for so-called 'non-productive' investments. For example, academics and policy makers have often bemoaned and criticized the high amounts of money that migrants tend to spend on housing. However, various empirical studies have reported that construction activities can generate considerable employment and income for non-migrants (Taylor et al. 1996). This also applies to many other expenses, for instance on feasts and funerals (Mazzucato et al. 2006). In this way, the benefits of remittances might accrue to households other than the ones that directly receive them (Taylor 1999). Emigration and remittance expenditure also have the tendency to increase wages in sending regions and countries.[11] Although (migrant) entrepreneurs might view increasing local wage levels as negative, this is obviously to the benefit of non-migrants and immigrants living in such regions.

Narrow and arbitrary definitions of investments

In addition to ignoring the indirect ways in which consumptive expenses and 'non-productive investments' can contribute to economic growth and employment, conventional views on migration and development also tend to rest on rather arbitrary definitions of what actually constitutes productive investments (Conway and Cohen 1998: 42). Expenditure in areas such as education, food, health care, medicines and investments in housing as well as community projects for education, health and recreational facilities (Nwajiuba 2005) can substantially enhance people's health, well-being and ability to lead the lives they have reason to value. From a capabilities perspective on development as proposed by Sen (1999), such improvements should be considered as 'developmental'.

Criticism of migrants' 'unproductive' or 'irrational' expenditure behaviour also reveals an apparent inability to comprehend the difficult social, economic, legal and political conditions that often prevail in migrant-sending countries. In such insecure contexts, spending money on relatively safe assets such as houses can be a rational strategy towards securing, diversifying and improving livelihoods (Adams 1991; Taylor 1994). Expenditure on items such as land, housing, education, transport and jewellery can be rational, as they frequently offer better rates of return or are safer stores of value than high-risk investments in, for instance, agriculture or industry (Russell 1992). Therefore, the distinction between consumption and investments is often blurred and the outcome of evaluations on the relative merits of such expenditure also partly depends on value judgements. In fact, by suggesting that people should stay in their 'mud brick houses', social scientists and policy makers risk applying different standards to others than they would to themselves.

Migration, remittances, community structures and care arrangements

The pivotal role of migration and remittances in social and economic reproduction of sending communities has been widely acknowledged. Remittances have been ascribed an essential role in assuring the survival and reproduction of households and their maintenance in origin countries. This is why Heinemeijer et al. (1977) interpreted migration from the Moroccan countryside to Europe as a livelihood strategy to *partir pour rester* ('to go away in order to stay').

While often maintaining the social and economic reproduction of communities, remittances also tend to transform social structures and care arrangements. As with the issue of remittances and inequality, it is important not to automatically interpret as negative any form of change from a real or imagined stable and traditional past. Although the social and psychological costs of separation often remain high, this gives reason to counter simplistic views on the supposedly devastating effects of migration and remittances on family life. On the one hand, migration can under certain circumstances disrupt traditional care arrangements for children and the elderly; on the other hand, remittances may enable households to improve their livelihoods and to substitute family carers for paid carers.

Despite the difficulties created by migration of household members, people tend to adapt to these new situations, which almost inevitably implies social change. For instance, King and Vullnetari (2006) contended that massive internal and international out-migration from rural Albania has disrupted traditional social and kinship systems. Although remittances cushion their social isolation, the loss of children and grandchildren through emigration has undermined elderly people's self-respect and raison d'être in Albanian family life. One of their coping mechanisms has been to follow their children abroad to care for the grandchildren, enabling their children to engage in paid work (King and Vullnetari 2006).

On the basis of his study of transnational family life in New York among Ecuadorian migrants, Pribilsky (2004) countered the commonly held view that male migration to the United States often leads to spousal abandonment. Despite the tensions and problems they face, couples often state that their relationship improved after migration. A study by Parrado (2004) found that although international migration deterred marriage while migrants were abroad, after returning to their home community the savings accumulated by migrants facilitated the purchase of housing, businesses and land and as such helped them to accumulate the necessary capital to start a family.

In summary, migration and remittances seem to be a transformative rather than a disruptive force. Evaluating 'the' effect of migration and remittances on wider community structures and traditional institutions is an equally ambiguous and potentially value-laden affair. In Moroccan oases, for instance, migration and the concomitant partial emancipation of formerly subordinate groups of black sharecroppers has undermined the functioning of tradition village institutions that regulate the maintenance of collectively managed irrigation systems. On the other hand, the influx of international remittances has enabled households to pump this water through individual pumping and to start new farms in the desert (de Haas 2006, 1998).

In an indigenous Oaxacan village in Mexico, it was found that villagers regard migration as necessary, yet problematic. Although migration provides income for families, it is said to undercut traditions of community service (Mutersbaugh 2002). On the other hand, also in rural Oaxaca, it was found that some communities can use the organizational capacity of traditional governance systems to access remittances from migrants for the benefit of the community as a whole. Instead of communal labour requirements, communities can require payment from migrants and may directly solicit remittances from migrants for community projects (VanWey et al. 2005).

Migration, remittances and gender

The selectivity and impacts of migration and remittances are unlikely to be gender-neutral. It is often taken for granted that female migration from 'patriarchal' societies forms part of household strategies such as family reunification and family formation (Chant and Radcliffe 1992; Salih 2001). However, a high and increasing number of independent migrants are in fact women (de Haan et al. 2000), even from 'patriarchal' societies such as Mexico and Morocco.[12]

Also, the literature on the *impacts* of migration and remittances on sending societies tends to ignore the gender dimension, or arguments have been based on assumption rather than on empirical inquiry. For instance, it is sometimes assumed that the migration of men encourages the emancipation of women who stay behind since in their husbands' absence, women's responsibilities, autonomy and power would increase (Fadloullah et al. 2000), while remittances would enable these women to assert this newly acquired independence.

However, the limited empirical evidence suggests that migration and remittances do not necessarily have a structural impact on changing traditional gender roles, and may actually serve to reproduce them. Empirical research in Turkey (Day and Içduygu 1997), Morocco (Van Rooij 2000), Albania (King et al. 2006), Egypt (Taylor 1984), Yemen (Myntti 1984) and Burkina Faso (Hampshire 2006) yielded similar conclusions that migration and remittances do not lead to any permanent shift in the patriarchal family structure. In addition, changes in gender roles are not necessarily positive. In case studies of Egyptian and Yemeni migrant-sending communities, Taylor (1984) and Myntti (1984) even suggested that the position of women might have worsened due to the growing influence of conservative interpretations of Islam, which some return migrants bring back.

Furthermore, the emotional burden of the increased responsibilities can be high. For Morocco, both Hajjarabi (1995) and Van Rooij (2000) showed that women do not necessarily appreciate the sudden increase in responsibilities and tasks, which were not theirs within the normative context of traditional society and to which they do not always aspire. As this new role is generally not assumed out of free choice, it should not be equated with emancipation in the sense of making independent and conscious choices against prevailing norms of gender roles (de Haas 2007a).

It is important to disentangle the effects of migration and remittances from more general processes of social and cultural change affecting migrant-sending communities. While the latter are often more important, migration may play an accelerating or reinforcing role in such processes. In particular, in the long term there may be (intergenerational) gains for women. For instance, international migration and remittances can have a distinct positive influence on the educational participation of younger women. In Albania and Morocco, it has been suggested that transformations of patriarchal power structures are more likely to be generational (King et al. 2006; de Haas 2007a). Based on their research in four Guatemalan sending communities, Taylor et al. (2006) concluded that migration and social remittances may permit a gradual erosion of traditional gender and ethnic roles, but that such changes are gradual because migrants, despite their increased earnings and awareness, run into a social structure that resists rapid change.

Both Courbage (1996) and Fargues (2006) hypothesized that migration from North African to European countries has contributed to the diffusion and adoption of European marriage patterns and small family norms, and so has played an accelerating role in the demographic transition. In the case of Egyptian migration to conservative Gulf countries, the effect would be the reverse. It has also been argued that female migrants show a deeper commitment than male migrants to providing more economic support to households that are left behind.[13] However, some empirical studies have reached opposite conclusions by showing that in some cases men remit more money, even when controlling for income differentials between men and women (Semyonov and Gorodzeisky 2005).

Remittances and human capital formation: Brain drain vs brain gain

Perhaps the most commonly used argument *against* migration as a potential source of development is that it deprives poor countries of their valuable human resources. In recent years, this brain drain hypothesis has been increasingly called into question, allowing for a much more nuanced picture.

First, not all migrants are highly skilled. Second, the brain drain seems to be significant only in a minority of countries. Adams (2003) concluded that international migration does not tend to involve a very high proportion of the best educated. The emigration of highly educated migrants seems to be truly massive only in a limited number of smaller countries, in particular small island states. However, even in these cases mass migration of high-skilled workers should primarily be seen as a symptom of development failure rather than the cause of this failure as such (Lowell and Findlay 2002: 30–1).

For instance, the migration of health workers is often said to have created labour shortages in the health sectors in countries such as Ghana and South Africa. However, there is limited data available to underpin such claims. A recent empirical study suggested that Africa's generally low health staffing levels and poor public health conditions are the result of factors entirely unrelated to international movements of highly trained health professionals, such as unattractive working conditions in the public health sector and the failure to provide basic health services, which do not require highly trained personnel to deliver (Clemens 2007). This corroborates another study that concluded that migration is a symptom, rather than a cause, of failing health systems, and that most elite health workers would not provide basic health care to those most in need if they had stayed (Development Research Centre on Migration, Globalisation and Poverty 2006).

Third, labour tends to be much more productive in wealthy countries, which may, therefore, increase the capabilities of migrants and their families to improve their livelihood. Moreover, many developing countries now face mass unemployment among the highly skilled, which is often the partial result of misguided education policies (Development Research Centre on Migration, Globalisation and Poverty 2006). This all casts some doubt on the assumption that the emigration of the highly skilled would *automatically* represent a loss. In several cases, the long-term individual and collective gains may effectively outweigh the immediate costs of migration.

Fourth, as in the case of remittance impacts, it is important to distinguish the negative short-term effects from the often more positive, long-term effects of the emigration of the highly skilled. Depending upon the social, economic and political conditions in the countries of origin, the departure of the highly skilled *may* have beneficial effects in the form of a counterflow of remittances, investments, trade relations, skills, knowledge, innovations, attitudes and information in the long run. Migrants have played an important role as innovating and transnationally operating entrepreneurs and investors in countries such as India, the Republic of Korea and Taiwan.

Finally, a 'brain drain' can be accompanied by a significant 'brain gain' (Lowell and Findlay 2002; Stark et al. 1997), because the prospect of moving abroad may stimulate the incentive to pursue education among stay-behinds (World Bank 2005: 68). This situation might explain how a country may end up with more educated workers (a brain gain) despite the existence of a brain drain and the 'educated unemployment' that is prevalent in a number of developing countries.[14] Several studies conducted in many parts of the developing world have shown that migration and remittances can have positive effects on educational expenditure and school attendance, especially of girls.[15]

On the other hand, there is evidence that under certain circumstances migration might also create negative incentives for education. If the opportunity to migrate decreases the return to education, individuals may be discouraged to invest in education. This seems specifically to be the case in migration systems predominated by low-skilled and often undocumented migration, where few, if any positive externalities of education can be expected. For instance, a Mexican or a Moroccan cleaner with a university education in Spain or the United States is unlikely to earn significantly more than a colleague with only a primary education. There is indeed some evidence from Mexican household surveys indicating that international migrations have a negative effect on the level of schooling of children (McKenzie 2006). This corroborates evidence that schooling has no effect on incentives for international migration from rural Mexico, whereas schooling has positive effects on internal migration incentives (Mora and Taylor 2006; Özden 2006). In other words, the wage gain is higher for less educated Mexicans who migrate to the United States rather than internally (Özden and Schiff 2006).

Migration and remittances can thus both encourage and discourage education of non-migrants. Depending upon the specific incentive structures, remittances and the opportunity to work in cities or abroad give individuals and their households the choice either to invest in or to disengage from education.

Migration, remittances and political reform

Migration and remittances also affect social and political life in countries of origin in a broader sense. Sending countries have often had ambiguous attitudes towards emigrants. Many states have considered migration as a safety valve to reduce unemployment, poverty and political unrest and saw migration as a direct way to get rid of political dissidents (Gammage 2006; de Haas 2007b). It has, therefore, been argued that emigration could diminish pressure for domestic reforms (Kireyev 2006). On the other hand, there are strong long-term economic incentives for emigration states to strengthen ties with their absent citizens (Barry 2006). Many sending states have, therefore, embarked upon more inclusive 'diaspora engagement policies' through extending special political and economic rights to emigrants and allowing dual citizenship (Østergaard-Nielsen 2003; Gamlen 2006).

Migrants often play a significant role in the societal and political debate and civil society in countries of origin. Migrants and their organizations often take an active stance in shaping their new role in the national life of their home countries. Migrants' considerable weight can eventually create a push for political and economic reforms, democratization, increasing political and bureaucratic transparency and the emancipation of minority groups in sending states.[16]

Although migrants have recently been celebrated for their ability to stimulate social, political and economic reform in origin countries, it is important to remember that migrants, through remittances and other factors, may also contribute to sustained conflicts, for instance, by providing support for warring parties (Van Hear 2004; Nyberg-Sorensen et al. 2002). Furthermore, migrants are often from middle-class or elite groups (see Guarnizo et al. 2003) and, therefore, might not necessarily represent the view of the poor and the oppressed, but instead effectively sustain oppressive political systems.

Again, this scenario exemplifies the difficulty of generalizing about the social, economic and cultural effects of migration and remittances. The direct effect of skilled emigration needs to be evaluated on a case-by-case basis (Lowell and Findlay 2002). Furthermore, such analyses tend to be value laden. This is particularly evident when assessing migrants' political influence. Migrants encompass all possible political colours. And, clearly, there is no objective, scientific yardstick for determining which direction of political change is ultimately desirable.

Remittances and national economic growth

Whereas recent views on the impact of international remittances on social and economic development in migrant-sending societies have inclined towards the positive side, the impact of remittances on national economic growth and employment remains rather unclear (World Bank 2006; Kapur 2003). Relevant studies on different regions have yielded contradictory findings (Leon-Ledesma and Piracha 2004; Kireyev 2006). Chami et al. (2005) questioned the whole assumption that remittances play the same role in economic development as foreign direct investment and other capital flows. Empirical tests of a model in which remittances were assumed not to be profit driven, but rather compensatory transfers, yielded a negative correlation between remittances and GDP growth. This suggests that remittances may not be a source of capital for economic development.

These apparently contradictory empirical findings do not necessarily conflict on a theoretical level. First, as with issues of inequality and development on the community and regional levels, the positive impacts of remittances on national development are likely to materialize only in the long term (Russell 1995). Second, their impact is disparate across countries and is ultimately contingent on the social relations and economic structures in which the foreign currency becomes embedded (Eckstein 2004).

It has also been commonly argued that large remittance inflows can contribute to a harmful currency appreciation (Dutch disease). However, there is little empirical evidence sustaining this hypothesis. A recent study claimed that Dutch disease is less likely to occur with remittances, primarily because remittances are distributed more widely and may avoid the sorts of exacerbating strains on institutional capacity that are often associated with natural resource booms (World Bank 2006: xiv).

Can remittances alone trigger economic growth? Probably not. Although remittances play an increasingly vital role in securing and actually improving the livelihoods of millions of people in the developing world, it would be naïve to expect that remittances alone could solve more structural development obstacles such as an unstable political environment, misguided macroeconomic policies, lack of security, bureaucracy, corruption or deficient infrastructure. Also, legal insecurity of property tends to have devastating effects on people's ability and willingness to invest (De Soto 2000).

If states fail to implement effective political and economic reform, migration and remittances are also unlikely to contribute to nationwide sustainable development (Taylor et al. 2006; Gammage 2006). However, if development in origin countries takes a positive turn, if countries stabilize politically and economic growth starts to take off, then migrants are likely to be among the first to join in and recognize such new opportunities, reinforcing these positive trends through investing, circulating and returning to their origin countries. This sort of investment has happened in the past few decades with several former emigration countries as diverse as the Republic of Korea, Spain, Taiwan and Turkey.

Conclusion

This chapter presents ample evidence that migration and remittances are often part of risk-spreading and co-insurance livelihood strategies pursued by households and other family groups. This evidence generally corroborates the new economics of labour migration theory that point to the development *potential* of migration and remittances. Remittances have the proven capacity to protect people from income shocks and lifecycle risks. They may also enable significant increases in income and improvements in living conditions, education, health and welfare in sending communities. In the absence of well-functioning credit markets, remittances can also provide migrants and their families with the financial resources to invest in enterprises. For national accounts, remittances have gained importance as a relatively stable source of foreign currency.

Although the direct poverty-alleviating impact of remittances is limited because migration is a selective process, remittances do have a substantial potential to reduce poverty indirectly through the multiplier effects generated by remittance expenditure and investment. The impacts of migration and remittances on social, economic and gender inequality as well as on community cohesion are much more ambiguous. The specific nature of such impacts depends partly upon migration selectivity and temporal and spatial scales as well as value judgements. This analysis also exemplifies that the developmental impacts of migration and remittances tend to change over the different stages of household- and community-level migration cycles.

However, it is important to emphasize that we are dealing with developmental *potential* rather than a predetermined impact. The extent to which migration and remittances can contribute to sustainable development fundamentally depends upon more general development conditions in migrant-sending societies. This conditionality of migration and remittance impacts on more general development conditions also indicates that the margin to manoeuvre for *targeted* policies aimed towards improving the developmental impact of migration and remittances is fundamentally limited.

The scope and effect of such targeted policies are fundamentally limited. For instance, it is often argued that governments should 'channel' remittances into productive investment (see, for instance, Zarate-Hoyos 2004; European Commission 2005) or 'mobilize' remittances for national development (Athukorala 1993). To expect that this is really possible is rather naïve as long as the general political and economic conditions in sending countries remain unfavourable. Moreover, such ideas imply that states should and can 'tap' individuals' remittances and assume (rather paternalistically) that states know better than individuals how to use income for welfare improvement. The extent to which remittances can and do contribute to development depends on the institutional environment of particular countries. Thus, the best policies for optimizing remittance impacts are *general* development policies aimed at restoring political trust, creating a stable investment climate and offering social protection to people.

It is also important to be aware that current interest and belief in remittances also have a strong ideological dimension, as remittances fit very well into (neo)liberal political philosophies. On a critical note, Kapur (2003) therefore wondered whether remittances are the newest 'development mantra'. He argued that remittances strike the right cognitive chords because they fit in with a communitarian, 'third way' approach and stress the principle of self-help. Soaring remittances fuel the impression or wish that 'immigrants, rather than governments, then become the biggest provider of "foreign aid"' (Kapur 2003: 10).

This discussion also raises the more fundamental question of whether the more optimistic tone of the debate over recent years reflects a genuine change in migration impacts, the use of better or other methodological and analytical tools or is the deductive echo of a general paradigm shift away from dependency to neoclassical and neodevelopmentalist views on migration and development. It appears that all of these factors have at least some explanatory value.

First, there is indeed evidence that the impacts of migration and remittances on development change over time, and that the positive effects tend to become more apparent as migration matures. Second, the overall quality of empirical research has certainly improved over the past few decades. Third, structuralist theory has become increasingly discredited, and this might have led to less negative interpretations of (remittance) dependency and a more positive value being attributed to the global incorporation and capitalization of regions and countries in the developing world, a process of which migration is an integral part.

There is a real danger that amnesia regarding a rich body of research will lead to naïve, uninformed optimism reminiscent of earlier developmentalist beliefs. The significant empirical and theoretical advances that have been made over the past several decades stress the fundamentally *heterogeneous* nature of migration–remittance–development interactions as well as their contingency on spatial and temporal scales of analysis. This heterogeneity should forestall any blanket assertions on the issue. Notwithstanding their often considerable blessings for individuals, households and communities, migration and remittances are no panacea for solving more structural development problems.

If states fail to implement more general political and economic reform, migration and remittances are unlikely to contribute to nationwide sustainable development. To a considerable extent, migration and remittances are a response to failing markets, institutions, nepotism and a lack of meritocratic incentive structures, which tend to exclude non-elite groups from upward social and economic mobility. Migration is partly a quest to overcome this lack of opportunities. Migration and remittances, if anything, are an investment in social security by households and families. However, migration and remittances are too limited in scale and too fragmented to remove more general development constraints. Unattractive economic and political conditions might prevent migrants from making investments. After all, remittance earnings not only enable migrants to invest, but also give them and their families the freedom to disengage from societies of origin.

Although the positive impacts of remittances (such as mitigating income risks, improving housing, education and health, financing investments and the collective financing by hometown associations of infrastructure including schools, roads and wells) tend to be celebrated, they also ironically point to the failure of states to provide basic public services and functioning markets. If states improved their social policies and created a less risky and more reliable institutional environment, people would not be compelled to spend so much of their remittances on securing their livelihoods. This would set free a larger part of remittance income for investment, instead of being spent on income insurance.

Migrants and remittances can neither be blamed for a lack of development nor be expected to trigger take-off development in generally unattractive investment environments. Paradoxically, development in migrant-sending countries is a prerequisite for social and economic investment by migrants rather than a consequence of migration. Therefore, policies aimed at increasing people's welfare, creating functioning markets and improving social security and public services, such as health and education, are also likely to enhance the contribution that migration and remittances can make to development.

Notes

1. This chapter is an abridged version of Programme Paper No. 34, *Remittances, Migration and Social Development: A Conceptual Review of the Literature*, previously published under the UNRISD Programme on Social Policy and Development, October 2007.
2. The author would like to thank Katja Hujo, Anna Lindley, Parvati Raghuram, Shea McClanahan and two anonymous reviewers for their useful comments on earlier drafts.
3. I interpret 'social' in its broader sense, that is, encompassing economic, cultural and political dimensions of change. Thus, the term 'social' is not employed in opposition to 'economic' because economic processes are seen as part of broader social processes.
4. This chapter will only review the empirical literature on remittances and development. In another, more extensive version, I have embedded this review of the empirical literature into a broader theoretical debate on migration and development (de Haas 2007c).
5. Itzigsohn (1995); Lindley (2006); Conway and Cohen (1998); de Haas (2006); Stark and Taylor (1989); Koc and Onan (2004); Nwajiuba (2005). For general overviews, see Rapoport and Docquier (2005) and World Bank (2001).
6. World Bank (2005); Ratha (2003); Buch et al. (2002).
7. Brown (1994); Fokkema and Groenewold (2003); de Haas and Plug (2006).
8. Stark et al. (1988); Rapoport and Docquier (2005); Jones (1998b).
9. Massey et al. (1998); Adams (1991); Taylor (1999); Woodruff and Zenteno (2007); de Haas (2006).
10. For instance, the income and remittances of internal and international migrant households may differ significantly.
11. Mishra (2007); de Haas (2006); Lucas (1987).
12. Salih (2001); Fadloullah et al. (2000); Organista et al. (1998).
13. Osaki (1999); Wong (2006); Carling (2005); Boyd (1989).
14. Stark et al. (1997); Fan and Stark (2007); Clemens (2007).
15. See, for example, Yang (2004), Cox Edwards and Ureta (2003), Hanson and Woodruff (2002), Rapoport and Docquier (2005), Edwards and Ureta (2003). Bencherifa (1996), de Haas (2003) and Thieme and Wyss (2005).
16. Newland and Patrick (2004); de Haas (2005); Van Hear et al. (2004); Massey et al. (1998); Eckstein (2004).

References

Adams, Richard H. (2003) *International Migration, Remittances, and the Brain Drain: A Study of 24 Labor-Exporting Countries* (Washington, DC: World Bank).
—— (1991) 'The economic uses and impact of international remittances in rural Egypt', *Economic Development and Cultural Change*, Vol. 39, No. 4, 695–722.

—— (1989) 'Worker remittances and inequality in rural Egypt', *Economic Development and Cultural Change*, Vol. 38, No. 1, 45–71.

Adams, Richard H. and John Page (2005) 'Do international migration and remittances reduce poverty in developing countries?', *World Development*, Vol. 33, No. 10, 1645–69.

Adelman, Irma, J. Edward Taylor and Stephen Vogel (1988) 'Life in a Mexican village: a SAM perspective', *Journal of Development Studies*, Vol. 25, No. 1, 5–24.

Agunias, Dovelyn Rannveig (2006) *Remittances and Development: Trends, Impacts, and Policy Options* (Washington, DC: Migration Policy Institute).

Alper, A.M. and B. Neyapti (2006) 'Determinants of workers' remittances: Turkish evidence from high-frequency data', *Eastern European Economics*, Vol. 44, No. 5, 91–100.

Athukorala, Premachandra (1993) 'Improving the contribution of migrant remittances to development: The experience of Asian labour-exporting countries', *International Migration*, Vol. 31, No. 1, 103–24.

Barry, K. (2006) 'Home and away: The construction of citizenship in an emigration context', *New York University Law Review*, Vol. 81, No. 1, 11–59.

Bauer, T. and K. Zimmermann (1998) 'Causes of international migration: A survey.' In P. Gorter, P. Nijkamp and J. Poot (eds.), *Crossing Borders: Regional and Urban Perspectives on International Migration* (Aldershot: Ashgate).

Bencherifa, Abdellatif (1996) *L'impact de la migration internationale sur le monde rural marocain* (Rabat: Centre d'Etudes et de Recherches Démographiques).

Birks, J.S. and C.A. Sinclair (1979) 'Migration and development: The changing perspective of the poor Arab countries', *Journal of International Affairs*, Vol. 33, No. 2, 285–309.

Black, R., C. Natali and J. Skinner (2005) *Migration and Inequality* (Washington, DC: World Bank).

Blue, S.A. (2004) 'State policy, economic crisis, gender, and family ties: Determinants of family remittances to Cuba', *Economic Geography*, Vol. 80, No. 1, 63–82.

Bovenkerk, Frank (1978) 'The Fable of Suleiman', *Netherlands Journal of Sociology*, Vol. 14, No. 2, 191–201.

Boyd, M. (1989) 'Family and personal networks in international migration: Recent developments and new agendas', *International Migration Review*, Vol. 23, No. 3, 638–70.

Brown, R.P.C. (1994) *Consumption and Investments from Migrants' Remittances in the South Pacific* (Geneva: ILO).

Buch, Claudia M., Anja Kuckulenz and Marie-Helene Le Manchec (2002) *Worker Remittances and Capital Flows* (Kiel: Kiel Institute for World Economics).

Carling, J. (2005) *Gender Dimensions of International Migration* (Geneva: Global Commission on International Migration).

CDR (Centre for Development Research) (2002) *The Migration–Development Nexus* (Copenhagen: CDR).

Chami, R., C. Fullenkamp and S. Jahjah (2005) 'Are immigrant remittance flows a source of capital for development?', *International Monetary Fund Staff Papers*, Vol. 52, No. 1, 55–81.

Chant, S. and S.A. Radcliffe (1992) 'Migration and development: The importance of gender.' In S. Chant (ed.), *Gender and Migration in Developing Countries* (London: Belhaven Press).

Clemens, Michael A. (2007) *Do Visas Kill? Health Effects of African Health Professional Emigration* (Washington, DC: Center for Global Development).

Conway, Dennis and Jeffrey H. Cohen (1998) 'Consequences of migration and remittances for Mexican transnational communities', *Economic Geography*, Vol. 74, No. 1, 26–44.

Courbage, Youssef (1996) 'Le Maroc de 1962 à 1994: Fin de l'explosion démographique?', *Monde Arabe/Maghreb Machrek*, Vol. 153, July–September, 69–87.

Cox Edwards, Alejandra and Manuelita Ureta (2003) 'International migration, remittances, and schooling: Evidence from El Salvador', *Journal of Development Economics*, Vol. 72, No. 2, 429–61.

Day, Lincoln H. and Ahmet Içduygu (1997) 'The consequences of international migration for the status of women: A Turkish study', *International Migration*, Vol. 35, No. 3, 337–71.

de Haan, Arjan, Karen Brock, Grace Carswell, Ngolo Coulibaly, Haileyesus Seba and Kazi Ali Toufique (2000) *Migration and Livelihoods: Case Studies in Bangladesh, Ethiopia and Mali* (Brighton: Institute of Development Studies, University of Sussex).

de Haas, Hein (2007a) *Impact of International Migration on Social and Economic Development in Moroccan Sending Regions: A Review of the Empirical Literature* (Oxford: International Migration Institute, University of Oxford).

—— (2007b) 'Morocco's migration experience: A transitional perspective', *International Migration*, Vol. 45, No. 4, 39–70.

—— (2007c) *Remittances, Migration and Social Development: A Conceptual Review of the Literature*, Programme on Social Policy and Development, Paper No. 34 (Geneva: UNRISD).

—— (2006) 'Migration, remittances and regional development in southern Morocco', *Geoforum*, Vol. 37, No. 4, 565–80.

—— (2005) 'International migration, remittances and development: Myths and facts', *Third World Quarterly*, Vol. 26, No. 8, 1269–84.

—— (2003) *Migration and Development in Southern Morocco: The Disparate Socio-Economic Impacts of Out-Migration on the Todgha Oasis Valley*, PhD Thesis, mimeo (Nijmegen: Radboud University).

—— (1998) 'Socio-economic transformations and oasis agriculture in southern Morocco.' In Leo de Haan and Piers Blaikie (eds.), *Looking at Maps in the Dark: Directions for Geographical Research in Land Management and Sustainable Development in Rural and Urban Environments of the Third World* (Utrecht: KNAG, and Amsterdam: FRW UvA).

de Haas, Hein and Roald Plug (2006) 'Cherishing the goose with the golden eggs: Trends in migrant remittances from Europe to Morocco 1970–2004', *International Migration Review*, Vol. 40, No. 3, 603–34.

De Soto, Hernando (2000) *The Mystery of Capital* (London: Bantam Press).

Development Research Centre on Migration, Globalisation and Poverty (2006) *Skilled Migration: Healthcare Policy Options* (Brighton: Development Research Centre on Migration, Globalisation and Poverty, University of Sussex).

Durand, J., W. Kandel, E.A. Parrado and D.S. Massey (1996) 'International migration and development in Mexican communities', *Demography*, Vol. 33, No. 2, 249–64.

Eckstein, S. (2004) 'Dollarization and its discontents: Remittances and the remaking of Cuba in the post-Soviet era', *Comparative Politics*, Vol. 36, No. 3, 313–30.

Edwards, A.C. and M. Ureta (2003) 'International migration, remittances, and schooling: Evidence from El Salvador', *Journal of Development Economics*, Vol. 72, No. 2, 429–61.

European Commission (2005) *Migration and Development: Some Concrete Orientations* (Brussels: European Commission).

European Investment Bank/Facility for Euro-Mediterranean Investment and Partnership (2006) *Study on Improving the Efficiency of Workers' Remittances in Mediterranean Countries* (Rotterdam: Ecorys).

Fadloullah, Abdellatif, Abdallah Berrada and Mohamed Khachani (2000) *Facteurs d'attraction et de répulsion des flux migratoires internationaux. Rapport national: Le Maroc* (Rabat: European Commission).

Fan, C. Simon and Oded Stark (2007) 'International migration and "educated unemployment"', *Journal of Development Economics*, Vol. 83, No. 1, 76–87.

Fargues, Philippe (2006) *The Demographic Benefit of International Migration: Hypothesis and Application to Middle Eastern and North African Contexts* (Washington, DC: World Bank).

Fokkema, Tineke and George Groenewold (2003) 'De migrant als suikeroom', *DEMOS*, Vol. 19, No. 6, 45–7.

Gamlen, Alan (2006) *Diaspora Engagement Policies: What Are They, and What Kinds of States Use Them?* (Oxford: Centre on Migration, Policy and Society, University of Oxford).

Gammage, S. (2006) 'Exporting people and recruiting remittances: A development strategy for El Salvador?', *Latin American Perspectives*, Vol. 33, No. 6, 75–100.

Ghosh, Bimal (2006) *Migrants' Remittances and Development: Myths, Rhetoric and Realities* (Geneva: International Organization for Migration, and The Hague: The Hague Process on Refugees and Migration).

Global Commission on International Migration (2005) *Migration in an Interconnected World: New Directions for Action* (Geneva: Global Commission on International Migration).

Guarnizo, Luis, Alejandro Portes and William Haller (2003) 'Assimilation and transnationalism: Determinants of transnational political action among contemporary migrants', *American Journal of Sociology*, Vol. 108, No. 6, 1211–48.

Hajjarabi, Fatima (1995) 'Femmes, famille et changement social dans le Rif.' *Le Maroc et la Hollande. Une approche comparative des grands intérêts communs* (Rabat: Université Mohammed V).

Hampshire, K. (2006) 'Flexibility in domestic organization and seasonal migration among the Fulani of northern Burkina Faso', *Africa*, Vol. 76, No. 3, 402–26.

—— (2002) 'Fulani on the move: Seasonal economic migration in the Sahel as a social process', *Journal of Development Studies*, Vol. 38, No. 5, 15–36.

Hanson, G.H. and C. Woodruff (2002) *Emigration and Educational Attainment in Mexico* (San Diego, CA: University of California).

Heinemeijer, W.F., J.A. van Amersfoort, W. Ettema, P. De Mas and H. van der Wusten (1977) *Partir pour rester, une enquête sur les incidences de l'émigration ouvrière à la campagne marocaine* (The Hague: NUFFIC).

Itzigsohn, J. (1995) 'Migrant remittances, labor markets, and household strategies: A comparative analysis of low-income household strategies in the Caribbean Basin', *Social Forces*, Vol. 74, No. 2, 633–55.

Jones, Richard C. (1998a) 'Introduction: The renewed role of remittances in the New World Order', *Economic Geography*, Vol. 74, No. 1, 1–7.

—— (1998b) 'Remittances and inequality: A question of migration stage and geographical scale', *Economic Geography*, Vol. 74, No. 1, 8–25.

Kapur, Devesh (2003) *Remittances: The New Development Mantra?* (Geneva: UNCTAD).

King, R., M. Dalipaj and N. Mai (2006) 'Gendering migration and remittances: Evidence from London and northern Albania', *Population Space and Place*, Vol. 12, No. 6, 409–34.

King, R. and J. Vullnetari (2006) 'Orphan pensioners and migrating grandparents: The impact of mass migration on older people in rural Albania', *Ageing and Society*, Vol. 26, 783–816.

Kireyev, A. (2006) *The Macroeconomics of Remittances: The Case of Tajikistan* (Washington, DC: International Monetary Fund).

Koc, I. and I. Onan (2004) '"International migrants" remittances and welfare status of the left-behind families in Turkey', *International Migration Review*, Vol. 38, No. 1, 78–112.

Kurosaki, T. (2006) 'Consumption vulnerability to risk in rural Pakistan', *Journal of Development Studies*, Vol. 42, No. 1, 70–89.

Leon-Ledesma, M. and M. Piracha (2004) 'International migration and the role of remittances in Eastern Europe', *International Migration*, Vol. 42, No. 4, 65–83.

Lindley, Anna (2006) *Migrant Remittances in the Context of Crisis in Somali Society* (London: Humanitarian Policy Group, Overseas Development Institute).

Lipton, Michael (1980) 'Migration from the rural areas of poor countries: The impact on rural productivity and income distribution', *World Development*, Vol. 8, No. 1, 1–24.

Lowell, L.B. and A. Findlay (2002) *Migration of Highly Skilled Persons from Developing Countries: Impact and Policy Responses* (Geneva: ILO, and London: United Kingdom Department for International Development).

Lucas, Robert E.B. (1987) 'Emigration to South-Africa's mines', *The American Economic Review*, Vol. 77, No. 3, 313–30.

Lucas, Robert E.B. and Oded Stark (1985) 'Motivations to remit: Evidence from Botswana', *Journal of Political Economy*, Vol. 93, No. 5, 901–18.

Massey, Douglas S., Joaquín Arango, Graeme Hugo, Ali Kouaouci, Adela Pellegrino and J. Edward Taylor (1998) *Worlds in Motion: Understanding International Migration at the End of the Millennium* (Oxford: Clarendon Press).

Mazzucato, V., M. Kabki and L. Smith (2006) 'Locating a Ghanaian funeral: Remittances and practices in a transnational context', *Development and Change*, Vol. 37, No. 5, 1047–72.

McKenzie, David J. (2006) 'Beyond remittances: The effects of migration on Mexican households.' In Çaglar Özden and Maurice Schiff (eds.), op. cit.

Merkle, L. and K.F. Zimmermann (1992) 'Savings, remittances and return migration', *Economic Letters*, Vol. 38, No. 1, 77–81.

Mishra, Prachi (2007) 'Emigration and wages in source countries: Evidence from Mexico', *Journal of Development Economics*, Vol. 82, No. 1, 180–99.

Mora, Jorge and J. Edward Taylor (2006) 'Determinants of migration, destination, and sector choice: Disentangling individual, household, and community effects.' In Çaglar Özden and Maurice Schiff (eds.), op. cit.

Mutersbaugh, T. (2002) 'Migration, common property, and communal labor: Cultural politics and agency in a Mexican village', *Political Geography*, Vol. 21, No. 4, 473–94.

Myntti, Cynthia (1984) 'Yemeni workers abroad', *Merip Reports*, Vol. 124, No. 5, 11–16.

Newland, Kathleen and Erin Patrick (2004) *Beyond Remittances: The Role of Diaspora in Poverty Reduction in Their Countries of Origin* (Washington, DC: Migration Policy Institute).

Nwajiuba, Chinedum (2005) *International Migration and Livelihoods in Southeast Nigeria* (Geneva: Global Commission on International Migration).

Nyberg-Sorensen, N., N. Van Hear and P. Engberg-Pedersen (2002) The migration–development nexus: Evidence and policy options state-of-the-art overview', *International Migration*, Vol. 40, No. 5, 3–47.

Organista, Pamela Balls, Kurt C. Organista and Pearl R. Soloff (1998) 'Exploring AIDS-related knowledge, attitudes, and behavior of female Mexican migrant workers', *Health and Social Work*, Vol. 23, No. 2, 96–103.

Osaki, Keiko (1999) 'Economic interactions of migrants and their households of origin: Are women more reliable supporters?', *Asian and Pacific Migration Journal*, Vol. 8, No. 4, 447–71.

Østergaard-Nielsen, Eva (ed.) (2003) *International Migration and Sending Countries: Perceptions, Policies and Transnational Relations* (Basingstoke: Palgrave Macmillan).

Özden, Çaglar (2006) 'Educated migrants: Is there brain waste?' In Çaglar Özden and Maurice Schiff (eds.), op. cit.

Özden, Çaglar and Maurice Schiff (2006) 'Overview.' In Çaglar Özden and Maurice Schiff (eds.), op. cit.

Özden, Çaglar and Maurice Schiff (eds.) (2006) *International Migration, Remittances, and the Brain Drain* (Washington, DC: World Bank).

Papademetriou, Demetrios G. (1985) 'Illusions and reality in international migration: Migration and development in post-World War II Greece', *International Migration*, Vol. 23, No. 2, 211–23.

Parrado, E.A. (2004) 'International migration and men's marriage in western Mexico', *Journal of Comparative Family Studies*, Vol. 35, No. 1, 51–72.

Pieke, Frank, Nicholas Van Hear and Anna Lindley (2005) *Informal Remittance Systems in Africa, Caribbean and Pacific (ACP) Countries* (London: United Kingdom Department of International Development, Brussels: European Community Poverty Reduction Effectiveness Programme, and New York: Deloitte and Touche).

Pribilsky, J. (2004) '"Aprendemos a convivir": Conjugal relations, co-parenting, and family life among Ecuadorian transnational migrants in New York City and the Ecuadorian Andes.' *Global Network: A Journal of Transnational Affairs*, Vol. 4, No. 3, 313–34.

Quinn, Michael A. (2006) 'Relative deprivation, wage differentials and Mexican migration', *Review of Development Economics*, Vol. 10, No. 1, 135–53.

Rapoport, Hillel and Frédéric Docquier (2005) *The Economics of Migrants' Remittances* (Bonn: Institute for the Study of Labor/IZA).

Ratha, Dilip (2003) 'Workers' remittances: An important and stable source of external development finance.' *Global Development Finance 2003* (Washington, DC: World Bank).

Regmi, G. and C. Tisdell (2002) 'Remitting behaviour of Nepalese rural-to-urban migrants: Implications for theory and policy', *Journal of Development Studies*, Vol. 38, No. 3, 76–94.

Russell, Sharon Stanton (2003) *Migration and Development: Reframing the International Policy Agenda* (Washington, DC: World Bank).

—— (1995) *International Migration: Implications for the World Bank* (Washington, DC: World Bank).

—— (1992) 'Migrant remittances and development', *International Migration*, Vol. 30, Nos. 3/4, 267–88.

Salih, Ruba (2001) 'Moroccan migrant women: Transnationalism, nation-states and gender', *Journal of Ethnic and Migration Studies*, Vol. 27, No. 4, 655–71.

Schiff, Maurice (1994) *How Trade, Aid, and Remittances Affect International Migration* (Washington, DC: International Economics Department, World Bank).

Semyonov, M. and A. Gorodzeisky (2005) 'Labor migration, remittances and household income: A comparison between Filipino and Filipina overseas workers', *International Migration Review*, Vol. 39, No. 1, 45–68.

Sen, Amartya (1999) *Development as Freedom* (New York: Anchor Books).

Stark, Oded (1991) *The Migration of Labor* (Cambridge and Oxford: Blackwell).

Stark, Oded, C. Helmenstein and A. Prskawetz (1997) 'A brain gain with a brain drain', *Economics Letters (Elsevier)*, Vol. 55, No. 2, 227–34.

Stark, Oded and David Levhari (1982) 'On migration and risk in LDCs', *Economic Development and Cultural Change*, Vol. 31, No. 1, 191–6.

Stark, Oded and J. Edward Taylor (1989) 'Relative deprivation and international migration', *Demography*, Vol. 26, No. 1, 1–14.

Stark, Oded, J. Edward Taylor and Shlomo Yitzhaki (1988) 'Migration, remittances and inequality: A sensitivity analysis using the extended Gini index', *Journal of Development Economics*, Vol. 28, No. 3, 309–22.

Taylor, J. Edward (1999) 'The New Economics of Labour Migration and the role of remittances in the migration process', *International Migration*, Vol. 37, No. 1, 63–88.

—— (1994) 'International migration and economic development: A micro economy-wide analysis.' In Edward J. Taylor (ed.), *Development Strategy, Employment and Migration* (Paris: OECD).

Taylor, J. Edward, Joaquín Arango, Graeme Hugo, Ali Kouaouci, Douglas S. Massey and Adela Pellegrino (1996) 'International migration and community development', *Population Index*, Vol. 62, No. 3, 397–418.

Taylor, J. Edward and T.J. Wyatt (1996) 'The shadow value of migrant remittances, income and inequality in a household-farm economy', *Journal of Development Studies*, Vol. 32, No. 6, 899–912.

Taylor, Elizabeth (1984) 'Egyptian migration and peasant wives', *Merip Reports*, Vol. 124, 3–10.

Taylor, M.J., M.J. Moran-Taylor and D.R. Ruiz (2006) 'Land, ethnic, and gender change: Transnational migration and its effects on Guatemalan lives and landscapes', *Geoforum*, Vol. 37, No. 1, 41–61.

Thieme, Susan and Simone Wyss (2005) 'Migration patterns and remittance transfer in Nepal: A case study of Sainik Basti in western Nepal', *International Migration*, Vol. 43, No. 5, 59–98.

Van Hear, Nicholas (2004) 'Diasporas, remittances, development, and conflict.' *Migration Information Source* (June) (Washington, DC: Migration Policy Institute). www.migrationinformation.org, accessed in September 2007.

Van Hear, Nicholas, Frank Pieke and Steven Vertovec (2004) *The Contribution of UK-Based Diasporas to Development and Poverty Reduction* (Oxford: Centre on Migration, Policy and Society, Department for International Development, Oxford University).

Van Rooij, Aleida (2000) *Women of Taghzoute: The Effects of Migration on Women Left Behind in Morocco*, MA Thesis (Amsterdam: University of Amsterdam).

VanWey, L.K., C.M. Tucker and E.D. McConnell (2005) 'Community organization migration, and remittances in Oaxaca', *Latin American Research Review*, Vol. 40, No. 1, 83–107.

Wong, M. (2006) 'The gendered politics of remittances in Ghanaian transnational families', *Economic Geography*, Vol. 82, No. 4, 355–81.

Woodruff, Christopher and Rene Zenteno (2007) 'Migration networks and microenterprises in Mexico', *Journal of Development Economics*, Vol. 82, No. 2, 509–28.

World Bank (2006) *Global Economic Prospects 2006: Economic Implications of Remittances and Migration* (Washington, DC: World Bank).

—— (2005) *Global Development Finance 2005* (Washington, DC: World Bank).

—— (2001) *Global Economic Prospects 2002* (Washington, DC: World Bank).

Wouterse, Fleur (2006) *Survival or Accumulation: Migration and Rural Households in Burkina Faso* (Wageningen: Wageningen University and Research Centre).

Yang, Dean (2004) *International Migration, Human Capital, and Entrepreneurship: Evidence from Philippine Migrants' Exchange Rate Shocks* (Ann Arbor, MI: University of Michigan).

Zarate-Hoyos, G.A. (2004) 'Consumption and remittances in migrant households: Toward a productive use of remittances', *Contemporary Economic Policy*, Vol. 22, No. 4, 555–65.

13
Remittances and Social Development: The Latin American Experience

Manuel Orozco

Introduction[1]

Improving development through the financing of social policies has long focused on certain approaches in the public sector, such as taxation, social insurance programmes and social pension funds. Only recently has the role of private flows such as remittances become a part of this discussion. Policy makers have become aware that remittances, as transfers between individuals, contribute to development in a variety of ways, including increasing opportunities for consumption and providing a form of social assistance for families in the country of origin.

This belief is based on the assumption that remittances support basic social provisions such as health and education in families that would otherwise struggle to afford these services. To date, few studies have linked the implications of remittance inflows to social policy that leads to policy recommendations for recipient countries. This chapter will address the following set of questions to evaluate these and other underlying implications in the context of Latin America. How do remittances influence the productive potential of receiving households and the economy? What are the gender dimensions of remittances? How do remittances act as social protection in times of economic downturn, crisis and natural disaster? What is the impact of remittances on poverty reduction and equity? What are the limitations of remittances? In evaluating these questions, this chapter finds that the effects of remittances on recipient's spending on social items like health and education are substantive and effective. However, these effects have limitations depending on the absorptive capacities of the economies, defined as the investment opportunities or choices economies offer remittance recipients. Moreover the chapter points to the issue that these personal expenditures resulting from remittance transfers are not in any way substitutes for government spending on social programmes and policies.

This chapter is organized into six sections. The first section provides a contextual background of remittances in Latin America and the Caribbean. The next part looks at research and survey data that corroborate the perception of remittances as social protection through spending on health care and education. Meanwhile, it evaluates the gender dimensions of remittances by analysing the implications

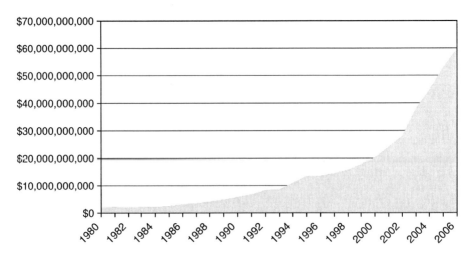

Figure 13.1   Annual remittance flows to Latin America and the Caribbean
Source: Central Bank of each country.

for senders, recipients and transnational families. Then, the role of remittances as social insurance during crises or natural disasters will be explored. The fifth section uses research and survey data to evaluate the impact of remittances on poverty reduction and inequality. In the final section, a discussion of the limitations of remittances as financial tools is highlighted. We argue, however, that remittances are not a substitute for the social policies mandated to the state in protecting its citizens. It is thus important to explore whether remittances have increased as a result of declines in social spending and to problematize the extent to which opportunism exists on the part of governments.

This analysis leads to conclusions that policy makers should consider strategies to best leverage the development effects of remittances. The chapter provides seven recommendations as pathways to better leverage remittances and social development. The study is based on an analysis of primary survey data and case study analysis in several Latin American and Caribbean countries.

Remittances to Latin America and the Caribbean: A brief overview

The volume of remittance flows to Latin America and the Caribbean has increased to over $60[2] billion in 2006 (see Figure 13.1). The increase is due to a number of factors that include reactions to economic downturns in Latin America and the Caribbean, strengthened ties between the United States and Latin America, improved competition in money transfers, increases in contact among members in a transnational family and improved accounting of the money received. For example, in 1980 only 17 countries reported flows on remittances; by 2004 the number was 30. Even these figures, reported by Central Banks, are considered to be conservative estimates.

Table 13.1 Central America in the global economy, 2005 (US$ millions)

Sector	Guatemala	El Salvador	Honduras	Nicaragua	Costa Rica	Dominican Republic
Remittances	2,992.8	2,830.2	1,763	850	362.0	2,410.8
Merchandise exports (not including maquiladora)	5,028.6	1,381.47	875.0	857.9	2,954.0	1,397.9
Maquiladora	352.4	1,920.7	886.4	682.1	4,072.3	4,734.6
Official Development Assistance*	218.4	211.5	641.7	1,232.4	13.5	86.9
Income from Tourism	868.9	542.9	472.2	207.1	1,598.9	3,519.7
GDP	27,400.0	17,244.0	8,000.0	5,000.0	20,014.5	29,333.2
R+X+A+T/GDP	35%	40%	58%	72%	45%	41%

Source: Central Bank of each country.

These flows have had an economic impact on several of these economies. First, the sheer volume has become an important source of foreign savings that helps to sustain foreign currency reserves. For example, in many Caribbean and Central American countries, remittances are the most important source of income and exhibit far more stable flows than other factors. Second, remittances respond to macroeconomic shifts, particularly to inflation, thus manifesting countercyclical tendencies. Third, in some countries, particularly in smaller ones, these savings affect the country's growth rate. Fourth, remittances represent an economic engine attached to an intermediating industry that includes other kinds of services and transactions. Fifth, remittances have a distributive impact in a country's economy.

In the broader Latin American and Caribbean context, remittances are increasingly taking on an important share of the national income. Although they only represent 2 per cent of regional gross domestic product, the impact of remittances varies across countries and regions and is greater in smaller economies.

At the national level, such variations are associated with the relationship to gross domestic product (GDP), to per capita flows and per capita GDP as well as to the cost of sending money. For example, Haiti, Honduras, Nicaragua, El Salvador and Jamaica are countries where the remittances received represent more than 10 per cent of total GDP. However, not all of these countries are relevant when remittances are measured in per capita terms. Those countries that receive more than $100 per capita include ten countries, among which are Mexico, Guatemala, Ecuador, Barbados and Grenada. These differences are noted in the average amounts sent as well as in the relationship between the annual amount sent and per capita income in these countries. Table 13.2 highlights these differences. Although the average amount sent is around $270 per month, when that figure is compared to per capita GDP, again the results vary. Recipients in Haiti, Honduras and Bolivia, for example, receive amounts that are nearly three times per capita GDP. The cost of sending

Table 13.2   Remittances and key economic indicators

Country	Remittance transfers … and GDP (%)	Per capita	Cost (%)	Average transfer	Annual volume
Mexico*	2.98	187.18	6.0	351.00	20,034,000,000
Brazil*	1.09	30.85	8.13	541.00	5,750,000,000
Colombia*	4.84	90.48	5.0	220.00	4,126,000,000
Guatemala*	11.42	237.54	5.6	363.00	2,992,770,000
El Salvador*	18.28	411.31	5.2	339.00	2,830,200,000
Dominican Republic*	13.35	271.03	6.4	176.00	2,410,800,000
Ecuador*	6.01	136.07	3.9	293.00	1,800,000,000
Jamaica*	18.33	622.78	8.2	209.00	1,651,000,000
Peru*	3.71	89.21	4.6	169.00	2,495,000,000
Honduras*	23.09	244.72	5.8	225.00	1,762,980,000
Haiti*	34.53	115.50	6.7	123.00	985,000,000
Nicaragua*	19.05	154.91	5.2	133.00	850,000,000
Paraguay*	8.52	89.31	9.11	263.00	550,000,000
Bolivia*	10.17	93.66	5.6	235.00	860,000,000
Costa Rica*	2.11	92.44	9.46	301.00	400,000,000
Argentina**	0.2	7	9.02	212.00	270,000,000
Panama*	1.36	61.90	10.50	196.00	200,000,000
Guyana*	36.89	359.52	10.14	179.00	270,000,000
Barbados	4.3	418	11.66	220.00	113,000,000
Trinidad and Tobago*	0.77	70.75	10.41	200.00	92,400,000
Uruguay**	0.3	71	11.28	198.00	93,000,000
Belize*	3.77	148.70	8.78	220.00	40,150,000
Surinam*	4.20	122.49	10.17	220.00	55,000,000
Grenada**	5.2	220		220.00	23,000,000
Venezuela, RB*	0.11	4.64	17.10	138.00	124,000,000
Chile**	0.0	1	8.90	279.00	13,000,000
Antigua and Barbuda**	1.5	140		220.00	11,000,000
Dominica**	1.5	56		220.00	4,000,000
St. Kitts and Nevis**	1.2	86		220.00	4,000,000
St. Lucia**	0.6	25		220.00	4,000,000
St. Vincent and the Grenadines**	0.8	27		220.00	3,000,000

Notes: * 2005; ** 2003.
Source: Central Banks of each country; World Bank Development Indicators; data collected by the author.

money also varies across countries and may be associated with volume; the lower the volume entering a country, the more expensive the transfer will be.

The differences in these trends are a function of specific country conditions as well as the history of migration. For example, although Central America, the Caribbean and Mexico have a historical relationship of migration to the United States, each migratory pattern and its subsequent remittance flows respond to the realities of these countries. Thus, Salvadorans and Dominicans may receive relatively similar volumes; however, their migrant populations are different in size and the timing of migratory flows responds to varying dynamics. In the case of

Table 13.3 Remittances and other indicators

	Rural areas	Female recipients (%)	Female Senders (%)	Recipients with bank accounts (%)	Non-recipients with bank accounts (%)	Senders with investment (%)	Recipients with investment (%)
Bolivia		52	71	44	35	4	
Colombia		68	54	52	45	5	14.5
Dominican Republic	40	73	45	66	58	3	21.1
Ecuador	57	74	28	46	34	1	29.8
El Salvador	39.5	72	46	31	19	3	10.6
Guatemala		80	29	41	17	2	5.1
Guyana	40	71	48	62		8	11.7
Haiti	54	53	32	68.4		25.5	17.7
Honduras			37	34	16	4	4
Jamaica			49	65	60	2	
Mexico	45.7	63	17	29	28	2	
Nicaragua	45	72	44	10	10	3	27
Peru		46		37	35		

Source: Central Banks of each country; World Bank Development Indicators; data collected by the author.

Table 13.4   Impact of remittances on Latin American and Caribbean economies

Impact of remittances

Strong	Medium	Low
Guatemala	Paraguay	Dominica
Ecuador	Colombia	Panama
Nicaragua	Peru	Antigua and Barbuda
El Salvador	Dominican Republic	St Vincent and the
Haiti	Brazil	Grenadines
Honduras	Surinam	Chile
Bolivia	Costa Rica	Trinidad and Tobago
Guyana	Belize	Argentina
Jamaica	Grenada	St Kitts and Nevis
Mexico	Barbados	Uruguay
		St Lucia
		Venezuela, RB

Notes: Ratio of remittances: 1: < .66; 2:0.67-1.5; 3: > 1.51; Remittances as % of GDP:
1: < 1%; 2: 1 to 4%; 3:>4%; Remittances per capita: 1<36; 2: 37-100; >100; Remittances
cost: 1: > 7.5; 2: 7.6-9.5; 3: <9.5.

El Salvador, they responded to the civil war and its post-conflict process, whereas
in the Dominican Republic there is a response to a longer historical tradition with
one reference point being emigration in order to escape the Trujillo dictatorship.

A look at these flows and their manifestations in the Latin American and
Caribbean region shows the presence of three distinct groups as they relate to
the impact these funds have in each country. One group is represented by those
countries whose flows have an effect on most, if not all of the indicators mentioned above. This means that remittances have an important presence both in
the country's national and per capita income, as well as in the inflow to a household's income, which is at least twice the average per capita income. A second
group is one wherein the effect of remittances is felt in half of these indicators, and
the third group is that which is minimally impacted by remittances.

Practices of social protection resulting from remittance flows

Although the relationship between remittances and development has been stressed
predominantly within the framework of economic and financial indicators as part
of asset-building approaches (Hamilton and Orozco 2006; Orozco 2007b), remittances exhibit a social development function allowing for the protection of the
recipient's well-being. In fact, remittances play a threefold role depending on
personal and structural circumstances; they can be a source of asset building,
social protection and livelihood survival. Social protection encompasses health and
education services that are two key expenses in remittance recipient households.

Health and education are directly related to the productive potential of households. The deficiencies in nutrition, illness and lack of access to quality education
that are common in low-income families will result in limited returns on the labour

Table 13.5 Monthly income, not including remittances

USD	Men	Women
Less than $150	31.7	50.0
Between $150 and $300	33.3	30.0
More than $300	35.1	19.9

Source: Orozco (2005).

market, perpetuating a cycle of poor households. As a result, attempts to measure the effects of migration on social development have focused on the levels of education, health and nutrition within remittance recipient households or households in which at least one member has migrated abroad, in comparison with levels within non-recipient households or households with no members abroad.

The existing literature often blurs the line between the impact of remittances and other non-tangible effects that migration may have on the habits of migrant-sending households. Levitt (2001) uses the term 'social remittances' to describe the types of ideas and practices that are transmitted as a result of migration, which may include health and education practices and expectations. For example, Menjívar (2002) provides evidence of the ways in which transnational relationships between Guatemalan migrants living in the United States and their families in Guatemala help to transmit medical knowledge, such as contraception practices and knowledge about diet, exercise and sanitation. However, such studies fail to take into account the opportunity costs associated with certain health, nutritional and educational practices. While changing attitudes and preferences about education and health practices are not insignificant, the economics of health and education decisions must be first examined in order to assess the real impact of remittances on household choices regarding health care and educational attainment.

In order to understand the trends in remittance recipient investment in the areas of nutrition, health and education, we examine recipient household survey data from eight countries:[3] Colombia, Cuba, the Dominican Republic, Ecuador, El Salvador, Guatemala, Guyana and Nicaragua. Of those remittance recipients surveyed, nearly three-quarters were women. Thirty-eight per cent of respondents had completed secondary school, while 34 per cent of respondents had a primary school education or less. Women recipients also exhibited lower levels of education than men, and the percentage of women who had not completed primary school was twice as high as the percentage of men. About half of the women surveyed earned less than $150 a month, not including remittances.

In the light of the lower levels of educational attainment and the lower incomes exhibited by the women in the survey, it is apparent that these respondents represent the most vulnerable population of remittance recipients. This is compounded by the fact that women tend to be the principal caregivers for children in the household, responsible for decisions regarding the child's nutritional intake, health care,

Table 13.6 Amount of money received per remittance transaction

USD	Men	Women
Between $1 and $100	33.8	35.8
Between $101 and $200	28.3	29.4
Between $201 and $300	13.2	14.8
Between $301 and $400	7.3	5.4
Between $401 and $500	5.5	5.4
More than $501	11.9	9.2

Source: Orozco (2005).

education and general well-being. A more vulnerable female caregiver can translate into more vulnerable children. Furthermore, women recipients care for larger households than male recipients.

Despite situational differences between males and females, these groups receive similar amounts of remittances. The majority of recipients, both men and women, receive less than $300 per remittance transaction, usually once or twice a month. Table 13.6 details the average amount received per transaction according to gender of the recipient.

Investment in nutrition

In the case of Mexico, Lopez-Cordova finds that infant mortality and birth weight improve among children in those households that receive remittances. According to a 2005 study, 'remittances may have a positive impact in reducing infant mortality by improving housing conditions, allowing mothers to stay home and care for the newborn baby, or by improving access to public services such as drinking water' (Lopez-Cordova 2005).

The aforementioned studies examine the relationships between educational attainment and health conditions and the existence of one or more members of a household who have emigrated. While a connection between remittance income and actual increases in investment in health, education and nutrition is assumed to play a part in these improvements in educational attainment, data on remittance expenditures are not examined as part of these studies. The following section will consider survey data on spending choices.

Nearly 80 per cent of all remittance recipients reported using remittances to purchase food for their households (Orozco 2005). The percentage of women who devote remittance money to food purchases is about ten percentage points higher than that of their male counterparts. The likelihood that a person will be more dependent upon remittances for their food purchases also increases for those with lower independent incomes and lower levels of education. For example, while nearly 90 per cent of those respondents who did not complete primary school rely on remittances for food purchases, only 70 per cent of college graduates report using remittances to buy food.

Table 13.7 Remittance expenditures on food by level of education

	Spends on food
University degree	69.5
Some university	70.2
High school degree	79.2
Primary school	83.6
Did not complete primary school	89.0

Source: Orozco (2005).

Table 13.8 Remittance expenditures on food by Haitian recipients, per every $100 received

	Men	*Women*
Between $1 and $20	31.70	34.95
Between $21 and $40	25.61	24.78
Between $41 and $60	17.68	16.81
Between $60 and $80	0.61	0.44
Between $81 and $99	2.43	2.21
Does not spend remittance on this	21.95	20.79

Source: Orozco (2006b).

This finding is consistent with the assumption that those with lower levels of education will earn less on the job market. The tendency for women to be dependent upon remittances to buy food may also be due to the fact that women are less likely than men to have a formal source of income, as many women are homemakers or do informal work inside the home. As a result, these recipients display a higher dependence on remittances to meet the basic needs of the household, including the provision of food.

In a separate survey of Haitian remittance recipients, respondents were asked to identify how much of every $100 in remittances they received was spent on food. More than half of Haitian respondents report dedicating up to $40 to purchasing food, or 40 per cent of their remittance (Orozco 2006b).

Remittances are widely used to purchase food for family consumption, and this has a positive effect on the diets of household members, especially children and the elderly, who may have unique caloric and nutrition requirements. The improvements in diet are apparent not only in the quantity of food consumed but also in terms of the quality. The extra income provided by remittances allows households to diversify their food intake, for example by allowing them to add vegetables and meat to their diets rather than relying on inexpensive staples such as rice and beans.

Of those households that report eating meat on a regular basis, the majority are home to one or more children under the age of 18. This number includes nearly 90 per cent of those recipient households in Guatemala and El Salvador which purchase meat (Orozco 2006a).

Table 13.9   Remittance recipient families who regularly purchase meat and milk

	Guatemala		El Salvador		Jamaica	
	Meat	Milk	Meat	Milk	Meat	Milk
Remittances	84.6	7.7	40.0	33.3	62.9	22.2
No remittances	37.5	0.0	20.0	20.0	22.2	11.1

Source: Orozco (2006a).

Table 13.10   Remittance expenditures on health care by Haitian recipients, per every $100 received

	Men	Women
Between $1 and $20	16.50	20.80
Between $21 and $40	1.20	1.80
Between $41 and $60	0.00	1.30
Between $60 and $80	0.00	0.40
Does not spend remittances on this	82.30	75.70

Source: Orozco (2006b)

Investing in health

Remittances are also used to pay for costs associated with health care, including preventive care. Indeed, 31 per cent of remittance recipient households surveyed reported spending remittance money on health-related expenses. An additional 17 per cent reported spending some or all of their remittances on medication. A smaller percentage of remittance recipients, about 5 per cent, are covered by life insurance or health insurance plans which are financed by their relatives abroad.

Among Haitian remittance recipients, nearly one-quarter of women report spending remittances on health care expenses. One-fifth of women, compared with about 16 per cent of men, spend up to $20 on health care for every $100 that they receive in remittances (Orozco 2006b).

A recent in-depth survey conducted by the International Organization for Migration (IOM) and the Vice-President's Office of Guatemala (2006) sheds further light on the medical expenses faced by remittance recipient households, and the kinds of investments that are made, using the experience of Guatemala as a case study. Nationwide, the majority of funds spent on health care by remittance recipient households come from remittances and not from income earned by family members in Guatemala. In 2006, a total of US$283 million in remittances sent to Guatemala were spent on health care. The proportion of social expenditures coming from remittances is higher in certain departments and also varies by gender, which may be an indication of more vulnerable populations. For example, on average about 60 per cent of health care expenditures made by the families of emigrants are funded by remittances, with that percentage reaching more than 85 per cent in the departments of Chimaltenango, Sololá and Totonicapán (IOM et al. 2006).

Table 13.11 Origin of recipient household investments in health care in Guatemala

	Men	*Women*
Remittances	55.4	63.7
Own resources	44.6	36.8

Source: IOM et al. (2006).

Table 13.12 Expenditures in hospital care by households with at least one member abroad

	Type of hospital						
	National hospital	*Private hospital*	*Social security*	*Health centre*	*Municipal hospital*	*Other*	*No response*
Male	50.0	28.1	11.6	4.2	1.0	2.0	3.2
Female	49.0	35.6	6.6	4.1	0.1	2.3	2.4

Source: IOM et al. (2006).

According to the survey, in 2006 about one-third of emigrant households in Guatemala used a private hospital, with household members over the age of 50 more likely to be seen at a private hospital than younger cohorts (IOM et al. 2006). There are several factors that contribute to a family's decision to seek private rather than public medical attention. These factors may include the cost of the consultation, the type of illness or treatment, the perceived quality of customer service and medical care and prior negative experiences in public medical facilities. A preference for private medical services may be indicative of weaknesses in local public services with regards to the number of patients they are able to efficiently serve given their available resources as well as the types of illnesses they can treat on site.

In addition to hospital care, in 2006 more than 400,000 Guatemalans with at least one relative abroad visited a medical specialist. Of these, 44 per cent made at least one visit to a dentist, 19.6 per cent saw an ophthalmologist, and 10.7 per cent saw a cardiologist. Around 28 per cent of those who saw a cardiologist were over the age of 65, as were 18 per cent of those who saw an ophthalmologist (IOM et al. 2006).

Investments were not limited to doctor visits, as households spent money on expenses such as medication and laboratory tests. About 57 per cent of those specialized health expenditures were made by women, and the vast majority of these expenditures, nearly 93 per cent, were on medicines (IOM et al. 2006).

Remittances and investment in education

Low-income families are often forced to use cost–benefit analyses to make choices surrounding preventative health care and educational attainment for children, and in many cases the opportunity and direct costs make investments in health and

Table 13.13   Expenditures in medicine and laboratory tests

| | Medical expenses | | | | | |
	Medicine	Vitamins	Laboratory exams	Ultrasounds or X-rays	Vaccines	Glasses
Male	42.2	42.9	35.1	25.1	33.8	46.4
Female	57.8	57.1	64.9	74.9	66.2	53.6

Source: IOM et al. (2006).

education impossible. For example, in the case of education, 'poor families have to juggle current subsistence needs against investments in schooling that carry a remote or uncertain payoff. The end result: they invest in climbing the educational ladder while it is cheap, but stop when it becomes costly', such as in the final years at the secondary level and at the tertiary level (Perry et al. 2006).

One of the most common factors that may make investment in education unattractive to low-income families is the opportunity cost of children and young adults who can work at home or in the formal labour market, especially among larger families or in rural or semi-rural areas where schools are remote (Basu 1999; Strauss and Thomas 1995).

Existing research suggests that remittances may ease some of the liquidity restraints that are faced by families, allowing investments in health and education services which might otherwise have been impossible. Two studies relating to educational attainment in Latin America suggest that the additional income that families derive from remittances has a positive effect on educational attainment for children in the household. Cox-Edwards and Ureta (2003) examine school retention rates in El Salvador at traditional 'exit points' for students: these are usually at the end of each three-year cycle of primary school, that is at third grade, sixth grade and ninth grade. Taking into account exogenous factors such as gender, lack of water or electricity (to serve as an indicator of local conditions), and parental schooling, the authors find that the increases in household income caused by the receipt of remittances do ease budget constraints and positively affect the dropout rate for children in rural areas. According to the study, retention rates improve at these critical junctions among children from households that receive remittances, regardless of the amount of money received (Cox-Edwards and Ureta 2003).

Hanson and Woodruff (2003) conduct a similar study in Mexico, focusing on accumulated schooling for 10–15 year olds in rural areas. In Mexico, primary school attendance is mandatory up to grade six, so before the age of ten there is little variation in student retention. The authors find that while the emigration of a family member may disrupt family life in a way that hinders educational attainment, remittances received by households seem to make more money available to finance education and increase the levels of educational attainment in certain households. Mexican children in migrant households complete significantly more years of schooling. Among girls whose mothers have low education levels,

Table 13.14 Education and income of recipients who use remittances to fund education

Education	Invest in education
University degree	41.2
Some university	52.1
High school degree	41.1
Completed primary school	37.1
Did not complete primary school	32.5
Monthly income	
Less than $150	39.3
Between $150 and $300	47.6
More than $300	36.9

Source: Orozco (2005).

Table 13.15 Remittance expenditures on education by Haitian recipients, per every $100 received

	Men	Women
Between $1 and $20	4.9	14.2
Between $21 and $40	26.2	16.8
Between $41 and $60	23.8	31.9
Between $60 and $80	3.7	3.5
Does not spend remittances on this	41.5	33.6

Source: Orozco (2006b).

this estimated increase ranges from an extra 0.2 years to 0.9 years (Hanson and Woodruff 2003).

Education is, in fact, among the most important expense allocated by migrants and their families. In a survey of remittance recipients across seven countries, nearly 42 per cent of women reported using remittances to fund expenditures in education. The number of men with similar responses was slightly lower, at 37 per cent. The income and level of educational attainment of the recipient seem to have little influence on recipients' likelihood to invest remittances in education, and respondents with more education are only slightly more likely to invest in education than those who have a primary school education or less, with the exception of those recipients who have attended university.

For every $100 in remittances received by Haitian beneficiaries, more than half of the respondents spend over $20 on investments in education. More than a third of Haitian women who receive remittances report devoting at least 40 per cent of the money they receive in remittances to expenditures in education (Orozco 2006b).

Again, IOM's Guatemalan national household survey sheds more light on the ways in which families use remittances to fund education (IOM et al. 2006). Nationwide, the majority of funds spent on health and education by remittance

Table 13.16   Origin of recipient household investments in education in Guatemala

	Men	Women
Remittances	67.0	64.5
Own resources	32.4	34.8
Scholarships or donations	0.6	0.7

Source: IOM et al. (2006).

recipient households come from remittances and not from income earned by family members in Guatemala. In 2006, a total of $203 million was spent on education. In the departments of Chimaltenango, Sololá, Quetzaltenango, Chiquimula and Jalapa, more than 80 per cent of expenditures on education were made by households with one or more family members abroad. The national average is about 68 per cent.

Overall, about 80 per cent of male youths between the ages of five and 19 were currently attending some sort of educational institution, while 76 per cent of female youths within the same age group were receiving a formal education (IOM et al. 2006).

According to the United Nations Educational, Scientific and Cultural Organization (UNESCO), about 91 per cent of girls and 95 per cent of boys in Guatemala were enrolled in a primary school in 2004 (UIS 2006). These figures are roughly the same as those found by the IOM in its survey of children from emigrant households between the ages of ten and 14. However, on a national level, enrollment in secondary school dropped to 32 per cent for girls and 35 per cent for boys in 2004. This drop in enrollment is consistent with Cox-Edwards and Ureta's (1999) description of traditional 'exit points' in education, where families choose whether or not to continue their children's schooling at certain periods, for example when a student is about to make the transition from primary to secondary school.

A case study of the community of Salcaja in Guatemala reveals that there are a variety of elements which may factor into a parent's decision to withdraw their child from school at the secondary level, including the poor quality of public schools at the secondary level, the absence of instruction at the secondary level in their communities or the high cost of private schools or associated expenses such as transportation and school supplies (Alvarez Aragón et al. 2006; Orozco 2006a). The data on secondary school enrollment collected by the IOM in its survey of emigrant households in Guatemala may suggest that remittances do relax households' financial restraints in such as way as to allow them to continue to invest in education over a longer period of time (IOM et al. 2006). While enrollment does drop among youths between the ages of 15 and 19, it remains higher than the national average, with nearly 70 per cent of boys and 62 per cent of girls remaining enrolled in an educational institution.

These increased investments in secondary and post-secondary education also become apparent when examining the types of institutions that are attended by

Table 13.17   Members of emigrants' families who are currently attending a formal educational institution (in the home country)

Age range	Male	Female	Total
5–9	75.5	77.3	76.4
10–14	94.0	91.0	92.6
15–19	69.9	61.6	65.8
20–24	28.5	20.4	23.9
25–29	16.3	7.6	10.8
30–34	10.0	2.7	5.0
35–39	4.6	0.9	2.1
40+	6.3	2.9	4.3

Source: IOM et al. (2006).

students. While public primary education in Guatemala is more accessible and has fewer costs associated with it than secondary education, we see that the majority of children from emigrant households attend public institutions. However, the balance begins to change around the first phase of Guatemalan secondary education, where there is almost a doubling in the amount of children in private schools or cooperatives. The proportion of students in private schools further increases in the second phase of secondary school, known as *diversificado*, where between 85 and 93 per cent of the investments made in education at this level are through private institutions or cooperatives. This would suggest that not only do these families have the resources necessary to continue their children's education beyond the traditional drop-out points where the costs associated with obtaining a formal education become greater; they are also opting for private institutions. This could be because the quality of private education is perceived to be better or that options for public instruction are simply not available or not feasible (IOM et al. 2006).

The expenses associated with pursuing a formal education are not limited to the costs of tuition. According to the IOM's survey, emigrant families in Guatemala spend a total of $325 million in school fees and accompanying expenses annually. The largest expenses faced by families include school tuition, registration fees and transportation. Of the total amount invested in education by households with at least one member abroad, expenditures were divided among multiple expenses (IOM et al. 2006).

Moreover, expenditures on these items increase during the beginning of any cycle of schooling, such as the first year of primary school or secondary school, further increasing the cost of progressing from one level of schooling to another.

Social protection in times of economic downturns and poverty

While remittances regularly support the basic needs of families, they also act as social protection in times of economic downturn and particularly in times of crises or natural disasters. Emigrants, who are in frequent contact with their family

Table 13.18   Expenditures in education by households with at least one member abroad

	Type of establishment				
	Public	*Private*	*Cooperative*	*Other*	*No response*
Pre-school	34.6	60.6	2.2	2.9	0.2
Primary incomplete	49.5	45.0	4.3	0.4	0.8
Primary complete	57.2	36.0	4.5	0.3	1.3
Secondary incomplete	23.6	65.4	10.3	0.7	0.1
Secondary complete	19.4	64.9	12.8	2.9	0.0
Vocational incomplete	14.3	80.1	5.3	0.2	0.1
Vocational complete	7.3	88.7	4.0	0.0	0.0
University incomplete	25.1	66.4	1.6	6.5	0.4
University complete	25.6	66.9	6.3	1.1	0.0
No response	14.3	50.1	4.6	0.0	31.1
Total	26.8	65.4	5.8	1.4	0.7

Source: IOM et al. (2006).

Table 13.19   Breakdown of expenditures in education

	%
Tuition	29.1
Transportation	17.4
School supplies	14.2
Registration fee	13.4
Meals	10.2
Uniforms	5.0
Shoes and/or sneakers	4.3
Computer and/or printer	3.6
Encyclopaedias	0.7
Internet	0.4
Computer disks and/or ink	0.4
Other expenses	1.3

Source: IOM et al. (2006).

members at home, react quickly and effectively by sending funds to address needs associated with conflict, financial crisis or natural disasters. As research has pointed out, remittances often reach areas that donors and aid organizations cannot.

Guatemala and Hurricane Stan

The case of Guatemala after Hurricane Stan in October 2005 is a prime example of how migrants abroad supported their relatives at home in a time of great need. Hurricane Stan primarily took its toll in rural areas, destroying homes, crops and infrastructure, such as bridges, roads and plumbing services, and causing death, illness and injury. The rural poor were especially affected by the torrential rains and subsequent landslides.

According to surveys carried out by the IOM and the Vice-President's office of Guatemala (2006), of the nearly 9,000 homes either fully or partially destroyed by Hurricane Stan, more than 5,000 were in rural areas. Research shows that people in rural areas typically receive more money in remittances than people in urban areas, and Guatemala is no exception to this finding. In fact, the areas that were hardest hit by the hurricane were also those that received the highest amount of remittances in October 2005. Just over 50 per cent of households affected by Hurricane Stan nationwide are remittance recipients (IOM et al. 2006).

In the same month as the hurricane, remittances increased by 15 per cent when compared with the national average. Sending money was also encouraged by money transfer operators, such as Wells Fargo & Company, who deeply discounted the transfer costs to Guatemala and other areas affected by the hurricane during October 2005 and who themselves contributed to the cause.

Remittance recipients had a comparative advantage over non-recipients in the post-Hurricane Stan environment. Prices rose for essential goods such as potable water, and after the destruction of the storm, many people were left without any form of income. Those who were able to count on money from abroad arguably were able to recover more quickly than had they not received the remittances. The IOM survey reported that nearly 70 per cent of homes affected by the hurricane were reconstructed with the aid of a total of $1.4 million in remittance money (IOM et al. 2006).

Family remittances were not the only type of money transfers to increase after the hurricane. Organizations, such as the United States–Guatemala Chamber of Commerce, held fundraisers to provide funding and assistance to families in need. Other groups sent medical supplies, personnel and foodstuffs (Hendrix and Constable 2005).

Likewise, when earthquakes hit El Salvador in 2001, hometown associations (HTAs) in the United States banded together to send in-kind donations and supplies to family members and towns in need. These HTAs also acted as facilitators for others who wanted to donate to the cause, as is the case of the Comunidad Unida de Chinameca that received a donation of construction materials from the French Embassy to help build a wall for the local Red Cross building after the earthquake (Orozco 2007a).

The Dominican Republic and the banking crisis

In mid-2002 the Dominican Republic entered a severe economic recession connected to the decline in tourist revenue from 2001 and a banking crisis that bankrupted four institutions and affected foreign exchange, savings and access to capital. Moreover, Dominicans in the United States were severely affected by the economic recession that started in 2001 and deepened after September 2001.

Senders found that because their dollar was stronger there was no need to send extra money during times of local currency devaluation in the Dominican Republic. An econometric analysis of remittance transfers before, during and after the period of the crisis shows that despite the banking crisis, migrants continued sending money back home (Orozco 2005). The analysis looked at how remittances

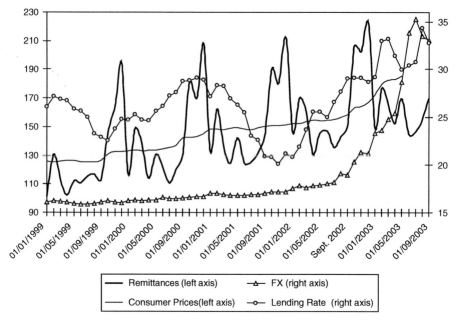

Figure 13.2   Dominican Republic: Remittances, prices, interest and exchange rates
Source: Central Bank of the Dominican Republic.

responded to inflation, exchange rates, unemployment and interest rates. The regression results showed that current inflation was the only statistically significant variable. Furthermore, they indicated that immigrants mostly respond to price changes in everyday activities, which is consistent with the evidence that the majority of remittances transferred go to cover basic household needs.

In the case of the Dominican Republic, these findings are particularly important because they indicate that the market of transfers occurs independently from exchange rate variations. Therefore, under conditions of economic crisis people seek to protect their families against external shocks.

Poverty

Studies have also shown that remittances tend to reduce poverty. The pivotal work by Richard Adams and John Page (2005) on remittances and poverty reduction analysed worldwide remittance and poverty trends and found a statistical relationship between these two variables. Their analysis showed that a 10 per cent increase in international remittances from each individual will lead to a 3.5 per cent decline in the share of people living in poverty. The study by Adams (2004) on remittances and poverty in Guatemala based on household survey data found that remittances also reduced poverty in that country. His findings in Guatemala showed that international remittances reduce the level of poverty by 1.6 per cent and the depth of poverty by 12.6 per cent.

Moreover, in his study on the effect of remittances on distribution of wealth in Ecuador, Orbe (2006) found that the Gini coefficient dropped from 0.54 to 0.52 as a result of incorporating remittances into the income equation, indicating that remittances reduce income inequality. In general, remittances make recipients wealthier across all income groups.

The limitations and challenges of the impact of remittances

Although remittances play an important role as a social protection mechanism in many instances and practices, it is important to bear two issues in mind. First, the overall effects of these flows will depend in large part upon the capacity of the local economy to absorb these savings. Secondly, remittance flows are not a substitute for government policies in relation to social welfare and protection. People have already migrated due in part to poor social protection in their countries, and an understanding on the part of governments of remittances as a private subsidy raises a number of problems and questions.

The local economy

A study conducted by the author in five communities in Latin America and the Caribbean looked at the extent to which services were matched by a demand from remittance recipients. In this section we provide a synthesis of the interplay between remittance transfers and the local economy.[4] The cities included a range of migration experiences. In the case of Jerez, Zacatecas or Suchitoto, El Salvador, migration has been part of a long-standing pattern dating at back least 30 years. More recent migrant communities were also studied, such as Salcaja, where residents predominantly started emigrating in the 1980s during the civil war in Guatemala, or Catamayo, Loja, Ecuador where emigration developed in the late 1990s as a result of the migratory waves resulting from the economic crisis of 2000. Overall, these communities are illustrative of places where at least one-third of the flow of remittances goes to these countries. Generally, one-third of the flow goes to the capital cities, one-third to provincial capitals, and one-third is captured by these types of semi-rural or rural communities.

The local economies of these communities struggle with structural and institutional challenges as well as with the current demands of the global economy. Productivity is constrained by relatively small labour forces, and subsistence agriculture is still a pattern in any of these cities. Moreover, in each community only one or two main sources of income exist, thus posing difficulties for diversifying sources of growth. Jerez is a mixture of agricultural activity and commerce. Salcaja operates on subsistence agriculture and the production of garments sold for the regional market. Suchitoto is also agriculturally oriented, focusing upon the production of basic staples with a small and emerging tourist industry; and Catamayo is a bifurcated economy with two enclaves, an airport and a sugar-cane farm, that coexist with local subsistence agriculture and entrepreneurs working in commercial activities. Although connected to larger urban centres, these cities maintain relationships of economic dependence on those centric places.

Table 13.20   Basic profile of five cities

	Jerez, Zacatecas Mexico	Salcaja, Quetzaltenango, Guatemala	May Pen, Jamaica	Suchitoto, El Salvador	Catamayo, Loja, Ecuador
Population	37,558	14,829	57,332	17,869	27,000
Labour force (%)	41	37		34	31
Population ages 5–19	34.7	36.81	32.3	34	30
	(ages 0–14)	(5,459)	(18,520)	(7 to 18)	
Main economic activities (%)	35	42		15.5	39
– Commerce and services	19	4 (excl. subs.)		52.2	20 (est.)
– Agriculture	13	6		7.6	8
– Manufacturing	11				
– Construction					
Proximity to major urban centre	45 km to Zacatecas	9 km to Quetzaltenango	58 km to Kingston	45 km to San Salvador	36 km to Loja

Source: Orozco (2006a); Egüez and Acosta (2006); Andrade-Eekhoff and Ortiz (2006); Reifsteck (2006); García Zamora (2006); Alvarez Aragón et al. (2006).

Table 13.21   Monthly cost of living, income and remittances

	Jerez	Catamayo	Suchitoto	Salcaja	May Pen
Cost of living ...					
Food	219	228	209	201	245
Services (utilities)	60	44	40	43	99
Education	13	32	29	56	98
Health	40	41	34	68	22
Entertainment	27	3	40	35	14
Total	359	348	352	403	478
Income ...					
Wages	323	303	125	162	295
Total earnings, remittances included	930	501	622	353	320
Monthly remittances amount received	637	331	515	181	247

Source: Orozco (2006a).

Moreover, these cities operate on a system of low wages and precarious employ-ment, making them unable to compete with other markets or in the global economy. Wages are often one-third or one-quarter of the cost of living. An agricul-tural worker in Catamayo working in sugar-cane fields earns $150 a month, and a store clerk in Salcaja earns $200. Such incomes make it hard for people to maintain a decent standard of living through their own employment. The cost of the basic food basket ranges between $150 and $350. This gap between earnings and cost of living has been a key factor in the decision to migrate for many people.

The productive base of the local economies is reduced to commercial activities, subsistence agriculture and some artisanal industrial work. Those segments that

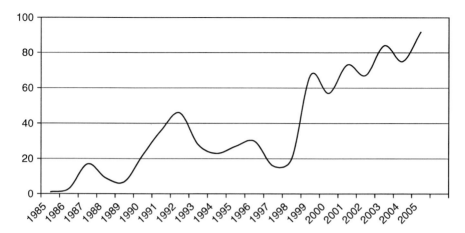

Figure 13.3 Salcaja: Number of businesses by starting year of operation
Source: Orozco (2006a); Alvarez Aragón et al. (2006).

are more productive are concentrated in some economic enclaves, such as sugar-cane production in Catamayo, vegetable production in Suchitoto or textiles and garment manufacturing in Salacaja. However, over the past six years there has been an overall increase in the number of registered businesses.

Remittance recipients and the local economy

Migrants who have left these communities regularly send money to their families so that they can take care of their basic needs and hopefully save. The number of remittance recipients in these cities is relatively variable, but is around 15 per cent of the population, representing between 2,000 and 6,000 households which each receive an average of $300 a month. Given the poor conditions of the local economy, the arrival of nearly one million dollars a month into the economy is more than a welcome flow; it is also a potential economic stimulus.

Remittance recipients spend money predominantly on the basic food items needed to take care of households composed of an average of six members. The majority of the foodstuffs purchased are locally or nationally produced, thus bene-fiting domestic producers and the economy. Most remittance recipients also spend money on education, health and other services, with an average expenditure of $500 a year on health and education. In fact, over the past five years half of the remittance recipients have made repairs to their homes or invested in buying a new home. One-third of those homebuyers did so at the investment request of the relative living abroad. Moreover, half of the remittance recipients have invested in some small business activity, most of which was also prompted by the remit-tance sender. What is more, those who are able to retain some disposable income after daily expenses open savings accounts. This is more prevalent when there are more financial intermediaries available in the community or financial institutions reach out to these costumers. In Catamayo, for example, there are three credit

Table 13.22   Business activities of local economies (number)

Type	Catamayo	Suchitoto	Jerez	May Pen	Total
Retail store	18	60	10	126	214
Food market	57	4	23	30	114
Restaurant	41	36	2	16	95
Professional services	15	17	13	19	64
Other commercial activities	3	39	1	6	49
Other services		36		91	127
Entertainment	13	13	9	15	50
Transportation		20	5	3	28
Construction and maintenance	2	11	10	10	33
Hardware and industrial warehouses	6	2	11	15	34
Auto and repairs	5		11	35	51
Food manufacturer	4	11	4		19
Gas	7	2	6	4	19
Hotel	13			2	15
Financial	6	1	10	10	27
Furniture	2		5	5	12
Bookstore		4		4	8
Media	1		2	10	13
Other industrial activities		3		4	7
Tourism	1			1	2

Sources: Orozco (2006a); Egüez and Acosta (2006); Andrade-Eekhoff and Ortiz (2006); Reifsteck (2006); García Zamora (2006); Alvarez Aragón et al. (2006).

Table 13.23   Remittance recipient households

	Jerez, Zacatecas Mexico	Salcaja, Quetzaltenango, Guatemala	Suchitoto, El Salvador	Catamayo, Loja, Ecuador	May Pen, Jamaica
Per cent of remittance recipient households	18.20	15	23	15	
Estimated number of remittance recipients	6,836	2,224	2,073	4,050	
Number of people in household	4	5	5	6	4
Number of children in household	1	2	3	2	2

Source: Estimates based on interviews and country census data.

and savings cooperatives and one bank that offer basic financial services to recipients. Similarly, Salcaja has one cooperative and two commercial banks. The Salcaja cooperative is proactive in reaching out to remittance beneficiaries and has several marketing tools to sell financial services to recipients.

Despite the fact that these families are investing or own bank accounts, the extent to which suppliers in the local economy cater and market their products to

Table 13.24 Remittance recipients who have invested in a small business or have savings accounts (%)

	Jerez	*Catamayo*	*Suchitoto*	*Salcaja*	*May Pen*
Invest	22.2	58.8	13.3	30.8	44.4
Savings account	11.1	29.4	86.7	61.5	88.9

Source: Orozco (2006a).

this market segment is at best very limited. This situation does not apply only to financial institutions but also to health, education and other services. The quality of services provided is rather poor and supply is sparse, with some exceptions. Local businesses do not target this population group as a source of wealth generation, thus missing opportunities to maximize on the multiplying effect of these flows. At most there is a tacit acknowledgement that their businesses benefit from the demand of products and services from remittance recipients.

Both education and health sectors perform poorly in these communities. Institutions do exist, predominantly in the public sphere, but they do not provide first-class services to people. Schools are understaffed, teachers are ill-prepared, and health provision is rather inadequate or expensive. For example, in Jerez, there are only two secondary schools in a city of more than 20,000 people, 30 per cent of whom are under the age of 18. A similar situation is to be found in Suchitoto. In both cases, many students are forced to travel to their closest economic centres in order to obtain education. In the case of Salcaja, private institutions have emerged to fill this gap. As a result, many remittance recipient parents have taken advantage of this sector, putting their children in private schools for an improved education.

Businesses do not seek to innovate or adapt to changing demands and realities accompanying the inflow of remittances. In education, for example, people invest predominantly in basic services and do not spend on greater educational opportunities such as putting children into extra-curricular activities, paying for tutoring lessons, or taking computer classes. This lack of approach is informed as much by limited knowledge on the part of parents as to what they should do for their children's education, as by the lack of supply of educational services. This latter issue is perhaps more relevant because remittance recipients are willing to spend on education but see few incentives to do so because the supply of services is relatively poor.

Looking to an inventory of all businesses operating in the community, there were very few, if any, education-related businesses except for school and office supply stores.

When businesses were interviewed about their business perspectives, their approach was relatively crude or simplistic and asserted that remittance recipients were not necessarily a business target. However, all of the businesses were quick to acknowledge that recipient patronage was important in bringing revenues to their stores, and that in many cases they have had to respond to changing demands from recipient households.

Table 13.25 Education, health and finance institutions

	Jerez, Zacatecas, Mexico	*Salcaja, Quetzaltenango, Guatemala*	*Suchitoto, El Salvador*	*Catamayo, Loja, Ecuador*	*May Pen, Clarendon, Jamaica*
Number of high schools	2	12 (public), 8 (private)	1 public high school, 1 vocational centre	8	4
Number of health centres	3 private hospitals, 4 public hospitals; 31 specialists; 24 general practitioners;	1 (public), 25 (private)	1 public hospital, 3 private medical clinics	25	1 public hospital, 3 private medical centres, 6 private practitioners
Number of commercial banks	4	2	0	1	6
Number of credit unions or MFIs	1	1	3	3	3

Source: Orozco (2006a); Egüez and Acosta (2006); Andrade-Eekhoff and Ortiz (2006); Reifsteck (2006); García Zamora (2006); Alvarez Aragón et al. (2006).

Table 13.26 Type of school obligations people engage (percentages)

	Jerez, Zacatecas Mexico	Salcaja, Quetzaltenango, Guatemala	Suchitoto, El Salvador	Catamayo, Loja, Ecuador	May Pen, Clarendon, Jamaica
Fees	15		37	57	
School registration	40	76	35	82	92
Transport		31		7	54
Food	23	5	26	2	54
School supplies, uniforms	36	71	62	61	96
Activities			22	8	33
Other	11	44		5	4

Source: Orozco (2006a); Egüez and Acosta (2006); Andrade-Eekhoff and Ortiz (2006); Reifsteck (2006); García Zamora (2006); Alvarez Aragón et al. (2006).

Table 13.27 Businesses operating in education-related activities

	Jerez	Suchitoto	Salcaja	Catamayo	May Pen
Private schools	11	0	8	4	0
Office supply	0	1	18	7	4
Internet	0	2	9	4	3
Total number of businesses	11	3	35	15	7

Source: Data provided by municipalities in every city.

Overall, local businesses respond to the local demands but provide insufficient resources to meet the market preferences of remittance recipients. One reason is their lack of access to finance or ability to scale up their businesses. In addition, their knowledge of recipients' market preferences and expectations of revenue generation are scant. They express frustration about the few opportunities or choices available. For example, one store owner expressed that 'there is no development that stimulates the municipality, and it is surprising to have a place with such rich resources as remittances where no one is taking advantage of them for anything productive'. A drugstore owner in Jerez said, 'Migrants visit or send money because they have roots here. But local businesses, commerce, do not know how to take advantage of these flows in investment or commercial projects. There isn't even a chamber of commerce that motivates economic activities.'

Government policy

Another limitation related to remittance transfers and social expenditure is that in spite of the multiplying effect of remittances, these foreign savings principally benefit only remittance recipients, which constitute no more than 30 per cent of the whole population. Therefore, these funds cannot be directly or indirectly perceived as a substitute for government policies in social spending. Instead, governments need to find ways to leverage these flows and their spending in ways that

Table 13.28 Per capita tax revenue in selected Latin American and Caribbean countries, 1980–2004 (US$)

	Bolivia	Colombia	Costa Rica	Dominican Republic	El Salvador	Guatemala	Mexico
1980		121		128			
1985	83	117	273	79	142	87	368
1990	62	118	365	108	93	59	433
1995	98	233	585	226	203	113	402
2000	125	266	491	353	227	174	692
2004	146	292	585		294	225	

Source: IMF Government Finance Statistics (several years).

Table 13.29 Per capita expenditure in health and education (H&E) in selected Latin American and Caribbean countries, 1980–2004 (US$)

H&E	Bolivia	Colombia	Costa Rica	Dominican Republic	El Salvador	Guatemala	Mexico
1980				43			
1985			132	21	46	24	79
1990	24	33	215	28	27	21	92
1995	48	101	283	56	54		136
2000	73		385	116	61	53	281
2004	92				115	67	

Source: IMF Government Finance Statistics (several years).

have greater distributive impacts on the local economies. From a normative stand-point, migrants leave to improve their families' social conditions partly because government policies do not create an adequate number of jobs in their countries. Therefore, expecting governments to see remittances as a measure to ease social spending responsibilities is not only insensitive but also irresponsible.

Moreover, an analysis of government spending over the course of the past 30 years shows that social spending has experienced slow growth. However, government revenue has increased at a somewhat higher pace than expenditure in health and education (see Tables 13.28 and 13.29). Part of the reason for this is a response to the state reforms that most Latin American countries have followed as a part of their neoliberal structuring. During the same period, migration and remittance inflows increased.

One important issue to consider about remittances, social spending and government revenues is that relative to the whole population remittance recipients make greater contributions to revenue collection. Their propensity to consume, generally around 90 per cent of all remittances received, often amounts to more than 30 per cent of revenue in sales taxes. This is partly due to the fact that remittances typically triple recipient income. Moreover, there is a positive correlation between

Table 13.30   OLS regression results on revenue

	B	Std. error
(Constant)	4.381	0.289***
Remittances per capita	0.161	0.027***
Per capita personal consumption	−0.164	0.083**
Per capita savings	0.302	0.075***

Notes: R2 = 0.355. Statistical significance: *** at 1%; ** at 5%.

Table 13.31   OLS regression results on expenditures in health and education

	B	Std. error
(Constant)	−0.19609	0.788255
Per capita remittances	−0.07684	0.021258***
Per capita GDP	−0.41041	0.14312***
Per capita revenue	1.46213	0.103875***
Per capita foreign aid	0.04469	0.03134
Per capita population growth	−0.04177	0.094201

Notes: R2 = 0.828. Statistical significance: *** at 1%; ** at 5%; at 1%.

remittances and revenue. An ordinary least squares (OLS) regression model was generated to look at the relationship between remittances and tax collection. The model employed was

$$\text{Revenue}_{t-1} = \text{Remittances} + \text{Consumption} + \text{Savings}.$$

The period collected is from 1980 to 2004 for which there are data available on revenue and remittances. The results show that there is a positive statistical relationship with remittances.[5] A dollar increase in remittances yields $0.16 increase in tax revenue.

Moreover, in examining whether remittances determine expenditure in health and education the relationship is significant but negative, whereas revenue is positively related. The regression model used included income growth, foreign aid and population growth, in addition to remittances and revenue. The results are presented in Table 13.31. Growth and remittances are negatively statistically related. Neither foreign nor population growth were statistically significant. The overall significance and interpretation of these results is relevant. A negative sign for economic growth and remittances denotes that social investment increases under conditions of hardship rather than under positive situations. That is, the more wealth available, the more resources are spent on activities other than health or education. Similarly, the positive relationship to tax revenues means that as long as tax collection exists, investments in health and education will occur.

Policy conclusions

For many people the contribution of remittance transfers and earnings to families in Latin America and the Caribbean provides more than a safety net. But the limitations that the flows often face require policy consideration as these initiatives can better leverage the flows on broader structural issues such as education and health.

Overall, the policy effort must aim at modernizing the productive base of local economies while leveraging resources from migrant foreign savings. In concrete terms this means linking investment opportunities, savings creation, local and central government enabling environments and increased risk propensity among local, national and transnational entrepreneurs.

We identify initiatives where donor activity can be critically important to promote leveraging schemes through remittance funds and migrant capital investment.

(i) Accelerating financial intermediation projects with credit unions and Monetary Financial Institutions (MFIs).

(ii) Engaging banking institutions more actively by identifying their opportunity costs in rural areas, including community reinvestment schemes by banking financial institutions.

(iii) Supporting projects on feasibility investment schemes to develop investment portfolios, including recommendations on business consolidation where microenterprise is ineffective or inefficient or technical assistance for business development, particularly among those seeking to return to their countries.

(iv) Providing tax breaks on the import of technology devices that can enhance the use of alternative payment instruments, such as debit cards or mobile banking.

(v) Linking investment opportunities to the transformation of subsistence agriculture, while relaxing investment red tape and including outreach for migrant investment in the investment promotion offices available in all of these countries.

(vi) Designing projects that include education and health services among a range of other services offered by MFIs in cooperation with schools, public or private:
   a. Education funds, tutoring classes, extra-curricular activities, Internet;
   b. Health insurance, specialized medicine funds;
   c. Goals and standards among community leaders, financial institutions and local governments to raise educational attainment from primary to secondary school completion levels.

(vii) Engaging local governments and the private sector to review their role as environment enablers to promote investment and increase productivity.

Accelerating financial intermediation projects with credit unions and MFIs

The experience to date has demonstrated that microfinance institutions and credit unions play key roles in transforming remittance recipient clients into bank clients at non-negligible rates (Orozco 2005), and in turn increasing savings

Table 13.32 Percentage distribution of locations by type of business

Type of payer

Country	Bank	Cooperative, credit union, popular bank	MFI	Bureau of exchange	Retail store	Post office	Home delivery
El Salvador	67.5	6.4	1.8	1.4	16.4		6.6
Honduras	61.5	1.1	1.7	8.9	26.8		
Ecuador	59.4	4.3			36.3		
Mexico	55.3	2.1	0.0	2.3	40.2		
Haiti	50.9	0.6	9.8		38.6		
Peru	50.8	3.5	3.2	6.6	35.1	0.8	
Bolivia	47.5	12.4	18.6	0.1	20.3	1.1	
Colombia	39.5			46.8	13.7		
Dominican Republic	39.1	2.4	0.1	10.3	48.2		
Jamaica	26.6	13.2	1.0	0.7	46.1	12.4	
Guatemala	23.5	3.3	0.4		72.8		
Nicaragua	17.7	18.6	9.7		53.9		
Guyana	7.7				56.9	35.4	

Source: Data compiled by the author.

and investment ratios in communities where remittances arrive. However, few institutions are involved in remittance transfers or receiving support to do so. In Latin America and the Caribbean, less than 10 per cent of remittance-paying institutions are credit unions or MFIs, yet they are reaching out to recipients more persistently.

Donors are slowly working towards support of these institutions, yet more is needed. The Inter-American Development Bank has invested more than $60 million to leverage remittance transfers by providing support to MFIs. The assistance pays attention to financial product design and marketing and technology. However, accelerating the support and participation of these financial institutions will be of critical importance to getting people into financial institutions and increasing their financial education and assets.

Credit unions, for example, are more oriented towards remittance recipients and have sold financial products and leveraged their funds. This is particularly the case for Salcaja Credit Union and Acoproduzca in Suchitoto (member of Fedecaces), both of which have developed strategies for attracting clients and turning them into members. Their banking rates are low, but may grow depending on their strategies and efforts. Currently, Salcaja has 1,000 remittance recipient clients, and Acoproduzca has 300 (Alvarez Aragón et al. 2006). Acoproduzca also attracts savings from remittance recipients who do not pick up their money: in April 2006, the cooperative received $20,000 in deposits, the majority of which came from remittance recipients. Banco de Loja in Catamayo is the third major competitor in the local remittance market controlled by two agents and offers financial products to recipients.

Engaging banking institutions

These efforts to bring people into savings and credit institutions do not exclude banking. Banks are at the core of providing the full range of financial opportunities while at the same time increasing profitable schemes. Governments and donors should work with banks to more actively identify their opportunity costs in rural areas. Moreover, there should be efforts to introduce initiatives that require community reinvestment schemes by banking financial institutions. These schemes should aim at encouraging banks to increase access to capital in rural and low-income areas, promoting entrepreneurialism and competitiveness.

Supporting projects on feasibility investment

Local communities often offer investment opportunities that can benefit from small-scale investors who can create new businesses or consolidate those businesses that already exist. To that effect, donors, in partnership with governments and private sector institutions, can work towards the creation of investment portfolios, including recommendations for business consolidation where microenterprise is ineffective or inefficient, linking investment opportunities to the transformation of subsistence agriculture, or technical assistance for business development, particularly among those seeking to return to their countries. These kinds of initiatives represent a step forward to enable an investment environment among migrants wishing to participate in small business development. In fact, part of this effort must include relaxing investment red tape and encouraging migrant outreach through the investment promotion offices.

Providing tax breaks on the import of technology

Remittance transfers are intimately related to their effective and efficient delivery, whereby technology plays an important role. Currently, there exist technology devices such as Point of Sale Terminals (POSTs) that can further enhance remittance spending. However, access to the technology is often expensive or cumbersome to acquire. The critical importance of POSTs in remittance transfers lies in the fact that these are instruments that enable the use of financial resources for payments on the streets using debit cards or mobile communication devices in lieu of cash. Modernizing small vendors and merchants with POSTs in developing countries creates a foundation for reducing cash on the street, increasing the level of savings among the public (remittance recipients in particular) and positively influencing revenue streams for MFIs and banks. Remittance recipients using debit cards at their typical places of economic activity, such as *colmados*, *pulperias* or small retail stores, would enjoy the use of this payment instrument, while better managing their resources and reducing the circulation of cash on the street.

Design projects that include education and health services

Although remittance recipients invest in health and education, the demand for good health and education services is often unmet due to lack of knowledge by the public or lack of public and private service delivery. One important strategy to provide these services is by forging business partnerships between MFIs and health and education providers to advertise and sell health insurance, utilizing already existing institutions, including public schools or clinics. Microfinance institutions can serve as financial and social service providers through contracts with these other institutions.

Among these services are the following:

(i) *Education funds, tutoring classes, extra-curricular activities, Internet lessons*:
   In cooperation with schools, public or private, MFIs can sell education packages, including loans or services, to remittance recipients. Children will benefit greatly from parents who purchase packages of extra-curricular education (for example, arts, crafts or sports) or tutoring lessons to raise their grades. Providing these services not only improves the educational status of children of emigrants but also motivates parents working abroad to continue investing in this long-term asset. Moreover, the satisfaction of parents that their children are obtaining a quality education is gratifying and a constant matter of attention (Orozco 2006a).

(ii) *Health insurance, specialized medicine funds*:
   At least 40 per cent of remittance recipients are minors or retired people, that is, individuals with a higher demand for health care services. MFIs can partner with insurance companies, clinics and health centres to sell affordable health services. These services should include emergency care, life insurance, medical insurance, body repatriation and child care. The effect of the supply of these services will enhance the quality of life of people while educating them about appropriate understandings of health care.

(iii) *Define goals and standards to raise educational attainment from primary to secondary school completion levels*:
   Lack of competitiveness in the global economy is a critical factor affecting economic development and outward migration. Communities where remittances arrive are places that require greater attention to the future of their societies. Education is one key component to improve local economic development, which can be leveraged through remittances. However, an economy with a mediocre educated class will not be able to fully absorb remittances. Therefore, communities need to consider goals and standards to raise educational performance during five-year periods in order to guarantee that children in communities with high levels of outbound migration are improving their educational attainment and achieving skills.

Enabling environment

One important consideration about remittances is that they exist predominantly as a consequence of an international pattern of labour mobility that results from necessity rather than choice. The condition of inequality and poor economic performance has forced many people to migrate in order to care for their families. Governments have yet to recognize the significant contributions that these flows make to the lives of families and society at large. Moreover, they have yet to implement policies that leverage the incoming flows, and they still struggle to mitigate the various structural challenges brought about by underdevelopment. Concentrating on the adverse effects of poor economic performance in the global economy is the first effort to address the causes of labour migration. However, given the reality of the transnational family, governments need to address the new demands and needs faced by these families, as well as to explore ways to leverage remittance flows in order to expand their development impact. Offering opportunities to build assets and improve the social conditions of people receiving remittances is an important step in enabling a development environment in societies where migration and remittances exist.

Not only do these efforts have an effect on improving the quality of life of people who receive remittances; they also add value to the local labour force. By increasing the demand for these services, new jobs are added and productivity is heightened. Thus, remittances will prove to have a greater multiplying effect beyond basic consumption and personal savings.

Notes

1. Rebecca Rouse and Jill Reifsteck provided research and writing assistance for parts of this chapter.
2. All $ amounts refer to US dollars.
3. The survey data analysed here is based on surveys conducted in 2004 as part of a project on transnational communities. See Orozco (2005).
4. The comparative study is found in Orozco (2006a); the authors of the independent reports are Egüez and Acosta (2006); Andrade-Eekhoff and Ortiz (2006); Reifsteck (2006); García Zamora (2006); and Alvarez Aragón et al. (2006).
5. Log values were used for remittances, revenue collection, savings and consumption. A one-year time lag was implemented to denote changes over the previous year on government revenue increases.

References

Adams, Richard (2004) *Remittances and Poverty in Guatemala*, World Bank Policy Research Working Paper No. 3418 (Washington, DC: World Bank).

Adams, Richard and John Page (2005) 'The impact of international migration and remittances on poverty.' In Samuel Munzele Maimbo and Philip Ratha (eds.), *Remittances: Development Impact and Future Prospects* (Washington, DC: World Bank).

Alvarez Aragón, Virgilio, Julia Gonzáles Decas, and Cristhians Manolo Castillo (2006) *Remesas y Mercado de Servicios: Estudio de Caso Salcaja, Quetzaltenango*, Report commissioned by the Inter-American Dialogue (Washington, DC: Inter-American Dialogue).

Andrade-Eekhoff, Katharine, and Xenia Ortiz (2006) *Mas Allá del Río de Plata Llamado Remesas Familiars: Un Vistazo al Hábitat de la Economía Local y la Inversión Social en el Caso de Suchitoto, El Salvador*, Report commissioned by the Inter-American Dialogue (Washington, DC: Inter-American Dialogue).

Basu, Susanto (1999) *Procyclical Productivity: Increasing Returns or Cyclical Utilization?*, NBER Working Paper No. 5336 (Cambridge, MA: NBER).

Cox-Edwards, Alejandra, and Manuelita Ureta (2003) 'International migration, remittances, and schooling: Evidence from El Salvador', *Journal of Development Economics*, Vol. 72, No. 2, 429–62.

—— (1999) *Income Transfers and Children's Schooling: Evidence from El Salvador*, mimeo.

Egüez, Pilar and Alberto Acosta (2006) *Economía Local y Remesas en América Latina: El Caso de Catamayo, Ecuador*, Report commissioned by the Inter-American Dialogue (Washington, DC: Inter-American Dialogue).

García Zamora, Rodolfo (2006) *Economía Local y Remesas en América Latina: El Caso de Jerez, Zacatecas*, Report commissioned by the Inter-American Dialogue (Washington, DC: Inter-American Dialogue).

Hamilton, Eve and Manuel Orozco (2006) *Remittances, Diasporas, and Economic Development*, report prepared for USAID (Washington, DC: Chemonics International).

Hanson, Gordon and Christopher Woodruff (2003) *Emigration and Educational Attainment in Mexico*, Working Paper (San Diego: University of California).

Hendrix, Steve and Pamela Constable (2005) 'Lifeline to a devastated Guatemala', *The Washington Post*, 23 October, p. A01.

International Organization for Migration and the Vice-President of Guatemala (2006) *Encuesta sobre Remesas 2006: Inversión en Salud y Educación*, Cuaderno de Trabajo sobre Migración No. 23 (Guatemala City: IOM Guatemala).

Levitt, Peggy (2001) *The Transnational Villagers* (Los Angeles, CA: University of California Press).

Lopez-Cordova, Ernesto (2005) *Globalization, Migration and Development: The Role of Mexican Migrant Remittances* (Washington, DC: Inter-American Development Bank).

Menjívar, Cecilia (2002) 'The ties that heal: Guatemalan immigrant women's networks and medical treatment', *International Migration Review*, Vol. 36, No. 2, 437–66.

Orbe, Mauricio (2006) *Capacidad de las Remesas*, report commissioned by the Inter-American Dialogue (Quito: Inter-American Dialogue).

Orozco, Manuel (2007a) 'Central American diasporas and Hometown Associations.' In Barbara J. Merz, Lincoln C. Chen and Peter F. Geithner (eds.), *Diasporas and Development* (Cambridge, MA: Harvard University Press).

—— (2007b) 'Migrant foreign savings and asset accumulation.' In Caroline O.N. Moser (ed.), *Reducing Global Poverty: The Case for Asset Accumulation* (Washington, DC: Brookings Institution Press).

—— (2006a) *Between Hardship and Hope: Remittances and the Local Economy in Latin America*, report commissioned by the Multilateral Investment Fund of the Inter-American Development Bank (Washington, DC: Inter-American Dialogue).

—— (2006b) *Understanding the Remittance Economy in Haiti*, report commissioned by the World Bank (Washington, DC: World Bank).

—— (2005) *Transnational Engagement, Remittances and Their Relationship to Development in Latin America and the Caribbean* (Washington, DC: Institute for the Study of International Migration. Georgetown University).

Perry, Guillermo, Omar S. Arias, J. Humberto Lopez, William F. Maloney and Luis Serven (2006) *Poverty Reduction and Growth: Virtuous and Vicious Circles* (Washington, DC: World Bank).

Reifsteck, Jill (2006) *Remittances and the Local Economy in May Pen, Jamaica*, report commissioned by the Inter-American Dialogue (Washington, DC: Inter-American Dialogue).

Strauss, John and Duncan Thomas (1995) *Empirical Modeling of Household and Family Decisions*, Paper No. 95–12, Reprint Series (Santa Monica, CA: RAND).

UIS (United Nations Education, Scientific and Cultural Organization/UNESCO Institute for Statistics) (2006) *UIS Statistics in Brief: Education in Guatemala* (Montreal: UIS). www.uis.unesco.org/profiles/EN/EDU/countryProfile_en.aspx?code=3200, accessed on 17 January 2007.

World Bank (2006) *World Development Indicators* (Washington, DC: World Bank).

14
Conclusions

Katja Hujo and Shea McClanahan

In this book, we have explored the potential and the developmental impact of different categories of resources for financing social policy in a development context. The chapters comprise contributions by a diverse range of scholars representing a wide range of disciplines. They outline broad patterns linking social policy outcomes in developing countries to a select set of what we have called, for lack of a better term, 'revenue sources', in order to denote their *potential* to be tapped for development purposes. For some of these resources, such as aid or social insurance, the relationship with social policy is more direct and in some sense intuitive, while for others, most notably remittances, the links are less direct, though not necessarily weaker. It is our view that the guiding principles for social policy instruments should be universality, solidarity, integration, efficiency and sustainability. These principles are often in tension, but they must not be treated as either/or options. Rather, difficult decisions about trade-offs should be taken in the spirit of optimizing the overall balance across all desirable principles. The chapters in this volume have identified several reasons why creating strong social policy systems, built on sustainable financial bases, is specifically challenging for developing countries. In the coming pages, we briefly review some of those reasons, identify some preliminary lessons for policy makers and advisors, and explore future directions for research.

Before turning to those challenges, a note of optimism is warranted. It is our hope that this project's focus on revenues will open up possibilities for new ways of thinking about social policies in a development context, one that takes their financing as a starting point rather than an afterthought. In the introduction to this volume, we noted the limitations of debates that emphasized controlling expenditures within predetermined and seemingly exogenous constraints. These 'affordability' arguments effectively foreclosed on discussions of possibilities for expanding and diversifying the existing resource base. This volume attempts to rectify this imbalance in scholarship, but it does not intend to suggest that merely generating more revenues to 'pay' for development is sufficient. To make the case that money is not enough, we need look no further than the paradoxical experience of many mineral-rich countries, which, despite enormous revenues, have performed poorly on important social indicators. On the contrary, the chapters in this volume go beyond the more obvious (even if somewhat neglected) point that 'revenues matter' for development, and begin to explore the complex challenges of mobilizing resources in a way that not only increases fiscal space for social policies, but also *reinforces* them. Delamonica and Mehrotra's chapter in this volume points out the utter futility of designing so-called 'pro-poor' social policies under the kinds of regressive tax regimes that characterize much of the developing world. Simply put, social policies cannot continue to 'row against the current' of economic and fiscal policies. If anything, this project has accentuated the importance of the quality, and not simply the quantity of fiscal resources, for creating and strengthening synergistic feedback with social policy systems.[1]

Both past and current United Nations Research Institute for Social Development (UNRISD) research demonstrate that economic and social policies have to work in tandem, at the micro and macro levels, in order to advance societies' well-being. Fair and just resource allocation decisions are critical for achieving positive human development outcomes, and the actors, processes and institutions involved in distribution are the centrepiece for reconciling the tensions among diverse policy goals and principles. These factors vary enormously from context to context. Therefore, attempting to derive potential 'lessons' or even 'implications' for different countries may, at times, seem futile. Recognizing the inherent limits to comparative research, this book (and research on 'development' more generally) has emphasized certain overarching commonalities among developing, and in some cases developed countries, in hopes of deriving broad, though somewhat qualified, conclusions.

Until very recently, scholarship on social policy literature has been dominated by studies on the more developed states in the North. This literature has focused, in one way or another, on an array of 'cost factors' that put pressure on advanced welfare states. The laudable achievement of near universal coverage through transfer programmes in contexts of rapidly ageing societies, puts real pressure on established welfare systems and requires creative policy – and political – solutions. In contrast, developing countries, by virtue of their underdeveloped welfare systems, are largely spared these particular burdens. However, recent UNRISD research on the so-called late industrializers reveals some interesting parallels between the challenges these 'successful' late developers faced at early stages of their development, and those confronting developing countries today. These latecomers in the industrialization process have shown that in a context of rapid structural change and social mobilization, combining economic development with political stability is paramount. In turn, stability in democratic contexts requires an extension of social rights, equality and opportunities to allow for some degree of social mobility. In addition, these countries had to find ways to mitigate the negative effects of structural transformation, especially when moving from an agrarian-rural setting to a more industrialized-urban economy. Their solutions, to a greater or lesser degree, put social policy at the centre of national development strategies. Indeed, the chapters in this volume on the development of the pensions systems in Finland and Norway attest to the fact that tying these policies to appropriate and sustainable financing mechanisms was critical to their success and sustainability.

However, when we look at most low- and middle-income countries today, we realize that they lag seriously behind in terms of social policies. In general, social expenditures per capita are comparatively low, and social protection schemes are fragmented, stratified and often inefficient. Consequently, coverage is far from universal and highly unequal – it is a general rule that those who are included are not among the neediest. Furthermore, the co-existence of market and government failures makes it difficult to opt for the right public–private mix in social protection. Low-income earners, and the poor generally, end up with low quality public services, targeted cash transfers (at best) or more commonly, alternative welfare arrangements that usually bypass the state entirely (for example, through self-provision, non-governmental organizations or informal clientelistic relationships). On the other hand, contribution-financed social insurance and private insurance, which are typically of much higher quality, are only accessible for the higher income quintiles.

Most importantly for this project, each of these deficiencies in social provisioning can be traced to very weak and notoriously regressive financial bases. The economic context – in particular low levels of investment and (formal sector) employment, low real wages and salaries, low public tax revenues, external debt and recurrent economic and financial crises – make it difficult to create a stable financial base for funding social policies. As a consequence, revenues from domestic sources like taxation or social insurance contributions are simply not sufficient to meet the basic demands regarding health, education, pensions, unemployment, family support and poverty reduction. On the flipside, external revenues like remittances, rents from natural resources or aid, pose their own challenges in terms of macroeconomic management as well as with regard to their potential effects on state legitimacy and accountability. Clearly, case-specific characteristics and the global environment influence the way countries cope with these challenges, that is, whether they are able to climb the ladder, or, in Ha-Joon Chang's words, have it 'kicked away'. As Ortiz emphasized in her chapter, it is an urgent imperative at the beginning of the twenty-first century to redress the world's gross inequities. For globalization to be accepted, it will have to be a globalization that benefits everyone. This requires multilateral coordinated action, better global governance, increased and improved Official Development Assistance (ODA), with more grants and fewer loans, with more budget support and less micromanagement, with more effective results to bring half of the world's population out of poverty, sharing responsibility for social development.

In a similar vein, Lo Vuolo's analysis in this volume of the 'revision of the Orthodoxy' – otherwise referred to as post-Washington consensus social policies – attests to how, sometimes, the very policies employed to fix the problem can actually exacerbate it. Recent history has amassed overwhelming evidence that the residual, safety-net social policies (for example, those that fall under the rubric of 'social risk management') are simply insufficient and unsuitable in contexts where large portions of the population are poor or near poor, and the market economy in which they find themselves is dysfunctional at best. Lo Vuolo's critique serves as a warning that 'revisionist' claims about the role of social policy should not be taken at face value. Given that the main champions of these policies consist of external actors like the international financial institutions and many developed countries, financial dependence on ODA coupled with high levels of debt continue to constrain the policy space and options for developing countries. That said, Ortiz points to some promising possibilities for limiting the influence of these actors through emerging regional and South–South development alternatives.

In our attempt to draw general conclusions from this volume, we realize that each revenue source examined in the project presents a specific set of challenges and varying degrees of potential. For this project, researchers were urged to expand their analyses beyond the predominant issue and disciplinary boundaries and attempt to simultaneously bring out the economic, social and political dimensions of each resource. A general observation that applies across virtually all of the resources, from taxation to mineral rents, is that the relationship between social and economic policies is mediated by political factors. Policy synergies cannot be created, strengthened or most importantly sustained, in the absence of political consensus, and political consensus, in turn, arguably reinforces the kinds of economic and social synergies that characterize more equitable systems.

In their respective chapters on *taxation and aid*, among other issues, researchers considered the implications of aid and other forms of external resource dependence for developing countries' own capacities to finance and implement social policies, and also to diversify their resource bases and reduce the volatility of state revenues. The chapters by both Sindzingre and Morrissey warned that excessive dependence on aid can have detrimental effects on democracy and state formation in developing countries if it undermines domestic policy space or accountability and responsiveness of state elites towards citizens. However, Morrisey's chapter also demonstrated that aid has a small, but positive impact on public social spending and welfare, especially in low-income countries. With regard to tax systems, Delamonica and Mehrotra make clear that the introduction of more progressive and solidarity-based tax structures remains a huge challenge for developing countries. A key lesson of both the Sindzingre and the Delamonica and Mehrotra chapters is that policy coherence is crucial for achieving optimal social outcomes. Tax reforms for low-income countries in recent decades have emphasized replacing volatile and 'distortionary' commodities and trade-based taxes with other 'easy-to-collect' indirect taxes, such as value added tax, which, besides being regressive, have not made up for the loss in trade-based tax revenue. In effect, these tax reforms work *against*, not in tandem with, any attempt to achieve social gains through the post-Washington consensus shift towards a focus, albeit residual, on social policies.

In fact, these chapters speak to the importance of recognizing taxation as an *intrinsic* dimension of the state and beginning to design tax systems that reflect a social contract to which citizens and the state are inextricably tied. They make a clear case as to why progressive forms of taxation are best suited for these long-term goals, although it is well known that direct and progressive taxation policies are difficult to implement in a context of highly unequal distributional patterns, low wages and a predominantly informal economy. More than with other revenue sources, therefore, it is central to establish a culture of taxation based on mutual trust, and to adopt systems to local circumstances. The challenge is to find ways of guaranteeing that both parties – taxpayers and the state – will comply.[2] Perhaps most importantly, though, the findings of the taxation and aid chapters seem to suggest that aid, taxation and expenditure are endogenously related. For instance, Morrissey's finding that aid has only a small positive effect on social spending may in fact be a reflection of the regressive effect of aid on taxation. Any additional positive gains from aid through social spending may be cancelled out due to the potentially larger loss in taxation revenues that could result from the 'crowding-out' effects of aid. Taken together, these findings suggest that future research in this area should analyse taxation *in relation to* both aid and state expenditure, as a function of the broader context of development and political governance in each country under consideration.

The chapters on *natural resource rents* focused on the enormous implications of mineral wealth for the design and delivery of social policies in developing countries. Avoiding 'Dutch disease' and other manifestations of the resource curse is, on the one hand, context-dependent. On the other hand, there are trade-offs as well as possible synergies between economic and social policy. In light of the diversity of experiences, UNRISD research is most concerned with the role that social policies can, and do, play in this process. As Holmøy's chapter demonstrated, the Norwegian oil pension fund is a good example of combining sustainable resource management with long-term social policy goals. As part of the fund can be invested abroad, it helps to relieve pressure on the exchange rate and adds to risk diversification, although international capital markets can also be a source of instability, as the current crisis has painfully demonstrated. In combination with budget surpluses, repayment of external debt and a monetary policy of inflation-targeting, policy makers have been able to safeguard macroeconomic stability in spite of the fact that generous social policies are being financed out of oil wealth.

Perhaps nowhere are political dynamics and institutions placed in sharper relief than in the case of mineral rents. While it may be more straightforward to look to successful countries for examples of how to avoid the potential macroeconomic manifestations of the 'resource curse', the political challenges involved in distributional decisions are clearly much more complex and context-specific. Indeed, as Rosser's chapter highlighted, much of the more recent literature on the resource curse has focused on the political implications, from increased conflict to authoritarianism, of natural resource wealth. At the other end of the spectrum, the Norwegian experience represents the epitome of political consensus, wherein arguably the entire validity of the pension funds rests on political adherence to the spending limit rule. Likewise in Norway, limits on domestic investment of pension fund assets have likely curbed or eliminated incentives for rent seeking among domestic actors. Clearly, developing countries with diverse institutional and political legacies will have to find their own rules appropriate to local circumstances and capabilities in order to manage revenues from natural resources in the interest of their people. Although it may be tempting to throw up our hands in exasperation and chalk Norway's success up to 'strong institutions' of the kind that seem unattainable in developing contexts, it is important to note that the path to

Norway's coveted political consensus involved explicitly linking mineral wealth, both present and future, to an intergenerational social contract. Future research into the links between social policy and natural resource abundance in developing countries[3] must explore specific policy options that link economic development objectives with social policies rooted in broad political constituencies.

With respect to *social insurance schemes* such as public pensions and health care, an important point of departure is to recognize the variety of forms these systems take in both the developing and the developed world. Research in this book has dealt with regional experiences, such as the relationship between labour markets, social insurance (pensions and health) and coverage in Latin America. A common theme is the challenge of reconciling the necessity of financial sustainability in these schemes with the imperatives of ensuring coverage and adequate levels of benefits. Global trends – including informalization, labour market flexiblization and deindustrialization, ageing and migration, and the shrinking importance of occupational social insurance in a context of strong wage cost competition – give reasons to question whether the traditional policy approach of supposedly 'fiscally neutral' insurance schemes is still the way to go. As research shows, these schemes are often heavily subsidized and as such are the most regressive part of social expenditures in many developing countries.

Mesa-Lago's chapter in this volume suggests that coverage levels vary with trends in labour market legislation – the more deregulated the labour market, the lower the social insurance coverage. As long as current labour market trends cannot be reversed, it seems unlikely that more social inclusion will be achieved via formal social insurance programmes. The recent trend to expand means-tested and conditional social assistance or workfare programmes, as analysed by Lo Vuolo in the case of Argentina, however, raises equally important questions with regard to their long-term impact on income security, redistribution, human capital formation, gender equality and citizenship rights, not to mention political sustainability.

In a related vein, research on *pension funds and economic development* focused on the challenge of reconciling the trade-offs – and maximizing the benefits – implied in the protective and productive functions of these kinds of social security systems. Case studies on Norway, Finland and a regional survey of Asian countries emphasized the role of these funds in national economic development. As with other revenues like taxation and social insurance, the pension fund cases highlight the importance of striking a delicate balance between the technical challenges of designing pensions, and the political challenges involved in aligning diverse interests in support of more equitable and sustainable pension schemes.

Furthermore, pension funds, once established, can either be used to finance important infrastructure investments, as demonstrated by the electricity or housing projects in Kangas's chapter on Finland, or they can end up in unproductive or low-return investment projects or government bonds to finance budget deficits. Whereas in the former case virtuous circles are created between pension funds and economic development, the latter situation erodes the values and support on which pensions depend and rarely makes a difference in terms of development. A preliminary conclusion, confirmed by the Asian studies, seems to be that the preconditions to make pension funds work for national development are rather stringent with regard to the economic and political environment; what we find more frequently is that these funds are used for political purposes (to serve the interests of a narrow or elite constituency), whereas economic and social efficiency is low. In his chapter, Asher demonstrates that the quality of investment decisions and the regulatory environment surrounding them are often more important than the type of investments themselves. The lessons developing countries can take from these experiences are not clear cut. Whether or not mineral-rich developing countries should follow the Norwegian example and invest part of their revenues in pension funds or, more generally, whether low-income countries should instead opt for small-scale voluntary funds while trying to extend tax-financed non-contributory pensions for the majority of citizens, are questions that definitely require more research and political debate.

If the previous resources were more clearly potential 'revenue sources' for social policy, the two chapters on *remittances* by de Haas and Orozco highlight the inherent difficulties of integrating private flows of money into the financing of the social policy framework. Findings in both chapters support the thesis that remittances cannot be a substitute for social policy; they can merely act as a complement. Research shows that remittances are indeed used for social protection, as recipients use them to invest in nutrition, health and education, as well as for the purpose of income smoothing in case of economic crises or natural disasters. The effectiveness of remittances for enhancing the welfare of recipients and their communities crucially depends on the economic and institutional environment of a particular country. Although our research findings reveal a broad consensus on both the desirability and legitimacy of facilitating remittance flows in a variety of ways, the question of creating incentives for specific investments or considering remittances as part of the taxable income of recipients remains controversial.

Equally, it became clear from both chapters that the relationship between social policy and migration, more generally, is a two-way street: while remittances can and do (under the right conditions) contribute to development in countries of origin, the poor quality or outright absence of social policy is among the primary causes of out-migration in the first place. To expect for remittances – which are in many ways a *symptom* of underdevelopment – to make up for a lack of resources and/or state initiative in developing countries, is not only short-sighted, it is arguably inefficient from a system-wide perspective, taking into account the huge social and economic costs to migrants as well as the high fees charged by the money transfer industry. Nevertheless, given the current landscape in which remittances outpace ODA in many countries, more immediate policies may be appropriate to minimize the pitfalls, outlined in the de Haas chapter, that tend to be associated with remittances.

The financing debate with regard to social policy has too often been neglected in the past, and this book is meant as a first step to fill this gap. However, without linking it to the broader set of questions that are inevitably confronted in developing contexts, we are not likely to give justice to the complexity of the problems at play. Rather than pretend to offer specific policy prescriptions, it is our hope that this volume will set the tone for future research and more balanced approaches to financing equitable social policies. In the light of the complex opportunities and constraints outlined with respect to the revenue sources presented in this volume, various broad policy 'lessons' emerge: first, to combine transformative social policy with employment-intensive development strategies; second, to go beyond the recommendations of the post-Washington consensus by stressing the importance of universal approaches, redistribution policies and the macro role of social policy; and finally, to forge political and external coalitions in support of reforms. Opting for such an approach would give due credit to the multiple roles of social policy that UNRISD research on *Social Policy in a Development Context* has emphasized, thereby enabling policy makers to reach beyond the presently circumscribed roles of social protection and poverty reduction. This volume has attempted to analyse each of the financing techniques and different revenue sources through the lens of these functions, and particularly, their effects on (i) production and reproduction, (ii) protection and redistribution, and (iii) social inclusion and democratization.

Given the range and complexity of topics covered in this volume, we can nevertheless distinguish some overarching guidelines for designing equitable financing regimes for social policy in a development context. First, policy makers, ideally in democratic conversation with citizens, must identify and articulate the basic normative principles that will guide their social policies. Second, it is necessary to assess fiscal space, not only with regard to reallocation of existing expenditures, but also with an eye towards the mobilization of additional revenues. Third, aspects of governance, including questions of implementation and capacity, cannot be ignored and indeed must be directly confronted early on in designing appropriate financing and social policy frameworks. Last but not least, it has been one of the central messages of this volume that the developmental impact of policies must be anticipated and evaluated as a function both of social policy measures *and* of funding decisions. In practice, choices between different options will be influenced by basic decisions regarding the desired balance of public versus private instruments, targeted versus universal schemes, the scope of solidarity and redistribution built into the system and the type of care regime that is implicitly or explicitly chosen. As the case studies in this volume made clear, these choices are not made in a vacuum; actors and external advisors must take into account the context of a country's social and economic policy regime, as well as historical trajectories.

We have established that revenues are important for social policy. More importantly, progressive and fair financing mechanisms are necessary in order to reinforce the myriad goals of social policy: economic development, horizontal and vertical equality, equitable distribution of paid and unpaid care work, and socio-economic security, to name but a few. Sufficient, stable and predictable financing sources are crucial for the performance and credibility of social policy. However, social policy is more than simply mobilizing revenues and the sum of social expenditure per capita – its scope is determined by more than just fiscal space. The same amount of money can be spent on different programmes and groups, the burden of financing can be carried by different income groups or production factors, and similar results can be achieved by different policy measures and types of institutions.

Here, it is important to note that even low-income countries have achieved good social outcomes by dedicating above-average resources and efforts to social policy. The political discourse must avoid focusing exclusively on issues of affordability and financing. If taken in isolation, the fiscal space discourse threatens to crowd out innovative thinking and a fundamental debate about how societies want to define their social contract in order to determine how to advance social cohesion and well-being.

Ultimately, though, the financing mix is country specific. The selection of resources in this volume does not represent the universe of possibilities for developing countries, and countries' financing choices will, at a very basic level, be dominated by those resources that are most readily available to them. Ideally, all countries should rely as much as possible on progressive taxation systems and social contributions to finance social policies, as these combine the potential advantages of impacting positively on macroeconomic stability, equity and social cohesion. The reality, however, is that external resources like aid, mineral rents and remittances are growing in importance in many developing countries. Despite the challenges these resources pose, they also have clear potential to bring positive social results. Policy makers, advisors and the research community must therefore strike a balance. They must look for ways to maximize the use of these external resources for social development, while simultaneously building and strengthening a sustainable financial 'core' – one that rests on domestic resource bases – for social policies.

Notes

1. This stance also implies that other financing mechanisms, such as printing money or issuing debt, in particular external debt, cannot be considered sustainable funding mechanisms for social policy. This rule obviously applies to all countries, although the negative consequences of not respecting it are much more rapidly felt in the South due to their weak monetary-financial system.
2. Decentralization and participatory budgets at the local level are two instruments that have the potential, if implemented well, to contribute to more trust and accountability in revenue collection and expenditure allocations.
3. To this end, UNRISD commissioned eight papers: four thematic papers and four country studies (on Norway, Chile, Indonesia and Nigeria), which were presented at a workshop in April 2008.

Index